CASES AND MATERIALS

# TAX LAW

# CASES AND MATERIALS

# TAX LAW

John Snape, MA (Oxon), Solicitor
Senior Lecturer, Nottingham Law School

BLACKSTONE
PRESS LIMITED

First published in Great Britain 1999 by Blackstone Press Limited,
Aldine Place, London W12 8AA.   Telephone 0181–740 2277

© Nottingham Law School, Nottingham Trent University, 1999

ISBN: 1 85431 744 X

British Library Cataloguing in Publication Data
A CIP catalogue record for this book is available from the British Library.

Typeset by Style Photosetting Limited, Mayfield, East Sussex
Printed by Livesey Limited, Shrewsbury, Shropshire

# FOREWORD

The books in the LLB series have been written for students studying law at undergraduate level. There are two books for each subject. The first is the *Learning Text* which is designed to teach you about the particular subject in question. However, it does much more than that. By means of Activities, Self Assessment, and End of Chapter Questions, the *Learning Text* allows you to test your knowledge and understanding as you work. Each chapter starts with 'Objectives' which indicate what you should be able to do by the end of it. You should use these Objectives in your learning — check them frequently and ask yourself whether you have attained them.

The second book is a volume of *Cases and Materials*. This is cross-referenced from the *Learning Text*. It contains the primary sources of law such as statutes and cases plus subsidiary sources such as extracts from journals, law reform papers and textbooks. This is your portable library. Although each volume can stand alone, they are designed to be complementary.

The two-volume combination aims to support your learning by challenging you to demonstrate your mastery of the principles and application of the law. They are appropriate whatever your mode of study — full-time or part-time.

# CONTENTS

# ACKNOWLEDGEMENTS

Nottingham Law School and the publishers would like to thank the following for permission to reproduce copyright material:

American Journal of Legal History: M. Emory, 'The Early English Income Tax: A Heritage for the Contemporary' (1965).

British Gas Trading Ltd: 'Customer Costs Down — VAT Reduction' (1997).

Butterworth & Co. (Publishers) Ltd: extracts from the *All England Law Reports, Simon's Tax Cases, Simon's Tax Cases (Special Commissioners' Decisions), Simon's Weekly Tax Intelligence, Blackstone's Commentaries on the Laws of England* (1825), *Encyclopaedia of Forms and Precedents (1993), Taxation (1997)* and the *Tax Journal* (various years).

Cavendish Publishing Ltd: extract from *The Student Law Review* (1994).

CCH Editions Ltd: extracts from the *Benefits Bulletin* (1997) and *The British Master Tax Guide* (1997).

Central Finance Board of the Methodist Church: specimen Deed of Covenant.

East Midlands Electricity plc: extract from the *Offering Circular for the Recommended Cash Offer for East Midlands Electricity on Behalf of DR Investments*.

Estates Gazette Ltd: extract from the *Estates Gazette Law Reports*.

Ewan Macnaughton Associates and the Telegraph Group Ltd: extracts from *The Daily Telegraph*.

Her Majesty's Stationery Office: for permission to reproduce Crown and Parliamentary copyright material and extracts from *Reports of Tax Cases*.

Incorporated Council of Law Reporting for England and Wales: extracts from the Law Reports and *Industrial Cases Reports*.

Inland Revenue: extracts from Booklet CWG2 (1997), IR20 (1993), IR34 (1994), IR123 (1994), Statements of Practice 7/84 and 1/90 and 'Guidance for employees about the employment records they may need to keep' (1996).

The Institute for Fiscal Studies: extract from the Meade Report (1978).

Law Society Gazette: B. McCutcheon, 'Interests in Possession Again — s. 31 of the Trustee Act 1925' (1980).

The Lawyer: S. Pye, 'Young Bar exempt from Professional Tax Charge' (1988).

Legalease Ltd: extract from the *In-House Lawyer*.

Macmillan Publishers Ltd: extract from M. Wilkinson, *Taxation*.

Oxford University Press: extracts from Kay and King, *The British Tax System* (1990) and *The Oxford English Dictionary*.

Penguin UK: extract from A. Smith, *The Wealth of Nations* (1996).

Routledge: extract from M. Beard, *English Landed Society in the Twentieth Century* (1989).

Sweet & Maxwell Ltd: extracts from Barlow and King, *Wills, Administration and Taxation — A Practical Guide* (1997), *The British Tax Review, Current Law, The Law Quarterly Review, Private Client Business, Property Law Bulletin* and *The Solicitors' Journal*.

Zeneca Group plc: extract from *Demerger Document on the Rights Issue by Zeneca Group plc* (1993).

# ABBREVIATIONS

| | |
|---|---|
| ACT | advance corporation tax |
| AEA | Administration of Estates Act 1925 |
| APA | additional personal allowance |
| APR | agricultural property relief |
| BPR | business property relief |
| CA 1985 | Companies Act 1985 |
| CA(s) | capital allowance(s) |
| CAA 1990 | Capital Allowances Act 1990 |
| CGT | capital gains tax |
| CIC | close investment-holding company |
| CTT | capital transfer tax |
| CYB | current year basis, i.e. the tax period is the accounting period ending in the tax period under consideration |
| DSS | Department of Social Security |
| EIS | enterprise investment scheme |
| ESC | extra statutory concession |
| EU | European Union |
| FA | Finance Act, e.g. FA 1998, Finance Act 1998 |
| FII | franked investment income, i.e. of a company |
| F (No. 2) A 1997 | Finance (No. 2) Act 1997 |
| FA 1998 | Finance Act 1998 |
| FRS | financial reporting standard |
| FSA 1986 | Financial Services Act 1986 |
| FYA(s) | first year allowance(s) |
| GAAP | generally accepted accounting principles |
| IA | indexation allowance |
| IBS(s) | industrial building or structure(s) |
| ICR | Industrial Cases Reports |
| ICTA 1988 | Income and Corporation Taxes Act 1988 |
| IHT | inheritance tax |
| IHTA 1984 | Inheritance Tax Act 1984 |
| IPT | insurance premium tax |
| ISA | Individual Savings Account |
| LCA 1972 | Land Charges Act 1972 |
| LEL | lower earnings limit (national insurance contributions) |
| LPA 1925 | Law of Property Act 1925 |
| Ltd | limited (as in limited company) |
| MCA | married couples' allowance |
| MIRAS | mortgage interest relief at source |
| NAA 1948 | National Assistance Act 1948 |
| NICs | national insurance contributions |
| NSB | National Savings Bank |
| NVQ | National Vocational Qualification |
| QCB | qualifying corporate bond |

| | |
|---|---|
| PAYE | pay as you earn |
| PEP | Personal Equity Plan |
| PET | potentially exempt transfer |
| PRR | private residence relief |
| plc | public limited company |
| PR | personal representative of a deceased individual |
| RPI | Retail Prices Index |
| SA | Société Anonyme (French limited company) |
| SA 1891 | Stamp Act 1891 |
| SERPS | State Earnings-Related Pension Scheme |
| SP | Inland Revenue Statement of Practice |
| SpA | Italian public company |
| SSAA 1992 | Social Security Administration Act 1992 |
| SSAP | statement of standard accountancy practice |
| SSCR 1979 | Social Security (Contributions) Regulations 1979 |
| SSCBA 1992 | Social Security Contributions and Benefits Act 1992 |
| STC | Simon's Tax Cases |
| STC(SCD) | Simon's Tax Cases (Special Commissioners' Decisions) |
| SVQ | Scottish Vocational Qualification |
| TA 1925 | Trustee Act 1925 |
| TC | Tax Cases |
| TCGA 1992 | Taxation of Chargeable Gains Act 1992 |
| TESSA | Tax-Exempt Special Savings Account |
| TLA 1996 | Trusts of Land and Appointment of Trustees Act 1996 |
| TMA 1970 | Taxes Management Act 1970 |
| UEL | upper earnings limit (national insurance contributions) |
| VAT | value added tax |
| VATA 1994 | Value Added Tax Act 1994 |
| VATR 1995 | Value Added Tax Regulations 1995 |
| VCT | venture capital trust |
| WBA | widow's bereavement allowance |
| WDA(s) | writing-down allowance(s) |

# TABLE OF CASES

# TABLE OF STATUTES

*Statutes, and sections thereof, which are set out in full or in part are shown in heavy type. The page at which the statute or section is printed is shown in heavy type.*

# CHAPTER ONE

# INCOME TAXATION: CONTEXTS AND HISTORY

## 1.1 Introduction

Tax law is part of everyday life.

**British Gas Trading Limited, 'Customer Costs Down — VAT Reduction', Leaflet, September 1997**

- VAT for domestic gas customers has been reduced from 8% to 5% from 1st September 1997.

- To ensure you enjoy the maximum benefit, British Gas Home Energy has charged VAT at 5%* on the whole of your current bill/statement, not just from 1st September. Everything you'd expect from the country's largest gas supply company.

- You will not need to take any action as we have applied the reduced VAT rate directly to your gas bill/statement.

- Customers with credit balances will also benefit from the reduced VAT rate immediately.

- Until the original credit runs out, the change in the VAT rate has no effect on customers who made an advance payment in March 1994.

- If you currently pay by Direct Debit, Standing Order or other regular payment scheme, your payment amount will be reviewed at your next annual reassessment. You will receive the benefit of the full VAT rate reduction.

*The new 5% VAT rate applies to gas chargeable at the domestic rate and includes small non-domestic users who use less than 145kWh of gas per day.

Consider this again when you have reached the end of **Chapter 19** of the *Learning Text*, especially **8.7**.

## 1.2 Tax and Taxation

NICs are charged partly to raise money for the national insurance fund and partly to fund the National Health Service.

**SOCIAL SECURITY CONTRIBUTIONS AND BENEFITS ACT 1992**

**1.  Outline of contributory system**
   (1)  The funds required—
     (a)  for paying such benefits under this Act as are payable out of the National Insurance Fund and not out of other public money; and
     (b)  for the making of payments under section 162 of the Administration Act towards the cost of the National Health Service,
shall be provided by means of contributions payable to the Secretary of State by earners, employers and others, together with the additions under subsection (5) below and amounts payable under section 2 of the Social Security Act 1993.

## 1.3   Income Taxation

The fundamental distinction between income and capital was propounded by Adam Smith (1723–1790).

**Smith, Adam, *The Wealth of Nations*, Book II, Chapter I, 'Of the Division of Stock', Skinner, A., ed., Penguin Books, 1986, pp. 373–374**

When the stock which a man possesses is no more than sufficient to maintain him for a few days or a few weeks, he seldom thinks of deriving any revenue from it. He consumes it as sparingly as he can, and endeavours by his labour to acquire something which may supply its place before it be consumed altogether. His revenue is, in this case, derived from his labour only. This is the state of the greater part of the labouring poor in all countries.

But when he possesses stock sufficient to maintain him for months or years, he naturally endeavours to derive a revenue from the greater part of it; reserving only so much for his immediate consumption as may maintain him till this revenue begins to come in. His whole stock, therefore, is distinguished into two parts. That part which, he expects, is to afford him this revenue, is called his capital. The other is that which supplies his immediate consumption; and which consists either, first, in that portion of his whole stock which was originally reserved for this purpose; or secondly, in his revenue, from whatever source derived, as it gradually comes in; or, thirdly, in such things as had been purchased by either of these in former years, and which are not yet entirely consumed; such as a stock of clothes, household furniture, and the like. In one, or other, or all these three articles, consists the stock which men commonly reserve for their own immediate consumption.

There are two different ways in which a capital may be employed so as to yield a revenue or profit to its employer.

First, it may be employed in raising, manufacturing, or purchasing goods, and selling them again with a profit. The capital employed in this manner yields no revenue or profit to its employer, while it either remains in his possession, or continues in the same shape. The goods of the merchant yield him no revenue or profit till he sells them for money, and the money yields him as little till it is again exchanged for goods. His capital is continually going from him in one shape, and returning to him in another, and it is only by means of such circulation, or successive exchanges, that it can yield him any profit. Such capitals, therefore, may very properly be called circulating capitals.

Secondly, it may be employed in the improvement of land, in the purchase of useful machines and instruments of trade, or in such-like things as yield a revenue or profit without changing masters, or circulating any further. Such capitals, therefore, may very properly be called fixed capitals.

Different occupations require very different proportions between the fixed and circulating capitals employed in them.

## 1.4 Contexts

### 1.4.1 THE PERSONAL CONTEXT

Don't forget the aphorism of Alexander Pope (1688–1744), the English poet and satirist, that a little learning is a dangerous thing.

**Pope, Alexander, 'An Essay on Criticism', Part II, lines 215–218, from *Collected Poems*, Probyn, C.T., ed., Everyman's Library, 1983**

> A little learning is a dangerous thing;
> Drink deep, or taste not the Pierian spring:
> There shallow draughts intoxicate the brain,
> And drinking largely sobers us again.

### 1.4.2 THE PROFESSIONAL LEGAL CONTEXT

If you did not know what the tax effect of the transaction or claim would be, your ignorance may have produced a tax charge on your client.

### *HURLINGHAM ESTATES LTD* v *WILDE AND PARTNERS* [1997] STC 627

LIGHTMAN J: . . . It is to be expected that an intelligent layman, in the sense of a person unfamiliar with the law of taxation (and I must include within this category not merely Hurlingham but also Mr Rowe), would not have imagined that there was any risk of Hurlingham incurring any such liability, since it was agreed that Hurlingham should occupy a neutral non-profit and non-loss-making role in the transaction. On the other hand, I would expect any reasonably competent solicitor practising in the field of conveyancing or commercial law to be aware of this concealed trap for the unwary. It is a matter he should have in mind in any transaction involving the grant of a lease and a related payment by the lessee to the lessor.

. . .

The judge was referring here to ICTA 1988, s. 34. This is discussed in **17.5** of the *Learning Text*.

### 1.4.3 THE ACCOUNTING CONTEXT

The balance sheet and the profit and loss account do not always use the same principles and rules as are used in taxation legislation.

**Cochrane, F.M., *Tolley's Accounting Principles for Tax Purposes*, 3rd edn, Croydon: Tolley Publishing Co. Ltd, 1998**

**The balance sheet**
**2.2** By far the most important document is the balance sheet. Normally it is in vertical format . . . and comprises no more than one page (possibly two). It lists the assets and shows who they belong to (the proprietors or 'shareholders').

. . .

**The profit and loss account**
**2.11** This can be confusing, particularly in the limited company context. In a sole trader or partnership situation, the profit and loss account is relatively straightforward. Usually in vertical format, the sales revenue is compared to the direct cost (i.e. purchases) to arrive at a gross profit from which the various expenses are deducted to arrive at the net profit.

. . .

### INCOME AND CORPORATION TAXES ACT 1988

**577.  Business entertaining expenses**
   (1)   Subject to the provisions of this section—
   (a)   no deduction shall be made in computing profits or gains chargeable to tax under Schedule A or Schedule D for any expenses incurred in providing business entertainment, and such expenses shall not be included in computing any expenses of management in respect of which relief may be given under the Tax Acts;
   (b)   no deduction for expenses so incurred shall be made from emoluments chargeable to tax under Schedule E; and
   (c)   for the purposes of Part II of the [Capital Allowances Act 1990], the use of any asset for providing business entertainment shall be treated as use otherwise than for the purposes of trade.

## 1.4.4   THE POLITICAL CONTEXT

The popular perception is that the Labour Party is the party of high taxation, and that the Conservative Party is the party of low taxation.

### Collins, N. and Fildes, C. 'Good Boy, Gordon', *The Daily Telegraph,* 18 March 1998, p. 16

GORDON BROWN has introduced his first Budget, at the third attempt. A quick tax grab in July before we had got used to calling him Chancellor and a green effort in November that we, and he, could have done without, were followed yesterday by one that was expected to thump the middle classes. It didn't. There's hardly a single detail that could be described as vindictive, or a paying-off of scores accumulated over 18 years of Tory rule.

No wonder the Tories slept uneasily through his speech, waking up only to cheer his reference to offshore trusts, a subject as dear to many of their own hearts as it is to the paymaster-general. That, and the booze cruisers, were the targets singled out for the traditional crackdown that rounds off the modern Budget. Mr Brown mumbled that he would get 1.5 billion over three years by taxing these tantalising trusts, and if you can get him to bet on that, you should have been at Cheltenham.

There are many good things in this Budget. Top of the list is the third penny off corporation tax since last May. This is enough to make a serious difference — he admitted that it will transfer £1.5 billion from the Exchequer to shareholders — and at 30 per cent the rate is competitive with most other proper economies.

The scrapping of advance corporation tax (ACT) that accompanied this largesse promises a painful transition, at least for some, but his pledge not to raise the rate is well worth the short-term cost. The best way to reward enterprise is to allow the entrepreneurs to keep their gains, something that earlier Labour chancellors never learnt. They would have been happier raising money from shareholders to back losers, which by definition never made any profits to be taxed on.

## 1.4.5   THE ECONOMIC CONTEXT

Adam Smith believed in a free market economy. In this famous extract, he expounded four 'maxims' of taxation. Later economists have added a fifth maxim, 'efficiency' or 'neutrality'.

### Smith, Adam, *The Wealth of Nations,* **Book V, Chapter II**

It is necessary to premise the four following maxims with regard to taxes in general.
   1. The subjects of every state ought to contribute towards the support of the government, as nearly as possible, in proportion to their respective abilities; that is, in proportion to the revenue which they respectively enjoy under the protection of the state.
. . .

2. The tax which each individual is bound to pay, ought to be certain, and not arbitrary. The time of payment, the manner of payment, the quantity to be paid, ought all to be clear and plain to the contributor, and to every other person. Where it is otherwise, every person subject to the tax is put more or less in the power of the tax-gatherer, who can either aggravate the tax upon any obnoxious contributor, or extort, by the terror of such aggravation, some present or perquisite to himself. The uncertainty of taxation encourages the insolence, and favours the corruption, of an order of men who are naturally unpopular, even where they are neither insolent nor corrupt. . . .

3. Every tax ought to be levied at the time, or in the manner, in which it is most likely to be convenient for the contributor to pay it. A tax upon the rent of land or of houses, payable at the same term at which such rents are usually paid, is levied at the time when it is most likely to be convenient for the contributor to pay; or, when he is most likely to have wherewithal to pay. Taxes upon such consumable goods as are articles of luxury, are all finally paid by the consumer, and generally in a manner that is very convenient for him. He pays them by little and little, as he has occasion to buy the goods. As he is at liberty, too, either to buy, or not to buy, as he pleases, it must be his own fault if he ever suffers any considerable inconveniency from such taxes.

4. Every tax ought to be so contrived, as both to take out and to keep out of the pockets of the people as little as possible, over and above what it brings into the public treasury of the state. A tax may either take out or keep out of the pockets of the people, a great deal more than it brings into the public treasury, in the four following ways. First, the levying of it may require a great number of officers, whose salaries may eat up the greater part of the produce of the tax, and whose perquisites may impose another additional tax upon the people. Secondly, it may obstruct the industry of the people, and discourage them from applying to certain branches of business which might give maintenance and employment to great multitudes. While it obliges the people to pay, it may thus diminish, or perhaps destroy, some of the funds which might enable them more easily to do so. Thirdly, by the forfeitures and other penalties which those unfortunate individuals incur, who attempt unsuccessfully to evade the tax, it may frequently ruin them, and thereby put an end to the benefit which the community might have received from the employment of their capitals. An injudicious tax offers a great temptation to smuggling. But the penalties for smuggling must rise in proportion to the temptation. The law, contrary to all the ordinary principles of justice, first creates the temptation, and then punishes those who yield to it; and it commonly enhances the punishment, too, in proportion to the very circumstance which ought certainly to alleviate it, the temptation to commit the crime. Fourthly, by subjecting the people to the frequent visits and the odious examination of the tax-gatherers, it may expose them to much unnecessary trouble, vexation, and oppression; and though vexation is not, strictly speaking, expense, it is certainly equivalent to the expense at which every man would be willing to redeem himself from it. It is in some one or other of these four different ways, that taxes are frequently so much more burdensome to the people than they are beneficial to the sovereign.

The evidence justice and utility of the foregoing maxims have recommended them, more or less, to the attention of all nations. All nations have endeavoured, to the best of their judgment, to render their taxes as equal as they could contrive; as certain, as convenient to the contributor, both in the time and in the mode of payment, and in proportion to the revenue which they brought to the prince, as little burdensome to the people. . . .

A tax law of 1696 provided that each window in houses above a certain size would attract a tax charge.

**Wilkinson, M., *Taxation*, London: Macmillan, 1992, p. 23**

*Windows and Vans*
In 1696 a tax was imposed on windows which were probably a fairish measure of the ability to pay. Revenue was raised from those with windows and this represented the minimum burden of the tax. However, this was not the only effect. People who wanted to reduce their tax liability had windows bricked up and new houses were built with

fewer windows. This type of tax-avoiding behaviour results in a distortion of choice and therefore causes an excess burden of the tax. Bricked-up windows and darker rooms reduced welfare but raised no revenue. In the 1950s and 1960s light vans were less heavily taxed than cars (a Mini van, for example, was cheaper than a Mini car). Some people chose to buy vans rather than cars in order to avoid the higher tax. Choice was distorted and welfare was reduced because vision was restricted and there was no light or view for passengers in the back. Again this welfare cost was not offset by the raising of any revenue.

## 1.5  History

### 1.5.1  THE INCOME TAX OF PITT AND ADDINGTON

Among eighteenth-century taxes, there had been a window tax.

**Brewer's Dictionary of Phrase and Fable**

**Pitt's Pictures** or *Billy Pitt's Pictures*. Blind windows; so called because many windows were blocked up when William Pitt augmented the Window Tax in 1784, and again in 1797.

With deduction at source and the Schedular System, Addington's income tax raised far more revenue than Pitt's had done.

**Emory, M., 'The Early English Income Tax: A Heritage For The Contemporary', (1965) 9 The American Journal of Legal History, pp. 286, 309–313**

. . . As previously noted, the reaction to the Income Tax Act of 1799 was very antagonistic. Although the opposition to the legislation gradually subsided and some pamphlets were to be seen favoring the Act, the general feeling remained very much opposed to the enactment. When hostilities ceased with the Treaty of Amiens, and the clamour for repeal increased, Addington, who had succeeded Pitt as Prime Minister and Chancellor of the Exchequer, proposed repeal as part of his first Budget in April 1802, which was subsequently enacted by Parliament. The public outcry against the tax was of such magnitude that the records pertaining to the earlier tax were ordered destroyed. The notion that such were 'cut into small pieces and conveyed to a paper manufacturer where, under the eyes of one of the Commissioners, they were to be committed to the mash tub' persisted until relatively recently when copies of statements and other data, previously thought unavailable, were discovered. Addington relied, for a time, on new excises and increased assessed taxes, but when the negotiations with France over British retention of Malta broke down, Britain declared war in May 1803, thus imposing the prospect of far greater fiscal burdens on the Addington government. In introducing his Budget on June 13, 1803, Addington proposed *inter alia*, a tax on 'land and property', in reality an income tax, but, of course, assuaged the House by stating: 'I wish it to be distinctly understood that I consider these duties as applicable to war only and I intend to propose that they should cease within six months after the restoration of peace.' The bill called for, generally speaking, an income tax of five per cent with an exclusion of income under £60. During the course of the debate upon the legislation several important issues, which were to shape the future of income taxation generally were discussed and resolved. Addington proposed a slightly preferential rate of tax for professional incomes and wages under £150. Income from land and investments, as well as commercial and industrial incomes, were to pay the full rate above the £60 exemption.

Once again Pitt was steadfastly opposed to any differentiation as to species of income. Noting that the modes of disposing of capital are various ('One man likes to employ his capital in a business which requires great labour', etc.), Pitt urged:

'Any attempt to meddle, by a legislative measure, with this, the usual and spontaneous distribution of property, would be highly unjust. . . . If taxes are to be levied, they should be accommodated to the present state of property, which should in no case be disturbed. . . . in a country like this, it would be unwise to encourage any man, by a partial tax, to give his capital a particular direction. . .'

Addington ultimately abandoned, 'with great difficulty', his rudimentary scheme of differentiation of income sources and agreed that a graduated scale of income should apply to all amounts between £60 and £150.

Probably the most novel feature of Addington's proposal was his plan for 'Taxation at the Source,' a true progenitor of the withholding system so successful in the United States. Admittedly, the plan advanced by Addington was aimed at increasing the efficiency of collection, and the prevention of evasion. Such, certainly, were the essential reasons for the inauguration of the withholding system in the United States. Equally important, however, is the conclusion that such a plan 'was calculated to avoid any disclosure of the circumstances or property of the parties paying the tax.' As proposed, the bill called for 'taxation at the source' on three levels. In the case of income from real property, the deduction of the tax was made the duty of the tenant. With respect to public securities, the tax was to be withheld prior to payment by the Bank of England. Finally, employers were to withhold the normal rate of tax on wages and salaries due their employees. Prevention of disclosure arose, therefore, since neither the landlord nor the creditor of money loaned would make any return of the rent or interest received since the tax on the amount received by them would already have been deducted. It would appear, therefore, that withholding, which is considered by many to be one of the cornerstones of a modern income tax owes its origin, in part at least, to a somewhat unrelated controversy. Pitt, however, steadfastly opposed taxation at the source on public securities by noting:

'To trench upon the public funds, so as to deduct a certain portion of the interest payable to the fundholders, was striking a first blow at the credit of the country. . . . Government had no right to avail itself of the circumstances of having borrowed money . . .'

The objection voiced is against both the schedular system of assessment proposed by Addington as well as against 'Taxation at the Source' on public securities. Part and parcel of Addington's 'Taxation at the Source' was a plan where, unlike Pitt's lump sum assessment in the 1799 Act, the taxpayer's income was divided into a convenient number of categories or 'schedules', as they are called in the Act. An official exposition of the Act explained that four main classes of income were envisaged, i.e., landed property, funded property, produce of industry, and government offices. The schedular assessment was, no doubt, designed to eliminate the full disclosure which was so greatly feared. If it accomplished this goal at all, however, it was in a most superficial sense. It was Addington's aim, as far as was possible, to impose the tax in each schedule upon the source of the income. If Pitt was objecting to the schedular system *per se*, it would seem that his position lacked merit.

It is more likely, however, that Pitt's dislike of the schedular plan was due to the fact that it represented the vehicle by which certain aspects of taxation at the source were to be accomplished. (There is, it should be noted, no evidence that Pitt opposed taxation at the source, as a general principle.) Pitt, nevertheless, won the day as respects the Addington proposal relative to taxation at the source on public securities. Since Pitt enjoyed the confidence of the City of London to an extent that Addington did not, his strongly voiced opposition to the proposal 'induced the directors of the Bank of England [the suggested withholding agent for the interest payable] to recede from their original agreement and to advise Addington that his proposals would prove unpracticable.'

As important as the earlier enactments were in the developmental process of the income tax, it is the Act of 1803 that must form a central position in any analysis of the history of the tax. The remarkable thing about the 1803 law is that the tax in England today remains strikingly similar to this early legislation. This contrasts sharply with the development of the tax in the United States, which, although coming into its own far later, and thus with a shorter history, has been shaped and molded by forces and pressures of all kinds to a point where it bears little, if any, resemblance to the earlier enactments. It is, one supposes, this aspect of durability which the English tax possesses, that makes consideration of the early tax a profitable endeavor. There have been, to be sure, numerous commissions and committees formed through the years which have made recommendations relating to the tax, many of which have been adopted. But the system adopted in 1803 has not been changed in any of its fundamental aspects. . . .

## 1.6   The Annual Budget

**Chancellor Gordon Brown, Budget Speech of 17 March 1998, *The Daily Telegraph*, 18 March 1998**

*This is an edited version of the Chancellor's Budget speech.*

ONLY once in a generation is the tax system fundamentally reformed. The Budget I bring before the House and country today begins the task of modernising not just taxation but the entire tax and benefits system of our country.

We do this to encourage enterprise; to reward work; to support families; to advance the ambitions not just of the few but of the many. For decades, under governments of both parties, the great economic strengths of our country have been undermined by deep-seated structural weaknesses — instability, under-investment and unemployment.

So behind the detailed measures of this Budget is the conviction that we must break for good from the conflicts and dogmas that have held us back and have for too long failed our country.

We must build a national economic purpose around new ambitions for Britain.

First: stability.

We must break from our history of stop-go and the false trade-offs between inflation and unemployment. The new ambition is long-term economic strength and stability based on an unshakeable commitment to prudent monetary and fiscal rules.

Second: enterprise.

Instead of punishing success by high taxation or offering the incentive of low taxation to only a few, the new ambition is a tax system that makes all work pay, that encourages skills and rewards enterprise and entrepreneurship throughout the economy.

Third: welfare reform.

The new ambition is a modern Welfare State that, instead of trapping people in poverty, provides opportunity for all.

And fourth: strong public services.

. . .

# CHAPTER TWO

# INCOME TAXATION: INCOME PROFITS, PERSONS AND CAPACITIES

## 2.1 Introduction

You may be acting in your personal capacity, the capacity of a partner or the capacity of a trustee or PR. This extract from the OED defines 'capacity'.

*The Oxford English Dictionary*, 2nd ed., vol II, Oxford: Clarendon Press, 1989

**capacity** . . .

**9. a.** Position, condition, character, relation.

*a* **1649** CHAS. I. *Wks.* 295 He should be in a capacity of Honor. **1655** FULLER *Ch. Hist.* III. 9 In what capacity these Jews came over, I finde not. **1710** POPE *Lett.* in *Wks.* V. 84, I am . . . dead in a natural capacity . . . dead in a poetical capacity . . . and dead in a civil capacity. **1747** HERVEY *Medit. & Contempl.* (1818) 266 The moon is . . . ready to act in the capacity of a guide. **1835** BUCHANAN *Ch. Establishm.* i. 7 Channels through which the mind of a people, in their collective capacity, can be expressed. **1848** MACAULAY *Hist. Eng.* I. 364 The King, in his individual capacity, had very little to give. **1871** SMILES *Charac.* iv. (1876) III.

†**b.** Relation, tenor, sense (of words). *Obs.*

**1720** WATERLAND *Vind. Christ's Divin.* 102 Irenæus understood those Texts . . . in that Capacity.

**10.** *Law.* Legal competency or qualification. *to be in capacity*: to be legally qualified.

## 2.2 *Income Profits* and *Income Losses*

### INCOME AND CORPORATION TAXES ACT 1988

**15. Schedule A**

  (1)  The Schedule referred to as Schedule A is as follows:—

SCHEDULE A

  1.—(1)  Tax is charged under this Schedule on the annual profits arising from a business carried on for the exploitation, as a source of rents or other receipts, of any estate, interest or rights in or over land in the United Kingdom.

  (2)  To the extent that any transaction is entered into for the exploitation, as a source of rents or other receipts, of any estate, interest or rights in or over land in the United Kingdom, it is taken to be entered into in the course of such a business.

  (3)  All businesses and transactions carried on or entered into by a particular person or partnership, so far as they are businesses or transactions the profits of which are chargeable to tax under this Schedule, are treated for the purposes of this Schedule as, or as entered into in the course of carrying on, a single business.

There are qualifications to this rule in the case of—

(a)   companies not resident in the United Kingdom (see subsection (1A) below); and

(b)   insurance companies (see sections 432AA and 441B(2A)).

(4)   The receipts referred to in the expression 'as a source of rents or other receipts' include—

(a)   payments in respect of a licence to occupy or otherwise to use land or the exercise of any other right over land, and

(b)   rentcharges, ground annuals and feu duties and other annual payments reserved in respect of, or charged on or issuing out of, the land.

2.—(1)   This Schedule does not apply to profits arising from the occupation of land.

(2)   This Schedule does not apply to—

(a)   profits charged to tax under Case I of Schedule D under—

section 53(1) (farming and market gardening), or

section 55 (mines, quarries and other concerns);

(b)   receipts or expenses taken into account as trading receipts or expenses under section 98 (tied premises);

(c)   rent charged to tax under Schedule D under—

section 119 (rent, etc. payable in connection with mines, quarries and other concerns), or

section 120(1) (certain rent, etc. payable in respect of electric line wayleaves).

(3)   The profits of a Schedule A business carried on by a company shall be computed without regard to items giving rise to—

credits or debits within Chapter II of Part IV of the Finance Act 1996 (loan relationships), or

exchange gains or losses within Chapter II of Part II of the Finance Act 1993 (foreign exchange gains and losses) . . .

### 18.   Schedule D

(1)   The Schedule referred to as Schedule D is as follows:—

SCHEDULE D

Tax under this Schedule shall be charged in respect of—

(a)   the annual profits or gains arising or accruing—

(i)   to any person residing in the United Kingdom from any kind of property whatever, whether situated in the United Kingdom or elsewhere, and

(ii)   to any person residing in the United Kingdom from any trade, profession or vocation, whether carried on in the United Kingdom or elsewhere, and

(iii)   to any person, whether a Commonwealth citizen or not, although not resident in the United Kingdom from any property whatever in the United Kingdom or from any trade, profession or vocation exercised within the United Kingdom, and

(b)   all interest of money, annuities and other annual profits or gains not charged under Schedule A or E, and not specially exempted from tax.

(2) Tax under Schedule D shall be charged under the Cases set out in subsection (3) below, and subject to and in accordance with the provisions of the Tax Acts applicable to those Cases respectively.

(3)   The Cases are—

Case I: tax in respect of any trade carried on in the United Kingdom or elsewhere but not contained in Schedule A;

Case II: tax in respect of any profession or vocation not contained in any other Schedule;

Case III: [income tax] in respect of—

(a)   any interest of money, whether yearly or otherwise, or any annuity or other annual payment, whether such payment is payable within or out of the United Kingdom, either as a charge on any property of the person paying the same by virtue of any deed or will or otherwise, or as a reservation out of it, as a personal debt or obligation by virtue of any contract, or whether the same is received and payable half-yearly or at any shorter or more distant periods, but not including any payment chargeable under Schedule A, and

(b)   all discounts, and

(c)  income from securities which is payable out of the public revenue of the United Kingdom or Northern Ireland;

Case IV: [income tax] tax in respect of income arising from securities out of the United Kingdom;

Case V: tax in respect of income arising from possessions out of the United Kingdom not being income consisting of emoluments of any office or employment;

Case VI: tax in respect of any annual profits or gains not falling under any other Case of Schedule D and not charged by virtue of Schedule A or E.

. . .

(4)  The provisions of Schedule D and of subsection (2) above are without prejudice to any other provision of the Tax Acts directing tax to be charged under Schedule D or under one or other of the Cases set out in subsection (3) above, and tax directed to be so charged shall be charged accordingly.

. . .

### 19.  Schedule E

(1) The Schedule referred to as Schedule E is as follows:—

### SCHEDULE E

1.  Tax under this Schedule shall be charged in respect of any office or employment on emoluments therefrom which fall under one or more than one of the following Cases—

Case I: any emoluments for any year of assessment in which the person holding the office or employment is resident and ordinarily resident in the United Kingdom, subject however to section 192 if the emoluments are foreign emoluments (within the meaning of that section) and to section 193(1) if in the year of assessment concerned he performs the duties of the office or employment wholly or partly outside the United Kingdom;

Case II: any emoluments, in respect of duties performed in the United Kingdom, for any year of assessment in which the person holding the office or employment is not resident (or, if resident, not ordinarily resident) in the United Kingdom, subject however to section 192 if the emoluments are foreign emoluments (within the meaning of that section);

Case III: any emoluments for any year of assessment in which the person holding the office or employment is resident in the United Kingdom (whether or not ordinarily resident there) so far as the emoluments are received in the United Kingdom; and tax shall not be chargeable in respect of emoluments of an office or employment under any other paragraph of this Schedule.

2.  Tax under this Schedule shall be charged in respect of every annuity, pension or stipend payable by the Crown or out of the public revenue of the United Kingdom or of Northern Ireland, other than annuities charged under paragraph (c) of Case III of Schedule D.

3.  Tax under this Schedule shall also be charged in respect of any pension which is paid otherwise than by or on behalf of a person outside the United Kingdom. . . .

### 20.  Schedule F

(1)  The Schedule referred to as Schedule F is as follows:—

### SCHEDULE F

1.  Subject to section 95(1A)(a), income tax under this Schedule shall be chargeable for any year of assessment in respect of all dividends and other distributions in that year of a company resident in the United Kingdom which are not specially excluded from income tax, and for the purposes of income tax all such distributions shall be regarded as income however they fall to be dealt with in the hands of the recipient.

2.  For the purposes of this Schedule and all other purposes of the Tax Acts . . . any such distribution in respect of which a person is entitled to a tax credit shall be treated as representing income equal to the aggregate of the amount or value of that distribution and the amount of that credit, and income tax under this Schedule shall accordingly be charged on that aggregate.

(2)  . . . no distribution which is chargeable under Schedule F shall be chargeable under any other provision of the Income Tax Acts. . . .

### 2.2.1  INCOME PROFITS

*ARIS-BAINBRIDGE* v *TURNER MANUFACTURING CO. LTD* **[1951] 1 KB 563, 564**

Income corresponds to the expressions *receipts* or *turnover.*

A company had agreed to pay a commission to its sales manager of a percentage of the company's 'turnover.' The issue was whether commission was payable on contracts with Government departments, terminated because of the end of the Second World War. McNair J held that it was so payable.

McNAIR J: . . . The question whether the commission ought to have been paid on the whole of the company's receipts or only on selected receipts turns primarily on the meaning of the phrase 'turnover of the company's annual business'. Giving to this phrase its ordinary grammatical meaning, I consider that it includes all sums received and receivable in the year in question as the result of the company's trading, whether normal or abnormal; in other words, it means all the money which the company turns over in the year for the purpose of making its gains or losses. I am reinforced in that view by the speech of Lord Dunedin in the well-known case of *Gliksten & Son Ld* v *Green* [1929] AC 381, which raised the question whether a company who were carrying on business as timber merchants were required to bring into their profit and loss account as a trading receipt, for the purpose of arriving at the company's profits for income-tax purposes, a large sum which they had recovered under a fire insurance policy upon their stocks. The House held that they were so obliged, and Lord Dunedin said [1929] AC 381, 385:

> The whole point is that the business of the company is to buy timber and to sell timber, and when they sell timber they turn it into money. This particular timber was turned into money, not because it was sold, but because it was burned and they had an insurance policy over it. The whole question comes to be whether that is a turnover in the ordinary course of their business. I think it was. They had that amount of timber, which they got rid of and for which they got a certain price, and then they could begin again. The more times you have a turnover — that is to say, the more sales you can get, provided that you are carrying on business at remunerative prices — the better for you. The result of this fire was that they got rid of so much timber and got the insurance money at that figure, and that seems to me precisely in the same position as if they got rid of it by giving it to a customer.

That seems to me to support the construction at which I have arrived on this particular contract.

I see no reason at all why there should not be included in the annual turnover of the company's business any receipts arising under the terms of the break clause; they are moneys due under the contract. The plaintiff is therefore entitled to judgment . . . in respect of unpaid commission . . .

## 2.3  Persons and Capacities

### 2.3.1  PERSONS

#### 2.3.1.1  Individuals

The basic charging provision for individuals resident in the UK in the current tax year is:

**INCOME AND CORPORATION TAXES ACT 1988**

**1.  The charge to income tax**

(1)  Income tax shall be charged in accordance with the provisions of the Income Tax Acts in respect of all property, profits or gains respectively described or comprised in

the Schedules, A, D, E and F, set out in sections 15 to 20 or which in accordance with the Income Tax Acts are to be brought into charge to tax under any of those Schedules or otherwise.

### 2.3.1.2  Companies

The rights conferred on the company and the obligations to which it is subject are different from the rights and obligations of each of the individuals who own the company. The following extract from a very famous company law case illustrates this point. The requirement for seven persons to form a company has long been repealed. The case none the less contains the cardinal principle of company law.

### *SALOMON* v *SALOMON & CO. LTD* [1895–99] All ER Rep 33, 46–49 (HL)

LORD MACNAGHTEN: . . . Mr Salomon, who is now suing as a pauper, was a wealthy man in July, 1892. He was a boot and shoe manufacturer, trading on his own sole account under the firm of 'A. Salomon & Co.,' in High Street, Whitechapel, where he had extensive warehouses and a large establishment. He had been in the trade over thirty years. He had lived in the same neighbourhood all along, and for many years past he had occupied the same premises. So far things had gone very well with him. Beginning with little or no capital he had gradually built up a thriving business, and he was undoubtedly in good credit and repute. It is impossible to say exactly what the value of the business was. But there was a substantial surplus of assets over liabilities. And it seems to me to be pretty clear that, if Mr Salomon had been minded to dispose of his business in the market as a going concern, he might fairly have counted upon retiring with at least £10,000 in his pocket. Mr Salomon, however, did not want to part with the business. He had a wife and a family consisting of five sons and a daughter. Four of the sons were working with their father. The eldest, who was about thirty years of age, was practically the manager. But the sons were not partners; they were only servants. Not unnaturally, perhaps, they were dissatisfied with their position. They kept pressing their father to give them a share in the concern. 'They troubled me,' says Mr Salomon, 'all the while.' So at length Mr Salomon did what hundreds of others have done under similar circumstances; he turned his business into a limited company. He wanted, he says, to extend the business and make provision for his family. In those words, I think, he fairly describes the principal motives which influenced his action.

All the usual formalities were gone through; all the requirements of the Companies Act 1862, were duly observed. There was a contract with a trustee in the usual form for the sale of the business to a company about to be formed. There was a memorandum of association duly signed and registered, stating that the company was formed to carry that contract into effect, and fixing the capital at £40,000 in 40,000 shares of £1 each. There were articles of association providing the usual machinery for conducting the business. The first directors were to be nominated by the majority of the subscribers to the memorandum of association. The directors, when appointed, were authorised to exercise all such powers of the company as were not by statute or by the articles required to be exercised in general meeting; and there was express power to borrow on debentures, with the limitation that the borrowing was not to exceed £10,000 without the sanction of a general meeting. The company was intended from the first to be a private company; it remained a private company to the end. No prospectus was issued; no invitation to take shares was ever addressed to the public. The subscribers to the memorandum were Mr Salomon, his wife, and five of his children who were grown up. The subscribers met and appointed Mr Salomon and his two elder sons directors.

The directors then proceeded to carry out the proposed transfer. By an agreement dated 2 August 1892, the company adopted the preliminary contract, and in accordance with it the business was taken over by the company as from 1 June 1892. The price fixed by the contract was duly paid. The price on paper was extravagant. It amounted to over £39,000, a sum which represented the sanguine expectations of a fond owner rather than anything that can be called a businesslike or reasonable estimate of value. That, no doubt, is a circumstance which, at first sight, calls for observation, but when the facts of the case and the position of the parties are considered, it is difficult to see what bearing it has on the question before your Lordships. The purchase money was paid in this way. As money came in sums amounting to £20,000 were paid to Mr Salomon, and then immediately returned to the company in exchange for fully-paid shares. The sum of £10,000 was paid in debentures for the like amount. The balance, with the exception of about £1,000, which Mr Salomon seems to have received and retained went in discharge of the debts and liabilities of the business at the time of the transfer, which were thus entirely wiped off. In the result, therefore, Mr Salomon received for his business about £1,000 in cash, £10,000 in debentures and half the nominal capital of the company in fully-paid shares for what they were worth. No other shares were issued except the seven shares taken by the subscribers to the memorandum, who, of course, knew all the circumstances, and had, therefore, no ground for complaint on the score of over-valuation.

The company had a brief career; it fell upon evil days. Shortly after it was started there seems to have come a period of great depression in the boot and shoe trade. There were strikes of workmen too, and in view of that danger, contracts with public bodies, which were the principal source of Mr Salomon's profit, were split up and divided between different firms. The attempts made to push the business on behalf of the new company crammed its warehouses with unsaleable stock. Mr Salomon seems to have done what he could; both he and his wife lent the company money, and then he got his debentures cancelled and re-issued to a Mr Broderip, who advanced him £5,000, which he immediately handed over to the company on loan. The temporary relief only hastened ruin. Mr Broderip's interest was not paid when it became due. He took proceedings at once and got a receiver appointed. Then, of course, came liquidation and a forced sale of the company's assets. They realised enough to pay Mr Broderip, but not enough to pay the debentures in full, and the unsecured creditors were consequently left out in the cold. In this state of things the liquidator met Mr Broderip's claim by a counterclaim, to which he made Mr Salomon defendant. He disputed the validity of the debentures on the ground of fraud. On the same ground he claimed rescission of the agreement for the transfer of the business, cancellation of the debentures, and repayment by Mr Salomon of the balance of the purchase money. In the alternative he claimed payment of £20,000 on Mr Salomon's shares, alleging that nothing had been paid on them.

When the trial came on before Vaughan Williams J, the validity of Mr Broderip's claim was admitted, and it was not disputed that the 20,000 shares were fully paid up. The case presented by the liquidator broke down completely. But the learned judge suggested that the company had a right of indemnity against Mr Salomon. The signatories of the memorandum of association were, he said, mere nominees of Mr Salomon, mere dummies. The company was Mr Salomon in another form. He used the name of the company as an alias. He employed the company as his agent; so the company, he thought, was entitled to indemnity against its principal. The counterclaim was, accordingly, amended to raise this point, and on the amendment being made the learned judge pronounced an order in accordance with the view he had expressed.

The order of the learned judge appears to me to be founded on a misconception of the scope and effect of the Companies Act 1862. In order to form a company limited by shares, the Act requires that a memorandum of association should be signed by seven persons, who are each to take one share at least. If those conditions are complied with, what can it matter whether the signatories are relations or strangers? There is nothing in the Act requiring that the subscribers to the memorandum should be independent or unconnected, or that they or any one of them should take a substantial interest in the undertaking, or that they should have a mind and will of their own, as one of the learned lords justices seems to think, or that there should be anything like a balance of power in the constitution of the company. In almost every company that is formed, the statutory number is eked out by clerks or friends, who sign their names at the request of the promoter or promoters without intending to take any further part or interest in the matter.

When the memorandum is duly signed and registered, though there be only seven shares taken, the subscribers are a body corporate 'capable forthwith' to use the words of the enactments, 'of exercising all the functions of an incorporated company'... Those are strong words. The company attains maturity on its birth. There is no period of minority; no interval of incapacity. I cannot understand how a body corporate thus made 'capable' by statute can lose its individuality by issuing the bulk of its capital to one person, whether he be a subscriber to the memorandum or not. The company is at law a different person altogether from the subscribers to the memorandum, and, though it may be that after incorporation the business is precisely the same as it was before, the same persons are managers, and the same hands receive the profits, the company is not in law the agent of the subscribers or trustee for them. Nor are the subscribers as members liable, in any shape or form, except to the extent and in the manner provided by the Act. That is, I think, the declared intention of the enactment. If the view of the learned judge were sound, it would follow that no common law partnership could register as a company limited by shares without remaining subject to unlimited liability.

Mr Salomon appealed, but his appeal was dismissed with costs, though the appellate court did not entirely accept the view of the court below. The decision of the Court of Appeal proceeds on a declaration of opinion embodied in the order which has been already read. I must say that I, too, have great difficulty in understanding this declaration. If it only means that Mr Salomon availed himself to the full of the advantages offered by the Companies Act 1862, what is there wrong in that? Leave out the words 'contrary to the true intent and meaning of the Companies Act 1862,' and bear in mind that 'the creditors of the company' are not the creditors of Mr Salomon, and the declaration is perfectly innocent. It has no sting in it. . . .

Among the principal reasons which induce persons to form private companies as is stated very clearly by Mr Palmer in his treatise on the subject, are the desire to avoid the risk of bankruptcy, and the increased facility afforded for borrowing money. By means of a private company, as Mr Palmer observes, a trade can be carried on with limited liability and without exposing the persons interested in it in the event of failure to the harsh provisions of the bankruptcy law. A company too can raise money on debentures which an ordinary trader cannot do; any member of a company acting in good faith is as much entitled to take and hold the company's debentures as any outside creditor. Every creditor is entitled to get and to hold the best security the law allows him to take. If, however, the declaration of the Court of Appeal means that Mr Salomon acted fraudulently or dishonestly, I must say that I can find nothing in the evidence to support such an imputation. The purpose for which Mr Salomon and the other subscribers to the memorandum were associated was 'lawful.' The fact that Mr Salomon raised £5,000 for the company on debentures that belonged to him seems to me strong evidence of his good faith and of his confidence in the company.

The unsecured creditors of A. Salomon & Co., Ltd, may be entitled to sympathy, but they have only themselves to blame for their misfortunes. They trusted the company, I suppose, because they had long dealt with Mr Salomon and he had always paid his way; but they had full notice that they were no longer dealing with an individual, and they must be taken to have been cognisant of the memorandum and of the articles of association. For such a catastrophe as has occurred in this case some would blame the law that allows such a thing as a floating charge. But a floating charge is too convenient a form of security to be lightly abolished. I have long thought, and I believe some of your Lordships also think, that the ordinary trade creditors of a trading company ought to have a preferential claim on the assets in liquidation in respect of debts incurred within a certain limited time before the winding-up. But that is not the law at present. Everybody knows that when there is a winding-up, debenture holders generally step in and sweep off everything. And a great scandal it is.

It has become the fashion to call companies of this class 'one-man companies.' That is a taking nickname, but it does not help one much in the way of argument. If it is intended to convey the meaning that a company which is under the absolute control of one person is not a company legally incorporated, although the requirements of the Act of 1862 may have been complied with, it is inaccurate and misleading; if it merely means that there is a predominant partner possessing an overwhelming influence and entitled practically to the whole of the profits, there is nothing in that that I can see contrary to the true intention of the Act of 1862, or against public policy, or detrimental to the interests of creditors. If the shares are fully paid up it cannot matter whether they are in the hands of one or many. If the shares are not fully paid it is as easy to gauge the solvency of an individual as to estimate the financial ability of a crowd.

One argument was addressed to your Lordships which ought perhaps to be noticed although it was not the ground of decision in either of the courts below. It was argued that the agreement for the transfer of the business to the company ought to be set aside, because there was no independent board of directors, and the property was transferred at an over-value. There are, it seems to me, two answers to that argument. In the first place, the directors did just what they were authorised to do by the memorandum of association. There was no fraud or misrepresentation and there was nobody deceived. In the second place the company have put it out of their power to restore the property which was transferred to them. It was said that the assets were sold by an order made in the presence of Mr Salomon, though not with his consent, which declared that the sale was to be without prejudice to the rights claimed by the company by their counterclaim. I cannot see what difference that makes. The reservation in the order seems to me to be simply nugatory. . . .

## INCOME AND CORPORATION TAXES ACT 1988

### 6. The charge to corporation tax and exclusion of income tax and capital gains tax

(1) Corporation tax shall be charged on profits of companies, and the Corporation Tax Acts shall apply, for any financial year for which Parliament so determines, and where an Act charges corporation tax for any financial year the Corporation Tax Acts apply, without any express provision, for that year accordingly.

. . .

### 8. General scheme of corporation tax

(1) Subject to any exceptions provided for by the Corporation Tax Acts, a company shall be chargeable to corporation tax on all its profits wherever arising.

. . .

(3) Corporation tax for any financial year shall be charged on profits arising in that year; but assessments to corporation tax shall be made on a company by reference to accounting periods . . .

### 2.3.2 CAPACITIES

### 2.3.2.1 Partners

An individual may act in the capacity of a partner in a partnership or firm.

## PARTNERSHIP ACT 1890

**1.**—(1) Partnership is the relation which subsists between persons carrying on a business in common with a view of profit.

(2) But the relation between members of any company or association which is—

(a) registered as a company under the Companies Act 1862, or any other Act of Parliament for the time being in force and relating to the registration of joint stock companies; or

(b) formed or incorporated by or in pursuance of any other Act of Parliament or letters patent, or Royal Charter; or

(c) a company engaged in working mines within and subject to the jurisdiction of the Stannaries:

is not a partnership within the meaning of this Act.

The concept of tax transparency or fiscal transparency is briefly considered in this extract from an article by Ashley Greenbank.

### Greenbank, A., 'Fiscal Transparency: Domestic Law and Treaty Interpretation', http://www.macfarlanes.com/bulletinfinanceleasing.html#fiscal (extract)

The classification of entities established or incorporated under another legal system is a difficult problem for any system of tax law. Attempts to shoe-horn unfamiliar forms of business organisation into domestic categories in order to apply the appropriate tax treatment will almost inevitably result in anomalies which can either be advantageous or disastrous in tax terms for those involved. Particular difficulties are experienced in relation to the classification of partnerships and other entities which under the law of state in which they are established are treated as 'fiscally transparent', that is, *the profits of which are taxed in the hands of the members rather than in the hands of the relevant business entity*. [emphasis added.]

### 2.3.2.2 Trustees and personal representatives

There are a number of crucial respects in which trustees and PRs are different from each other.

### CORBETT v IRC [1938] 1 KB 567, 575–576 (CA)

Sir Wilfred Greene MR [referring to *Dr Barnardo's Homes v Special Commissioners of Income Tax* [1921] 2 AC 1]: . . . It is quite obvious . . . that . . . the principle underlying the *Barnardo* case was not a limited principle turning entirely on the precise language of the provisions of the Income Tax Act . . . I read it as deciding . . . that, until the residue is ascertained in the due course of administration, the beneficiaries have no title to that residue. . . .

That that was the view of the House of Lords, or must be taken to be the view of the House of Lords, quite apart from what Lord Buckmaster said, appears, I think, from a consideration of a passage in the speech of Lord Finlay . . .

. . . [T]he language of Lord Finlay is, in my opinion, just as applicable to the case where the residue is settled as to the case where the residue is not settled. In neither case are the executors trustees; in neither case is the income the income of anybody but the executors; in each case the executors and not the beneficiaries are the recipients of the income, and there is no relation back; in each case, if no right of deduction at the source had existed, it is the executors and the executors only who could have been made liable for the tax. I myself attach great importance to the distinction drawn between the position and estate of executors and the position and estate of trustees, for this reason, that where trustees are in receipt of income which it is their duty to pay over to beneficiaries, either with or without deduction of something for trustees' expenses on the way, that income is at its very inception the beneficiaries' income. It is perfectly true that for assessment purposes the trustees may fall to be assessed, but the income is the beneficiaries' income from the very first and the expenses so paid out of it are paid out of it, so to speak, on the way. But, in the case of executors, it is not true to say (and this is how I read the opinion of Lord Finlay) that the income when received by executors pending the conclusion of the administration is the income of the beneficiaries in that sense . . .

### STAMP DUTIES COMMISSIONER (QUEENSLAND) v LIVINGSTON
### [1964] 3 All ER 692, 696 (PC)

The question in this case was whether the deceased, Mrs Coulson, had a 'beneficial interest' in her husband's *un*administered estate.

VISCOUNT RADCLIFFE: . . . When Mrs Coulson died she had the interest of a residuary legatee in his testator's unadministered estate. The nature of that interest has been conclusively defined by decisions of long established authority, and its definition no doubt depends on the peculiar status which the law accorded to an executor for the purposes of carrying out his duties of administration. There were special rules which long prevailed about the devolution of freehold land and its liability for the debts of a deceased, but subject to the working of these rules whatever property came to the executor virtute officii came to him in full ownership, without distinction between legal and equitable interests. The whole property was his. He held it for the purpose of carrying out the functions and duties of administration, not for his own benefit; and these duties would be enforced on him by the Court of Chancery, if application had to be made for that purpose by a creditor or beneficiary interested in the estate. Certainly, therefore, he was in a fiduciary position with regard to the assets that came to him in the right of his office, and for certain purposes and in some aspects he was treated by the court as a trustee. Kay J, in *Re Marsden, Bowden* v *Layland, Gibbs* v *Layland*, said [1881–85] All ER Rep 993, 996]

> An executor is personally liable in equity for all breaches of the ordinary trusts which, in courts of equity, are considered to arise from his office.

He is a trustee 'in this sense'.

It may not be possible to state exhaustively what those trusts are at any one moment. Essentially, they are trusts to preserve the assets, to deal properly with them, and to apply them in a due course of administration for the benefit of those interested according to that course, creditors, the death duty authorities, legatees of various sorts, and the residuary beneficiaries. They might just as well have been termed 'duties in respect of the assets' as trusts. What equity did not do was to recognise or create for residuary legatees a beneficial interest in the assets in the executor's hands during the course of administration. Conceivably, this could have been done, in the sense that the assets, whatever they might be from time to time, could have been treated as a present, though fluctuating, trust fund held for the benefit of all those interested in the estate according to the measure of their respective interests; but it never was done. It would have been a clumsy and unsatisfactory device, from a practical point of view; and, indeed, it would have been in plain conflict with the basic conception of equity that to impose the fetters of a trust on property, with the resulting creation of equitable interests in that property, there had to be specific subjects identifiable as the trust fund. An unadministered estate was incapable of satisfying this requirement. The assets as a whole were in the hands of the executor, his property; and, until administration was complete, no one was in a position to say what items of property would need to be realised for the purposes of that administration or of what the residue, when ascertained, would consist or what its value would be. Even in modern economies, when the ready marketability of many forms of property can almost be assumed, valuation and realisation are very far from being interchangeable terms. . . .

Saying that the beneficiaries have an immediate entitlement to the trust income is another way of saying that the income accrues directly to the beneficiary.

### WILLIAMS v SINGER [1921] 1 AC 65, 68 (HL)

The legislation discussed by Viscount Cave in this extract, the Income Tax Act 1842 and the Finance Act 1914, have been superseded, although the basic principle discussed is still generally accepted today.

VISCOUNT CAVE: . . . In *Williams* v *Singer* the respondents are the trustees of a settlement under which the Princesse de Polignac is the beneficial tenant for life in possession. The settlement is in English form, and the trustees are all domiciled and resident in the United Kingdom; but the Princess (who is a widow) is a French subject by marriage, and is domiciled and resident abroad. The settled fund, so far as it comes into question in these proceedings, consists of certain foreign investments of considerable value, and under orders signed by the trustees the whole income from these investments is paid to the account of the Princess at a bank in New York, no part thereof being remitted to this country. . . .

. . . counsel for the [Revenue] . . . contended that as the income in question in the cases under appeal 'accrued' to the trustees as the legal holders of the investments, and the trustees are the persons legally entitled to receive it, they are the persons chargeable under the Act. Indeed, I understood Mr Cunliffe [counsel for the Revenue] to go so far as to say that, when funds are vested in trustees, the revenue authorities are entitled to look to those trustees for the tax, and are neither bound nor entitled to look beyond the legal ownership.

My Lords, I think it clear that such a proposition cannot be maintained. It is contrary to the express words of s. 42 of the Income Tax Act 1842, which provides that no trustee who shall have authorised the receipt of the profits arising from trust property by the person entitled thereto, and who shall have made a return of the name and residence of such person in manner required by the Act, shall be required to do any other act for the purpose of assessing such person. And, apart from this provision, a decision that in the case of trust property the trustee alone is to be looked to would lead to strange results. If the legal ownership alone is to be considered, a beneficial owner in moderate circumstances may lose his right to exemption or abatement by reason of the fact that he has wealthy trustees, or a wealthy beneficiary may escape [tax] by appointing a number of trustees in less affluent circumstances. Indeed, if the Act is to be construed as counsel for the appellants suggests, a beneficiary domiciled in this country may altogether avoid the tax on his foreign income spent abroad by the simple expedient of appointing one or more foreign trustees. Accordingly I put this contention aside.

On the other hand, I do not think it would be correct to say that, whenever property is held in trust, the person liable to be taxed is the beneficiary and not the trustee. Section 41 of the Income Tax Act 1842, renders the trustee, guardian or other person who has the control of the property of an infant, married woman, or lunatic chargeable to income tax in the place of such infant, married woman, or lunatic; and the same section declares that any person not resident in Great Britain shall be chargeable in the name of his trustee or agent having the receipt of any profits or gains. Section 108 of the same Act, which deals with the profits or gains arising from foreign possessions or foreign securities, provides that in default of the owner or proprietor being charged, the trustee, agent or receiver of such profits or gains shall be charged for the same. And even apart from these special provisions I am not prepared to deny that there are many cases in which a trustee in receipt of trust income may be chargeable with the tax upon such income. For instance, a trustee carrying on a trade for the benefit of creditors or beneficiaries, a trustee for charitable purposes, or a trustee who is under an obligation to apply the trust income in satisfaction of charges or to accumulate it for future distribution, appears to come within this category; and other similar cases may be imagined.

The fact is that if the Income Tax Acts are examined, it will be found that the person charged with the tax is neither the trustee nor the beneficiary as such, but the person in actual receipt and control of the income which it is sought to reach. The object of the Acts is to secure for the State a proportion of the profits chargeable, and this end is attained (speaking generally) by the simple and effective expedient of taxing the profits where they are found. If the beneficiary receives them he is liable to be assessed upon them. If the trustee receives and controls them, he is primarily so liable. If they are under the control of a guardian or committee for person not sui juris or of an agent or receiver for persons resident abroad, they are taxed in his hands. But in cases where a trustee or agent is made chargeable with the tax the statutes recognise the fact that he is a trustee or agent for others and he is taxed on behalf of and as representing his beneficiaries or principals. This is made clear by the language of many sections of the Act of 1842. For instance, s. 41 provides that a person not resident in Great Britain shall be chargeable 'in the name of' his trustee or agent. Section 44 refers to the trustee or agent of any person as being assessed 'in respect of' such person, and gives him a right to retain the tax out of any money of such person coming to his hands. Section 51, under which trustees and others are bound to make returns, refers to the event of the beneficiary being charged either 'in the name of' the trustee or other person making the return, or in his own name. Section 53 refers to the trustee or agent as being charged 'on account' of the beneficiary; and similar expressions are found in other sections. In short, the intention of the Acts appears to be that where a beneficiary is in possession and control of the trust income and is sui juris, he is the person to be taxed; and that while a trustee may in certain cases be charged with the tax, he is in all such cases to be treated as charged on behalf or in respect of his beneficiaries, who will accordingly be entitled to any exemption or abatement which the Acts allow.

Applying the above conclusions to the present case, it follows in my opinion, first, that the respondent trustees, who have directed the trust income to be paid to the beneficial tenants for life and themselves receive no part of it, are not assessable to tax in respect of such income; and secondly, that even if they were so assessable, they would be assessable as trustees on behalf of the life tenants, who would accordingly be entitled to the benefit of the exemption contained in the proviso in s. 5 of the Finance Act 1914.

### *REID'S TRUSTEES v IRC* (1929) 14 TC 512, 527 (HL)

LORD SANDS: [explaining *Williams v Singer*] . . . The income never came into the coffers of the trustees, they never touched nor handled it. But they were the owners of the securities, and it was by their own mandate, which presumably they might have recalled, that payment was made directly to the beneficiary. It was, therefore, open to argument that theoretically the income must be held to have been received by them. This contention, however, was rejected. It was found that the substance of the matter and not only mere theory was to be regarded. That was all that was determined by the judgment in *Williams* v *Singer*. It was not held, and the decision does not involve, that when a body of trustees receive income of the trust estate not taxed at the source and proceed to distribute it among beneficiaries, they are not assessable to income tax and are bound to pay over the income to the beneficiaries without deduction, leaving it to the Revenue to pursue the beneficiaries.

## 2.4   End of Chapter Assessment Question

Amber Ltd manufactures metal fastenings at its factory in Grimetown. It sells the metal fastenings to wholesalers. On 6 April 1998, it has four shareholders, Alan, Bertram, Charlie and Deborah, each of whom own 25% of the issued ordinary share capital of the company. Alan and Bertram are brothers, Deborah is their sister, and Charlie is the father of all three of them. They are all directors of the company, including even Charlie, who is exactly 85 years old on 6 April 1998, and in failing health. All four are employed under service contracts with the company, and all receive a relatively small salary.

On 28 September 1998, Charlie dies. Bertram is his sole executor, although he did not witness the execution of the will, which took place in 1988. Under Charlie's will, cash gifts of £2,000 each are made to Alan, Bertram and Deborah. The will provides for them to receive interest on their cash gifts, from the date of Charlie's death, to the date of the receipt of the cheques by them. They are likely to receive the separate cheques for the gifts and the interest sometime in March 1999.

Besides being a director of, and shareholder in, Amber Ltd, Deborah is a partner in Brown & Co., a firm of solicitors in Grimetown. Brown & Co. has three partners, including Deborah. Deborah is single, and lets a room in her house to her cousin, Edwina, for £150 per month. She also receives interest on securities held for her by Georgina and Harry, who are the trustees of Deborah's uncle Frederick's will trust. Frederick died in 1993, and she has a life interest in possession under the will trust.

On 30 November 1998, Alan, Bertram and Deborah declared, and Amber Ltd paid, a dividend, which is divided equally between the four shareholders.

Identify the persons involved in these facts, the capacities which they have, and the sources of income which they possess.

## 2.5   End of Chapter Assessment Outline Answer

There are eight persons involved in the facts of this question: Amber Ltd, Alan, Bertram, Charlie, Deborah, Edwina, Georgina and Harry. Amber Ltd is a company and, as such, is a person separate from its four shareholders: *Salomon v Salomon & Co. Ltd* [1897] AC 22.
   The four shareholders in Amber Ltd are all individuals. Bertram has a capacity as an executor of Charlie's will. Deborah has a capacity as one of the partners in Brown & Co., the three-partner firm of solicitors. Georgina and Harry have a capacity as trustees of the will trust of Deborah's uncle Frederick. Alan and Edwina, as also Charlie before his death, are individuals who simply act in their personal capacity.
   The sources of income which these persons have are as follows. Amber Ltd has a source of trading income from manufacturing and selling metal fastenings. Each of Alan, Bertram, Charlie and Deborah have a source of income, although a relatively small one, from their contracts of employment with Amber Ltd. Alan, Bertram and Deborah have a second source of income, namely the interest payable on the gifts which they are to receive under Charlie's will. They also have a third source of income, in the form of the dividends declared and paid on their shareholdings in Amber Ltd.
   This deals with Alan and Bertram's sources of income, although Deborah has income from three further sources. These are the income from her partnership in Brown & Co., as well as the income from the trust fund in which she has a life interest in possession, plus income from the letting to Edwina.
   In his capacity as the executor of Charlie's will, Bertram has two sources of income. The first is any of Charlie's salary unpaid at Charlie's death, the second being the dividend declared and paid on 30 November 1998.
   Georgina and Harry, the trustees of Frederick's will, have a source of income in that capacity, although Deborah is entitled to the interest on the securities.

# CHAPTER THREE

# INCOME TAXATION: CAPITAL PROFITS, DIRECT AND INDIRECT TAXATION AND VAT

## 3.1 Introduction

The problematic distinction between direct and indirect taxation is explored in the following sophisticated analysis.

**Kay, J. A., and King, M. A., *The British Tax System*, 5th ed, Oxford: Oxford University Press 1990, pp. 120–121**

The *Oxford English Dictionary* defines an indirect tax as one which is 'not levied directly upon the person on whom it ultimately falls, but charged in some other way, especially upon the production or importation of articles of use or consumption, the price of which is thereby augmented to the consumer, who thus pays the tax in the form of increased price'. We argued [earlier in the book] that the economic analysis contained in this definition is shaky, and in general such a distinction cannot be made. We mean by indirect taxes only what is usually meant by them and attach no special significance, and particularly no economic significance, to the classification.

Nevertheless, many people do. Indeed, it has almost been part of the conventional political wisdom of British fiscal policy that the tax structure relied too much on direct taxation — especially income tax — and too little on indirect taxes. In a period of inflation, a progressive income tax takes an ever-increasing proportion of real incomes while the real yield of indirect taxes (which are in many cases levied as fixed monetary amounts) declines. This shift was not intended, and it reinforces the case for indexation, which is the only way in which inflation can be prevented from accidentally bringing about changes that no one wants to bring about by design. So it is not surprising that the balance of direct and indirect taxation should have been a subject of attention.

But some of the reasons that people had for believing that the balance of direct and indirect taxation was wrong were bad ones. One is that it is thought that the disincentive effects of high rates of direct taxation can be reduced or avoided by a shift to indirect taxes. This argument is quite simply false. Ignore for the moment the role of savings, since it is the incentive to work rather than the incentive to save which is at the centre of this concern. Then anyone considering whether to work longer hours or assume more responsibility will weigh the obvious costs against the benefits in terms of increased consumption which he or she would derive. The additional effort would, we shall assume, generate additional earnings of £10 per week. Now compare a 50% tax on all income with a 100% tax on all expenditure, since that is the rate which is needed to maintain the same revenue. Then our worker would discover that the extra £10 per week was reduced to a net £5 per week by the income tax; with taxes on expenditure, it would remain £10 but would only buy the same bundle of goods, the additional £5 being absorbed by the indirect taxes. The reality of the final outcome is exactly the same in both cases. It is possible that for a time people might be misled into working harder to earn larger monetary amounts before they noticed the reduced purchasing power of what they were receiving; but it is improbable that this irrationality would persist for long. If it did, then inflation — which puts larger quantities of less valuable money into wage-packets in just the same way — would have precisely the same beneficial effect on incentives to work, and few people would find this easy to believe.

## 3.2 Income Profits and Capital Profits

### 3.2.1 INTRODUCTION

**Chancellor James Callaghan's Budget Speech, 6 April 1965, Hansard, col 245**

. . .

First, I begin with tax reform. The failure to tax capital gains is widely regarded, outside as well as inside the Labour Party, as the greatest blot on our existing system of direct taxation. There is little dispute nowadays that capital gains confer much the same kind of benefit on the recipient as taxed earnings more hardly won. Yet earnings pay tax in full while capital gains go free. This is unfair to the wage and salary earner. It has in the past been one of the barriers to the progress of an effective incomes policy, but now my right hon. Friend the First Secretary of State has carried this policy forward to a point which many did not believe was possible six months ago. This new tax will provide a background of equity and fair play for his work.

Moreover, there is no doubt that the present immunity from tax of capital gains has given a powerful incentive to the skilful manipulator of which he has taken full advantage to avoid tax by various devices which turn what is really taxable income into tax-free capital gains. We shall only make headway against avoidance of this sort when capital gains are also taxed.

I have already given a general outline of my proposals. Broadly the tax will be levied on gains realised on all assets, with limited exceptions: of these exceptions the most important will be the owner-occupied house, and goods and chattels realised for not more than £1,000.

. . .

(Note: The reference to a very low annual exemption at the end of this extract.)

### 3.2.2 IS THE CLASSIFICATION IMPORTANT?

Exploitation of the distinction between income and capital was identified as one of the most frequently-used devices to avoid paying income tax.

**The Institute For Fiscal Studies — Report of a committee chaired by Professor J. E. Meade, *The Structure and Reform of Direct Taxation*, London: George Allen & Unwin, 1978, pp. 30–31**

INCOME AS THE TAX BASE

A taxpayer's *income* is an obvious candidate to serve as the base for his tax liability; but there are unfortunately difficulties in establishing what in principle is meant by a taxpayer's income, quite irrespective of any practical difficulties of ascertaining and measuring his income when it has been defined. A natural and commonsensical approach is to draw a distinction between a man's capital and his income by regarding his *capital* as the stock of resources from which the flow of income proceeds; in terms of the familiar analogy, the tree is the capital from which the annual income of the fruit crop is derived.

But on examination this distinction is found to involve many difficulties. Should the whole of the fruit crop be counted as taxable income if the fruit trees are ageing and depreciating in value, so that part of the proceeds of the crop must be used to maintain the productive power of the orchard? Or to take an example at the other extreme, if a forester is growing trees from which there is no annual crop but which are ultimately cut down and sold for timber, does he have no income at any time but only a realisation of the gain in the capital value of his trees when he cuts them down and sells them? Or consider two Government bonds both of which are issued at a price of £100, the difference being that on bond A the government undertakes to pay no interest but to redeem the bond at a price of £110 in a year's time, whereas on bond B the government undertakes to redeem the bond at its issue price of £100 in a year's time but meanwhile to pay £10 in interest on its borrowing. Is there no income but only gain in capital value on bond A, while there is income but no capital gain on bond B?

The above are only some extremely simple and obvious examples of the relationships between gains and losses in capital values on the one hand and net income on the other. As rates of income tax have risen to their present high levels, the distinction between income and capital gains has become more and more important; more and more sophisticated ways have been devised by taxpayers to turn highly taxable income into less highly taxable capital gains; and the importance of finding, if it is possible, a definition of income which does not permit these uncertain and often irrelevant distinctions to continue has correspondingly increased.

Inflation is an economic effect which causes the real value of money to fall. This means that the cost of property decreases in real terms with the passage of time.

### Segall, A., 'Cost of living up by 2,000 per cent', *The Daily Telegraph*, 29 August 1997

THE pound in your pocket is definitely not what it used to be. Prices have risen 20-fold since 1947 or by more than 2,000 per cent and statisticians have been struggling to keep up with it all.

The decision to keep a regular check on prices was made by the Attlee government half a century ago at a time when many goods were still being rationed, beer was watered down and a woolly cost £4 3s 2d plus six coupons.

Since then, prices have risen in most years and at a frightening pace in some. During the mid-Seventies the inflation rate reached a peak of 26.9 per cent and even today prices are rising annually by around three per cent. As consumer choice has expanded, so has the task of deciding what should be included in the Retail Prices Index, which aims to cover the cost of a 'typical' basket of consumer goods and services.

In the good old days, officials were sent off with pen and paper to scribble down the cost of items such as wild rabbits, radio sets, condensed milk, back-lacing corsets and gramophone records.

These days, market researchers are despatched with hand-held computers to keep tabs on 600 commodities such as Internet subscriptions, alcopops and aerobic classes by visiting 146 shops and offices. They punch the prices of 12,000 items into their machines and transmit the results automatically into the computer data bank run by the Office for National Statistics.

While prices have almost invariably gone up over the past 50 years, the cost of some goods and services has far outpaced others. Household goods and high-tech products such as computers and videos have become relatively cheap over time.

Despite rising prices, living standards have improved enormously. The Office for National Statistics, which yesterday celebrated the 50th anniversary of the Retail Prices Index, estimates that people these days can afford two and half times more than they could back in 1947 because wages have far outstripped prices.

Then, average pay for a manual worker was £6 a week against over £300 now — a 50-fold increase. That means it took two and a half times longer to earn the money to pay for a typical shopping basket of goods and services compared to now.

As people have become richer, they have had to devote a smaller proportion of their incomes to basics such as food and clothing, leaving more to spend on eating out and other services and luxuries.

The average family now spends 14 per cent of its income on food against 35 per cent in 1947 and 33 per cent on services against eight per cent then.

As spending power, tastes and products have changed, statisticians have had to alter their assessment of what constitutes a 'typical' basket of consumer goods and services. They do so every year, using the results of the family expenditure survey.

The 20-fold increase in prices since 1947 represents an average annual rate of inflation of 6.3 per cent — enough to reduce the value of the pound in your pocket to 5p. Put another way, it would cost £21.50 today to buy what could have been bought for a pound in 1947.

The statisticians responsible for compiling the monthly retail prices index are proud of their efforts and believe that they have performed a valuable role over the years. Jon McGinty, the statistician in charge of compiling the Retail Prices Index, claims that it is 'the statistic that affects the lives of individuals more than any other'.

The idea of keeping tabs on prices goes back to 1914. The Cost of Living Index for the Working Classes covered what Government officials thought of as essentials. Potatoes were the only vegetable included; tobacco was in but alcohol was out.

The post-war index was based for the first time not on what someone in Whitehall thought people needed, but on what households typically bought. Gramophone records, cinema tickets and football admission charges were included for the first time.

In the Fifties, statisticians added ice-cream, Tupperware and televisions. In the Sixties they brought in fish fingers and crisps, jeans and motor scooters. And in the Seventies, mortgage payments, yogurt, wine, cassette recorders and home perms were added to the index. The following decade saw the inclusion of condoms and unleaded petrol.

The 'deeming' provisions for investments in offshore roll-up funds are in ICTA 1988, ss. 757 to 764. Parts of ss. 757 and 761 are extracted below.

## INCOME AND CORPORATION TAXES ACT 1988

**757. Disposal of material interests in non-qualifying offshore funds**

(1) This Chapter applies to a disposal by any person of an asset if—

(a) at the time of the disposal, the asset constitutes a material interest in an offshore fund which is or has at any material time been a non-qualifying offshore fund;

. . .

(2) Subject to the following provisions of this section and section 758, there is a disposal of an asset for the purposes of this Chapter if there would be such a disposal for the purposes of the [TCGA 1992].

**761. Charge to income tax or corporation tax of offshore income gain**

(1) If a disposal to which this Chapter applies gives rise . . . to an offshore income gain, then, subject to the provisions of this section, the amount of that gain shall be treated for all the purposes of the Tax Acts as—

(a) income arising at the time of the disposal to the person making the disposal, and

(b) constituting profits or gains chargeable to tax under Case VI of Schedule D for the chargeable period in which the disposal is made.

### 3.2.3 INCOME PROFIT OR CAPITAL PROFIT?

The 'fixed capital' test.

### *DAVIS v SHELL COMPANY OF CHINA LTD* (1951) 32 TC 133, 155–157 (CA)

The taxpayer, a company resident in the UK, sold and distributed petrol in China. It required its agents in China to deposit a security with it in Chinese dollars. This resulted in a profit to the company because, as a result of a war between China and Japan, the Chinese dollar was devalued. The company therefore had to repay only part of the value it had taken as security from its agents, leaving a windfall profit for the company.

The Court of Appeal held that this profit was not taxable as an income profit, since it related to fixed capital of the company.

JENKINS LJ: . . . Sir Andrew Clark presented his argument for the Crown, if I may say so, in his usual clear and attractive manner but he has not succeeded in convincing me that the Special Commissioners were wrong. He argues with force that this is an English company, trading in China; the results of its operations must ultimately be stated in terms of sterling. It does business in dollars and in particular receives these agency deposits in dollars. If as a result of those transactions it makes a profit through the difference in exchange between the sterling and Chinese dollars, why should that not be a profit of its trade? He says that the deposits received from agents were trading receipts giving rise to corresponding trade liabilities. He puts his argument as to that in effect in two ways. First, he says that you cannot regard each of those deposit transactions by itself as if it were a separate and isolated transaction. He says that it was the Company's regular practice to conduct the bulk of its business through agents, of whom it employed no fewer than 600. He says that the appointment of agents was a common and customary operation in the course of the Company's trading as the Company chose to carry it on, and he points to the opening statement in the findings of the Commissioners, that 'In the ordinary course of business the Appellant Company received deposits in dollars from its agents, as and when they were appointed.'

The answer to that branch of Sir Andrew Clark's argument is I think provided by Mr Grant's [counsel for Shell's] contention that the mere fact that a certain type of operation is done in the ordinary course of a company's business and is frequently repeated, does not show that the transaction in question is a trading transaction; you have to look at the transaction and see what its nature was; and on that Mr Grant gave the illustration of a retail trader who, as and when he opens new branches, buys shops in which to carry on his business, and from time to time may make a profit by selling one of the shops so bought. Now it may be said of such a trader that he buys shops and from time to time disposes of shops that he no longer wants to operate, in the ordinary course of business but it would by no means follow that the price he spends on a shop when he buys it is an outgoing of his trade or that the price he gets for a shop when he sells it is a trading receipt. In fact in the case of an ordinary retail trader the contrary would be the case and expenditure and receipts such as these would, I apprehend, clearly be in respect of fixed capital.

Mr Grant referred, on this branch of the argument, to the case of *Eastmans, Ltd* v *Shaw*, 14 TC 218, which was the case of a multiple butcher's concern which had several hundred retail shops. It was the company's policy to close shops or to open shops in accordance with the needs of their business as a whole, and advantageous to dispose of the fixtures and fittings in a shop given up rather than to transfer them to a newly acquired shop. In such circumstances the company debited in their trading account the difference between the cost of new fixtures and the price obtained for old fixtures, and these items had been added back in computing the company's liability to Income Tax and Corporation Profits Tax. The decision was to the effect that no deduction was admissible in computing the company's profits in respect of the excess of the cost of new fixtures over the price obtained for the old fixtures.

Mr Grant has satisfied me that this branch of Sir Andrew Clark's argument fails. The mere fact that it was the Company's regular practice to appoint agents does not in my view invest the deposits taken from the agents with the character of trading receipts any more than the fact that it is the practice of a multiple trader to buy shops up and down the country whenever he sees fit to open a new branch invests his expenditure on such shops with the character of trade outgoings.

'Next', Sir Andrew Clark says, 'look at the character of the agent's deposit itself and the terms of the agreement under which it was made.' He points out that on the face of the agreement the deposit was made to secure the due performance by the agent of his obligations; to secure, in other words, the due discharge of the liabilities which might arise from time to time from the agent to the Company as a result of the agent carrying on business as agent for the Company, selling the Company's petroleum and so forth. Sir Andrew argued that a deposit so closely linked with the actual trading operations to be carried on by the agent must itself be regarded as a trading receipt. In that I venture to differ from him. If the agent's deposit had in truth been a payment in advance to be applied by the Company in discharging the sums from time to time due from the agent in respect of petroleum products transferred to the agent and sold by him the case might well be different and might well fall within the *ratio decidendi* of *Landes Bros* v *Simpson* 19 TC 62 and *Imperial Tobacco Co.* v *Kelly* 25 TC 292. But that is not the character of the deposits here in question. The intention manifested by the terms of the agreement is that the deposit should be retained by the Company, carrying interest for the benefit of the depositor throughout the terms of the agency. It is to be available during the period of the agency for making good the agent's defaults in the event of any default by him; but otherwise it remains, as I see it, simply as a loan owing by the Company to the agent and repayable on the termination of the agency; and I do not see how the fact that the purpose for which it is given is to provide a security against any possible default by the agent can invest it with the character of a trading receipt.

Mr Grant described the agents' deposits as part of the Company's trading structure, not trade receipts but anterior to the stage of trade receipts, and I think that is a fair description of them. It seems to me that it would be an abuse of language to describe one of these agents, after he had made a deposit, as a trade creditor of the Company; he is a creditor of the Company in respect of the deposit, not on account of any goods supplied or services rendered by him in the course of its trade, but simply by virtue of the fact that he has been appointed an agent of the Company with a view to him trading on its behalf, and as a condition of his appointment has deposited with or, in other words, lent to the Company the amount of his stipulated deposit.

After paying the best attention I can to the arguments for the Crown and those for the Respondent Company, I find nothing in the facts of this case to divest those deposits of the character which it seems to me they originally bore, that is to say the character of loans by the agents to the Company, given no doubt to provide the Company with a security, but nevertheless loans. As loans it seems to me they must *prima facie* be loans on capital not revenue account; which perhaps is only another way of saying that they must *prima facie* be considered as part of the Company's fixed and not of its circulating capital. As appears from what I have said above, the evidence does not show that there was anything in the Company's mode of dealing with the deposits when received to displace this *prima facie* conclusion.

In my view, therefore, the conversion of the Company's balances of Chinese dollars into sterling and the subsequent re-purchase of Chinese dollars at a lower rate, which enabled the Company to pay off its agents' deposits at a smaller cost in sterling than the amount it had realised by converting the deposits into sterling, was not a trading profit, but it was simply the equivalent of an appreciation in a capital asset not forming part of the assets employed as circulating capital in the trade. That being so it was a profit of the nature not properly taxable under Schedule D, and the Special Commissioners in my view came to a right conclusion, which was rightly affirmed by the learned Judge, and I would therefore dismiss the appeal.

## 3.3 Income Taxation and Indirect Taxation

### 3.3.1 INDIRECT TAXES GENERALLY

Examples of indirect taxation are customs duties. Here is an eighteenth-century discussion of them by Sir William Blackstone (1723–1780).

**Sir William Blackstone, *Commentaries on the Laws of England*, Book I, 16th ed, Coleridge, C.J.T., ed), London: Butterworths, 1825, pp. 316–317**

These customs are then, we see, a tax immediately paid by the merchant, although ultimately by the consumer. And yet these are the duties felt least by the people; and, if prudently managed, the people hardly consider that they pay them at all. For the merchant is easy, being sensible he does not pay them for himself; and the consumer, who really pays them, confounds them with the price of the commodity: in the same manner, as Tacitus observes, that the emperor Nero gained the reputation of abolishing the tax of the sale of slaves, though he only transferred it from the buyer to the seller; so that it was, as he expresses it '*remissum magis specie, quam vi: quia cum venditor pendere juberetur, in partem pretii emptoribus accrescebat.*' But this inconvenience attends it on the other hand, that these imposts, if too heavy, are a check and cramp upon trade; and especially when the value of the commodity bears little or no proportion to the quantity of the duty imposed. This in consequence gives rise also to smuggling, which then becomes a very lucrative employment; and it's natural and most reasonable punishment, viz confiscation of the commodity, is in such cases quite ineffectual; the intrinsic value of the goods, which is all that the smuggler has paid, and therefore all that he can lose, being very inconsiderable when compared with his prospect of advantage in evading the duty. Recourse must therefore be had to extraordinary punishments to prevent it; perhaps even to capital ones: which destroys all proportion of punishment, and puts murderers upon an equal footing with such as are really guilty of no natural, but merely a positive, offence.

There is also another ill consequence attending high imposts on merchandise, not frequently considered, but indisputably certain; that the earlier any tax is laid on a commodity, the heavier it falls upon the consumer in the end: for every trader through whose hands it passes must have a profit, not only upon the raw material, and his own labour and time in preparing it, but also upon the very tax itself, which he advances to the government; otherwise he loses the use and interest of the money which he so advances. To instance in the article of foreign paper. The merchant pays a duty upon importation, which he does not receive again till he sells the commodity, perhaps at the end of three months. He is therefore equally entitled to a profit upon that duty which he pays at the custom-house, as to a profit upon the original price which he pays to the manufacturer abroad; and considers it accordingly in the price he demands of the stationer. When the stationer sells it again, he requires a profit of the printer or bookseller upon the whole sum advanced by him to the merchant; and the bookseller does not forget to charge the full proportion to the student or ultimate consumer; who therefore does not only pay the original duty, but the profits of these three intermediate traders, who have successively advanced it for him. This might be carried much farther in any mechanical, or more complicated, branch of trade.

Having read this extract, you may wish to re-read the extract at **3.1**.

### 3.3.2   VAT: A SPECIAL TYPE OF INDIRECT TAX

VAT is charged on supplies of goods or services made in the UK, by a taxable person, in the course or furtherance of a business, which are not exempt or zero-rated.

### VALUE ADDED TAX ACT 1994

**4.   Scope of VAT on taxable supplies**
    (1)   VAT shall be charged on any supply of goods or services made in the United Kingdom, where it is a taxable supply made by a taxable person in the course or furtherance of any business carried on by him.
    (2)   A taxable supply is a supply of goods or services made in the United Kingdom other than an exempt supply.

A supply is anything done by the supplier for a consideration.

### VALUE ADDED TAX ACT 1994

**5.   Meaning of supply: alteration by Treasury order**
. . .
    (2)   Subject to any provision made by [sch. 4] and to Treasury orders under subsections (3) to (6) below—
    (a)   'supply' in this Act includes all forms of supply, but not anything done otherwise than for a consideration,
    (b)   anything which is not a supply of goods but is done for a consideration (including, if so done, the granting, assignment or surrender of any right) is a supply of services.

Charities which do not make taxable supplies at all carry large burdens of input VAT which cannot be reclaimed by them. The concept of 'profit-shedding', an income tax/corporation tax concept referred to in this extract is discussed in **Chapter 9** of the *Learning Text*.

### Dawes, I., 'Can the VAT Burden be Relieved?' *The Tax Journal*, 3 August 1995, p. 10

The idea of taxing charities, the objects of which provide for the relief of poverty, sickness, infirmity and other beneficial purposes, somehow seems difficult to justify; yet a report published recently by London Economics confirms that United Kingdom charities are suffering from an estimated £350 million annual irrecoverable VAT bill on what they buy in to support their non-business, charitable activities. This figure does not include VAT attributable to exempt activities, such as the provision of education or residential accommodation, which are treated as being by way of business. Such a drain on financial resources, taken with a perceived fall in funding as a result of the National Lottery, means that the Treasury is facing strong pressure to reduce the VAT burden on charities.

Although in principle the taxing of charities appears unfair, since they are essentially non-profit-making organisations, it is the way in which the VAT legislation is drafted that causes charities to be the unintended victim of irrecoverable VAT. The basic rule is that the VAT legislation permits recovery of input tax on purchases, where they have been incurred in making taxable supplies — that is, incurred in the course of business activities. Consequently, given that the activities of charities in fulfilling their objectives are largely non-business and do not involve making taxable supplies, those activities fall outside the scope of United Kingdom VAT and input tax on purchases accordingly becomes irrecoverable.

VAT treatment from a charity's perspective is inconsistent with direct tax legislation, which exempts the income of charities from being assessed to corporation tax on business profits, unless it can be demonstrated that the activities constitute trading — that is, that they are for a profit-making purpose. The adage 'what is good for the goose is good for the gander' does not hold where on the one hand VAT is recoverable on costs relating to trading activity, but on the other, any profits are subject to corporation tax.

Observers to the charitable field may offer trading as the solution. Indeed, 'profit shedding' is often used by charities to mitigate corporation tax liabilities, whereby a separate trading company operates the trading activity, covenanting all profits to the charity, so eliminating the profit and consequently mitigating the corporation tax. Profit shedding may only be used up to a point, however, since a charity's objects — that is, its raison d'être — as set out in its articles of association, can be compromised by excessive trading. Moreover, many activities of charities in fulfilment of their objects do not by their nature involve the making of taxable supplies by way of business for VAT purposes: they are either statutory exempt, or treated as non-business (even when charges are made, charitable provision to the natural 'clients' of a charity of social welfare services will be treated as non-business when the subsidy exceeds 15 per cent).
. . .

The Treasury has already made concessions in respect of the charitable sector in specific circumstances, by allowing zero-rating of construction services, advertising services, certain items for the handicapped, donated goods and donated medical and scientific equipment, to mention a few. As a result of receiving these goods and services at 0 per cent VAT, the problem of irrecoverable VAT is avoided by the charity.

Some of these reliefs, it should be noted, represented the continuation of zero-rating for charities when it was removed for everyone else.

From March 1995, zero-rating of charities' exports was given statutory status, and the zero-rating reliefs were extended to allow zero-rating on the construction of a self-contained annexe used for a relevant charitable purpose, even where there is secondary access through an existing building. . . .

## 3.4   End of Chapter Assessment Question

Amber Ltd is registered for VAT. It makes only supplies taxable at the standard rate. Comment on the implications of these facts, paying particular attention to the question of whether, in your opinion, VAT is a form of income taxation for Amber Ltd.

## 3.5   End of Chapter Assessment Outline Answer

VAT is an indirect tax, which means that it is incorporated into the price of goods or services supplied. In manufacturing and selling metal fastenings, Amber Ltd is carrying on a trade, i.e. a form of business activity. Amber Ltd would seem to be a supplier of goods, rather than a supplier of services, although this has no bearing on the relevant law here.

VAT is charged on supplies of goods or services which are not exempt or zero-rated, made in the UK by a taxable person in the course or furtherance of a business: VATA 1994, s. 4. A supply is anything done by the supplier for a consideration: VATA 1994, s. 5(2)(b). Since Amber Ltd is a taxable person, it being registered for VAT, and since it makes only taxable supplies, it is obliged to charge VAT on those supplies.

VAT is not charged by a taxable person on the profit element of the price of goods or services, but on the whole price charged by the taxable person.

Since Amber Ltd makes supplies taxable at the standard rate, it must account to the tax authority for the VAT collected on the prices charged. This is referred to as its output VAT, or output tax, and is charged by Amber Ltd to its customers, on the prices charged for the goods and services supplied. By the same token, VAT charged on supplies made to Amber Ltd by other taxable persons is referred to as Amber Ltd's input VAT, or input tax.

Fundamentally important for Amber Ltd, as a taxable person, is that if it makes only standard-rated or zero-rated supplies, it can deduct its input VAT from its output VAT in full. Every quarter, Amber Ltd will account to HM Customs and Excise for the excess of output VAT over input VAT in that quarter. If its input VAT is more than its output VAT in that quarter, the difference can be reclaimed from the taxation authority.

This all depends on Amber Ltd being a taxable person making only taxable supplies. If it were not such a taxable person, it would not be able to reclaim all its input VAT.

Since Amber Ltd is a taxable person making only taxable supplies, its input VAT will not be a form of income taxation, since it will be entitled to deduct it all.

# CHAPTER FOUR

# INCOME TAXATION: TAX PERIODS, TAX AVOIDANCE AND RESIDENCE

## 4.1  Introduction

The way in which reading tax law should be approached by the lawyer.

### PEPPER v HART [1993] 1 All ER 42 (HL)

FA 1976, s. 63(2), now ICTA 1988, s. 156(2), provided that the cost of a benefit provided to an employee was '. . . the amount of any expense incurred in or in connection with its provision': see *Learning Text* at **14.3.4**. Ten members of staff at Malvern College were charged for their sons' education at the college at concessionary rates. The concessionary rates were one-fifth of the rates charged to parents of pupils generally. The point at issue was whether they should be taxed on the cash equivalent of the expense ('the average cost'), as the Revenue argued, or the marginal cost, as argued by the members of staff.

The House of Lords held that the members of staff should be taxed on the marginal cost. In doing so, six of the seven law lords relied on Parliamentary materials to find the true meaning of ICTA 1988, s. 156(2). The relevant extracts from the speech of Lord Browne-Wilkinson are set out in **4.5** below. The appeal to the House of Lords was the taxpayers', who had lost the argument before Vinelott J and the Court of Appeal.

## 4.2  Tax periods

### 4.2.1  INCOME TAX

The tax year begins on 6 April in one calendar year and ends on 5 April in the following calendar year.

### INCOME AND CORPORATION TAXES ACT 1988

**2.  Fractions of a pound, and yearly assessments**
. . .
   (2)   Every assessment and charge to income tax shall be made for a year commencing on the 6th April and ending on the following 5th April.

The reason for a tax year beginning on 6 April in one calendar year and ending on 5 April in the following calendar year is historical.

### *Correspondence on the Timing of the Tax Year* (1985) British Tax Review 56

A copy of the following correspondence has been sent to us.

Dear Mr Jeffrey-Cook,

*A Year Beginning on April 6.*

When I wrote to Somerset House recently to ask why the tax year starts on April 6, rather than April 5 (which is what Lady Day, March 25, the former New Year's Day, became after 1752), I was referred to your article in *British Tax Review* ([1977] BTR 68–69) for the statement that 1753 would have been a leap year on the old (Julian) calendar. That sounded wrong, though, because Pepys's *Diary* had leap days in 1659/1660, 1663/1664 and 1667/1668.

So I looked up the correspondence in *The Times* that you had referred to. There was indeed a letter from I. T. Barclay on February 8, 1977, that said what you did, but a week later one from Hugh Peskett denied it: we had February 29 in 1747/1748, 1752 and 1756; the Calendar Act did not alter February 1753.

The real answer to the problem seems to lie concealed in the letter from R. R. Cockcroft on February 2, 1977. The end of the government's financial year (of 366 days, including February 29, 1752) at Michaelmas 1752 was delayed (like all periods for payments bridging the jump from September 2 to 14) by 11 days from September 29 to October 10; the other Quarter Days were shifted likewise, Lady Day to April 5. The change of the end of the financial year to January 5 (old Christmas) in 1799 and the introduction of an income tax year to April 5 were simply to different old Quarter Days, each being the *end* of an accounting period.

So April 5 is the *end* of the tax year in its old capacity of a quarter day ending an accounting period and not the *beginning* that one might have expected from the former status of Lady Day as the first day of a new calendar year.

This explanation was not brought out in the correspondence in *The Times*; nor have I seen it elsewhere. Do you agree that it makes sense?

Yours sincerely,
G. C. R. MORRIS

Dear Mr Morris

*British Tax Review 1977 No 2*
*A Year Beginning on April 6*

Thank you for your letter of September 14.

I am sorry for the delay in replying, but you will appreciate that a certain amount of research was necessary and the appropriate documents are only available at certain libraries.

I think you will agree that correspondence in *The Times* needs to be treated with caution and no statements (or denials) can be relied upon without independent verification. The evidence of Pepys's *Diary* is, however, very helpful and shows that Leap Years were calculated according to years beginning on January 1.

I agree with you that all evidence points to the conclusion in your penultimate paragraph.

Yours sincerely,
JOHN JEFFREY-COOK

## 4.2.2  CORPORATION TAX

Corporation tax on both the income and capital profits of companies is charged by reference to a financial year.

### INCOME AND CORPORATION TAXES ACT 1988

**834.  Interpretation of the Corporation Tax Acts**

(1) . . . 'accounting date' means the date to which a company makes up its accounts and 'period of account' means the period for which it does so;

. . .

'the financial year 1988' means the financial year beginning with April 1988, and similarly with references embodying other dates; . . .

## 4.3   Tax Avoidance

As a taxpayer, I am entitled to order my affairs in the most tax advantageous way.

### *IRC* v *DUKE OF WESTMINSTER* [1935] All ER Rep 259, 267–68 (HL)

The facts of this case are discussed in the **Learning Text** at **9.3.1**. In the course of his speech, Lord Tomlin set out the following statement of principle, with which the other Law Lords, except Lord Atkin, concurred.

LORD TOMLIN: [I]t is said that in revenue cases there is a doctrine that the court may ignore the legal position and regard what is called 'the substance of the matter,' and that here the substance of the matter is that the annuitant was serving the Duke for something equal to his former salary or wages and that, therefore, while he is so serving the annuity must be treated as salary or wages. This supposed doctrine (upon which the commissioners apparently acted) seems to rest for its support upon a misunderstanding of language used in some earlier cases. The sooner this misunderstanding is dispelled and the supposed doctrine given its quietus the better it will be for all concerned, for the doctrine seems to involve substituting 'the uncertain and crooked cord of discretion' for 'the golden and straight mete wand of the law' (4 Inst. 41).

   Every man is entitled, if he can, to order his affairs so that the tax attaching under the appropriate Acts is less than it otherwise would be. If he succeeds in ordering them so as to secure this result, then however unappreciative the Commissioners of Inland Revenue or his fellow taxpayers may be of his ingenuity, he cannot be compelled to pay an increased tax. This so-called doctrine of 'the substance' seems to me to be nothing more than an attempt to make a man pay notwithstanding that he has so ordered his affairs that the amount of tax sought from him is not legally claimable.

### Anonymous Note, *Law Notes*, December 1938, p. 355

The *Observer* had a paragraph last month to the effect that some artful dodger had discovered how to dodge the very latest Finance Act, and the writer of the paragraph wanted to know what the Law Society and the Institute of Chartered Accountants proposed to do to their members who advise the adoption of the dodge. And the answer is, nothing! A great judge of the past said that it was neither illegal nor immoral to avoid a taxation Act, and, he added with a grin, 'if you can do it.' If the Act does not expressly provide for the dodge, well, then the dodge is not illegal. But none of these dodges lasts long. The draftsman keeps a fatherly eye on his statutory child and Parliament can soon pass an amending section in the annual Finance Act.

The *Ramsay* principle:

### *WT RAMSAY LTD* v *IRC* [1982] AC 300, 323G–324B (HL)

The facts of this case are discussed in the **Learning Text** at **25.4.1**. In the course of his speech, Lord Wilberforce set out the following statement of principle, with which the other law lords concurred:

Given that a document or transaction is genuine, the court cannot go behind it to some supposed underlying substance. This is the well-known principle of *Inland Revenue Commissioners* v *Duke of Westminster* [1936] AC 1. This is a cardinal principle but it must not be overstated or overextended. While obliging the court to accept documents or transactions, found to be genuine, as such, it does not compel the court to look at a document or a transaction in blinkers, isolated from any context to which it properly belongs. If it can be seen that a document or transaction was intended to have effect as part of a nexus or series of transactions, or as an ingredient of a wider transaction intended as a whole, there is nothing in the doctrine to prevent it being so regarded: to do so is not to prefer form to substance, or substance to form. It is the task of the court to ascertain the legal nature of any transaction to which it is sought to attach a tax or a tax consequence and if that emerges from a series or combination of transactions, intended to operate as such, it is that series or combination which may be regarded. For this there is authority in the law relating to income tax and capital gains tax: see *Chinn* v *Hochstrasser* [1981] AC 533 and *Inland Revenue Commissioners* v *Plummer* [1980] AC 896.

Tax avoidance in terms of income taxation usually involves manipulating the rules as to the availability of deductions and reliefs, but continued attempts have been made to derive tax advantages from the distinction between income and capital: see **Learning Text** at **3.3.2**.

### IRC v McGUCKIAN [1997] 3 All ER 817, 823 and 829–830 (HL)

This case involved a scheme to avoid income tax under ICTA 1988, s. 739 (see **Learning Text** at **18.4.2**), by dressing up certain moneys received by trustees as capital, rather than income ones. The effect of the House of Lords' using the *Ramsay* principle was to turn the receipts into income ones. In the course of their speeches, Lord Browne-Wilkinson and Lord Cooke, made the following statements on the *Ramsay* principle. Edward Nugee QC appeared for Mr McGuckian.

LORD BROWNE-WILKINSON: . . . Finally, Mr Nugee submitted that the *Ramsay* principle only requires the artificial steps inserted for tax purposes to be disregarded if, apart from the *Ramsay* principle, they would have been effective to achieve a tax advantage. My Lords, I emphatically reject this submission. The approach pioneered in the *Ramsay* case and subsequently developed in later decisions is an approach to construction, viz that in construing tax legislation, the statutory provisions are to be applied to the substance of the transaction, disregarding artificial steps in the composite transaction or series of transactions inserted only for the purpose of seeking to obtain a tax advantage. The question is not what was the effect of the insertion of the artificial steps but what was its purpose. Having identified the artificial steps inserted with that purpose and disregarded them, then what is left is to apply the statutory language of the taxing Act to the transaction carried through, stripped of its artificial steps. It is irrelevant to consider whether or not the disregarded artificial steps would have been effective to achieve the tax-saving purpose for which they were designed.

LORD COOKE OF THORNDON: . . . The principle of looking on a planned series of steps as a whole transaction appears to be, as one would expect, perfectly natural and orthodox. It is surely decidedly more natural and less extreme than the decision which in 1935 a majority of their Lordships felt forced to reach in the *Duke of Westminster*'s case. One can well understand that in the *Ramsay* case this House was unwilling to carry the latter decision further. Nor can the position of the taxpayer plausibly be improved for the purposes of the *Ramsay* principle by the argument that the planned series of steps in question were incidental to an even wider scheme of tax avoidance devised against wealth tax.

. . .

The principle which your Lordships have been developing in *WT Ramsay Ltd* v *IRC* [1981] 1 All ER 865, *IRC* v *Burmah Oil Co Ltd* [1982] STC 30 and *Furniss (Inspector of Taxes)* v *Dawson* [1984] 1 All ER 530, is not uncommonly seen as special to the construction of taxing Acts. Perhaps more helpfully, however, it may be recognised as an application to taxing Acts of the general approach to statutory interpretation whereby, in determining the natural meaning of particular expressions in their context, weight is given to the purpose and spirit of the legislation. So, in the *Ramsay* case [1981] 1 All ER 865 at 873, Lord Wilberforce said that it was well and indeed essentially within the judicial function to determine whether there was such a loss (or gain) as the legislation was dealing with. In the *Burmah* case [1982] STC 30 at 38 Lord Fraser of Tullybelton echoed those words in saying that there was no real loss and no loss in the sense contemplated by the legislation. In *Furniss*'s case [1984] 1 All ER 530 at 543, Lord Brightman said that in conditions which he defined the court must look at the end result; precisely how it would be taxed depended on the terms of the taxing statute.

*Craven (Inspector of Taxes)* v *White* [1988] 3 All ER 495, where the facts were distant from those of the present case, is a difficult case, partly because of the differences of opinion in your Lordships' House, but at least it can be said that one cardinal point of agreement was that essentially the question is one of construction (see [1988] 3 All ER 495 at 500, 506, 520 and 524, 531 and 541, per Lord Keith of Kinkel, Lord Templeman, Lord Oliver of Aylmerton, Lord Goff of Chieveley and Lord Jauncey of Tullichettle respectively).

My Lords, this approach to the interpretation of taxing Acts does not depend on general anti-avoidance provisions such as are found in Australasia. Rather, it is antecedent to or collateral with them. In *Furniss*'s case [1984] 1 All ER 530 at 543, Lord Brightman spoke of certain limitations (a preordained series of transactions including steps with no commercial or business purpose apart from the avoidance of a liability to tax). The present case does fall within these limitations, but it may be as well to add that, if the ultimate question is always the true bearing of a particular taxing provision on a particular set of facts, the limitations cannot be universals. Always one must go back to the discernible intent of the taxing Act. I suspect that advisers of those bent on tax avoidance, which in the end tends to involve an attempt to cast on other taxpayers more than their fair share of sustaining the national tax base, do not always pay sufficient heed to the theme in the speeches in *Furniss*'s case, especially those of Lord Scarman, Lord Roskill and Lord Bridge of Harwich, to the effect that the journey's end may not yet have been found. I will profit from the example of Lord Roskill in *Furniss*'s case (see [1984] 1 All ER 530 at 534) by refraining from speculating about whether a sharper focus on the concept of 'wages' in the light of the statutory purpose and the circumstances of the case would or would not have led to a different result in the *Duke of Westminster*'s case [1935] All ER Rep 259. . . .

## 4.4 Residence and Domicile

### 4.4.1 RESIDENCE OF INDIVIDUALS

To be resident in the UK in the tax year under consideration, I must be physically present in the UK during some part of that tax year. The extract below deals with the residence of those coming to the UK from abroad.

**Inland Revenue, International Series IR20, *Residents and Non-Residents — Liability to Tax in the United Kingdom*, November 1993, Crown Copyright pp. 11–15**

### 3   Coming to the UK

*Coming to the UK permanently or indefinitely*
3.1   You are treated as **resident and ordinarily resident** from the date you arrive if your home has been abroad and you come to the UK

- to live here **permanently**, or
- intending to stay here for **three years or more**.

*Visitors to the UK*
3.2   If you come to the UK other than to live here permanently as in paragraph 3.1, the guidelines in the rest of this Chapter will govern your residence and ordinary residence position in the UK.

The Chapter deals in turn with three main groups coming to this country

- **short term visitors** — where you visit the UK for only limited periods in one or more tax years
- **those coming for employment**
- **longer term visitors** — where you come to the UK to stay indefinitely or for an extended period, perhaps stretching over several tax years.

You may fall within one or more of these categories, depending on your precise circumstances.

*Short term visitors*

*Residence*
3.3   You will be treated as resident for a tax year if
- you are in the UK for 183 days or more in the tax year . . ., or
- you visit the UK regularly and after four tax years your visits during those years average 91 days or more a tax year. You are treated as resident from the fifth year. However

  - any days spent in the UK for exceptional circumstances beyond your control, for example the illness of yourself or a member of your immediate family, are not counted for this purpose
  - you are treated as resident from 6 April of the first year if it is clear when you first come to the UK that you **intend** making such visits
  - you are treated as resident from 6 April of the tax year in which you **decide** that you will make such visits, where this decision is made before the start of the fifth tax year.

For example

- you come to the UK with no definite intentions but your visits during the tax years 1993–94 to 1996–97 average at least 91 days a tax year; you are resident from 6 April 1997
- you first come to the UK during 1993–94, intending that between then and 5 April 1997 your visits will average at least 91 days a tax year; you are resident from 6 April 1993
- you first come to the UK during 1993–94 with no definite intentions and you spend, say, 60 days here; you come again during 1994–95 and decide you will come regularly in future years and your visits will average at least 91 days a tax year; you are resident from 6 April 1994.

For tax years before 1993–94, you were treated as **resident** if you had accommodation in the UK available for your use and you visited the UK, no matter how short the visit . . .

*Ordinary Residence*
3.4   You will be treated as **ordinarily resident** if you come to the UK regularly and

- your visits average 91 days or more a tax year; any days spent in the UK for exceptional circumstances beyond your control, for example the illness of yourself or a member of your immediate family, are not normally counted for this purpose, or
- for tax years before 1993–94, you had accommodation in the UK available for your use.

3.5   The date from which you are treated as ordinarily resident depends upon your intentions. You will be ordinarily resident

- from 6 April of the tax year of your first arrival, if it is clear when you first come here that you **intend** visiting the UK regularly for at least four tax years
- from 6 April of the fifth tax year after you have visited the UK over four years, if you originally came with no definite plans about the number of years you will visit
- from 6 April of the tax year in which you **decide** you will be visiting the UK regularly, if that decision is made before the start of the fifth tax year.

For example

- you first come to the UK during 1993–94, you intend visiting regularly until at least 5 April 1997 and your visits will average at least 91 days a tax year. You are ordinarily resident from 6 April 1993
- you come to the UK with no definite intentions but you visit regularly during the tax years 1993–94 to 1996–97 and your visits average at least 91 days a tax year. You are ordinarily resident from 6 April 1997
- you first come to the UK during 1993–94 with no definite intentions; you come again in 1994–95 and 1995–96 and during 1995–96 you decide you will come regularly in future years, and your visits will average at least 91 days a tax year. You are ordinarily resident from 6 April 1995.

*Those coming for employment*
3.6   You are treated as resident in the UK from the day you arrive to the day you depart . . . if you come to the UK to work for at least **two years**. If you come to work for less than two years or do not know how long you will be here, you will **only** be treated as resident for the tax year if

- you spend 183 days or more in the UK in the tax year, or
- for tax years before 1993–94, you had accommodation in the UK available for your use. . . .

For your ordinary residence status see paragraphs 3.8–3.11.

*Longer term visitors*
3.7   For your **residence** status see paragraph 3.3.
3.8   You will be **ordinarily resident** in the UK from the date you arrive, whether to work here or not, if it is clear that you intend to stay for at least **three years**.
**If you come to the UK as a student** for an extended period of study or education, see paragraph 3.13.
3.9   You will be treated as ordinarily resident from the beginning of the tax year after the third anniversary of your arrival if you come to, and remain, in the UK but you

- do not originally intend to stay for at least three years, and
- do not buy accommodation or acquire it on a lease of three years or more.

For example, if you arrive in the UK on 21 November 1993 and are still in the UK on 6 April 1997, you are ordinarily resident from 6 April 1997.
3.10   If, after you have come to the UK, you **decide** to stay for at least **three years** from the date of your original arrival, you will be treated as ordinarily resident from

- the day you arrive if your decision is made in the year of arrival, or
- the beginning of the tax year in which you make your decision when this is after the year of arrival.

For example, you arrive in the UK on 4 January 1994 and decide to stay permanently on 16 May 1994. You are ordinarily resident from 6 April 1994.
3.11   If you come to and remain in the UK, you will be treated as ordinarily resident

- from the day you arrive, if
  - you already own accommodation here
  - you buy accommodation during the tax year of arrival, or
  - you have or acquire accommodation on a lease of three years or more during the tax year of arrival
    or
- from 6 April of the tax year in which such accommodation becomes available, when this occurs after the year of arrival.

3.12   If you are treated as ordinarily resident **solely** because you have accommodation here (paragraph 3.11) and you dispose of the accommodation and leave the UK within three years of your arrival, you may be treated as not ordinarily resident for the duration of your stay if this is to your advantage.

3.13   If you are a **student** who comes to the UK for a period of study or education and you will be here for less than **four years**, you will be treated as not ordinarily resident, providing

■  you do not own or buy accommodation here, or acquire it on a lease of three years or more, and

■  on leaving the UK you will not be returning regularly for visits which average 91 days or more a tax year.

### 4.4.2   RESIDENCE OF COMPANIES

Compared with the rules on individuals, the rules for companies are quite straightforward.

#### Inland Revenue Statement of Practice 1/90, 9 January 1990

#### Company residence

**1**   . . . FA 1988, s. 66 introduced the rule that a company incorporated in the UK is resident here for the purposes of the Taxes Acts. Case law still applies in determining the residence of companies excepted from the incorporation rule or which are not incorporated in the UK.

#### A   THE INCORPORATION RULE

**2**   The incorporation rule applies to companies incorporated in the UK subject to the exceptions in FA 1988, sch. 7 for some companies incorporated before 15 March 1988. Paragraphs 3 to 8 below explain how the Revenue interpret various terms used in the legislation.

*Carrying on business*

**3**   The exceptions from the incorporation test in sch. 7 depend in part on the company carrying on business at a specified time or during a relevant period. The question whether a company carries on business is one of fact to be decided according to the particular circumstances of the company. Detailed guidance is not practicable but the Revenue take the view that 'business' has a wider meaning than 'trade'; it can include transactions, such as the purchase of stock, carried out for the purposes of a trade about to be commenced and the holding of investments including shares in a subsidiary company. Such a holding could consist of a single investment from which no income was derived.

**4**   A company such as a shelf company whose transactions have been limited to those formalities necessary to keep the company on the register of companies will not be regarded as carrying on business.

**5**   For the purposes of the case law test (see B below) the residence of a company is determined by the place where its real business is carried on. A company which can demonstrate that in these terms it is or was resident outside the UK will have carried on business for the purposes of sch. 7.

*'Taxable in a territory outside the UK'*

**6**   A further condition for some companies for exception from the incorporation test is provided by sch. 7, para. 1(1)(c), para. 5(1). The company has to be taxable in a territory outside the UK. 'Taxable' means that the company is liable to tax on income by reason of domicile, residence or place of management. This is similar to the approach adopted in the residence provisions of many double taxation agreements. Territories which impose tax on companies by reference to incorporation or registration or similar criteria are covered by the term 'domicile'. Territories which impose tax by reference to criteria such as 'effective management', 'central administration', 'head office' or 'principal place of business' are covered by the term 'place of management'.

**7**   A company has to be liable to tax on income so that a company which is, for example, liable only to a flat rate fee or lump sum duty does not fulfil the test. On the other hand a company is regarded as liable to tax in a particular territory if it is within the charge there even though it may pay no tax because, for example, it makes losses or claims double taxation relief. . . .

### B   THE CASE LAW TEST

**9**   This test of company residence is that enunciated by Lord Loreburn in *De Beers Consolidated Mines* v *Howe* (5 TC 198) at the beginning of this century—

> A company resides, for the purposes of Income Tax, where its real business is carried on . . . I regard that as the true rule; and the real business is carried on where the central management and control actually abides.

**10**   The 'central management and control' test, as set out in *De Beers*, has been endorsed by a series of subsequent decisions. In particular, it was described by Lord Radcliffe in the 1959 case of *Bullock* v *Unit Construction Company* 38 TC 712 at p. 738 as being—

> as precise and unequivocal as a positive statutory injunction . . . I do not know of any other test which has either been substituted for that of central management and control, or has been defined with sufficient precision to be regarded as an acceptable alternative to it. To me . . . it seems impossible to read Lord Loreburn's words without seeing that he regarded the formula he was propounding as constituting *the* test of residence.

Nothing which has happened since has in any way altered this basic principle for a company the residence of which is not governed by the incorporation rule; under current UK case law such a company is regarded as resident for tax purposes where central management and control is to be found.

*Place of 'central management and control'*

**11**   In determining whether or not an individual company outside the scope of the incorporation test is resident in the UK, it thus becomes necessary to locate its place of 'central management and control'. The case law concept of central management and control is in broad terms, directed at the highest level of control of the business of a company. It is to be distinguished from the place where the main operations of a business are to be found, though those two places may often coincide. Moreover, the exercise of control does not necessarily demand any minimum standard of active involvement: it may, in appropriate circumstances, be exercised tacitly through passive oversight.

**12**   Successive decided cases have emphasised that the place of central management and control is wholly a question of fact. For example, Lord Radcliffe in *Unit Construction* said that 'the question where control and management abide must be treated as one of fact or "actuality"' (p. 741). It follows that factors which together are decisive in one instance may individually carry little weight in another. Nevertheless the decided cases do give some pointers. In particular a series of decisions has attached importance to the place where the company's board of directors meet. There are very many cases in which the board meets in the same country as that in which the business operations take place, and central management and control is clearly located in that one place. In other cases central management and control may be exercised by directors in one country though the actual business operations may, perhaps under the immediate management of local directors, take place elsewhere.

**13**   But the location of board meetings, although important in the normal case, is not necessarily conclusive. Lord Radcliffe in *Unit Construction* pointed out (p. 738) that the site of the meetings of the directors' board had *not* been chosen as 'the test' of company residence. In some cases, for example, central management and control is exercised by a single individual. This may happen when a chairman or managing director exercises powers formally conferred by the company's Articles and the other board members are little more than cyphers, or by reason of a dominant shareholding or for some other reason. In those cases the residence of the company is where the controlling individual exercises his powers.

**14** In general the place of directors' meetings is significant only insofar as those meetings constitute the medium through which central management and control is exercised. If, for example, the directors of a company were engaged together actively in the UK in the complete running of a business which was wholly in the UK, the company would not be regarded as resident outside the UK merely because the directors held formal board meetings outside the UK. While it is possible to identify extreme situations in which central management and control plainly is, or is not, exercised by directors in formal meetings, the conclusion in any case is wholly one of fact depending on the relative weight to be given to various factors. Any attempt to lay down rigid guidelines would only be misleading.

**15** Generally, however, where doubts arise about a particular company's residence status, the Inland Revenue adopt the following approach—

(i) They first try to ascertain whether the directors of the company in fact exercise central management and control.

(ii) If so, they seek to determine where the directors exercise this central management and control (which is not necessarily where they meet).

(iii) In cases where the directors apparently do *not* exercise central management and control of the company, the Revenue then look to establish where and by whom it is exercised.

. . .

### Conclusion

**18** In outlining factors relevant to the application of the case law test, this statement assumes that they exist for genuine commercial reasons. Where, however, as may happen, it appears that a major objective underlying the existence of certain factors is the obtaining of tax benefits from residence or non-residence, the Revenue examine the facts particularly closely in order to see whether there has been an attempt to create the appearance of central management and control in a particular place without the reality.

**19** The case law test examined in this Statement is not always easy to apply. The courts have recognised that there may be difficulties where it is not possible to identify any one country as the seat of central management and control. The principles to apply in those circumstances have not been fully developed in case law. In addition, the last relevant case was decided almost 30 years ago, and there have been many developments in communications since then, which in particular may enable a company to be controlled from a place far distant from where the day-to-day management is carried on. As the statement makes clear, while the general principle has been laid down by the courts, its application must depend on the precise facts.

. . .

### 4.4.3 DOMICILE

**Inland Revenue, International Series IR20, *Residents and Non-Residents — Liability to Tax in the United Kingdom*, November 1993, Crown Copyright pp. 18–19**

### 5 Domicile

5.1 Domicile is a general law concept. It is not possible to list all the factors that affect your domicile but some of the main points are explained in this Chapter.

5.2 Broadly speaking you are domiciled in the country where you have your permanent home. Domicile is distinct from nationality or residence. You can only have one domicile at any given time.

### Domicile of origin

5.3 You normally acquire a **domicile of origin** from your father when you are born. It need not be the country in which you are born. For example, if you are born in France while your father is working there, but his permanent home is in the UK, your domicile of origin is in the UK.

*Domicile of dependency*

5.4   Until you have the legal capacity to change it — see paragraph 5.5 — your domicile will follow that of the person on whom you are legally dependent. If the domicile of that person changes, you automatically acquire the same domicile (a **domicile of dependency**), in place of your domicile of origin.

*Domicile of choice*

5.5   You have the legal capacity to acquire a new domicile (a **domicile of choice**) when you reach age 16. To do so, you must broadly leave your current country of domicile and settle in another country. You need to provide strong evidence that you intend to live there permanently or indefinitely. Living in another country for a long time, although an important factor, is not enough in itself to prove you have acquired a new domicile.

*Married women*

5.6   Before 1974, when you married you automatically acquired your husband's domicile. After marriage this domicile would change at the same time as your husband's domicile changed. If your marriage ended, you kept your husband's domicile until such time as you legally acquired a new domicile.

5.7   From 1 January 1974 your domicile is no longer necessarily the same as your husband's domicile. It is decided by the same factors as for any other individual who is able to have an independent domicile. If, however, you were married before 1974 and had acquired your husband's domicile (see paragraph 5.6), you **retain** this after 1 January 1974 until such time as you legally acquire a new domicile.

## 4.5   Reading Tax Law

No-where is the precise meaning of words more important than in tax law. Do not be discouraged by the following words of a famous American judge!

**Judge Learned Hand, 'Thomas Walter Swan' (1947) 57 *Yale Law Journal* pp. 167, 169**

In my own case the words of such an act as the Income Tax, for example, merely dance before my eyes in meaningless procession: cross-reference to cross-reference, exception upon exception — couched in abstract terms that offer no handle to seize hold of — leave in my mind only a confused sense of some vitally important, but successfully concealed, purport, which it is my duty to extract, but which is within my power, if at all, only after the most inordinate expenditure of time. I know that these monsters are the result of fabulous industry and ingenuity, plugging up this hole and casting out that net, against all possible evasion; yet at times I cannot help recalling a saying of William James about certain passages of Hegel: that they were no doubt written with a passion of rationality; but that one cannot help wondering whether to the reader they have any significance save that the words are strung together with syntactical correctness.

### *R v IRC, EX PARTE FULFORD-DOBSON* [1987] STC 344, 351

In this passage, McNeill J states his attitude, as a judge, to ESCs. Under discussion was ESC D2 (see *Learning Text* at **25.3.1.1**), and he begins by referring to Walton J's words in *Vestrey (No. 2)* v IRC [1979] 2 All ER 225 (see *Learning Text* at **4.6**). For 'the rubric' referred to by McNeill J, see **25.1.1**.

McNEILL J: . . . It is, however, to be noted that although extra-statutory concessions were criticised, Walton J appears to have accepted that if there was some published code of concessions which applied indifferently to all who fall or can bring themselves within its scope the position might be different. There was no such code in *Vestey*'s case. . . .

   . . . [E]xtra-statutory concessions have persisted. Parliament has not sought to legislate to provide for concessions, despite the words of Scott LJ in 1943, cited by Lord Edmund-Davies ([1980] STC 10 at 36):

The fact that such extra legal concessions have to be made to avoid unjust hardships is conclusive that there is something wrong with the legislation.

Counsel for the taxpayer argued that the existence of concession D2 meant that s. 2 of the [TCGA 1992] was unworkable. The reality was, he said, that the assessment was not made under the section but under the concession as limited by the rubric. His difficulty was that if he successfully established that the concession itself was unlawful, it is unnecessary to consider the rubric; it falls with the concession. The taxpayer is then left with s. 2 and in no way can counsel for the taxpayer argue that he would not be caught by that. Nor am I persuaded that the rubric is discriminatory. It is, in terms, of general application to all those who come within its words. This, of course, does not decide what those words mean; that is the next question to be answered.

So far as the argument based on *Vestey's* case is concerned, I am not prepared to hold that concession D2 is unlawful. I consider it as falling well within the concept of good management or of administrative common sense, as those words were used by their Lordships and already cited by me, and they are within the proper exercise of managerial discretion.

There is really no additional argument of any substance advanced by counsel for the taxpayer to isolate the rubric from the concession to say that the concession is lawful but the rubric unlawful. In my judgment, the rubric is effectively part of each concession. It loses none of its force by being given a special and early place in the booklet: indeed, perhaps, it gains force from that. And, indeed, why should a taxpayer have the advantage of a concession when he is attempting to use it for tax avoidance?

### *PEPPER v HART* [1993] 1 All ER 42, 69–74 (HL)

Here, Lord Browne-Wilkinson sets out the conditions under which Parliamentary material may be consulted in statutory interpretation. Under discussion is FA 1976, s. 63(2), now ICTA 1988, s. 156(2). The exclusionary rule referred to at the beginning of the extract is the rule that references to Parliamentary material as an aid to statutory construction are not permissible.

LORD BROWNE-WILKINSON: . . . I . . . reach the conclusion, subject to any question of parliamentary privilege, that the exclusionary rule should be relaxed so as to permit reference to parliamentary materials where: (a) legislation is ambiguous or obscure, or leads to an absurdity; (b) the material relied on consists of one or more statements by a minister or other promoter of the Bill together if necessary with such other parliamentary material as is necessary to understand such statements and their effect; (c) the statements relied on are clear. Further than this, I would not at present go.

2.    DOES THIS CASE FALL WITHIN THE RELAXED RULE?

(a)   *Is s. 63 ambiguous?*
   I have no hesitation in holding that it is. The 'expense incurred in or in connection with' the provision of in-house benefits may be either the marginal cost caused by the provision of the benefit in question or a proportion of the total cost incurred in providing the service both for the public and for the employee (the average cost).
   In favour of the marginal cost argument, it is submitted by the taxpayers that there has to be a causal link between the benefit in kind taxed under s. 61(1) and its 'cash equivalent': s. 63(1) defines the cash equivalent of the benefit as being an amount equal to the cost of the benefit. Therefore, it is said, one is looking for the actual cost of providing that benefit for the employee. The basic expense of providing and running the school would have been incurred in any event; therefore that expenditure is not caused by the provision of the benefit for the employee. The test is whether the cost would have been incurred but for the provision of the benefit. Therefore, when one comes to s. 63(2) one is looking for the additional expense incurred in or in connection with the provision of the benefit. . . .
   On the other side, the Revenue contend that, once one has identified the benefit under s. 61, s. 63 contains a code for establishing its cash equivalent. Section 63(1) defines the cash equivalent as the cost of the benefit and s. 63(2) defines 'the cost of a benefit' as

being the expense 'incurred in or in connection with' its provision. The benefit in this case consists of the enjoyment of the facilities of the school. What is the cost of providing those facilities? It must be the total cost of providing the school. However, the total cost of providing the school is incurred not only in connection with the provision of the benefit to the employee but also in providing the school with fee-paying boys. This provision is expressly covered by the final words of s. 63(2) 'and includes . . . a proper proportion of any expense relating partly to the benefit and partly to other matters'. Therefore, says the Revenue, the cost of the benefit is a proportion of the total cost of providing the services. . . .

I find these arguments nicely balanced. The statutory words are capable of bearing either meaning. There is an ambiguity or obscurity.

(b)    *Are the words of the Financial Secretary [to the Treasury] clear?*

It is necessary by way of preface to emphasise that in no circumstances can in-house benefits give rise to no taxable benefit or only a small taxable benefit if that benefit is to be assessed on an average cost basis. The average cost basis means that the cost will approximate to the open market charge (less any profit element) and therefore must in all circumstances be substantial.

The Finance Bill 1976 as introduced proposed to charge in-house benefits on a different basis from that applicable to external benefits, i.e. on the open market price charged to the public (see cl. 54(4)). Once the government announced its intention to withdraw cl. 54(4) a number of members were anxious to elucidate what effect this would have on classes of taxpayers who enjoyed in-house benefits: concessionary transport for railway-men, airline employees and merchant seamen; concessionary accommodation for hotel employees; concessionary education for the children of teachers. In answer to these inquiries the Financial Secretary gave similar answers in relation to each class, namely (1) that in all the cases (except that of the teachers' concessionary education) the benefits would be taxed on the same basis as under the existing law and (2) that in all cases the amount of the charge would be nil, small or, in the case of the schoolteachers, 'very small indeed'. In my view these repeated assurances are quite inconsistent with the minister having had, or communicated, any intention other than that the words 'the expense incurred in or in connection with' the provision of the benefit would produce a charge to tax on the additional or marginal cost only, not a charge on the average cost of the benefit.

It may be said that the Financial Secretary's reference to the taxpayers being liable to tax as under the pre-existing law (i.e. under the Finance Act 1948, s. 39, as re-enacted by the Income and Corporation Taxes Act 1970) shows that he was saying that the position was unchanged: nothing the minister said could affect the proper construction of legislation already on the statute book. To this contention there are, in my judgment two answers. First, the old Acts were repealed by the 1976 Act; the provisions were re-enacted in different language, albeit that the phrase 'incurred in or in connection with the provision of the benefit' appeared in both statutes. In this case the court is concerned to construe the 1976 Act; what is relevant is the ministerial statement as to the effect of that Act. Second, the existing practice of the Revenue under the pre-1976 law was not to tax benefits in kind on the average cost basis and those who were asking questions on behalf of their constituents would have been well aware of this fact. For example, in the case of the airline employees the Revenue had sought to tax concessionary travel on the average cost basis but their claim had failed before the commissioners and they had not persisted in that claim. The minister's answer in Parliament that the cost to the airlines of providing concessionary travel for airline employees would be nothing was exactly what in practice had been happening under the old law.

The question then arises whether it is right to attribute to Parliament as a whole the same intention as that repeatedly voiced by the Financial Secretary. In my judgment it is. It is clear from reading Hansard that the committee was repeatedly asking for guidance as to the effect of the legislation once cl. 54(4) was abandoned. That Parliament relied on the ministerial statements is shown by the fact that the matter was never raised again after the discussions in committee, that amendments were consequentially with-drawn and that no relevant amendment was made which could affect the correctness of the minister's statement.

Accordingly, in my judgment we have in this case a clear statement by the responsible minister stating the effect of the ambiguous words used in what became s. 63 of the 1976 Act which the parliamentary history shows to have been the basis on which that section was enacted.

### 3.  IF REFERENCE TO HANSARD IS PERMISSIBLE, WHAT IS THE TRUE CONSTRUCTION?

In my judgment there can be no doubt that, if parliamentary privilege does not prohibit references to Hansard, the parliamentary history shows that Parliament passed the legislation on the basis that the effect of ss. 61 and 63 of the 1976 Act was to assess in-house benefits, and particularly concessionary education for teachers' children, on the marginal cost to the employer and not on the average cost. Since the words of s. 63 are perfectly capable of bearing that meaning, in my judgment that is the meaning they should be given.

I have had the advantage of reading in draft the speech of my noble and learned friend on the Woolsack. In construing the 1976 Act without reference to the parliamentary proceedings, he treats it as decisive that in this case the taxpayers' children were only occupying surplus accommodation and that it lay in the discretion of the school whether to grant such benefit to the taxpayers. This approach draws a distinction which is not reflected in the parliamentary proceedings. Concessionary travel for railwaymen is not discretionary nor is it dependent on there being surplus seats on any train. Similarly, in many cases the education of teachers' children at concessionary rates is neither discretionary nor dependent on there being surplus capacity. Yet in both cases in Parliament the section was put forward as providing that only the marginal cost would be treated as taxable. I can therefore find no ground for drawing the narrow distinction and would hold that in the case of all in-house benefits the same test applies, viz the cost of the benefit to the employer is the additional or marginal cost only.

Therefore if reference to Hansard is permissible, I would allow the appeal.

### 4.  IF REFERENCE TO HANSARD IS NOT PERMISSIBLE, WHAT IS THE TRUE CONSTRUCTION?

Having once looked at what was said in Parliament, it is difficult to put it out of mind. I have the advantage that, after the first hearing and before seeing the parliamentary materials, I had reached the conclusion, in agreement with Vinelott J and the Court of Appeal, that the Revenue's submissions were correct. If it is not permissible to take into account what was said by the Financial Secretary, I remain of the same view.

My reasons are the same as those given by the Court of Appeal. I accept [counsel for the taxpayers'] submission that there must be a causal link between the benefit provided for the taxpayers and the cost of the benefit referred to in s. 63(1). But in my judgment s. 63(2) provides a statutory formula for quantifying such cost: it requires one to find 'the amount of any expense incurred in or in connection with' the provision of the benefit, such expense to include 'a proper proportion of any expense relating partly to the benefit and partly to other matters'.

To apply s. 63(2) it is first necessary to identify 'the benefit'. It has throughout been common ground that the benefit in this case to each taxpayer is that 'his son is allowed to participate in all the facilities afforded by the school to boys who are educated there'. These facilities are exactly the same as those afforded to every boy in the school, whether his parents are paying the full or concessionary fees. Therefore the relevant question is: what is the expense incurred in or in connection with providing those facilities? On the literal meaning of the words, the expense to the school of providing those facilities is exactly the same for each boy in the school, i.e. a proportion of the total cost of running the school.

Even if it could be said that, because the school would have incurred the basic expense of running the school in any event, such expense was not incurred 'in' providing the facilities for the taxpayer's child, on the literal meaning of the words such expense was in any event incurred 'in connection with' the provision of such facilities. The words 'in connection with' have the widest connotation and I cannot see how they are to be restricted in the absence of some context permitting such restriction.

The strongest argument in favour of the taxpayers is the anomaly which would arise if the employer's business were running at a loss or was subsidised by endowment: as I have explained, in such a case the adoption of the literal meaning of the statutory words would lead to a result whereby the taxpayer is assessed at an amount greater than that charged by the employer to the public for the same service. The Crown has no answer to this anomaly as such. But there are other anomalies which arise if the taxpayers' argument is correct. For example, if, unlike the present case, the school could have been filled with boys paying the full fee, the school would have lost the fee income from the places occupied by the children of the taxpayers for whom only the concessionary fee was payable. Without deciding the point, it seems to me arguable that, on the taxpayers' argument, such loss or part of it would be an expense incurred by the school in providing the concessionary places. If so, the amount on which the taxpayer would be assessed to tax would vary from year to year depending on the success of the school in attracting applicants. To my mind such a variation on a year-by-year basis by reference to an extraneous factor would be a most anomalous result, and would involve great difficulties in quantifying the cost to the employer in each case.

In the circumstances, if I could detect from the statute any statutory purpose or intention pointing to one construction rather than the other, I would certainly adopt it. But the statute yields no hint. The basic problem is this. What is taxable is the benefit to the employee and one would have expected the quantum of that benefit to be assessed by reference to the value of the benefit to the employee. But the statutory formula does not seek to value the benefit to the employee as such, but requires the quantum of the benefit to be fixed by reference to the cost to the employer in providing it. Given this dislocation between the benefit which is assessable to tax and the basis on which its value is to be assessed it is impossible to gain any guidance in the statute as to the parliamentary intention. In the circumstances there is in my judgment no option but to give effect to the literal meaning of the words as did the Court of Appeal. In the result, the Revenue's argument should succeed and the appeal should be dismissed.

5.   PARLIAMENTARY PRIVILEGE

It follows from what I have said that in my view the outcome of this appeal depends on whether or not the court can look at parliamentary material: if it can, the appeal should be allowed; if it cannot, the appeal should be dismissed. For the reasons I have given, as a matter of pure law this House should look at Hansard and give effect to the parliamentary intention it discloses in deciding the appeal. The problem is the indication given by the Attorney General that, if this House does so, your Lordships may be infringing the privileges of the House of Commons.

For the reasons I have given, in my judgment reference to parliamentary materials for the purpose of construing legislation does not breach s. 1, art 9 of the Bill of Rights. However, the Attorney General courteously but firmly warned your Lordships that this did not conclude the question. He said that art 9 was an illustration of the right that the House of Commons had won by 1688 to exclusive cognisance of its own proceedings. He continued:

> I remain convinced . . . that the House of Commons would regard a decision by your Lordships to use Hansard to construe a statute as a grave step and that the House of Commons may well regret that its views were not sought on such an important matter before your Lordships reached a decision.

My Lords, this House and the courts have always been, and I trust will always continue to be, zealous in protecting parliamentary privileges. I have therefore tried to discover some way in which this House can fulfil its duty to decide the case before it without trespassing on the sensibilities of the House of Commons. But I can find no middle course. Although for a considerable time before the resumed hearing it was known that this House was to consider whether to permit Hansard to be used as an aid to construction, there was no suggestion from the Crown or anyone else that such a course might breach parliamentary privilege until the Attorney General raised the point at the start of the rehearing. Even then, the Attorney General did not ask for an adjournment to enable the House of Commons to consider the matter. Your Lordships therefore heard the case through to the end of the argument.

Although in the past the courts and the House of Commons both claimed the exclusive right to determine whether or not a privilege existed, it is now apparently accepted that it is for the courts to decide whether a privilege exists and for the House to decide whether such privilege has been infringed (see *Erskine May Parliamentary Practice* (21st edn, 1989) pp. 147–160). Thus, *Erskine May* p. 150 says:

> In the 19th century, a series of cases forced upon the Commons and the courts a comprehensive review of the issues which divided them, from which it became clear that some of the earlier claims to jurisdiction made in the name of privilege by the House of Commons were untenable in a court of law: that the law of Parliament was part of the general law, that its principles were not beyond the judicial knowledge of the judges, and that it was the duty of the common law to define its limits could no longer be disputed.

Again it is said (p 154):

> Though events have revealed no single doctrine by which all issues of privilege arising between Parliament and the courts may be resolved, many of the problems of earlier years which are dealt with above have been substantially solved. Neither House is by itself entitled to claim the supremacy over the courts of law enjoyed by the undivided medieval High Court of Parliament. Since neither House can by its own declaration create a new privilege, privilege may be considered to be capable of being ascertained and thus judicially known to the courts.

Accordingly, if the nature of the privilege going beyond the Bill of Rights had been identified, your Lordships could have determined whether or not such privilege exists, although it would be for the House of Commons to determine whether or not there was an infringement of any privilege found to exist. In fact, neither the letter from the Clerk of the Commons nor the Attorney General has identified or specified the nature of any privilege extending beyond that protected by the Bill of Rights. In the absence of a claim to a defined privilege as to the validity of which your Lordships could make a determination, it would not in my view be right to withhold from the taxpayers a decision to which, in law, they are entitled. I would therefore allow the appeal.

I trust that, when the House of Commons comes to consider the decision in this case, it will be appreciated that there is no desire to impeach its privileges in any way. Your Lordships are motivated by a desire to carry out the intentions of Parliament in enacting legislation and have no intention or desire to question the processes by which such legislation was enacted or of criticising anything said by anyone in Parliament in the course of enacting it. The purpose is to give effect to, not thwart, the intentions of Parliament.

A number of commentators were unhappy with *Pepper v Hart*, however.

**Harris, D.R., 'A High Price For Justice',** *The Tax Journal,* **28 January 1993, pp. 15, 17**

Notwithstanding his Lordship's robust denial, it is submitted that, by departing from the established principle, the Judges are in danger of becoming mere lackeys of the executive. In particular:

- ■ The 'highly technical rules of construction' have been developed over many years as aids to the interpretation of statutes. They are familiar to practitioners and, insofar as they are examined at length in legal textbooks, available in context to an intelligent layman. No such rule applies to the interpretation of Parliamentary pronouncements, other than the dubious one of 'clarity'.
- ■ There is a confusion of thought here between the purpose of the legislation and its expected effect . . .
- ■ If there is a Parliamentary statement governing the matter, which is sufficiently clear to be admissible, the Court has no alternative but to accept it at face value, since it cannot be questioned.

More importantly, perhaps, both the case in question and the extra-judicial observations of Lord Wilberforce, referred to by Lord Browne-Wilkinson in the course of his judgment, are concerned with the individual pitted against a Department of State. The relaxation of the rule will apply equally to both sides, so that not only does the appropriate Department have the power, via the executive, to have the law changed, often with retrospective effect, but it also has the ability to ensure that its interpretation is made the subject of appropriate Parliamentary enunciation, that its comprehensive access to Parliamentary proceedings is used to the full in seeking out evidence admissible under this head, and that selective amnesia is applied to other statements which are either less favourable or in direct conflict. . . .

In my view, this relaxation in the rules of evidence will cause a good deal of extra work and expense, disproportionate to any benefit arising, and its constitutional implications are sinister.

In 1966, the late Sir Hilary Scott, then President of the Law Society, warned:

It will indeed be a bad day for the country if we allow ourselves to be talked into a state of acquiescence and into regarding something as having the force of law just because someone in authority has said it . . .

That is exactly what the House of Lords — for the best of motives — has allowed to happen here.

## 4.6   End of Chapter Assessment Questions

(a)   'Every tax avoidance scheme involves a trick and a pretence. It is the task of the Revenue to unravel the trick and the duty of the court to ignore the pretence.' (*Matrix-Securities Ltd* v *IRC* [1994] 1 All ER 769, 780 (Lord Templeman).)

Briefly discuss the issues raised by this quotation.

(b)   Refer to **2.4**, and note the following additional facts. Amber Ltd makes its accounts up to 31 December in each calendar year. Amber Ltd was incorporated in the UK on 20 April 1990.

The firm of solicitors in which Deborah is a partner, Brown & Co., makes its accounts up to 30 November in each calendar year. The same firm has been in business for many years, although one of the partners retired from the firm on 30 November 1997.

Comment on the significance of these facts, in terms of income tax and corporation tax.

## 4.7   End of Chapter Assessment Outline Answers

(a)   The idea of tax avoidance arouses fierce emotions. It is to be distinguished from tax evasion, which is illegal, since tax avoidance is in principle legal. It is interesting that Lord Templeman uses the word 'scheme', which implies a distinction between operations involving detailed planning, and the straightforward use of rights conferred by the tax legislation.

In suggesting that the Revenue must expose such schemes, leaving the courts to negative their effects, he is referring to the effect of a line of cases, beginning with *WT Ramsay Ltd* v *IRC* [1982] AC 300 and *Furniss* v *Dawson* [1984] BTC 71, which have established that the Courts may nullify a tax advantage sought to be obtained where there is a pre-ordained series of transactions or a single composite transaction, having steps inserted which have no commercial purpose other than the avoidance of tax. This principle is referred to as the *Ramsay* principle. It has represented a departure from *IRC* v *Duke of Westminster* [1936] AC 1, which is often cited as establishing the principle that taxpayers are entitled to order their affairs in the most tax advantageous way.

Tax avoidance, in the context of income taxation, usually seems to involve manipulating the rules on the availability of deductions, reliefs and exemptions.

(b)   The fact of Amber Ltd's being incorporated in the UK on 20 April 1990 indicates that it is *resident* in the UK. This is because, with effect from 15 March 1988, a company is generally resident in the UK for the purposes of corporation tax if it is either incorporated in the UK, or, even if it was not incorporated in the UK, if its central management and control is located in the UK: FA 1988, s. 66, sch. 7; SP 1/90.

For professional partnerships such as Brown & Co., whose profits fall under Schedule D, Case II, the tax period is generally the accounting period ending in the tax year under consideration. Brown & Co.'s tax period is therefore generally the 12-month period ending with the 30 November in the tax year under consideration.

The tax period is different for corporation tax purposes. Corporation tax is charged on both income profits and capital profits of companies, although according to different rules for each type of profit. Tax on both the income and capital profits of companies is charged by reference to a financial year, which begins on 1 April in one year and ends on 31 March in the following year: ICTA 1988, s. 834(1). The financial year 1998 is thus the period from 1 April 1998 to 31 March 1999.

However, corporation tax is payable on a company's total profits chargeable to corporation tax, not for each financial year, but for each of the company's accounting periods. For a company, an accounting period begins either at the end of the previous one or, when a new business of the company begins, as soon as the company becomes liable to pay corporation tax on the income profits of the business. It ends 12 months later unless, basically, it ceases in the meantime to be liable to corporation tax.

If, therefore, an accounting period of a particular company runs across two financial years in which the corporation tax rates are different, then the profits of the accounting period must be apportioned and the rate for each financial year applied to each part of the profits apportioned in this way.

# CHAPTER FIVE

# INCOME TAX AND CORPORATION TAX: LIABILITY AND INCOME SOURCES

## 5.1 Introduction

**Kay, J. A., and King, M. A., *The British Tax System*, 5th edn, Oxford: Oxford University Press 1990, pp. 200–201,**

The most important tax on factors of production is the income tax on individuals. If labour income is taxed too heavily in country A, you can often reduce the burden by working in country B instead. Again, this is an issue which generates more anecdote than evidence of serious effect. The study by Fiegehen and Reddaway (1981) showed that even the high tax rates of the 1970s appeared to have had little effect on the mobility of senior managers in practice. For most people, the ties of family, home, culture, and language outweigh fiscal incentives to work in other countries, and the opportunities for advancement within multinational companies dominate the fiscal benefits of a lower tax rate on a lower salary. There are obvious exceptions — entertainers and professional sportsmen and women. But when the Inland Revenue published a consultation document on changes to the concept of residence for tax purposes, most of the practitioner response was to the effect that mobile managers were being penalised too heavily rather than moving to minimise tax. The competition between countries in the 1980s to lower their top rates of income tax . . . is essentially a political rather than an economic competition.

The most significant distortions are those introduced by corporation tax. Some of these distortions are, of course, intentional. When the Republic of Ireland set a corporation tax rate of 10% for much of manufacturing industry, its principal objective was to induce companies to establish plants in that country when it might otherwise have been uneconomic to do so. Most of the gains from this policy will be earned at the expense of other countries. Indeed, since the output which such a policy creates is necessarily high-cost production, it is likely that the high-cost output which results has the consequences that the gains to Ireland, or any other country acting in this way, will be less than the costs imposed on the rest of the world. Other countries may then react by making similar changes in their own tax systems, and the outcome may have negative results for everyone.

There is therefore a common interest in refraining from this destructive competition. The provisions of the Treaty of Rome which restrict the use of state aids are designed for this purpose but, although they have enjoyed some success in limiting the use of industrial subsidies and ensuring that regional policies across the European Community are co-ordinated rather than competitive, the opportunity to apply similar principles to corporate tax systems has proved limited.

## 5.2 Persons Liable to Pay Income Tax and Corporation Tax

**British Master Tax Guide 1997–98, para. 1783, CCH Editions Ltd, 1997**

There are different kinds of relief from double taxation.

■ *Relief by treaty exemption* — certain categories of income are exempted from tax in whole or in part in one or other of the countries which are parties to the 'double taxation agreement' or 'double tax treaty' . . .

■ *Relief by treaty credit* — tax charged in one country may be available as a credit in the other.

■ *Unilateral relief* — where there is no provision for double taxation relief, any foreign tax paid may nevertheless be available as a credit in calculating UK tax.

■ *Relief by deduction* — the taxpayer can treat the foreign tax paid as a deduction from his taxable income (for example, the foreign tax suffered may be 'inadmissible' for credit relief . . .).

Provision for double tax relief is made by ICTA 1988, s. 788–816. Those provisions apply also to capital gains (TCGA 1992, s. 277(1)) and chargeable gains of companies (ICTA 1988, s. 788(1)(b)).

Whether the Revenue will admit a foreign tax for unilateral double taxation relief in relation to business profits is determined by examining the tax within its legislative context in the foreign territory and deciding whether it serves the same function as income tax and corporation tax serve in the UK in relation to such profits . . .

### 5.2.1   INDIVIDUALS

#### 5.2.1.1   UK taxpayers

### INCOME AND CORPORATION TAXES ACT 1988

**192.   Relief from tax for foreign emoluments**

(1)   In this Part 'foreign emoluments' means the emoluments of a person not domiciled in the United Kingdom from an office or employment under or with any person, body of persons or partnership resident outside, and not resident in, the United Kingdom, but shall be taken not to include the emoluments of a person resident in the United Kingdom from an office or employment under or with a person, body of persons or partnership resident in the Republic of Ireland.

(2)   Where the duties of an office or employment are performed wholly outside the United Kingdom and the emoluments from the office or employment are foreign emoluments, the emoluments shall be excepted from Case I of Schedule E.

#### 5.2.1.2   Foreign taxpayers

The mechanics of tax collection: rental income.

**Soares, P.C., 'New Rules For Payments To Overseas Landlord: Obligations to Account for Tax', (1996) 16 *Property Law Bulletin* 63**

The new regulations which govern the payment of rent and other sums relating to land made on or after 6 April 1996 to a landlord or landowner whose usual place of abode is outside the United Kingdom are contained in the Taxation of Income from Land (Non-Residents) Regulations 1995 (SI No 2902).

Under the Tax Act 1988, s. 42A(1) the Inland Revenue may make regulations for the charging, assessing and collection and recovery of tax from prescribed persons in respect of the tax which is or may become chargeable under Schedule A on the income of any person who has his usual place of abode outside the United Kingdom (the non-resident).

A payer falls within this legislation if he is:

*tenant or tenant's agents*

(a)   a person by whom any such sums are payable to a non-resident as fall, or would fall, to be treated as receipts of a Schedule A business carried on by the non-resident; or

*agents of landlord*

(b)   a person who acts on behalf of a non-resident in connection with the management or administration of any such business.

The class therefore broadly comprises tenants and agents.

The Revenue has the power to designate a person as a prescribed person (presumably not with retrospective effect) provided he is a tenant or an agent (within the Tax Act 1988, s. 42A(2)) but agents and tenants are automatically prescribed persons (whether or not the Revenue have given them a notice to that effect) provided their usual place of abode is in the United Kingdom. That is a curious restriction on the legislation and there is no such restriction in the Tax Act 1988, s. 43 which applies to payments made on or before 5 April 1996.

Maybe the restriction is an acknowledgement of fiscal reality on the part of the Inland Revenue.

It should also be noted that the provisions apply to a Schedule A business and the various lease premiums sections have been carefully amended to ensure that as far as income tax is concerned, the charges which were formerly under Sched D come within Schedule A (see the Tax Act 1988, ss. 36 and 35).

Thus, if an overseas landlord grants a short lease at a premium or there is an assignment of a lease originally granted at an undervalue within s. 35 or land is sold with a right to a re-conveyance within s. 36 the deduction at source provisions will apply even though under the original legislation the charges were under Schedule D. There is therefore no loophole in that area.

Regulation 17 provides that a non-resident may apply to the Revenue for the obligation imposed under the Regulations to make payments to the Board not to apply to him because, for example, he has an excellent tax record. The Board will provide the non-resident landlord with a form requiring various particulars as set out in reg 17(3).

The following points can also be noted:

(1)   If the agent is an excluded person then he will not be a prescribed person within reg 3(3). 'Excluded person' means an agent whose activity, on behalf of the non-resident in connection with the management or administration of a Schedule A business or part thereof as the case may be, is confined to the provision of legal advice or legal services.

(2)   In any case where a liability to make payment to the Revenue arises from amounts payable or things done in the course of a business carried on by any persons in partnership, that partnership as such shall be treated for the purposes of the Regulations as the person who is prescribed, i.e. a person falling within s. 42A(2).

### 5.2.2   COMPANIES

#### 5.2.2.1   UK companies

All income profits of a UK company are liable to corporation tax wherever they are made.

### INCOME AND CORPORATION TAXES ACT 1988

**8.   General scheme of corporation tax**

(1)   Subject to any exceptions provided for by the Corporation Tax Acts, a company shall be chargeable to corporation tax on all its profits wherever arising.

#### 5.2.2.2   Overseas companies

Income profits, other than those from a trade carried on within the UK through a branch or agency, are subject to income tax.

### INCOME AND CORPORATION TAXES ACT 1988

**6.   The charge to corporation tax and exclusion of income tax and capital gains tax**

. . .

(2)   The provisions of the Income Tax Acts relating to the charge of income tax shall not apply to income of a company (not arising to it in a fiduciary or representative capacity) if—

(a)   the company is resident in the United Kingdom, or

(b)   the income is, in the case of a company not so resident, within the chargeable profits of the company as defined for the purposes of corporation tax by section 11(2).

INCOME AND CORPORATION TAXES ACT 1988

### 11.  Companies not resident in United Kingdom

. . .

(2)   For purposes of corporation tax the chargeable profits of a company not resident in the United Kingdom but carrying on a trade there through a branch or agency shall be—

(a)   any trading income arising directly or indirectly through or from the branch or agency, and any income from property or rights used by, or held by or for, the branch or agency (but so that this paragraph shall not include distributions received from companies resident in the United Kingdom) . . .

## 5.3   The Schedular System

*FRY* v *SALISBURY HOUSE ESTATE LTD* [1930] All ER Rep 538, 551–552 (HL)

A property management company owned a big property which it let to a large number of tenants as unfurnished offices. Its income profits from lighting, cleaning, caretaking, etc, fell under Schedule D, Case I. The Revenue contended that the income profits from the rentals also fell within Schedule D, Case I. The House of Lords held that the rental profits fell under Schedule A, and did not fall under Schedule D, Case I.

LORD ATKIN: . . . I think that this case should be decided in favour of the respondents on the simple ground that annual income derived from the ownership of lands, tenements, and hereditaments can only be assessed under Schedule A and in accordance with the rules of that schedule. In my opinion it makes no difference that the income so derived forms part of the annual profits of a trading concern. For the purpose of assessing such profits for the purpose of Schedule D the income so derived is not to be brought into account. The option of the revenue authorities to assess under whichever schedule they prefer in my opinion does not exist and is inconsistent with the provisions of the Income Tax Acts throughout their history.

The scheme of the Income Tax Acts is and always has been to provide for the taxation of specific properties under schedules appropriated to them and under a general Schedule D to provide for the taxation of income not dealt with specifically. . . . It is unnecessary to go further back than the Income Tax Act 1842, the provisions of which were incorporated in every Customs and Inland Revenue or Finance Act up to 1918, when the present consolidation Act was passed. I need not repeat the familiar schedules altered and extended by the Act of 1853. It is only necessary to refer to s. 100 of the Act of 1842, which defined the tax to be imposed under Schedule D:

The duties hereby granted, contained in the schedule marked (D) shall be assessed and charged under the following rules, which rules shall be deemed and construed to be a part of this Act and to refer to the said last-mentioned duties, as if the same had been inserted under a special enactment.

Schedule D: The said last-mentioned duties shall extend to every description of property or profits which shall not be contained in either of the said Schedules . . ., and to every description of employment or profit not contained in Schedule (E).

Nothing could be clearer to indicate that the schedules are mutually exclusive: that the specific income must be assessed under the specific schedule: and that D is a residual schedule so drawn that its various cases may carry out the object so far as possible of sweeping in profits not otherwise taxed. For this reason no doubt the actual schedule was drawn in the widest terms.

For and in respect of the annual profits or gains arising or accruing to any person residing in the United Kingdom from any kind of property whatever, whether situate in the United Kingdom or elsewhere, etc. Such language covers income from land in Schedule A . . . Its true meaning is made apparent by s. 100. Moreover, the dominance of each schedule . . . over its own subject-matter is confirmed by reference to the sections and rules which respectively regulate them in the Act of 1842. They afford a complete code for each class of income dealing with allowances and exemptions, with the mode of assessment and with the officials whose duty it is to make the assessments. . . . I find it impossible to conceive that these various commissioners had an option to encroach on the duties of one another: or that the taxpayer was exposed to having his income freed from the restrictions and exemptions imposed by statute under one schedule in order to be subject to a different set of restrictions and exemptions imposed by statute under another schedule. . . . Believing as I do that the specific Schedules . . ., and the rules thereunder contain definite codes applying exclusively to their respective defined subject-matters I find no ground for assessing the taxpayer under Schedule D for any property or gains which are the subject-matter of the other specific schedules. In the present case the income from the offices should be and has been assessed under Schedule A . . . as prescribed by statute. It therefore is not the subject-matter of assessment under Schedule D. I should add that if there had been an option to assess under Schedule A or Schedule D I cannot conceive a more conclusive election under the option than the assessment and receipt of payment under Schedule A, but this point need not be determined.

## 5.4   End of Chapter Assessment Question

Reflect on the facts relating to Amber Ltd and its shareholders: **2.3**, **3.4** and **4.6**. Note the following additional facts. Charlie was a shareholder in Megabucks plc. Amber Ltd exports metal fastenings to Malaysia.

Answer, with reference to the appropriate authority, the following questions:

(a)   Which of the eight persons involved is liable to income tax or corporation tax on their income profits?

(b)   In what capacity are each of the eight liable to income tax or corporation tax on their income profits?

(c)   On which of their income profits are they liable to income tax?

(d)   Under which of the Schedules and Cases do their income profits fall?

## 5.5   End of Chapter Assessment Outline Answer

All seven of the individuals involved in the facts of this question are resident in the UK in the 1998/99 tax year. There is nothing in the facts to cast doubt on this assumption.

Amber Ltd is resident in the UK. Since it is a UK company, Amber Ltd is liable to pay corporation tax on the whole of its income profits in an accounting period, wherever they arise: ICTA 1988, s. 8(1). This includes trading profits made on the sale of goods exported to Malaysia, and sold through its representative office there, as well as trading profits made on the sale of goods in the UK: ICTA 1988, s. 18(3).

Alan merely has a personal capacity. He is liable to income tax on his salary from Amber Ltd, the interest on the gift under Charlie's will, and the dividend income from Amber Ltd. Of the income received in his personal capacity, his salary from Amber Ltd falls under Schedule E, Case I; the interest payable on the gift under Charlie's will falls under Schedule D, Case III; and the dividends received from Amber Ltd fall under Schedule F.

Besides his personal capacity, Bertram has a capacity as the executor of Charlie's will, following the death of Charlie on 28 September 1998. In his personal capacity, he is liable to income tax on his salary from Amber Ltd. He is also liable to income tax on the interest payable on the gift he is to receive under Charlie's will, as well as on the dividend income received from Amber Ltd. In his capacity as the executor of Charlie's estate, he will be liable to income tax on all the income profits of Charlie's estate, wherever they come from. This is because we assume that Bertram is resident in the UK in the 1998/99 tax year, and because Charlie was resident, ordinarily resident and domiciled in the UK.

The same comments apply in relation to the income received in his personal capacity as for Alan: see above. Of the income received in his capacity as PR, the salary falls under Schedule E, Case I, whilst the dividend income falls under Schedule F.

Charlie dies part-way through the 1998/99 tax year although, prior to his death, his salary fell under Schedule E, Case I, whilst his dividend income fell under Schedule F.

Besides her personal capacity, Deborah has a capacity as a partner in Brown & Co. In her personal capacity, she is liable to income tax on her salary from Amber Ltd, the interest on the gift under Charlie's will, the dividends from Amber Ltd, her partnership in Brown & Co., and the income from the letting.

The same rules apply to Edwina, although there are no details of her income.

Georgina and Harry, although they have personal capacities, are relevant only in their capacity as trustees. They are liable to pay income tax on the income profits of the trust. There is nothing to suggest they are not resident in the UK in the 1998/99 tax year.

# CHAPTER SIX

# NATIONAL INSURANCE CONTRIBUTIONS: LIABILITY AND EARNINGS

## 6.1 Earnings

*S & U STORES* v *WILKES* **[1974] ICR 645 (National Industrial Relations Court)**

This case is a decision of the now-defunct National Industrial Relations Court. The issue at stake was whether 'remuneration' included amounts paid by way of expenses to the employee. In dealing with the issue, Sir John Donaldson P discussed 'remuneration' generally.

SIR JOHN DONALDSON P: Mr Wakerley [counsel for the employer] submits that 'remuneration' . . . means 'payment for work done' and that whether any particular payment or part of a payment made under a contract of employment falls within this description is a question of fact in each case. In his submission payments which are labelled as being in respect of expenses can arise in three different ways: (1) the employer can agree to re-imburse the employee for expenditure incurred by him; (2) the employer can agree a genuine pre-estimate of the expenditure which is likely to be incurred by the employee and pay that sum; (3) the employer can make a payment which though labelled as being in respect of expenses has no very precise relationship to the expenditure incurred or likely to be incurred by the employee. For completeness it should be added that an employer can also pay an increased wage or salary, because he recognises that the employee will be involved in expenditure and would not take the job if he were paid less.

Mr Wakerley rightly says that money paid in reimbursement of expenditure is no part of the employee's remuneration and that the *whole* of an increased wage or salary which merely reflects the fact that expenditure will be involved is part of that remuneration. There remain cases (2) and (3) above. Mr Wakerley submits that the tribunal must decide whether the whole or, if not, how much of the expenses element of the payment to the employee is a genuine attempt to reimburse the employee. To that extent, but no more, the payment is excluded from the calculation of the employee's 'average weekly rate of remuneration.'

Faced with *S & U Stores Ltd* v *Lee* [1969] 1 WLR 626, Mr Wakerley submits that it can be distinguished. The basis of the distinction is that the £3 paid to Mr Lee did not depend upon whether he used any or any particular car and that the Divisional Court treated the payment as if it was not, or might well not be, a genuine pre-estimate of the employee's expenditure on travelling: see p. 629. In the present case the tribunal has found:

Had we felt free to override the decision of the Divisional Court we would probably have held that this was a genuine estimate of actual expenses incurred for which the [employee] was to be re-imbursed and we do not think that we, had we had a free hand, would have been able to concur with the original tribunal decision in *Lee's* case.

The factual distinction may well exist, but we do not think that it is material in the light of the court's reasoning. This was that wages or salary mean direct payment for work done and that remuneration is not 'mere payment for work done, but is what the doer expects to get as a result of the work he does in so far as what he expects to get is quantified in terms of money.'

Alternatively Mr Wakerley submits that this court is not bound by *Lee's* case, although it is of great persuasive authority, and should not follow it: see *Chapman* v *Goonvean and Rostowrack China Clay Co. Ltd* [1973] ICR 50.

It seems to us that in construing the word 'remuneration' regard should be had to the purpose of a redundancy payment. It is intended to cushion long service employees against the vicissitudes of dismissal in a redundancy situation. The higher they have risen (in terms of wage and salary levels) and the longer they have been doing it, the greater is their potential fall. But their need of support, and Parliament's intention to provide it, cannot depend on whether they earned £x free of all expenses or £x free of all expenses plus £y to meet expenditure of £y incurred as a result of performing the contract of employment. Yet this is the result of the application of the decision in *Lee's* case. There is a further consideration. If both *S & U Stores Ltd* v *Lee* [1969] 1 WLR 626 and *NG Bailey & Co. Ltd* v *Preddy* [1971] 1 WLR 796 are right, Parliament is applying a different standard in the case of those who have a normal working week from that applicable in other cases. The wording of the paragraphs [i.e. of the relevant statutory provision] has to be different to take account of the different bases of remuneration, but we think that it is improbable that a different standard was intended. In our judgment the test for determining the 'average weekly rate of remuneration' is as follows. (1) Any sum which is paid as a wage or salary without qualification is part of the employee's remuneration. (2) The value of any benefit in kind (e.g. free accommodation) or paid in cash by someone other than the employer (e.g. the Easter offering) is to be disregarded as not forming part of the remuneration. (3) Any sum which is agreed to be paid by way of reimbursement or on account of expenditure incurred by the employee has to be examined to see whether in broad terms the whole or any part of the sum represents a profit or surplus in the hands of the employee. To the extent that it does represent such a profit or surplus it is part of the employee's remuneration. This is not a matter which calls for an involved accountancy exercise. It is for the tribunal of fact to form a broad common sense view of the realities of the situation as revealed by the evidence assessed in the light of their expert knowledge and experience. . . .

### Inland Revenue and Contributions Agency, Booklet CWG2 (1997), *Employer's Further Guide To PAYE and NICs*, December 1996, p. 68 (edited version)

The text below is directed at an employer operating the PAYE machinery (*Learning Text* at **19.3.7**).

### What to include as gross pay on form P11

The chart which follows tells you what to include as gross pay on form P11 for PAYE and NICs purposes. It lists the type of payments that can be made to employees.

Some entries will refer you to more detailed information elsewhere. This is because there may be special conditions for that type of payment.

If the chart does not show the type of payment you are making or if you are not sure whether to include the payment on form P11, contact

- for PAYE queries, your PAYE Tax Office
- for NICs queries, the Employer's Helpline by calling 0345 143 143. Calls will be charged at the local rate.

**Important** even if the payment does not need to be shown on form P11 it may need to be shown on forms P9D or P11D for tax purposes. [. . .]

| Type of payment | Include on P11 for | |
| --- | --- | --- |
| | NICS? | PAYE? |
| **Car fuel** supplied for private motoring including when the fuel is supplied using your own pump, credit card, or garage account, an agency card or petrol vouchers | No but there may be Class 1A liability [...] | No |
| **Car parking fees at the normal place of employment** paid for or reimbursed to employees | | |
| ■ contract is between the car park company and you | No | No |
| ■ all other circumstances | Yes | No |
| **Car parking fees** for **business related journeys** paid or reimbursed to employees | No | No |
| **Cars made available for private use** | No but there may be Class 1A liability [...] | No |
| **Christmas boxes in cash** | Yes | Yes |
| **Clothing or uniforms** | | |
| ■ clothing or uniforms provided by you | No | No |
| ■ payments to employees for non-durable items such as tights or stockings | No | Yes |
| ■ other payments to employees to purchase clothing or uniforms which can be worn at any time | Yes | Yes |
| ■ other payments to employees to purchase clothing or clothing which can be worn only at work | No | Yes |
| **Council tax** on employee's living accommodation | | |
| ■ employee provided with accommodation and the accommodation is within one of the categories where the value does not have to be included for tax purposes on form P9D or P11D [...] | No | No |
| ■ all other circumstances | Yes | No |
| **Credit card, charge cards** and so on — employees use your card to purchase **goods or services bought on your behalf** | | |
| ■ prior authority given by you to make the purchase **and** the employee explained in advance of the contract being made **and** the supplier accepted that the purchase was made on your behalf | No | No |
| ■ above condition not **fully** satisfied | Yes | No |
| ■ **Credit card, charge card** and so on — employees use your card for expenditure **other than** goods or services bought on your behalf | | |

| Type of payment | Include on P11 for | |
|---|---|---|
| | NICS? | PAYE? |
| ■ payments relating to business expenses actually incurred | No | No |
| [. . .] | | |
| ■ any other payments not reimbursed to you | Yes at the date you decide not to seek reimbursement | No |
| **Damages or similar payment** made to an employee injured at work | | |
| ■ there is a contractual liability to make it | Yes | Yes |
| ■ all other circumstances | No | No |
| **Director's personal bills** charged to loan account and so on | | |
| ■ the transaction makes the account overdrawn (or more overdrawn) **and** it is normal practice for you to pay the director's earnings into the same account | Yes on the overdrawn (or additional overdrawn) amount | No |
| ■ all other circumstances | No | No |
| **Director's remuneration,** salary, bonuses, fees and so on, including any advance or anticipatory payments paid, voted or credited | Yes | Yes |
| **Dividends** from shares | No | No |
| **Employee liability insurance —** reimbursements of payments made by employees for insurance cover or uninsured liabilities (such as legal costs) for claims against the employee arising out of his or her work | No | No |
| **Expenses payments or reimbursements** covered by a dispensation | [See extract below] | [See extract below] |
| [. . .] | | |
| [. . .] | | |
| **Inducement payment** such as 'golden hello' to recruit or retain employees | Yes | Yes |
| [. . .] | | |
| **Insurance premiums** for pension, annuities, or health cover and so on, **paid or reimbursed by you** where contract is between | | |
| ■ you and the insurance provider | No | No |
| ■ employee and the insurance provider | Yes | No |
| **Loans** | No | No |

| Type of payment | Include on P11 for | |
| --- | --- | --- |
| | NICS? | PAYE? |
| Loans written off | Yes at time of write off | No |
| **Lost time** payments | | |
| ■ payments made by a third party or by you on behalf of a third party | No | Yes |
| ■ all other circumstances | Yes | Yes |
| **Meal allowances and vouchers** | | |
| ■ cash payments for meals | Yes | Yes |
| ■ vouchers redeemable for food and drink or a cash alternative | Yes | Yes |
| ■ vouchers redeemable for food and drink only. | No | No |
| [. . .] | | |
| **Mortgage payments** met directly by you for employees | | |
| ■ mortgage provided by you or mortgage contract is between you and mortgagee | No | No |
| ■ mortgage contract is between employee and mortgagee | Yes | No |
| **Payments in kind** but not tradeable assets — [. . .] | | |
| ■ which can be turned into cash **by surrender** such as Premium Bonds, and so on | Yes | Yes |
| ■ which can be turned into cash only **by sale** such as furniture, kitchen appliances, holidays and so on | No | No |
| [. . .] | | |
| **Pensions** | No | Yes |
| **Personal bills paid** for goods and services supplied to employees, club memberships and so on | | |
| ■ contract to supply goods and services is between you and the provider | No | No |
| ■ contract to supply goods and services is between the employee and the provider — | | |
| payment made direct to the provider | Yes | No |
| payment made or reimbursed direct to the employee | Yes | Yes |
| **Personal incidental expenses** (PIEs) | [See extract below] | [See extract below] |
| [. . .] | | |

| Type of payment | Include on P11 for | |
| --- | --- | --- |
| | NICS? | PAYE? |
| **Prize money** paid in cash to employees for competitions you run in connection with your business, which are not open to the public | Yes | Yes |
| [. . .] | | |
| **Sickness, maternity and other absence** from work payments | Yes | Yes |
| **Statutory Sick Pay and Statutory Maternity Pay** (SSP & SMP) | Yes | Yes |
| [. . .] | | |
| **Subscriptions or fees** to professional bodies paid or reimbursed by you | | |
| ■ contractual or professional requirement for employee to be a member of the body | No | No |
| ■ membership of the body is voluntary | Yes | No |
| **Suggestions schemes** awards to employees | | |
| ■ it is not part of the employee's normal duties to make staff suggestions **and** the award is wholly discretionary with no contractual entitlement or expectation | No | Ask your PAYE Tax Office about Extra Statutory Concession A57 |
| ■ above condition not **fully** satisfied. | Yes | (as above) |
| **Telephone charges and/or rental paid** or reimbursed where the employee is the subscriber and the telephone is **not used exclusively for business use** | | |
| ■ payments covered by an Inland Revenue dispensation | No | No |
| ■ payments not covered by an Inland Revenue dispensation that can nevertheless be identified as relating to business calls by reference to itemised bills or diary and so on | No | No |
| ■ all other payments | Yes | No |
| **Telephone charges and/or rental paid** or reimbursed where you are the subscriber **or** the employee is the subscriber but the telephone is used **exclusively for business use** | No | No |
| [. . .] | | |

| Type of payment | Include on P11 for | |
| --- | --- | --- |
| | NICS? | PAYE? |
| **Training** — payments for such things as course fees, books and so on | | |
| ■ training is work related or is encouraged or required by you in connection with the employment | No | No |
| ■ all other circumstances | Yes | Yes |
| **Transport vouchers**, such as season tickets and so on | | |
| ■ contract to provide the voucher or ticket is between you and the provider | No | No |
| ■ contract to provide the voucher or ticket is between the employee and the provider | Yes | No |
| **Travel and subsistence payments** | [see extract below] | [see extract below] |
| **Travelling time** payments | Yes | Yes |
| **Vouchers** which can be redeemed or exchanged for | | |
| ■ goods alone (but not tradeable assets) | No | No |
| ■ both goods and cash or cash alone | Yes | Yes |
| [. . .] | | |
| **Wages, salaries, fees, overtime, bonuses, commission** and so on | Yes | Yes |

### [Notes]

A **dispensation** is a notice sent to you by the Inspector of Taxes, authorising you not to report on forms P11D the expenses payments and benefits specifically covered by the dispensation. The Inspector will issue the dispensation if he or she is satisfied that

■ your employees would be able to obtain a deduction for the expenses or benefits in arriving at their tax liability **and**

■ payments are properly controlled by you.

The following guidance on what can and cannot be included in a dispensation should be noted.

■ Scale rate payments can be included for such things as travelling and subsistence provided they are reasonable.

■ Round sum allowances are specifically excluded.

■ There are no other restrictions on the types of expenses payments or reimbursements which can be included.

Provided the conditions under which the dispensation was granted have not changed, the Contributions Agency will accept a dispensation as evidence that the payments it covers

■ are expenses incurred in carrying out employment

■ are not to be included in gross pay for NICs purposes.

. . .

### Personal incidental expenses

Employees staying away from home overnight on business will often incur additional expenses to cover such things as telephone calls home, laundry and newspapers. These are commonly referred to as personal incidental expenses.

Do not include in gross pay any payment you make to pay for or contribute towards personal incidental expenses incurred by an employee when they stay away from home overnight on business, up to a limit of

■ £5 a night in the United Kingdom, and

■ £10 a night outside the United Kingdom.

If you pay over the relevant maximum, then the whole amount must be included in gross pay for both PAYE and NICs purposes.

. . .

### Travel and subsistence payments

The treatment for both PAYE and NICs purposes of employees' travel or subsistence payments, depends upon the circumstances under which the payments are made. . . .
Unless made under one of the circumstances [elsewhere in the booklet apply] any payment made to an employee towards the cost of travelling between his or her home and normal place of employment must be included in gross pay for both for PAYE and NICs purposes. (Only rarely can an employee's home be regarded for tax or NICs purposes as the normal place of employment.)

## 6.2    End of Chapter Assessment Question

Refer to the facts concerning Amber Ltd and its shareholders: **2.3**, **3.4**, **4.6** and **5.4**. Note the following additional facts. The salaries of Alan, Bertram, Charlie and Deborah, as directors of Amber Ltd, are £8,000 each, before income tax and NICs. Up to his death on 28 September 1998, Charlie has lived in a house in Knightsbridge, owned by the company, at a very subsidised rent, Amber Ltd paying the council tax on the property. Deborah had a car provided for her general use by Amber Ltd on 6 April 1998.

On the basis of the information in this chapter, comment on the NIC implications of these facts for the persons involved.

## 6.3    End of Chapter Assessment Outline Answer

For NIC purposes, each of Alan, Bertram, Charlie and Deborah are employed earners. Each of them are liable to pay Class 1 primary NICs on their earnings of £8,000 each, as directors of Amber Ltd. In addition, Amber Ltd is liable to pay Class 1 secondary NICs in respect of the earnings of each of them.

In relation to Charlie, the value of his subsidised living accommodation will *not* have ranked as part of his earnings for the purpose of Class 1 primary NICs, although the payment of his council tax by Amber Ltd *will* have done so.

In relation to Deborah, the provision to her of the car for her general use will mean that Amber Ltd is liable to pay Class 1A NICs. These will be payable once annually by Amber Ltd, in relation to the relevant tax year. The value of the use of the car will not form part of Deborah's earnings for the purposes of Class 1 primary NICs.

# CHAPTER SEVEN

# INCOME TAXATION: CALCULATION (1)

## 7.1   Introduction

No distinction is made in this chapter between earned and unearned income, although the distinction *is* made in ICTA 1988, s. 833.

### INCOME AND CORPORATION TAXES ACT 1988

**833.   Interpretation of Income Tax Acts**

. . .

   (4)   Subject to subsections (5) and (6) below, in the Income Tax Acts 'earned income' means, in relation to any individual—
   (a)   any income arising in respect of—
      (i)   any remuneration from any office or employment held by the individual, or
      (ii)   any pension, superannuation or other allowance, deferred pay or compensation for loss of office, given in respect of the past services of the individual or of the husband or parent of the individual in any office or employment, or given to the individual in respect of past services of any deceased person, whether the individual or husband or parent of the individual shall have contributed to such pension, superannuation allowance or deferred pay or not; and
   (b)   any income from any property which is attached to or forms part of the emoluments of any office or employment held by the individual; and
   (c)   any income which is charged under Schedule D and is immediately derived by the individual from the carrying on or exercise by him of his trade, profession or vocation, either as an individual or, in the case of a partnership, as a partner personally acting in the partnership.

. . .

Reference is made to this section in the *Learning Text* at **7.3**.

## 7.2   Calculating the *Total Income Tax Due* from an Individual

Total charges on income are deducted from statutory income, in order to give total income: ICTA 1988, s. 835.

### INCOME AND CORPORATION TAXES ACT 1988

**835.   'Total income' in the Income Tax Acts**
   (1)   In the Income Tax Acts 'total income', in relation to any person, means the total income of that person from all sources estimated in accordance with the provisions of the Income Tax Acts.

(2)   Any person who, on his own behalf or on behalf of another person, delivers a statement of the amount of his or that other person's total income shall observe the rules and directions contained in section 836.

(3)   Where deductions reduce a person's total income and the order in which they are made or in which income of different descriptions is reduced thereby may affect his liability to income tax the deductions shall be made and treated as reducing income in accordance with [subsection (4)] below.

(4)   Subject to any express provisions of the Income Tax Acts, any deductions allowable in computing a person's total income or to be made from a person's total income shall be treated as reducing income of different descriptions in the order which will result in the greatest reduction of his liability to income tax.

. . .

(6)   In estimating the total income of any person—

(a)   any income which is chargeable with income tax by way of deduction at the basic rate in force for any year or which for the purposes of Schedule F comprises an amount which is or (apart from section 78(3) of the Finance Act 1993) would be equal to a tax credit calculated by reference to the rate of advance corporation tax in force for any year shall be deemed to be income of that year; and

(b)   any deductions which are allowable on account of sums payable under deduction of income tax at the basic rate in force for any year out of the property or profits of that person shall be allowed as deductions in respect of that year;
notwithstanding that the income or sums, as the case may be, accrued or will accrue in whole or in part before or after that year.

(7)   Where an assessment has become final and conclusive for the purposes of income tax for any year of assessment—

(a)   that assessment shall also be final and conclusive in estimating total income; and

(b)   no allowance or adjustment of liability, on the ground of diminution of income or loss, shall be taken into account in estimating total income unless that allowance or adjustment has previously been made on an application under the special provisions of the Income Tax Acts relating thereto.

. . .

## 7.3   Calculating the *Mainstream Corporation Tax Liability* of a Company

Dividend income is *not* included in Stage One of a company's corporation tax calculation.

### INCOME AND CORPORATION TAXES ACT 1988

**208.   UK company distributions not generally chargeable to corporation tax**
Except as otherwise provided by the Corporation Tax Acts, corporation tax shall not be chargeable on dividends and other distributions of a company resident in the United Kingdom, nor shall any such dividends or distributions be taken into account in computing income for corporation tax.

## 7.4   End of Chapter Assessment Question

Alan, Bertram, Charlie and Deborah (see **6.2**) have a cousin called Hugh. Hugh is a barrister in private practice, aged 28. At 6 April 1998, he has been in private practice for five years. He owns a few investments, and he supplements the income from his practice at the bar by lecturing. He makes up his accounts for his bar practice to 30 June in each calendar year.

In the tax year 1998/99, he has the following income and expenditure:

|  | £ |
|---|---|
| Brief fees (to 30 June 1998) (Schedule D, Case II) | 15,000 |
| Allowable deductions in bar practice (to 30 June 1998) | 8,000 |
| Lecturing pay (Schedule E) | 6,000 |
| | |
| Schedule E allowable deductions | 650 |
| | |
| Rental income | 10,000 |
| Allowable deductions on rented-out properties: | |
| Insurance | 2,500 |
| Repairs | 9,000 |
| | |
| Dividend income (gross) | 2,000 |

Hugh has covenanted to pay £1,500 gross per annum to a registered charity. The dividend income above includes an ACT credit of £400. The rental income and expenditure shown relates to three houses in Stepney, which he owns.

Hugh is married to Jane.

Calculate the total income tax due from Hugh in the 1998/99 tax year.

(The personal allowance for 1998/99 is £4,195 and the married couples' allowance is £1,900.)

## 7.5   End of Chapter Assessment Outline Answer

(Square bracketed figures refer to notes at the end.)

INCOME TAX CALCULATION OF HUGH FOR THE TAX YEAR 1998/99

|  | £ |
|---|---|
| Profit from employment (Schedule E) [1] | 5,350 |
| *Plus* Profit from bar (Schedule D, Case II) [2] | 7,000 |
| *Plus* Profit from lettings [3] | NIL |
| *Plus* Dividend income (gross) | 2,000 |
| | |
| *Statutory income* | 14,350 |
| | |
| *Less* Charge on income (gross) | (1,500) |
| | |
| *Total income* | 12,850 |
| | |
| *Less* Personal allowance | (4,195) |
| | |
| *Taxable income* | 8,655 |
| | |
| £4,300 at 20% | 860 |

| | |
|---|---:|
| Next £4,355 at 23% | 1,002 |
| *Total tax* | 1,862 |
| *Less* MCA [4] | (285) |
| *Tax liability* | 1,577 |
| *Less* Tax credited as paid [5] | (400) |
| SUB-TOTAL TAX DUE | 1,177 |
| *Plus* Tax on charges paid [6] | 345 |
| TOTAL INCOME TAX DUE | 1,522 |

*Notes*:
[1] i.e. £6,000 − £650.
[2] i.e. £15,000 − £8,000.
[3] i.e. £10,000 − £2,500 — £9,000. This gives a rental loss of £(1,500), which will be available for relief as discussed in *Learning Text* at **Chapter 13**.
[4] i.e. 15/100 × £1,900.
[5] i.e. ACT on the dividends.
[6] i.e. 23/100 × £1,500.

# CHAPTER EIGHT

# INCOME TAXATION: CALCULATION (2)

## 8.1 Introduction

The ACT is an 'up-front' payment of corporation tax.

### INCOME AND CORPORATION TAXES ACT 1988

**239. Set-off of ACT against liability to corporation tax**

(1) ... advance corporation tax paid by a company (and not repaid) in respect of any distribution made by it in an accounting period shall be set against its liability to corporation tax on any profits charged to corporation tax for that accounting period and shall accordingly discharge a corresponding amount of that liability.

ICTA 1988, s. 1A ensures that, as a basic rate taxpayer, you have no extra tax to pay on the dividend.

### INCOME AND CORPORATION TAXES ACT 1988

**1A. Application of lower rate to income from savings and distributions**

(1) Subject to sections 469(2) and 686, so much of any person's total income for any year of assessment as—
    (a) comprises income to which this section applies, and
    (b) in the case of an individual, is not income falling within section 1(2)(b),
shall, by virtue of this section, be charged for that year at the lower rate, instead of at the rate otherwise applicable to it in accordance with section 1(2)(aa) and (a).
(2) Subject to subsection (4) below, this section applies to the following income—
    (a) any income chargeable under Case III of Schedule D other than—
        (i) relevant annuities and other annual payments that are not interest; and
        (ii) amounts so chargeable by virtue of section 119;
    (b) any income chargeable under Schedule F; and
    (c) subject to subsection (4) below, any equivalent foreign income.
. . .
(5) So much of any person's income as comprises income to which this section applies shall be treated for the purposes of subsection (1)(b) above and any other provisions of the Income Tax Acts as the highest part of his income.
(6) Subsection (5) above shall have effect subject to section 833(3) but shall otherwise have effect notwithstanding any provision requiring income of any description to be treated for the purposes of the Income Tax Acts . . . as the highest part of a person's income.

Further changes will take effect from 6 April 1999.

**Gammie, M., 'The Future of ACT',** *Taxation Practitioner*, **March 1998, p. 8**

The tax landscape for companies and their shareholders is changing dramatically. Out goes advance corporation tax. In comes advanced corporation tax. This article takes stock of the changes to date and anticipates some changes to come.

*Company taxation*

*The rate of corporation tax*

The mainstream tax rate on corporate profits earned on or after 1 April 1997 has been reduced from 33 to 31 per cent. There is a corresponding reduction from 23 to 21 per cent for companies with profits of £300,000 or less. The marginal rate of corporation tax for those companies that earn profits between £300,000 and £1.5m is 33.5 per cent.

The Chancellor proposes to reduce the mainstream corporation tax rate to 30 per cent for profits earned on or after 1 April 1999. With this in mind, companies should seek whatever advantage they can gain by taking deductions in periods ending before April 1999 and deferring income to later periods. In periods that straddle the date of the reduction, the benefit of such timing is negated, as net taxable profits are time apportioned over the period.

The Chancellor announced no corresponding reduction to 20 per cent in the small companies rate to bring it into line with the lower rate of income tax. The reduction in rate to 30 per cent was to compensate companies for the introduction of quarterly payments on account (see below). Quarterly payments will not affect companies that pay tax at the small companies rate. Even at 21 per cent, however, the small companies rate on retained profits compares well with the higher rate of income tax borne by unincorporated businesses.

*Advance Corporation Tax (ACT)*

From 6 April 1999 companies will be able to pay dividends without accounting for ACT and without otherwise having to withhold tax. Until then, companies must continue to pay ACT at 25 per cent of their dividends. Up to 6 April 1999, group companies remain entitled to elect to pay dividends within the group without ACT.

Thereafter group income elections cease to be relevant for dividends. This resolves for the future the first issue raised in the *Hoechst* case. Hoechst UK is arguing that it is entitled on non-discrimination grounds to pay dividends gross to its German parent company. This is now relevant only for the past and the time remaining until April 1999.

*Foreign income dividends*

Companies may continue to elect to pay cash dividends as foreign income dividends ('FIDs') until 6 April 1999. Schedule 7 of the Finance Act 1997 also continues until then to treat distributions on the repurchase or repayment of shares and certain special dividends as FIDs. Companies must pay ACT on FIDs, unless they qualify as international headquarters companies ('IHCs'). They may, however, match their FIDs against their foreign taxed income and reclaim the ACT if they are unable to offset the ACT against their mainstream corporation tax due to foreign tax credits.

Prior to July 1997 few companies paid FIDs. FIDs were unpopular with tax exempt investors, who were unable to recover the tax credit on such dividends. As pension funds are no longer able to recover the tax credit on any dividend, many more companies have begun to pay FIDs as a way of managing their ACT liabilities. As a result, other tax exempt shareholders, such as charities and personal equity plan holders, have suffered an immediate reduction in their income rather than as anticipated in April 1999 when repayable tax credits disappear for virtually everyone.

The FIDs regime incorporated special provisions for IHCs — essentially foreign-owned companies based in the UK. IHCs may pay foreign taxed profits as FIDs without accounting for ACT on the dividends. As all UK companies (irrespective of ownership) will be able to pay dividends on or after 6 April 1999 without accounting for ACT and without otherwise withholding tax, the IHC provisions will be withdrawn from that date. It seems unlikely that the government will be persuaded to introduce a new international holding company regime incorporating, for example, a special exemption for chargeable gains on interests in foreign subsidiaries.

*Surplus ACT and shadow ACT*

The abolition of ACT in April 1999 eliminates for the future the problem of surplus ACT, especially for those companies with substantial taxed foreign earnings. Until then, companies may use their ACT to reduce their mainstream corporation tax bills in the normal way. Thereafter, surplus ACT carried forward will continue to reduce corporation tax liabilities but only to the extent permitted by a 'shadow ACT' system.

The basic theory of shadow ACT is that a company must calculate the ACT that it would have paid on distributions made after 5 April 1999. This shadow ACT reduces its capacity to offset real ACT carried forward from before April 1999. The 1998 Finance Act will contain the enabling legislation for the shadow ACT system. The substantive provisions, however, are to be in Regulations. This will provide more time for consultation and to get the provisions right.

With an estimated £7 billion of surplus ACT, there is a considerable amount at risk for the government if the scheme is unduly generous to companies. At the same time, the government wishes to be fair. Its intention is that 'companies' existing expectations as regards past surplus ACT will be substantially preserved, no more and no less'. The government is not expecting to repay ACT — possibly as much as £5 billion in aggregate — that represents long run structural ACT, much of it already written off in companies' accounts.

ACT abolition provides a permanent solution to surplus ACT while shadow ACT offers the potential for fair treatment of existing surpluses. The shadow ACT system is unlikely to incorporate all the features of the current ACT system. Thus, companies may be unable to surrender shadow ACT. Companies will also be unable to pay shadow FIDs and it is unclear how surplus shadow ACT will be dealt with. It may also be unwise to expect the shadow ACT system to survive long-term. A new Chancellor might justify abolishing shadow ACT after a few years by claiming that any remaining surpluses must be structural surpluses that companies could not expect to recover.

*Planning for surplus ACT*

The scope for maximising the use of past surplus ACT under the shadow system will become apparent only later this year. In the meantime, the optimum strategy for companies is to minimise the surplus ACT that they will carry into the shadow system. This may involve increasing current taxable profits and also making maximum use of the facility to carry back ACT.

Income generated in the UK by a company with surplus ACT bears tax at effectively 11 per cent. Such a company may therefore want to take advantage of any legitimate opportunities it has to earn income in the UK and incur expenses abroad where they may be relieved at a higher tax rate. The reduction in the UK corporation tax rate may produce excess foreign tax credits and UK companies may look to utilise them by mixing high and low taxed foreign income through a foreign subsidiary. The Inland Revenue will no doubt be watching carefully for any signs of abuse in this area.

Companies may also want to minimise their new ACT liabilities. In this way they will free current mainstream corporation tax to absorb surplus ACT carried forward. The most straightforward method is to postpone paying dividends until after 5 April 1999. If the government thinks that this may become a significant issue it might consider legislation to impose some notional dividend standard, based on the average dividend payments of recent years. As an alternative, companies may consider paying current dividends as scrip or perhaps as non-qualifying distributions. A non-qualifying distribution in the form of bonus redeemable shares or securities may create shadow ACT on redemption and a restriction on the company's capacity at that point to use any surplus ACT.

Companies have already taken to paying FIDs as a means of being repaid ACT and minimising any increase in surplus ACT. Companies that have been unable to pay FIDs by election (because, for example, they have more than one class of share capital) have used the anti-avoidance provisions of FA 1997, Sch. 7 to convert ordinary dividends into deemed FIDs.

For those companies that wish to return more substantial sums to shareholders, the trick is now to do so in capital form without ACT rather than, as previously, as a distribution with a repayable tax credit. Companies may be able to achieve this in a variety of ways. They may, for example, use their share premium account or reorganise their share capital to attribute contributed capital to a class of share that is repaid. Alternatively, they may consider inserting a new group holding company for the issue of a mixture of ordinary and redeemable shares and loan notes.

### Payments on account

The abolition of ACT leaves a gap in the government's revenues. To fill this, large and medium sized companies will have to pay corporation by instalments, starting with CT self-assessment, i.e. for accounting periods *ending* on or after 1 July 1999.

The current proposals envisage that those companies that pay tax at the full main-stream rate (i.e. with taxable profits of £1.5m or more) will pay by four equal instalments in months 7, 10, 13 and 16. This involves two in-year payments with some acceleration of the balance. To mitigate the cash flow impact on companies, there will be a transition from ACT to payments on account running from 1999 for four years.

Companies that pay tax at the marginal rate (i.e. with taxable profits falling between £300,000 and £1.5m) will pay half their tax in quarterly instalments and the balance nine months after the year-end. Companies liable to tax at the small companies rate will continue to pay their tax nine months after the year-end.

Instalments are based on current estimated tax liabilities and the Inland Revenue has said that there will be a relatively light compliance regime, with interest only on over- and under-payments. They will seek penalties only if they believe that there has been a deliberate and flagrant opting out of the instalment regime. Nevertheless, many bodies, including the Chartered Institute, have criticised the proposals. Companies may not know for a particular period whether they are large, medium or small (and their status may change during the period) and may not be able accurately to estimate their profits for the period. Some change in the detail of the proposals seems likely.

### Shareholders

### The tax credit and tax rate on dividends

From 6 April 1999, the tax credit rate for all shareholders will reduce from 20 per cent to ten per cent and the ordinary rate of tax on dividend income becomes ten per cent. Lower and basic rate shareholders will continue to have no further liability to tax on their dividend income. Higher rate shareholders will pay tax on their dividend income at the special rate of 32.5 per cent. This produces the same after tax return on dividend income as compared with a 40 per cent tax rate and a 20 per cent tax credit. The special dividend tax rate applies also to dividends from foreign companies.

Pension funds and corporate investors (in particular insurance companies) have been unable to recover the tax credit on dividends paid since 2 July 1997. Under current proposals, only shares held in the new individual savings account are proposed to be eligible to be repaid the tax credit (for a five-year period). From 6 April 1999 charities cease to be repaid the tax credit but benefit until 2004 from a transitional relief designed to mitigate the impact of this change on their income.

### Foreign shareholders

The reduction in the tax credit is entirely related to the dividend articles in the UK's double taxation treaties. Foreign shareholders remain entitled under treaties to be repaid all or half the tax credit. With a ten per cent tax credit, however, the 15 or five per cent withholding permitted by treaties from the sum of the dividend and applicable tax credit, eliminates the treaty benefit for portfolio shareholders and reduces it to negligible proportions for direct investors.

The UK has given notice to its treaty partners of the change but it is too early to say whether treaty partners, in particular the USA, will seek to renegotiate dividend articles. The government's hope for UK investors abroad is that they will remain entitled to reduced dividend withholding rates under existing treaty articles. The tax credit is, however, little more than a fig leaf and post-1999 is no longer backed by ACT. In those limited cases where the credit or part is repaid, the Treasury may effectively repay foreign tax.

Foreign investors entitled to the tax credit will get a better UK result from repatriating profits with a real credit before April 1999 than with a fig-leaf credit afterwards. The restriction on the tax credit repayment solves the second issue in the *Hoechst* case, namely that Hoechst AG should get the benefit of the tax credit. The change gives impetus for EC parent companies generally to argue that the withholding under UK treaties is contrary to the Parent/subsidiary directive (EC Directive 90/435).

*The Future*

It is unlikely that the measures that we will see in the 1998 Finance Bill will mark an end to change. The reforms may lead to higher gearing by UK companies and put pressure on the UK's foreign tax credit system. It is quite possible that at some stage government may consider restricting interest relief for foreign investment (or more generally) and limiting foreign tax credit planning. For the time being, however, corporate tax advisers have quite enough to cope with.

## 8.2   Calculation of National Insurance Contributions

A percentage rate is applied to the earnings figure.

### SOCIAL SECURITY CONTRIBUTIONS AND BENEFITS ACT 1992

**15.   Class 4 contributions recoverable under the Income Tax Acts**

. . .

(3)   A Class 4 contribution for any tax year shall be an amount equal to 6 per cent. of so much of the profits or gains referred to in subsection (1) above (as computed in accordance with Schedule 2 to this Act) as exceeds £7,310 and does not exceed £25,220.

## 8.3   When a Person Must Account for Value Added Tax

**¶8222 Zero-rating groups**
There is a statutory list of items to be zero-rated . . . it consists of a series of 'groups' each of which contains a number of 'items' specifying supplies which are to be zero-rated (VATA 1994, sch. 8). The groups are structured so as to contain items which are linked in some general way. For instance, the group headed 'Books, etc.' provides zero-rating for supplies of books and also for supplies of newspapers: essentially, the zero-ratings for supplies of published material are contained in this group.

Although each zero-rating group has a heading, these headings are of no legal force (VATA 1994, s. 96(10)). The headings are there merely to assist in identifying which groups may provide zero-rating for a particular supply. In order to determine whether a zero-rating does, in fact, exist it is necessary to study the items within the groups, to see whether the supply fits precisely into one or other of the descriptions.

Furthermore, there are notes to each group which amplify or modify the meanings of the zero-ratings contained in the items, and these must be studied as well to see whether zero-rating is available (VATA 1994, s. 96(9)).

Since the UK zero-rating provisions do not generally derive from the EC legislation, but are derogations from it, they must be interpreted in accordance with UK principles. However, the provisions for zero-rating exports of goods, and various other supplies connected with international trade, do arise from the EC legislation, so that recourse can be had to this in interpreting the legislation.

The zero-rating groups, and a brief description of the supplies zero-rated by them, are set out below.

**Group 1 — food**
Group 1 zero-rates many supplies of food for human consumption, animal food, seeds for food plants, and live animals used for food purposes. Certain supplies are excluded, particularly supplies in the course of catering (including supplies of hot take-away food) and confectionery.

**Group 2 — sewerage services and water**
Group 2 zero-rates supplies relating to the bulk treatment of sewage, emptying cess pools, etc. and most supplies of water for non-industrial purposes.

**Group 3 — books, etc.**
Most books, booklets, leaflets, pamphlets, newspapers and periodicals, printed music, maps, etc. are zero-rated, as are ancillary objects such as covers included in the price. The zero-rating does not extend to stationery.

**Group 4 — talking books for the blind and handicapped and wireless sets for the blind**
Group 4 zero-rating covers supplies (including hire) of certain goods to the Royal National Institute for the Blind, the National Listening Library and similar charities. It also covers supplies (including hire) to any charity of certain equipment which is to be lent, free of charge, to blind persons.

**Group 5 — construction of buildings, etc.**
Group 5 zero-rating relates only to dwellings and certain buildings for communal residential use, non-business use by charities, or use by a charity as a village hall or similarly in providing social and recreational facilities.
   Zero-rating is provided for:

■  supplies in the course of constructing the building; and
■  the sale of the freehold or long lease of the building by the person constructing it (or, in some instances, the person who created it by converting a non-residential building). This means the person who constructed the building rather than a person who is currently constructing it (*C & E Commrs* v *Link Housing Association Ltd* [1992] BVC 113).

   In addition, services in the course of construction of a civil engineering work necessary for the development of a permanent park for residential caravans are zero-rated. However, the sale of such a caravan park does not qualify for zero-rating.
   A number of conditions must be met to secure zero-rating.

**Group 6 — protected buildings**
A further zero-rating is available for certain protected buildings, if they are qualifying buildings (see above), relieving from tax some alteration works. As with the construction zero-rating, there is one relief for supplies for such buildings by their owners, and a separate one for the supplies made to their owners by contractors. The buildings to which the reliefs apply are qualifying buildings which are also:

■  buildings which are listed buildings under the *Planning (Listed Buildings and Conservation Areas) Act* 1990, or its Scottish or Northern Irish equivalents; or
■  scheduled monuments within the meaning in the *Ancient Monuments and Archaeological Areas Act* 1979 or the *Historic Monuments (Northern Ireland) Act* 1971.

**Group 7 — international services**
Before 1 January 1993 there were many more zero-rating categories under the 'International services' heading, which are now implemented as place of supply provisions.
   The two zero-ratings which remain are for work carried out on goods for export from the EC, and for the making of arrangements for such a supply, for an export of goods from the EC, or for a supply of services made outside the EC.
   There is also a concessionary relief, from 1 September 1993, for similar services supplied to businesses elsewhere in the EC.

**Group 8 — transport**
Group 8 provides zero-rating for supplies of ships and aircraft, for the public transport of passengers, for the international transport of goods and passengers, and for international freight handling and storage facilities.

The zero-ratings fall into five main categories:
(1)   supplies of ships and of aircraft, including repair, maintenance, hire, etc.;
(2)   supplies of lifeboats;
(3)   supplies of public transport services;
(4)   supplies of freight transport and related supplies; and
(5)   certain supplies by tour operators outside the EC.

### Group 9 — caravans and houseboats
Group 9 provides zero-rating, broadly, for supplies of caravans and houseboats likely to be used as private residences, putting these on the same basis for VAT as private houses.

### Group 10 — gold
Group 10 is of little general interest, and zero-rates supplies of gold held in the UK between Central Banks and members of the London Gold Market.

### Group 11 — bank notes
Group 11 is of interest mainly to the Bank of England and the Scottish banks, and zero-rates the issue of bank notes by banks.

### Group 12 — drugs, medicines, aids for the handicapped, etc.
The zero-ratings provided by Group 12 are multifarious, tightly defined, and highly specialised.

The group zero-rates a number of supplies of goods and services for use by people who are handicapped. The supply must be made to the handicapped person or to a charity which makes it available to the handicapped person.

The supplies which can qualify for zero-rating are tightly defined, but include items such as specialised equipment, modifications to buildings, etc. . . .

It should be noted that, to the extent that zero-rating is given for supplies of goods designed or adapted for use by handicapped persons, the tribunals have tended to take a narrow view and deny zero-rating where items have been of particular use to handicapped persons but also of use to the population generally (see, for instance, *Portland College* [1993] BVC 827).

The group also zero-rates the supply of drugs and medicines on prescription.

### Group 13 — imports, exports, etc.
Group 13 provides certain peripheral zero-ratings in relation to international trade.

### Group 14 — tax-free shops
Group 14 zero-rates limited supplies of tobacco products, etc. to certain intra-EC travellers when supplied in a tax-free shop, or supplied on board an aircraft or ship by the person supplying the transport (or someone authorised by him).

### Group 15 — charities, etc.
Group 15 zero-rates a number of supplies to or by charities and related bodies. However, it should be noted that it does not provide any general zero-rating for matters relating to charities. In the main, charities are subject to exactly the same VAT rules as other entities.

The zero-ratings cover some supplies by charities and some supplies to charities. In all cases there are a number of conditions to be met.

### Group 16 — clothing and footwear
Group 16 zero-rates supplies of children's clothing, of protective boots and helmets for industrial use, and of motor cycle helmets.

## EXEMPT SUPPLIES

. . .

### ¶8230   VAT exemption groups
The groups contained in the statutory list of exempt supplies and a brief description of the supplies exempted by them, are set out below.

**Group 1 — land**
Group 1 exemption covers the grant or assignment of:

■   any interest in land;
■   any right over land; or
■   any licence to occupy land.

As a matter of principle, a right to call for or be granted such an interest, right or licence is itself an interest in land, and so capable of falling within the exemption. However, in Scotland such a personal right is not considered to be a right over land, and the legislation therefore makes specific provision bringing such a right within the exemption.

Some supplies falling within these categories, such as holiday lettings, supplies of sporting rights, etc. are excluded from the exemption.

From 1 August 1989 it is possible to elect to waive the land exemption — the so-called 'option to tax'. The effect is to make taxable those supplies which would otherwise be exempt (VATA 1994, sch. 10, para. 2). The election is irrevocable so, once made, all future supplies of the land concerned by the elector are standard-rated. The operation and scope of the election to waive exemption are complex.

The European Court of Justice decision in the case of *Lubbock Fine & Co.* v *C & E Commrs* (Case C-63/92) [1993] BVC 287 established that the surrender, as well as the grant or assignment, of an interest, etc. in land is an exempt supply. In legislating to incorporate this exemption in the UK law from 1 March 1995, Customs have also extended it to exempt reverse surrenders (i.e. cases where the tenant pays the landlord to accept a surrender).

**Group 2 — insurance**
The Group 2 exemption in VATA, sch. 9, as it applies from the enactment of the *Finance Act* 1997 covers the provision of insurance or reinsurance by recognised insurance companies, and the provision of various intermediary services.

Most intermediary services provided by insurance brokers or insurance agents are covered, but not market research, promotional activities, etc., valuation or inspection services, or supplies of loss adjusters, etc. (except where handling a claim with full written authority to conclude it).

**Group 3 — postal services**
Group 3 exemption covers supplies of the conveyance of postal packets by the Post Office, and the supply by the Post Office of services in connection with the conveyance of postal packets (other than the hire of goods).

**Group 4 — betting, gaming and lotteries**
Group 4 exemption applies to supplies of:

■   the provision of facilities for placing bets;
■   the provision of facilities for playing games of chance;
■   the granting of a right to take part in a lottery.

However, excluded from the exemption are admission charges, charges made at premises or clubs licensed under Pt. II of the *Gaming Act 1968*, subscriptions to clubs, and supplies made through gaming machines, or of gaming machines.

**Group 5 — finance**
Group 5 provides exemption for a wide range of financial transactions, including loans, dealings in money, the sale of stocks and shares, etc.

The exemption applies to supplies deemed to be made in the UK. As a general rule the place of supply will be outside the UK if there is a non-EC customer or an EC customer receiving the supply in a business capacity. Where the customer is based outside the EC, or the supply is directly linked with the export of goods from the EC, related input tax will be recoverable for a supply which would be exempt under this head if made in the UK (*Value Added Tax (Input Tax) (Specified Supplies) Order 1992* (SI 1992/3123)).

### Group 6 — education

Group 6 provides exemption, in broad terms, for the provision of education or vocational training by schools, universities, and other 'eligible bodies'. Supplies of research by an eligible body to another eligible body are exempted. Supplies of examination services are exempt if the supply is either by or to an eligible body, and also if supplied to a person receiving exempt education or training.

All persons teaching English as a foreign language are regarded as being eligible bodies in respect of these supplies, but this does not necessarily mean that they are eligible bodies in respect of other supplies of education.

Group 6 also exempts certain ancillary supplies, and also the provision of facilities by youth clubs to their members.

### Group 7 — health and welfare

Group 7 provides exemption for a number of supplies connected with the provision of health and welfare services, and related goods. . . . It covers supplies by doctors and other qualified health workers, the provision of care in hospitals and other approved institutions, and various related services.

### Group 8 — burial and cremation

Group 8 exempts supplies of the disposal of the remains of the human dead, and the making of arrangements for and in connection with such disposal.

### Group 9 — trade unions and professional bodies

Exemption is provided for supplies made in return for subscriptions by:

- trade unions;
- professional associations;
- learned societies and the like;
- certain trade associations;
- bodies which are made up of the exempt bodies above and which have the same objectives.

In each case, the body seeking exemption must be non-profit making.

### Group 10 — sport, sports competitions and physical education

Group 10 exemption applies to the right to enter a sporting competition where all entry fees are returned as prizes, and also the right to enter a sporting competition promoted by a non-profit making body established for the purposes of sport or physical recreation. However, the latter exemption does not apply if the competition involves the free use of facilities for the use of which the body normally makes a charge.

Exemption also applies to supplies of sporting and physical education services to individuals by non-profit making bodies (such as many sports clubs). If the non-profit making body operates a membership scheme exemption only applies to supplies made to members.

### Group 11 — works of art, etc.

Group 11 applies to the disposal of certain works of art, etc. exempted from capital taxes when disposed of by private treaty sale, or by way of acceptance in lieu of tax, under the douceur arrangements.

### Group 12 — fund-raising events by charities and other qualifying bodies

Group 12 exempts the supply of goods or services in connection with a one-off fund-raising event (such as a fete, performance, etc.) by:

- a charity, if the event is organised for charitable purposes by one or more charities; or

■ a trade union or professional body within Group 9 above, or certain bodies with objects of a 'public' nature (VATA 1994, s. 94(3)), if the event is organised solely for the benefit of the body concerned.

In the case of a charity, relief is also available for supplies by a wholly owned subsidiary which covenants the whole of its profits to the charity.

### Group 13 — cultural services

Group 13 provides exemption for supplies by public bodies and eligible bodies of admission to museums, galleries, art exhibitions and zoos, and theatrical, musical, etc. performances of a cultural nature.

Public bodies are local authorities, government departments, and other bodies listed as such by the Office of Public Service. Eligible bodies are non-profit making bodies managed on a voluntary basis by persons with no financial interest in their activities.

The exemption for supplies by public bodies only applies where it is not likely to cause distortions of competition with taxable persons.

## 8.4   End of Chapter Assessment Questions

Refer to the facts concerning Amber Ltd and its shareholders: **2.3**, **3.4**, **4.6**, **5.4** and **6.2**.

(a)  On 30 November 1998, the three surviving directors declare, and the company pays, a dividend of £12,000 gross, which is divided equally between each of the four shareholders of Amber Ltd.

Calculate:

(i)   the amount of the *net* dividend received by each of the shareholders; *and*
(ii)  the amount of the tax credit which each receives in respect of the dividend received.

(b)  On the basis that Alan's earnings from his directorship of Amber Ltd are £8,000 in the 1998/99 tax year, what amount of NICs is he liable to pay in that tax year?

(c)  In the 1998/99 tax year, Deborah receives £800 net in interest from debentures in Megabucks plc held by the trustees of the will trust of her uncle Frederick (died 1993), under which she has a life interest in possession. What figure must be included for this interest in Stage One of her income tax calculation, and deducted by way of credit at Stage Six?

(d)  Amber Ltd makes taxable supplies of £250,000 (excluding VAT) in the three-month period ending on 31 December 1998. What will be the *output* VAT on those supplies? What would be the VAT element of VAT-*in*clusive standard-rated supplies of £293,750?

## 8.5   End of Chapter Assessment Outline Answers

(a)(i)   Net dividend received by each of the shareholders:

$$ACT = 20/100 \times £3,000 = £600$$
$$= £3,000 - £600$$
$$\text{Net dividend} \qquad = £2,400$$

(ii)   Amount of tax credit received by each of them:

$$£2,400 \times 25/100 = £600.$$

(b)  As an employee who is also a director, Alan is liable to pay primary Class 1 NICs. The earnings period applicable to him is the tax year. The LEL is therefore £3,328. However, he is only liable to pay NICs on his earnings up to the UEL of £25,220 (i.e. £485 × 52). The first £3,328 of his earnings are therefore charged at 2% (i.e. £66.56), whilst the remaining £4,672 are charged at 10% (i.e. £467.20).

(c)  The grossed-up amount must be included in Stage One, i.e.:

$$£800 \times \frac{100}{80} = £1,000.$$

Stage Six: £200, i.e. £1,000 − £800.

(d)  The output VAT on VAT-*ex*clusive taxable supplies of £250,000 will be £43,750. The VAT component in VAT-*in*clusive taxable supplies of £293,750 is *the same*, i.e. £293,750 × 7/47 = £43,750.

# CHAPTER NINE

# REDUCING INCOME TAXATION (1)

## 9.1 Charges on Income of Individuals

### 9.1.1 ANNUAL PAYMENTS

A reduction in the basic rate of income tax will not affect the amount paid to the charity under a deed covenanting a *net* amount.

**Specimen Deed of Covenant, Central Finance Board of the Methodist Church**

## *Deed of Covenant*

*To: The Central Finance Board of the Methodist Church*

| | Cov Section Checklist |
|---|---|

Item 1    I promise that for four years from ............................. *(enter the Effective Commencing Date)* or until I die if earlier, I shall pay to you or, with your consent, into one or more charitable central or local funds of the Methodist Church, such a sum as after deduction of income tax at the basic rate amounts to ☐

Item 2            £........................... per calendar year ☐

which sum is intended to be contributed on one of the following bases:—

Item 3    * Tick appropriate box

     * ☐      as a single annual payment

     * ☐ **OR** *(when the Deed commences 6th April)* is the total contribution in the tax year

     * ☐ **OR** *(when the Deed commences other than on 6th April **and** the intended payments are not single annual amounts)*

              at the rate of ........................... each week / month / quarter / half-year *(circle the appropriate frequency)* ☐

to be applied for any purposes of the Methodist Church.

Item 4  **NOTE: This section is only applicable for superseding deeds that commence 6th April.**
This Deed is to Cancel and Supersede the following deed(s):—

Deed Number    Original Effective Date    Equivalent Annual Value

.....................    .....................................    £                    ☐

.....................    .....................................    £                    ☐

Item 5  Signed as a deed and delivered

.................................................................    Date.......................    ☐
*(which date must not be later than the Effective Commencing Date)*

Item 6  Full Name (Rev/Mr/Mrs/Miss) .....................................................
(BLOCK CAPITALS, SURNAME UNDERLINED)

Address .................................................................................

.................................................................................

Item 7  First Witness *(and the only one for a Deed signed in England or Wales)*    Second Witness *(if the Deed is signed in Scotland and the Covenantor's signature is not Adopted as Holograph)*

Signature ................................    Signature ...............................    ☐

Address ................................    Address ...............................

................................    ...............................

### 9.1.1.1  Covenanted payments to charity

#### INCOME AND CORPORATION TAXES ACT 1988

### 347A.  General rule

. . .

(7)  In subsection (2)(b) above 'a covenanted payment to charity' means a payment made under a covenant made otherwise than for consideration in money or money's worth in favour of a body of persons or trust established for charitable purposes only whereby the like annual payments (of which the payment in question is one) become payable for a period which may exceed three years and is not capable of earlier termination under any power exercisable without the consent of the persons for the time being entitled to the payments.

#### INCOME AND CORPORATION TAXES ACT 1988

### 348.  Payments out of profits or gains brought into charge to income tax: deduction of tax

(1)  Subject to any provision to the contrary in the Income Tax Acts, where any annuity or other annual payment charged with tax under Case III of Schedule D, not being interest, is payable wholly out of profits or gains brought into charge to income tax—

(a)  the whole of the profits or gains shall be assessed and charged with income tax on the person liable to the annuity or other annual payment, without distinguishing the annuity or other annual payment; and

(b)  the person liable to make the payment, whether out of the profits or gains charged with income tax or out of any annual payment liable to deduction, or from which a deduction has been made, shall be entitled on making the payment to deduct and retain out of it a sum representing the amount of income tax thereon; and

(c)  the person to whom the payment is made shall allow the deduction on receipt of the residue of the payment, and the person making the deduction shall be acquitted and discharged of so much money as is represented by the deduction, as if that sum had been actually paid; and

(d)  the deduction shall be treated as income tax paid by the person to whom the payment is made.

(2)  Subject to any provision to the contrary in the Income Tax Acts, where—

(a)  any royalty or other sum paid in respect of the user of a patent;

. . .

is paid wholly out of profits or gains brought into charge to income tax, the person making the payment shall be entitled on making the payment to deduct and retain out of it a sum representing the amount of the income tax thereon.

. . .

## 9.2   Charges on Income of Companies

### INCOME AND CORPORATION TAXES ACT 1988

**349.  Payments not out of profits or gains brought into charge to income tax, and annual interest**

(1)  Where—

(a)  any annuity or other annual payment charged with tax under Case III of Schedule D, not being interest; or

(b)  any royalty or other sum paid in respect of the user of a patent;

. . .

is not payable or not wholly payable out of profits or gains brought into charge to income tax, the person by or through whom any payment thereof is made shall, on making the payment, deduct out of it a sum representing the amount of income tax thereon.

. . .

(2)  Subject to subsection (3) below and to any other provision to the contrary in the Income Tax Acts, where any yearly interest of money chargeable to tax under Case III of Schedule D is paid—

(a)  otherwise than in a fiduciary or representative capacity, by a company (other than a building society) or local authority; or

(b)  by or on behalf of a partnership of which a company is a member; or

(c)  by any person to another person whose usual place of abode is outside the United Kingdom;

the person by or through whom the payment is made shall, on making the payment, deduct out of it a sum representing the amount of income tax thereon for the year in which the payment is made.

(3)  Subsection (2) above does not apply—

(a)  to interest payable on an advance from a bank, if at the time when the interest is paid the person beneficially entitled to the interest is within the charge to corporation tax as respects the interest; or

(b)  to interest paid by a bank in the ordinary course of its business . . .

## 9.3   End of Chapter Assessment Question

Refer to the facts concerning Brown & Co. the firm of solicitors in which Deborah is a partner: see **2.3**. The partners make their accounts up to 30 November in each calendar year. It is 20 September 1998. The three partners in Brown & Co., Deborah, Emerald and Frances, are contemplating making a £100,000 investment in machinery and plant on which they are entitled to claim capital allowances, at some point in the period to 30 November 1999. The partners share profits and suffer losses equally. They tell you that they propose to borrow this amount, and a loan has been arranged with Dogger Bank plc. They would like you to advise them on the deductibility of the interest payments under the loan for tax purposes.

They also tell you that Gerald, who retired from the firm on 30 November 1997, is being paid a retirement annuity by them. They ask you to advise them also on the deductibility of the annuity payments.

## 9.4   End of Chapter Assessment Outline Answer

Each of the partners should be able to claim relief for their proportionate part of the interest on the loan. It seems clear that the loan is for the acquisition of machinery and plant. 'Machinery' is a self-explanatory term, whilst 'plant' was defined by Lindley LJ in *Yarmouth v France* (1887) 19 QBD 647 as including ((1887) 19 QBD 647, 658): '. . . whatever apparatus is used by a businessman for carrying on his business — not his stock in trade but all goods and chattels, fixed or moveable . . . which he keeps for permanent employment in his business'.

The conditions which the three partners will need to satisfy are as follows (ICTA 1988, s. 359), i.e. that: (a) The interest is paid by each of them as a partner; (b) They are entitled to claim capital allowances in relation to the plant or machinery acquired by them with the loan; and (c) Not more than three years has elapsed from the end of the tax year in which they incurred the debt on which the interest will be paid by them. All of these conditions would appear to be satisfied by them here.

Gerald's partnership retirement annuity is an annual payment. As continuing partners, each of Deborah, Emerald and Frances will pay a proportion of the annuity. They will be able to deduct that proportion from their statutory income at Stage Two of their income tax calculations. The conditions which must be satisfied are as follows (ICTA 1988, ss. 347A(2) and 660A(9)). The payment must have been made: (a) Under the terms of the partnership agreement; (b) To a former partner or his or her spouse or other dependants; and (c) Under a liability incurred for full consideration. There is insufficient information here to know whether all of these conditions are satisfied on the facts. It is worth the partners noting that the annuity payments should have been made *net* of basic rate income tax (ICTA 1988, ss. 348 and 349), and that the basic rate tax deducted will form part of the total income tax due from them for the 1997/98 tax year.

# CHAPTER TEN

# REDUCING INCOME TAXATION (2)

## 10.1   Income Tax: Personal Reliefs

### 10.1.1   INDIVIDUALS: PERSONAL RELIEFS DEDUCTED FROM TOTAL TAX

### INCOME AND CORPORATION TAXES ACT 1988

**257A.   Married couple's allowance**

(1)   If the claimant is, for the whole or any part of the year of assessment, a married man whose wife is living with him, he shall be entitled for that year to an income tax reduction calculated by reference to £1,900.

(2)   If the claimant is, for the whole or any part of the year of assessment, a married man whose wife is living with him, and either of them is at any time within that year of the age of 65 or upwards, he shall be entitled for that year to an income tax reduction calculated by reference to £3,305 (instead of to the reduction provided for by subsection (1) above).

(3)   If the claimant is, for the whole or any part of the year of assessment, a married man whose wife is living with him, and either of them is at any time within that year of the age of 75 or upwards, he shall be entitled for that year to an income tax reduction calculated by reference to £3,345 (instead of to the reduction provided for by subsection (1) or (2) above).

(4)   For the purposes of subsections (2) and (3) above a person who would have been of or over a specified age within the year of assessment if he had not died in the course of it shall be treated as having been of that age within that year.

(5)   In relation to a claimant whose total income for the year of assessment exceeds £16,200, subsections (2) and (3) above shall apply as if the amounts specified in them were reduced by—

(a)   one half of the excess, less

(b)   any reduction made in his allowance under section 257 by virtue of subsection (5) of that section,

(but not so as to reduce the amounts so specified below the amount specified in subsection (1) above).

(6)   A man shall not be entitled by virtue of this section to more than one income tax reduction for any year of assessment; and in relation to a claim by a man who becomes married in the year of assessment and has not previously in the year been entitled to relief under this section, this section shall have effect as if the amounts specified in subsections (1) to (3) above were reduced by one twelfth for each month of the year ending before the date of the marriage.

In this subsection 'month' means a month beginning with the 6th day of a month of the calendar year.

## 10.2   Income Tax: Deductions and Reliefs *Outside* Your Income Tax Calculation

### 10.2.1   MIRAS: ICTA 1988, ss. 369–379

**Inland Revenue Leaflet IR123, *Mortgage Interest Relief — Buying Your Home*, May 1994**

*What if I have more than one place to live?*
You can have tax relief for the one which is actually your home, or your main home. You cannot just pick one residence as your main home for mortgage interest relief purposes but actually live somewhere else.

*Can I use the loan for anything else?*
No. You can get tax relief only on a loan used for buying your own home. Tax relief will not be given if the loan is

- for home improvements, renovations or repairs
- to buy a home for someone else such as a dependent relative or a former husband or wife.

However, if you own a share in your home, you can get tax relief on a loan to buy a further share. For example, you may wish to buy the share of a former partner with whom you bought jointly. And if you own a lease on your home, you can get tax relief on a loan to buy the freehold.

*How much relief can I get?*
For the tax year 1994–95 (6 April 1994 to 5 April 1995) the rate of tax relief is 20 per cent. For the tax year 1995–96 the rate will be 15 per cent. Tax relief is available on a loan up to £30,000.

**Example**
You have a loan for £30,000. The interest rate is 10%.

| | |
|---|---:|
| Interest due in 1994–95 £30,000 × 10% | £3,000 |
| Tax relief on the interest paid £3,000 × 20% | £600 |
| Total interest payable less tax relief £3,000 − £600 | £2,400 |

If your loan is more than £30,000 you can still have tax relief, but only on the interest on £30,000. So, in the example above, if the mortgage was for £60,000, the tax relief would still be £600.

*What if I am not a taxpayer?*
You will receive the same amount of relief as everyone else so long as your loan is in MIRAS. . . .

*I am buying with someone else. Do we both get the £30,000 limit?*
No. The £30,000 limit is attached to the home you are buying. It makes no difference whether the home is occupied by one person, by a married couple, or by unmarried sharers. . . .

## 10.3   Income Tax: Exempt Income

### 10.3.1   THE RENT-A-ROOM SCHEME

**Williams, D., 'Rent-A-Room', *The Tax Journal*, 30 July 1992, p. 8**

Note: The figures used are for the tax year in which the scheme was introduced. 'RR' is the abbreviation for 'Rent a Room'.

RR is only due where the furnished accommodation is in a 'qualifying residence' or residences. . . . This is defined as a residence which is the individual's *only or main residence* in the basis period for the year concerned (see below). 'Residence' includes a part of a building (so that RR could be available to a flat-owner who lets a spare room as well as to a house-owner), a caravan or houseboat. . . . It would not, however, seem to include a letting of a self-contained flat, since that would not itself be the owner's residence but a separate residence — a matter of some importance for capital gains tax purposes . . .

There is no facility to deem a residence to be the owner's main residence where he has more than one — so the position appears to be the same as for that which applies for the purposes of mortgage interest relief under section 355(1)(*a*), Income and Corporation Taxes Act 1988 (and unlike the position for capital gains tax in section 222(5), Taxation of Chargeable Gains Act 1992), in that it will be a question of fact whether a property is the main residence and factors such as the length of time spent at the property by the owner in the year will be relevant. Any claim for RR in respect of a property subject to a mortgage, on which a claim for mortgage interest relief has been rejected by the Revenue on the ground that it is not the only or main residence of the payer, would thus seem doomed unless there has been a change in the relevant facts . . .

While referring to mortgages it is important to note, from a practical viewpoint, that anyone wishing to let rooms in a mortgaged property should check that by so doing he is not in breach of the mortgage deed. Most lenders would normally give any necessary permission when approached but it would be foolish to risk having one's home repossessed merely to save relatively small amounts of income tax.
. . .

Where more than one individual is entitled to the income from letting within RR, the limit of £3,250 is halved for each resident lessor . . . In a simple case of husband and wife jointly owning and letting the room(s) this will give them an exemption of £1,625 each. It could of course be advantageous to arrange for only one spouse to undertake the letting so that all of the income accrued to that spouse and a full exemption was available. In the absence of such arrangements, non-trading income accruing from a letting of jointly owned property by a married couple would appear to be treated as arising to them in equal shares, even if in fact only one spouse undertook the letting, by the rule in section 282A, Income and Corporation Taxes Act 1988, in the absence of an election under *ibid.*, section 282B.

However, the legislation appears to be so drafted that even if one of the joint lessors does not live in the property, the exemption available to the resident lessor is still reduced to £1,625 — even though the non-resident lessor is taxable in full on the normal basis, since he cannot qualify for RR at all — . . . . which halves the exemption limit where 'sums accrue to *a person or persons other than the individual*' (emphasis added). Those 'other persons' do need to be resident in the property (and therefore eligible for RR) to trigger the restriction for the resident lessor.

If a person moves house in the basis period and lets room(s) in both his main residences in that period, it is clear that he is still entitled only to one £3,250 exemption against his total gross receipts for the year.

## 10.4   End of Chapter Assessment Question

Refer to the facts concerning Amber Ltd: **2.3** and **3.4**. As stated, usually it makes only standard rated supplies. However, by mistake, in the return period from 1 January 1999 to 31 March 1999, it makes certain supplies of financial services, i.e. exempt supplies (VATA 1994, sch. 9, Group 5). Amber Ltd's input VAT in that period is:

(a)   input VAT attributed to *taxable* supplies: £40,000;

(b)   input VAT attributed to *exempt* supplies: £12,000; and

(c)   residual input VAT: £25,000.

Amber Ltd therefore has total input VAT in that period of £77,000, i.e. £40,000 + £12,000 + £25,000. In the same period, Amber Ltd has made exempt supplies of £30,000 and taxable supplies of £100,000.

Applying the standard method, how much of Amber Ltd's residual input VAT is recoverable?

## 10.5   End of Chapter Assessment Outline Answer

(a)   Amber Ltd attributes the residual input VAT according to the ratio of taxable supplies made by Amber Ltd in the return period, to all supplies and non-supplies:

= £100,000 (taxable supplies): £130,000 (taxable and exempt supplies together).

(b)   Amber Ltd then reduces that ratio to a percentage of taxable supplies to all supplies made by it in the return period under consideration:

$$= \frac{£100,000}{£130,000} \times 100 = 77\%.$$

(c)   Finally, Amber Ltd multiplies the residual input VAT by the percentage of taxable supplies to all supplies, in order to arrive at the residual input tax recoverable by Amber Ltd:

$$£25,000 \times 77\% = £19,250.$$

# CHAPTER ELEVEN

# REDUCING INCOME TAXATION (3)

## 11.1 Allowable Deductions from Trading Income

### 11.1.1 INDIVIDUAL TRADERS

#### 11.1.1.1 *Wholly and exclusively* for the purpose of the trade

### *MALLALIEU* v *DRUMMOND* [1983] 2 All ER 1095 (HL)

The facts of this case are given in the *Learning Text* at **11.5.1.1**.

LORD BRIGHTMAN: My Lords, the immediate issue in this appeal concerns the right of a female barrister, in computing the profits of her profession, to deduct the cost of upkeep of a wardrobe of clothes of a design and colour suitable to be worn under her gown during court appearances. But during the course of the argument this issue was found to resolve itself into a far more general and fundamental question: whether any person carrying on a trade, profession or vocation on his own account is entitled to a similar deduction if he chooses to set apart clothes, underclothes and footwear for use only at his place of work, and when proceeding to and from his place of work. . . .

The effect of [ICTA 1988, s. 74 (a)] is to exclude, as a deduction, the money spent by the taxpayer unless she can establish that such money was spent exclusively for the purposes of her profession. The words in the paragraph 'expended *for the purposes* of the trade, profession or vocation' mean in my opinion 'expended *to serve the purposes* of the trade, profession or vocation', or as elaborated by Lord Davey in *Strong & Co of Romsey Ltd* v *Woodifield (Surveyor of Taxes)* [1904–7] All ER Rep 953 at 956 'for the purpose of enabling a person to carry on and earn profits in the trade, &c.' The particular words emphasised do not refer to 'the purposes' of the taxpayer as some of the cases appear to suggest. They refer to 'the purposes' of the business which is a different concept although the 'purposes' (ie the intentions or objects) of the taxpayer are fundamental to the application of the paragraph.

The effect of the word 'exclusively' is to preclude a deduction if it appears that the expenditure was not only to serve the purposes of the trade, profession or vocation of the taxpayer but also to serve some other purposes. Such other purposes, if found to exist, will usually be the private purposes of the taxpayer: see for example *Prince* v *Mapp (Inspector of Taxes)* [1970] 1 All ER 519.

To ascertain whether the money was expended to serve the purposes of the taxpayer's business it is necessary to discover the taxpayer's 'object' in making the expenditure: see *Morgan (Inspector of Taxes)* v *Tate & Lyle Ltd* [1954] 2 All ER 413 at 416, 423. As the taxpayer's 'object' in making the expenditure has to be found, it inevitably follows that (save in obvious cases which speak for themselves) the General Commissioners need to look into the taxpayer's mind at the moment when the expenditure is made. After events are irrelevant to the application of s. [74] except as a reflection of the taxpayer's state of mind at the time of the expenditure.

If it appears that the object of the taxpayer at the time of the expenditure was to serve two purposes, the purposes of his business and other purposes, it is immaterial to the application of [s. 74(a)] that the business purposes are the predominant purposes intended to be served.

The object of the taxpayer in making the expenditure must be distinguished from the effect of the expenditure. An expenditure may be made exclusively to serve the purposes of the business, but it may have a private advantage. The existence of that private advantage does not necessarily preclude the exclusivity of the business purposes. For example a medical consultant has a friend in the South of France who is also his patient. He flies to the South of France for a week, staying in the home of his friend and attending professionally on him. He seeks to recover the cost of his air fare. The question of fact will be whether the journey was undertaken solely to serve the purposes of the medical practice. This will be judged in the light of the taxpayer's object in making the journey. The question will be answered by considering whether the stay in the South of France was *a* reason, however subordinate, for undertaking the journey, or was not a reason but only the effect. If a week's stay on the Riviera was not an object of the consultant, if the consultant's only object was to attend on his patient, his stay on the Riviera was an unavoidable effect of the expenditure on the journey and the expenditure lies outside the prohibition in [s. 74]

There is no dispute between the parties as to the true meaning of [s. 74(a)], and it is common ground that the principles which I have outlined are those which fall to be applied. The appeal before your Lordships is basically concerned with the distinction between object and effect. The inspector of taxes disallowed the deduction claimed by the taxpayer, with the result that she appealed to the General Commissioners against the assessment made on her. The General Commissioners, who had themselves been in practice at the Bar, confirmed the assessment subject to a small adjustment on which there was agreement. The taxpayer successfully appealed to the High Court, and the decision of the Chancery judge was upheld on appeal. The inspector of taxes now appeals to this House with the leave of your Lordships.

The primary facts found by the General Commissioners are contained in para. 4 of the printed case. . . . The clothes which the taxpayer maintained for professional purposes were, broadly speaking, worn by her only in connection with her work. That is to say, she travelled in them to her chambers or directly to court, wore them throughout the day and changed out of them when she arrived home at the end of her working day. There were odd occasions on which the taxpayer might find it convenient to remain in her working clothes after her work was done. But no point is taken by the Revenue in relation to such occasions nor is any point taken that the clothes were worn not only at work but also when travelling to and from work.

The critical findings of fact as set out in paras 4 and 8 of the case are these: . . .

4 . . . (c) The rules for guidance are . . . normally complied with and it would be virtually impossible for a lady barrister to practice unless she complied with the rules laid down . . . (f) At all material times the taxpayer had a private wardrobe of clothes and shoes which was amply sufficient to keep her clothed and shod in comfort and decency, without having to resort to any of the disputed items. She would not have purchased any of the disputed items had it not been for the requirement of her profession that she should comply with the notes for guidance when appearing in court . . . (j) . . . She bought such items only because she would not have been permitted to appear in court if she did not wear, when in court, them or other clothes like them. Similarly the preservation of warmth and decency was not a consideration which crossed her mind when she bought the disputed items. (k) The white blouses and black clothing bought by the taxpayer were items of ordinary civilian clothing readily available for purchase by anyone at many clothing stores . . .

8. We consider that the evidence shows that when she bought the clothes she bought them to wear in court and that she would not have bought them but for the exigencies of her profession . . .

In addition there are certain statements in a proof of evidence of a senior executive of Marks and Spencer Ltd. These were accepted by the taxpayer as accurate statements of fact. They are summarised in the commissioners' decision in the following terms:

(i)   that it is important for a major retail outlet to design garments likely to have a broad popular appeal, (ii) that the colours in which garments are produced must necessarily be what are called 'safe' colours, including black, (iii) that a black velvet jacket is a perennial favourite, and (iv) that black clothing is always acceptable whether it is a fashion colour or not and always represents a proportion (which he put at over 10%) of sales in ladies' outerwear.

I refer to this evidence only to emphasise the point that the clothing in question consists of perfectly ordinary articles of apparel which many ladies wear from choice. On the basis of those findings of fact the commissioners had to draw an inference and decide whether or not the taxpayer had expended money on her professional wardrobe exclusively to serve the purposes of her business, or alternatively to serve both purposes of her business and her own private purposes. The inference drawn by the commissioners and the determination reached by them are contained in the second part of para. 9 of their written decision, which reads as follows:

> We consider, in the present case, that when [the taxpayer] laid out money on clothes for wearing in court her purpose in making that expenditure was to enable her to earn profits in her profession and also to enable her to be properly clothed during the time she was on her way to chambers or to court and while she was thereafter engaged in her professional activity, and in the other circumstances indicated in para. 2. We do not consider that the fact that her sole motive in choosing the particular clothes was to satisfy the requirements of her profession or that if she had been free to do so she would have worn clothes of a different style on such occasions altered the purpose of the expenditure which remained the purpose of purchasing clothes that would keep her warm and clad during the part of the day when she was pursuing her career as well as the purpose of helping her to earn profits in that career. We think, therefore, that the expenditure had a dual purpose, one professional and one non-professional . . .

. . .

I return to the question for your Lordships' decision whether there was evidence which entitled the commissioners to reach the conclusion that the object of the taxpayer in spending this money was exclusively to serve the purposes of her profession, or was also to serve her private purposes of providing apparel with which to clothe herself. Slade J felt driven to answer the question in favour of the taxpayer because he felt constrained by the commissioners' finding that, in effect, the only object present in the mind of the taxpayer was the requirements of her profession. The conscious motive of the taxpayer was decisive. The reasoning of the Court of Appeal was the same. What was present in the taxpayer's mind at the time of the expenditure concluded the case.

My Lords, I find myself totally unable to accept this narrow approach. Of course the taxpayer thought only of the requirements of her profession when she first bought (as a capital expense) her wardrobe of subdued clothing and, no doubt, as and when she replaced items or sent them to the launderers or the cleaners she would, if asked, have repeated that she was maintaining her wardrobe because of those requirements. It is the natural way that anyone incurring such expenditure would think and speak. But she needed clothes to travel to work and clothes to wear at work, and I think it is inescapable that one object, though not a conscious motive, was the provision of the clothing that she needed as a human being. I reject the notion that the object of a taxpayer is inevitably limited to the particular conscious motive in mind at the moment of expenditure. Of course the motive of which the taxpayer is conscious is of a vital significance, but it is not inevitably the only object which the commissioners are entitled to find to exist. In my opinion the commissioners were not only entitled to reach the conclusion that the taxpayer's object was both to serve the purposes of her profession and also to serve her personal purposes, but I myself would have found it impossible to reach any other conclusion.

It was inevitable in this sort of case that analogies would be canvassed; for example, the self-employed nurse who equips herself with what is conveniently called a nurse's uniform. Such cases are matters of fact and degree. In the case of the nurse, I am disposed to think without inviting your Lordships to decide, that the material and design of the uniform may be dictated by the practical requirements of the art of nursing and the maintenance of hygiene. There may be other cases where it is essential that the self-employed person should provide himself with and maintain a particular design of clothing in order to obtain any engagements at all in the business that he conducts. An example is the self-employed waiter, mentioned by Kerr LJ, who needs to wear 'tails'. In his case the 'tails' are an essential part of the equipment of his trade, and it clearly would be open to the commissioners to allow the expense of their upkeep on the basis that the money was spent exclusively to serve the purposes of the business. I do not think that the decision which I urge on your Lordships should raise any problems in the uniform type of case that was so much discussed in argument. As I have said, it is a matter of degree.

. . .

## 11.2 Allowable Deductions from the Income of an Office or Employment

### 11.2.1 NON-TRAVELLING EXPENDITURE

**Ridgway, P., 'Old Law Revisited — the distinction between Schedule E and Schedule D; and the Deductibility of Schedule E Expenses', *Student Law Review*, Summer 1994, p. 68**

This extract is very useful for *students* of tax law!

There are certain areas of the law which appear to be reasonably well settled, although there may be the occasional case where there is a dispute on a finding of fact. These topics are often highly examinable, usually by way of problem question. Two of these areas are: the distinction between employment and self-employment; and the deductibility of expenses under Schedule E. This year, however, they may be more examinable than usual. There has been a major case in each area, one in the Court of Appeal and one in the House of Lords. This brief article examines both areas and looks at how these cases affect the law.

The first case is that of *Hall* v *Lorimer* [1993] BTC 473 heard by the Court of Appeal. Only one judgment was given by Nolan LJ who, whilst at the bar, practised in Revenue Chambers.

Mr Lorimer was employed by television production companies as a vision mixer. Each employment usually lasted only one or two days. During the period February 1985 to April 1989 he had about 480 engagements. The Inland Revenue sought to assess Mr Lorimer under Schedule E on the basis that he had a number of employments. The consequence of this would be that PAYE would be deductible and the expenses he incurred would only be deductible if the very stringent tests in s. 198, ICTA 1988 were satisfied. Mr Lorimer argued that he was assessable under Schedule D Case I. If this was the case, there would be no PAYE, his expenses would only have to be wholly and exclusively incurred, not necessarily incurred, and he would be assessed on the preceding year basis.

It was agreed by both parties that the answer to the question was to be found in whether the contract was one for services (Schedule D) or one of service (Schedule E). In *Davies* v *Braithwaite* [1951] 2 KB 628 Rowlatt J stated that an employment was more or less analogous to an office which in *Great Western Railway Co.* v *Bater* 8 TC 231 he had described as 'a subsisting, permanent, substantive position which has an existence independent of the person who fills it, and which is filled in succession by successive holders'. However, in *Fall* v *Hitchen* [1973] STC 66 it was held that an employment was akin to a contract of service, this now appears to be the accepted test.

The distinction between a contract for services and one of service is usually explained by reference to *Davies* v *Braithwaite* and *Fall* v *Hitchen*. In the former case the taxpayer was Lilian Braithwaite, an actress. Between 1924 and 1928 she appeared in a number of plays and films. She also recorded programmes for the wireless and gramophone. During this time, she also appeared in a play on Broadway, New York. The case is interesting because the taxpayer was arguing that earnings from her appearance on Broadway should be taxed under Schedule E, which at that time would not be taxed until remitted to the UK. The Inland Revenue argued that her performance was merely an incident of her profession as an actress and should therefore be taxed under Schedule D. The Inland Revenue won. Rowlatt J stated that 'where one finds a method of earning a livelihood which does not contemplate the obtaining of a post and staying in it, but essentially contemplates a series of engagements and moving from one to the other . . . then each of these engagements could not be considered an employment, but a mere engagement in the course of occupying a profession . . .'

The test in *Davies* v *Braithwaite* is therefore to examine the taxpayer's overall activities and see how any particular contract fits in.

In *Fall* v *Hitchen* a ballet dancer was employed by the Sadler's Wells Company for a period of 22 weeks, during which time he was not to work for anyone else. Pennycuick V-C held the contract looked at in isolation was one of service and therefore taxable under Schedule E. The approach in *Fall* v *Hitchen* was therefore to look at the particular contract, regardless of the number of contracts entered into [at] a particular time.

A number of cases have been decided since *Fall* v *Hitchen* which have examined the indicia of a contract of service. These cases have been in the employment law field but have been used by the Commissioners when having to decide whether someone was to be taxed under Schedule E or Schedule D.

Factors which need to be examined when deciding are, amongst other things, whether a person provides his or her own tools, the degree of control exercised, the manner of payment, i.e. whether it is a fee for the job or a salary or wages, and the degree of financial risk, i.e. whether or not the person could make a loss.

In *Hall* v *Lorimer* the Court of Appeal in effect reverted to the *Davies* v *Braithwaite* test whilst accepting that the distinction was between a contract of service and one for services. In other words, in looking to see what type of contract existed one has to look at the overall picture. Nolan LJ adopted the words of Mummery J at first instance when he said, 'In order to decide whether a person carries on business on his own account, it is necessary to consider many different aspects of that person's work activity. This is not a mechanical exercise of running through items on a check list to see whether they are present in, or absent from, a given situation. The object of the exercise is to paint a picture from the accumulation of detail. The overall effect can only be appreciated by standing back from the detailed picture which has been painted, by viewing at a distance and by making an informed, considered, qualitative appreciation of the whole.'

The case does leave a number of questions which may be fertile ground for examiners. One of the questions looked at was, 'what is a casual employee?' What is the distinction between a person who has a large number of casual employments and a person exercising a trade or profession? One of the factors which influenced the Court of Appeal was the amount of expenditure incurred by Mr Lorimer, £9,250 which was out of all proportion to that which would be expected of an employee.

How many engagements make a trade or profession? If Mr Lorimer failed to find work or only found a minimal amount would the overall picture be any different? Does a trade or profession depend on the success or failure of finding work? If a person had a large number of successive contracts with only one television company would that point towards employment? At what point is the balance tipped as far as the number of engagements is concerned?

Prior to *Hall* v *Lorimer*, the Inland Revenue placed heavy reliance on *Fall* v *Hitchen*. They changed the basis of assessment from Schedule D to Schedule E for a large number of actors and actresses. It has just been announced that a test case (which was called such until the Inland Revenue lost it) is not to be appealed. *Hall* v *Lorimer* may have stopped the Inland Revenue's crusade to put as many people on to PAYE as their view of the law would allow.

The second case involves the deduction of expenses in employment. For an employee to deduct expenses, they must be wholly, exclusively and necessarily incurred in the performance of the duties. This test is notoriously difficult to satisfy. Vaisey J in *Lomax* v *Newton* 34 TC 558 said that the allowable expenses amounted to 'nearly nothing at all'.

Certain rules are well established. The 'wholly and exclusively' test precludes the deduction of expenditure where it has a dual purpose as under Schedule D (*Mallalieu* v *Drummond* 57 TC 330).

The 'in the performance of the duties' test prevents a deduction unless the employee was actually doing the job whilst the expenditure was incurred, see *Elderkin* v *Hindmarsh* [1988] STC 267. This prevents a deduction for, eg, food and hotel accommodation.

The 'necessarily' test means that each and every holder of the employment must be obliged to incur it, see *Ricketts* v *Colquhoun* 10 TC 118 *Owen* v *Pook* 45 TC 571 and *Taylor* v *Provan* 49 TC 579. These last two cases are open to criticism in that it is arguable that it was not necessary for each [h]older to incur the expenses.

In *Owen* v *Pook*, Edmund-Davies LJ said in the Court of Appeal that had the doctor lived next to the hospital, he could 'stroll up the hill to the hospital by the expenditure of nothing except a little shoe leather.'

In *Taylor* v *Provan*, the consultant was the only one capable of performing the job. However, this does not mean the expense had to be incurred. The case also calls into question whether, although he was called a director he had an office or employment if the post had no existence independent of the holder, see *Abbott* v *Philbin* 39 TC 82. If he did hold an office or employment, which had a degree of independence, whether every holder would be obliged to incur the expense of flying between England and Canada is open to question.

So what was the argument about in *Fitzpatrick* v *IRC* and *Smith (HMIT)* v *Abbott*? Put simply, in each case a number of journalists bought newspapers each day which they read before they went to work. The purpose of the reading was to give them some ideas for stories, layout and graphics, and to ensure that they did not repeat news which had been reported by competitors. The problem was that in the *Fitzpatrick* case in Scotland, it was held that the expenses were not necessarily incurred, in the *Abbott* case in England it was held that they were. Therefore, there were two cases of identical facts which came to the opposite conclusion. This is not the first time this has happened, see for example the cases of *Balgownie Land Trust* v *IRC* 14 TC 684 and *IRC* v *Hyndland Investment Co* 14 TC 694.

The result is a consequence of a system which places great reliance on the finding of fact. If the evidence is sufficient to support the finding, in the absence of mistake of law the finding cannot be overturned, see *Edwards* v *Bairstow and Harrison* 36 TC 207.

The House of Lords (Lord Browne-Wilkinson dissenting) held that the question of whether an expense was necessarily incurred was a mixed question of fact and law. Therefore, the determination of the Commissioners was open to review. Lord Templeman said that the two decisions could not stand together. The two sets of Commissioners could not both be right. He reviewed the cases, and decided that in law the expenses were not necessary. He also held that, like the schoolmaster in *Humbles* v *Brooks* 40 TC 500, the journalists read the papers to enable them to perform their duties, not in the performance of their duties.

Lord Browne-Wilkinson, on the other hand, held that in a real world, Lord Templeman would be right, but because Parliament had only given a limited right of appeal discrepancies would occur.

Perhaps the real reason for Lord Templeman's decision is to be found towards the end of his judgment. He states that if journalists are allowed to deduct these expenses, assuming 30,000 journalists deducting £1,000 a year, a total deduction of £30 million would be given. However, it is submitted that there are two things wrong with this approach. First, it assumes that 30,000 journalists each go to the Commissioners and get a finding in their favour; secondly, and more importantly, the loss to the exchequer would be irrelevant when deciding the case. Tax policy is a matter for the government. Many taxpayers have failed in the high court because of the combination of the *Edwards* v *Bairstow and Harrison* test and an adverse finding of fact before the Commissioners. Why should the Inland Revenue be in any different position?

So how might the journalists' problem be solved? If the newspaper owners bought the papers and provided them to the journalists, the newspaper owners would get a deduction. Maybe the newspapers ought to make it a term of the contract that the journalists should work from home for some part of each day and have the newspapers sent round. If the newspapers were provided in the office, they would not be a benefit in kind. The journalists could then bring the newspapers in and hand them back to the newspaper owners. The journalists ought not to be taxed on the benefit. The provision of newspapers would amount to a hefty deduction in the accounts of the newspaper owners, perhaps as much as £30 million. If the journalists did contractually have to work at home reading the papers for a couple of hours each day, when they travelled into the office, would they not be travelling from one place of work to another? Why then should their travelling expenses not also be deductible? Maybe policy will dictate otherwise.

**Cockfield, R. and Mulholland, M., 'The Taxman and the Scruffy Teacher',**
*The Tax Journal*, **13 February 1997, p. 18**

This article appeared against the background of the possibility of a special dress-code for teachers. Would the cost of complying with the code be tax-deductible?

. . .

### Fiscal politics

It is interesting to consider to what extent judges are influenced by the fiscal consequences of their decisions. Is there a need to keep employee expenses under a greater degree of control because of their greater number? The following cases indicate that judges are acutely aware of the revenue implications of decisions in Schedule E cases, whilst aware that Schedule D decisions will not open the floodgates to claims against the Inland Revenue. There are obvious exceptions to this. *Horton* v *Young* 47 TC 60, which allowed sub-contractors in the building industry to claim what was effectively their home to office travel, led to every building sub-contractor similarly claiming.

The Master of the Rolls (Lord Evershed) in *Brown* v *Bullock* at page 9 pointed:

Once again to the distinction between the two Schedules, which I for my part regard as somewhat regrettable as something which tends to bring the law into a measure of disrepute and to make the income tax obligations of the taxpayer a game of ingenuity divorced from principle or ethical or other common-sense considerations.

Dankwerts J in *Brown* v *Bullock* 40 TC said at page 6:

Now, that Rule has again and again been criticised judicially for being extremely narrow, and it is undoubtedly in terms much more severe and much more narrow than the corresponding Rule which occurs in the question of expenses for the purpose of Schedule D.

The case of *Ward* v *Dunn* 52 TC 517 is particularly interesting as Walton J, after rejecting Mr Dunn's claim for clothing in the now familiar manner, then goes on to let the cat out of the fiscal bag (at page 521):

I think that if he reflects upon what the situation would be if apportionment of the kind that he really would like to make is allowable, he will probably come to the conclusion that the staff of the Inland Revenue would require to be at least trebled to deal with the claims which would be put in, because virtually every taxpayer uses his clothing in the course of his work.

Lord Brightman in *Mallalieu* v *Drummond* at page 369 commented:

This appeal has inevitably opened up a far wider and more fundamental point, namely the right of any self-employed person to maintain, at the expense of his gross income and therefore partly at the expense of the general body of taxpayers, a wardrobe of every-day clothes which are reserved for work.

This philosophy is not applied to any other aspect of business expenditure. Contrast the Social Security Acts where business expenditure must also be reasonable. Travelling expenses under Schedule E also have to be reasonable (*Marsden* v *CIR* 42 TC 326).

However, home to office travel is effectively allowed for senior employees and company directors by the generous tax treatment of company cars. The tax actually paid on a company car is less than such a car would cost to buy and run privately. For many years the element of personal choice was ignored by basing the scale charge on engine size (and very broad *spectra* of original cost). Even after the present reforms (effective from April 1994), the upper limit of £80,000 means the personal choice of the fat cat is still subsidised.

In *Smith* v *Abbott* [1994] 1 All ER 673 the House of Lords was mindful of the loss of tax if the journalist's claim for the cost of buying newspapers were allowed. Lord Templeman said at page 683:

> If a journalist was allowed to deduct expenses incurred in improving his usefulness to his employer, the imposition of income tax would be distorted and the amount of the expenses would depend only on the taxpayer's own choice . . . the ramifications of a decision in their favour would be enormous.

It is the authors' opinion that the House of Lords should act in accordance with the law and not for the benefit and convenience of the Treasury.

It is ironic that we have one half of the government urging employers and employees to improve efficiency and performance, whilst the other half go out of their way positively to discourage those employees who are trying to do their job better by spending their own money over and above what their firms are prepared to spend.

**Conclusion**

Where the headteacher has imposed a dress code to improve the effectiveness of the teacher as a role model, there is a strong case for allowing a tax deduction. Such a case should be the end of the artificial and unjustifiable difference of whether an item of expenditure can be apportioned or not. In view of the numbers involved, the Inland Revenue would have to agree a flat rate allowance.

**11.2.2   TRAVELLING EXPENSES**

**CCH Editions Ltd, 'Going Round in Triangles',** *Benefits Bulletin***, November 1997, p. 1**

A new regime for travel and subsistence expenses applies from 6 April 1998. Although the basic premise that relief is available for expenses necessarily incurred in the performance of the employee's duties is unchanged, the new rules aim to address two situations which have caused problems under the existing rules — site-based employees and triangular travel.

*Site-based employees*

Unlike employees with a 'travelling appointment', under the existing rules, site-based employees are not entitled to tax relief for journeys to and from the site. A site-based employee is one who:

■ works at a succession of places as part of the same employment, spending a few days or weeks or months at each;
■ has no permanent place of work with that employer; and
■ does not hold a travelling appointment.

From 6 April 1998, such employees will be entitled to relief in full.

Where employers have a number of site-based employees and meet their travelling expenses, they should consider applying for a dispensation [see **6.1**] to remove the need to report the expense payments on the P11D and for the employee to make a corresponding claim for tax relief.

*Triangular travel*

The situation commonly described as triangular travel arises where an employee with a normal place of work travels directly from home to the temporary place of work. Under the existing rules, the employee is entitled to relief equal to the lesser of:

- the actual journey between home and work; and
- a journey between the normal place of work and the temporary place of work.

This rule was criticised as being unfair, as it enabled some employees to obtain a tax-free profit, whereas others were not able to obtain full relief for their out-of-pocket expenses. In addition, it is cumbersome to apply, as it is necessary to ascertain the cost of a theoretical journey from the normal place of work to the temporary place of work.

The new rules initially aimed to simplify this by allowing relief for the additional cost of triangular travel. That is to say, the cost which the employee has to occur over and above his 'ordinary commuting costs' if he is to go to the temporary place of work rather than to his normal place of work. Although this sounds fair in theory, in practice it would have been a nightmare to apply, as it would require details to be maintained of each employee's ordinary commuting costs. This would not be a simple task, even if it were possible in every case to ascertain what constitutes an individual's 'normal commuting'.

People vary the way they come to work, when they come to work and the place from which they start their journeys. Even if every employee started his journey from home each morning, took the same route to work, using the same mode of transport each day, leaving home at the same time and, in the evening, returned home at the same time each day and in the same way, the administrative task of collating this information is something most people could do without.

Fortunately, having listened to public pressure, the Revenue have seen sense and removed the need to offset the ordinary commuting costs. This means that when an employee travels from home to a temporary place of work, relief for the journey will be available in full.

This change of heart, although very welcome, comes at the eleventh hour. Legislation to remove the need to offset 'ordinary commuting costs' is to be included in the 1998 Finance Bill. The new regime goes live in less than six months time and employers need to ensure that their systems can cope. The Revenue have indicated that they plan to issue detailed guidance shortly, and the feeling is that this cannot come soon enough. Many employers will have already wasted time and energy getting together procedures for capturing details of employees' commuting habits, and this will now be time wasted. Given that public consultation preceded the Finance Act 1997 legislation, one may be forgiven for asking why this could not have been addressed earlier.

The Contributions Agency are, however, one step ahead of the Revenue. Prior to the Revenue's press release of 24 September 1997, they had already announced that they would be allowing relief from NIC on the full cost of the employee's journey to the temporary place of work without attempting to offset the costs of ordinary commuting. The Revenue's new stance aligns the tax and NIC rules — something to be welcomed.

A further piece of good news concerns dispensations already in force — the Revenue have indicated that these will remain valid under the new regime. Employers will not need to renegotiate these with the Revenue, as previously thought. . . .

    . . .

## 11.3   End of Chapter Assessment Questions

Refer to the facts concerning Amber Ltd and Bertram, one of its directors.: **2.3**, **5.4** and **6.2**. Note these additional facts.

  (a)   Bertram is Amber Ltd's finance director. In the 1998/99 tax year, he has the following expenditure:

      (i)    £500 on bus fares from his home to Amber Ltd's premises every working day;

      (ii)   £250 on financial newspapers, which he reads to keep abreast of the financial markets; and

      (iii)  £150 on 12 issues of a specialist professional accountancy journal.

  (b)   In the accounting period to 31 December 1998, Amber Ltd has the following expenditure:

      (i)    £8,000 plus VAT on entertaining clients from Malaysia;

      (ii)   £300,000 gross wages; and

      (iii)  £80,000 plus VAT factory premises rental.

Comment on whether the items in (a) will rank as allowable deductions from Bertram's employment income, and whether the items in (b) will rank as allowable deductions from Amber Ltd's trading income.

## 11.4   End of Chapter Assessment Outline Answers

  (1)   (a)   The bus fares are deductible from Bertram's Schedule E income only if they are qualifying travelling expenses: ICTA, 1988, s. 198(1)(a). Qualifying travelling expenses are amounts necessarily expended on travelling in the performance of the duties of the office or employment or, briefly, other expenses of travelling which are not expenses of ordinary commuting or private travel. These expenses are clearly those of ordinary commuting, and the travel takes place outside the duties of the employment. Therefore, no deduction is available here from Bertram's employment income.

        (b)   The £250 on financial newspapers, which he reads to keep abreast of the financial markets are deductible only if it is incurred wholly, exclusively and necessarily in the performance of the duties of the employment: ICTA, 1988, s. 198(1)(b). On the basis on *Smith* v *Abbott* [1994] 1 All ER 673, this expenditure does not satisfy that test. Therefore, no deduction is available here from Bertram's employment income.

        (c)   The £150 on 12 issues of a specialist professional accountancy journal is strictly deductible only if it satisfies the test in (b) above. However, by concession, the cost of subscribing to the accountancy journal should be deductible, even though it does not satisfy this rule. In practice, the subscription to *Accountancy* is treated as augmenting a chartered accountant's annual membership subscription to The Institute of Chartered Accountants.

  (2)   (a)   The £8,000 plus VAT on entertaining clients from Malaysia will not be deductible from Amber Ltd's trading income, because of the ban on such deductions in ICTA 1988, s. 577.

(b)   The £300,000 gross wages will only be deductible if they are incurred wholly and exclusively for the purpose of Amber Ltd's trade, of a revenue nature, and not specifically disallowed by legislation: ICTA 1988, s. 74(1). Each of these three conditions will be satisfied here.

(c)   The £80,000 plus VAT factory premises rental will be deductible on the same basis as the wages in (b): ICTA 1988, s. 74(1)(c).

The VAT element of (a), i.e. £1,400 will be an allowable deduction for corporation tax purposes, to the extent that full input credit is unavailable. No allowable deduction can be made if full credit is obtainable, however. The same comment applies to the VAT of £14,000 in (c).

# CHAPTER TWELVE

# REDUCING INCOME TAXATION (4)

## 12.1  Qualifying Assets: *Machinery* and *Plant*

### CAPITAL ALLOWANCES ACT 1990

SCHEDULE AA1
EXCLUSIONS FROM EXPENDITURE ON MACHINERY OR PLANT

*Buildings*

1.—(1)   For the purposes of this Act expenditure on the provision of machinery or plant does not include any expenditure on the provision of a building.

(2)   For the purposes of this Schedule 'building' includes any asset in the building—

(a)   which is incorporated into the building, or

(b)   which, by reason of being moveable or otherwise, is not so incorporated, but is of a kind normally incorporated into buildings;

and in particular includes any asset in or in connection with the building included in any of the items in column 1 or column 2 of the following Table ('Table 1').

(3)   Sub-paragraph (1) above does not affect the question whether expenditure on the provision of—

(a)   any asset falling within column 2 of Table 1,

(b)   any cold store,

(c)   any caravan provided mainly for holiday lettings,

(d)   any building provided for testing aircraft engines run within the building, or

(e)   any moveable building intended to be moved in the course of the trade,

is for the purposes of this Act expenditure on the provision of machinery or plant.

(4)   Table 1 is to be read subject to the notes following it.

TABLE 1

| (1)<br>Assets included in the expression 'building' | (2)<br>Assets so included, but expenditure on which is unaffected by the Schedule |
|---|---|
| A. Walls, floors, ceilings, doors, gates, shutters, windows and stairs. | 1. Electrical, cold water, gas and sewerage systems—<br>    (a)   provided mainly to meet the particular requirements of the trade, or<br>    (b)   provided mainly to serve particular machinery or plant used for the purposes of the trade.<br>2. Space or water heating systems; powered systems of ventilation, air cooling or air purification; and any ceiling or floor comprised in such systems. |

| (1)<br>*Assets included in the expression 'building'* | (2)<br>*Assets so included, but expenditure on which is unaffected by the Schedule* |
|---|---|
| B. Mains services, and systems, of water, electricity and gas. | 3. Manufacturing or processing equipment; storage equipment, including cold rooms; display equipment; and counters, checkouts and similar equipment.<br>4. Cookers, washing machines, dishwashers, refrigerators and similar equipment; washbasins, sinks, baths, showers, sanitary ware and similar equipment; and furniture and furnishings. |
| C. Waste disposal systems. | 5. Lifts, hoists, escalators and moving walkways.<br>6. Sound insulation provided mainly to meet the particular requirements of the trade. |
| D. Sewerage and drainage systems. | 7. Computer, telecommunication and surveillance systems (including their wiring or other links).<br>8. Refrigeration or cooling equipment. |
| E. Shafts or other structures in which lifts, hoists, escalators and moving walkways are installed. | 9. Sprinkler equipment and other equipment for extinguishing or containing fire; fire alarm systems.<br>10. Burglar alarm systems.<br>11. Any machinery (including devices for providing motive power) not within any other item in this column. |
| F. Fire safety systems. | 12. Strong rooms in bank or building society premises; safes.<br>13. Partition walls, where moveable and intended to be moved in the course of the trade.<br>14. Decorative assets provided for the enjoyment of the public in the hotel, restaurant or similar trades.<br>15. Advertising hoardings; and signs, displays and similar assets.<br>16. Swimming pools (including diving boards, slides and structures on which such boards or slides are mounted). |

*Notes:*

1.  An asset does not fall within column 2 if its principal purpose is to insulate or enclose the interior of the building or provide an interior wall, a floor or a ceiling which (in each case) is intended to remain permanently in place.

2.  'Electrical systems' include lighting systems.


*Structures, assets and works*

2.—(1)  For the purposes of this Act expenditure on the provision of machinery or plant does not include any expenditure on—

(a)  the provision of structures or other assets to which this paragraph applies, or

(b)  any works involving the alteration of land.

(2)  This paragraph applies to any structure or other asset which falls within column 1 of the following Table ('Table 2').

(3)  Sub-paragraph (1) above does not affect the question whether—

(a)  any expenditure falling within column 2 of Table 2, or

(b)   any expenditure on the provision of any asset of a description within any of the items in column 2 of Table 1,
is for the purposes of this Act expenditure on the provision of machinery or plant.

(4)   Table 2 is to be read subject to the notes following it.

TABLE 2

| (1)<br>*Structures and assets* | (2)<br>*Expenditure which is unaffected by<br>the Schedule* |
|---|---|
| A. Any tunnel, bridge, viaduct, aqueduct, embankment or cutting. | 1. Expenditure on the alteration of land for the purpose only of installing machinery or plant. |
| B. Any way or hard standing, such as a pavement, road, railway or tramway, a park for vehicles or containers, or an airstrip or runway. | 2. Expenditure on the provision of dry docks.<br>3. Expenditure on the provision of any jetty or similar structure provided mainly to carry machinery or plant. |
| C. Any inland navigation, including a canal or basin or a navigable river. | 4. Expenditure on the provision of pipelines, or underground ducts or tunnels with a primary purpose of carrying utility conduits.<br>5. Expenditure on the provision of towers provided to support floodlights. |
| D. Any dam, reservoir or barrage (including any sluices, gates, generators and other equipment associated with it). | 6. Expenditure on the provision of any reservoir incorporated into a water treatment works or on the provision of any service reservoir of treated water for supply within any housing estate or other particular locality. |
| E. Any dock. | 7. Expenditure on the provision of silos provided for temporary storage or on the provision of storage tanks.<br>8. Expenditure on the provision of slurry pits or silage clamps. |
| F. Any dike, sea wall, weir or drainage ditch.<br>G. Any structure not within any other item in this column. | 9. Expenditure on the provision of fish tanks or fish ponds.<br>10. Expenditure on the provision of rails, sleepers and ballast for a railway or tramway.<br>11. Expenditure on the provision of structures and other assets for providing the setting for any ride at an amusement park or exhibition.<br>12. Expenditure on the provision of fixed zoo cages. |

*Notes:*
1.   'Dock' includes—
    (a)   any harbour, wharf, pier, marina or jetty, and
    (b)   any other structure in or at which vessels may be kept or merchandise or passengers may be shipped or unshipped.
2.   An industrial structure, that is, anything (other than a building) which is or is to be an industrial building or structure as defined in section 18, is not within item G in column 1; and that section, as it applies for the purposes of this note, shall have effect as if—
    (a)   in subsection (1)(b), after 'electricity' there were inserted 'gas',
    (b)   after that paragraph there were inserted—

'(ba)  for the purposes of a trade which consists in the provision of telecommunication, television or radio services; or', and

(c)  in subsection (9), after the definition of 'foreign plantation', there were inserted—

'"gas undertaking" means an undertaking for the extraction, production, processing or distribution of gas'.

### Land

3.—(1)  For the purposes of this Act expenditure on the provision of machinery or plant does not include expenditure on the acquisition of any interest in land.

(2)  This paragraph does not apply for the purposes of Part II to any asset which is so installed or otherwise fixed in or to any description of land as to become, in law, part of that land.

### General exemptions

4.  Paragraphs 1(1) and 2(1) above do not apply to any expenditure to which section 67, 67A, 68, 69, 70 or 71 applies.

### Interpretation

5.—(1)  In this Schedule—

(a)  'structure' means a fixed structure of any kind, other than a building, and

(b)  references to the provision of any building, structure or other asset include references to its construction or acquisition.

(2)  Nothing in this Schedule affects the question whether expenditure on the provision of any glasshouse which is constructed so that the required environment (that is, air, heat, light, irrigation and temperature) for growing plants is provided automatically by means of devices which are an integral part of its structure is, for the purposes of this Act, expenditure on the provision of machinery or plant.

(3)  The definition of 'land' in Schedule 1 to the Interpretation Act 1978, in its application for the purposes of this Schedule, shall have effect with the omission of the words 'buildings and other structures'; and, subject to that, 'interest in land' in paragraph 3 above has the same meaning as in Chapter VI of Part II.'

## WIMPY INTERNATIONAL LTD v WARLAND [1988] STC 149

(Findings of the Special Commissioner on Items of Plant and Machinery.)

This case is discussed the **Learning Text** at **12.6**. Hoffman J agreed with all of the Special Commissioner's findings, except 6 below. They did not accept that the light fittings were plant, whereas Hoffman J *did* do so, as being important to fast-food restaurants.

### 1 Shop Fronts

None of the shop fronts or doors qualifies as plant, in our opinion. Their principal function is to form a necessary part of the premises since restaurants, in our climate, are normally conducted within walled premises: and doors are needed for ingress and egress.

The fascia boards on the other hand qualify as plant, being equipment used in the trade. They are in effect advertising signs which are attached to the building for display purposes but do not become part of it.

### 2 Floor Tiles and Wall Tiles

None of the floor or wall tiles can in our opinion be classed as plant. This conclusion is most obvious in relation to the white tiles in the utility and rubbish rooms, but it applies equally to the others. The surfaces left by the builder, or the stripped down interiors, have to be covered before the premises can be used; and the tiles provide a hard wearing hygienic surface suitable as the setting for a fast food restaurant such as Wimpy operates. Naturally enough they are chosen so as to create an attractive setting in which customers will be pleased to sit for the short time required to consume a fast food meal; but we are not persuaded that their function in the trade goes beyond that. They cannot be regarded as embellishments creating an ambience which forms part of the product sold to the customers.

### 3 Suspended Ceilings

It (the suspended ceiling) is said to be a design feature drawing attention to the stairwell and encouraging customers to use the basement area. In our opinion it is simply a part of the premises like the stairwell with which its design is integrated. We cannot regard it as plant.

It (a different ceiling) incorporates fluorescent lights, air conditioning grills, loud-speakers and sprinkler heads, but its principal function is said to be the creation of atmosphere by reducing the height of the ceiling and giving it visual interest. This ceiling (including the voids) is in our opinion on the borderline. If it served only to contain or to conceal light fittings and other apparatus it would fail to qualify as plant on the reasoning applied to the false ceiling in *Fortes Autogrill*. But we think that on balance the case for regarding it as an embellishment of the premises designed to create atmosphere has been made out and it is properly to be regarded as apparatus used in the trade.

### 4 Wall Panels and Mirrors

We have to resolve the problem by considering the function of the wall panels and mirrors in the conduct of Wimpy's trade.

We cannot ignore the evidence that the wall panels were chosen to create the right environment for the particular trade; nor can it be said that the claim in respect of these moveable items is so extreme as to fall outside the scheme of capital allowances for commercial premises. They are again near the borderline between apparatus and mere setting, but we conclude on balance that they too qualify as plant under the general description of embellishments.

### 5 Mezzanine Floor, Raised Floor Areas, Ballustrading and Stairs

We group these items together because we reject the claim in each case for the same reason, that the expenditure was on alterations to the place in which the trade is conducted and not apparatus to be used in the trade.

### 6 Light Fittings and Wiring

The object (of the light fittings) is to create an atmosphere of brightness and efficiency, suitable to the service and consumption of fast food meals and attractive to potential customers looking in from outside.

Light fittings may qualify as plant if they perform a positive function in the trade; but we are not satisfied on the evidence that these light fittings do that. General illumination of this kind cannot, in our opinion, be classed as apparatus used in the particular trade of, in this case, preparing and serving meals. It is no more than a necessary feature of the setting in which that trade is conducted.

[The Revenue] concedes that wiring which serves exclusively items of plant should be included in the plant and we endorse that approach. The dispute is over mixed wiring circuits.

If its [i.e. the mixed wiring circuits] purpose is to supply electricity to plant then even if, for convenience, other items are served as well we would consider it to be plant. Conversely the fact that items of plant are served by a circuit installed for a general purpose would not make that circuit plant.

### Moriarty, S., 'Restricted Plant and Machinery Allowances', *The Tax Journal*, 27 January 1994, p. 8

Shortly after what was to become CAA 1990, Sched AA1 appeared in the 1994 Finance Bill, this article appeared in *The Tax Journal*, criticising heavily the contents of the proposed legislation.

When it was announced on 30 November that legislation would be included in the Finance Bill to clarify the boundaries between plant and machinery and buildings and structures for capital allowances purposes, the obvious concern was whether the Inland Revenue would be able to clarify matters without drafting legislation which would be as baffling as the complex existing case law on machinery and plant. The proposed legislation issued in draft on 17 December 1993 answers this question in the negative. What is proposed adds 'building' and 'structure' to 'plant' as words likely to generate even more case law.

Taxpayers were reassured on Budget Day that the new legislation would not disturb current case law definitions of plant and machinery. Accordingly, the proposals incorporate lists of specific items for which allowances will be preserved. This will lead to difficulties in many individual cases, because who other than an expert building services engineer or architect is going to know what is and what is not included in 'powered systems of ventilation', for example? One also suspects that the Inland Revenue will always start from a position of denying that a particular item of expenditure falls within these lists (finding a cause, particularly a minor one, for distinguishing the item will not be difficult); similarly, taxpayers will be encouraged to try to fit expenditure within a definition, rather than trying to argue that it qualifies for allowances in its own right.

The way in which the legislation seeks to give wide, all-encompassing definitions to the now excluded 'buildings' and 'structures' also means that the legislation is going to have a greater impact than some perhaps anticipated when it was first announced.

### Defects

The defects in the proposals can be illustrated by a few examples (though there are bound to be many others). The basic structure is simple enough. Buildings and structures will not qualify as plant but certain assets and types of expenditure that would otherwise fall within the new definitions are specifically excluded. These assets will continue to be subject to the existing case law on plant and machinery. The possibility of machinery and plant allowances has also been preserved for a few specific items, including cold stores and specialist greenhouses. This is how the Inland Revenue has sought to meet the intention stated in the 30 November Press Release that specific decisions of the Courts would be unaffected.

The first example of confusion comes in the definition of buildings. 'Building' is to include any asset incorporated into a building and assets which, though not incorporated in a particular case, are of a kind which is normally incorporated. Whilst this clearly extends the definition beyond simple bricks and mortar, what exactly does 'normally incorporated' mean? Does it extend so far as carpets and carpet tiles?

Clearly, depending on how widely this phrase is to be interpreted, the reference to assets normally incorporated may well result in the new legislation having an impact on the capital allowance claims of most taxpayers. Table 1, Column 2 preserves allowances for '. . . washing machines, dishwashers . . . furniture and furnishings' (which should mean that carpets are saved). However, the very fact that these items appear under the heading of assets included in the definition of building, but expenditure on which is unaffected by the rest of the proposed legislation, is a startling indication of how widely the definition of building could extend.

Even more baffling to a lay person (including, one suspects, an Inspector of Taxes) will be to know exactly what some of the items referred to in the lists incorporated into the draft legislation actually mean. Fire safety systems appear in the non-exclusive list of items which illustrate assets within the definition of a building. These items will not qualify. Yet alongside this, in the list of assets expenditure on which is to be unaffected, appears 'Sprinkler equipment and other equipment for extinguishing or containing fire; fire alarm systems'. What sort of fire system is therefore excluded? Moreover, what is the policy behind excluding allowances for some measures taken to avoid the risk of fire, but giving allowances for others? It may be that the exclusion is designed to cover detection systems as opposed to systems which extinguish fire, but I would be surprised if manufacturers such as Chubb and Thorn conveniently package their products in this way.

### Decisions of Commissioners

Although the lists incorporated into the draft legislation seek to preserve past decisions of the Courts, there is no provision for taxpayers who have obtained a favourable decision of the Special or General Commissioners on an asset which falls within the definition of building or structure but where the Inland Revenue did not appeal the decision. It is true that if the lists incorporated into the legislation covered all those items they would run to several pages and in many cases those decisions will be particular to the trade of the taxpayer involved, but why should such a taxpayer now lose the benefit of a decision obtained at his own cost which, lest we forget, still cannot be recovered from the Inland Revenue? If the decision has been upheld in the High Court that would presumably have been reflected in the list of items.

The proposals should incorporate a provision stating that taxpayers who have obtained favourable decisions from the Commissioners which have not been overruled should be able to continue to apply those decisions to the relevant assets used in their own particular businesses, regardless of the rest of the draft legislation.

One further example will demonstrate the confusion which the draft legislation will cause. False ceilings and raised floors which form part of a heating and ventilation system have been accepted as plant for many years. The proposals recognise this by including such assets in the list of assets included in the definition of building for which expenditure is to be unaffected. However, the notes accompanying Table 1 state that if the principal purpose of the ceiling or floor is to provide a ceiling or floor which is intended to remain permanently in place, the expenditure will not qualify. It cannot be denied that a false ceiling or raised floor forming part of a heating and ventilation system serves both of these functions. How will a taxpayer and his Inspector be able to agree which is predominant? Where also is the justification for this approach in the existing case law, which the new legislation is supposed to reflect?

These examples illustrate that the basic approach of the proposed legislation will only serve to increase the difficulties of taxpayers in trying to work out where the boundary of machinery and plant allowances lies. If this were legislation of relevance to no more than a few taxpayers who regularly employ specialist advisers to assist them, it might be possible to put up with the proposals. However, the fact that the legislation is likely to impact upon the affairs of a large number of taxpayers means that the proposals in their current form are unworkable and should not be enacted.

**Change of Policy**

More fundamental, however, is the change of policy which these proposals represent. A fundamental principle which underlies the case law on the meaning of plant is that if a taxpayer incurs capital expenditure on an asset which, to use the words of Mr Justice Megarry in *Cooke* v *Beach Station Caravans Ltd* [1974] STC 402, is 'the means whereby his trade is carried on', that asset qualifies as plant unless it forms part of his stock in trade. If the asset is the premises in which the trade is carried on, it will not qualify unless the whole premises is part of the means by which the trade is carried on.

As taxpayers have become more and more sophisticated in the nature of their operations, it is not surprising that they have been able to demonstrate that items such as electrical installations have been designed in a way which is dictated by the needs of the trading operation. It is frequently the case that having an asset designed and built specifically in a way that meets the particular needs of the trade involves the taxpayer in greater expense than if an asset of a standard design had been purchased. This is particularly the case for retailers.

The draft legislation is the Inland Revenue's reaction to the success of taxpayers in being able to demonstrate to the General and Special Commissioners that the sort of items now to be excluded form part of the means whereby they carry on their trades. If that is what capital allowances are for, why should taxpayers now be prevented from benefiting from such tax relief? That is the fundamental question which the Inland Revenue should be called upon to answer in the process of lobbying that will be triggered by these proposals.

This is particularly so in the case of commercial operations, such as retailing, in which the taxpayer cannot benefit from an equivalent relief to industrial buildings allowances. At the very least, a commercial buildings allowance should be introduced as a *quid pro quo* for the new legislation.

That would, however, be no more than a sop to taxpayers for whom industrial buildings allowances are of no relevance. The point is that if the taxpayer goes to the trouble and (frequently additional) expense of obtaining an asset that forms part of the apparatus with which he trades, why should he be prevented from obtaining the same level of tax relief as he does for a computer system? If no one has raised that question with the Chancellor so far, it should be raised now.

## 12.2   End of Chapter Assessment Question

Refer to the facts concerning Amber Ltd in **2.6** and **3.6**. Consider the following additional facts.

Amber Ltd bought two items of plant and machinery, respectively, on 1 July 1993 and on 5 December 1993, for £1,600 and £6,500. It sold two other items of plant and machinery on 1 November 1995 and 15 September 1996 for £1,900 and £3,700 respectively. The qualifying expenditure in its pool of plant and machinery at 31 December 1992 was £10,000. Deborah's car is not pooled with this plant and machinery.

Calculate the balance of the pool at the end of the accounting periods ending on 31.12.93, 31.12.94, 31.12.95, 31.12.96 and 31.12.97.

## 12.3   End of Chapter Assessment Outline Answer

1.   The numbers in square brackets refer to the Notes at the end.
2.   FYAs were given for expenditure on plant and machinery, between 1 November 1992 and 31 October 1993: see *Learning Text* at **12.5.2**. Here, there was expenditure on plant and machinery on 1 July 1993 and 5 December 1993. Therefore, only the plant and machinery acquired on 1 July 1993 qualifies for 40% FYAs.

### CAPITAL ALLOWANCES: AMBER LTD

| Accounting period to 31.12.93 | £ | £ |
|---|---|---|
| Opening balance of pool of machinery brought forward | | 10,000 |
| Amber buys plant and machinery: | | |
| on 1.7.93 | 1,600 | |
| on 5.12.93 | | 6,500 |
| *Less*: FYA at 40% | (640) | |
| | 960 | |
| Qualifying expenditure for purposes of WDA | | 16,500 |
| *Less*: WDA at 25% | | (4,125) |
| Expenditure left in pool after WDA made | | 12,375 |
| *Plus*: Balance of expenditure on which FYA made [1] | | 960 |
| BALANCE OF POOL OF PLANT AND MACHINERY | | |
| FOR CARRYING FORWARD | | 13,335 |

The figure of £13,335 is carried forward as the opening balance of the pool for the accounting period ending on 31 December 1994. For the accounting period ending 31 December 1993, Amber Ltd can deduct total CAs from its trading income of £4,765, i.e. £640 (the 40% FYA), plus £4,125 (the WDA).

| Accounting period to 31.12.94 | £ | £ |
|---|---|---|
| Opening balance of pool of machinery brought forward | | 13,335 |
| *Less*: WDA at 25% · | | (3,334) |
| Expenditure left in pool after WDA made | | 10,001 |
| BALANCE OF POOL OF PLANT AND MACHINERY | | |
| FOR CARRYING FORWARD | | 10,001 |

The figure of £10,001 is carried forward as the opening balance of the pool for the accounting period ending on 31 December 1995. For the accounting period ending 31 December 1994, Amber Ltd can deduct total CAs from its trading income, of £3,334 (the WDA).

| **Accounting period to 31.12.95** | £ | £ |
|---|---|---|
| Opening balance of pool of machinery brought forward | | 10,001 |
| *Less*: Sale proceeds of 1.11.95 sale | | (1,900) |
| Balance of qualifying expenditure after sale [2] | | 8,101 |
| *Less*: WDA at 25% | | 2,025 |
| BALANCE OF POOL OF PLANT AND MACHINERY | | |
| FOR CARRYING FORWARD | | 6,076 |

The figure of £6,076 is carried forward as the opening balance of the pool for the accounting period ending on 31 December 1996. For the accounting period ending 31 December 1995, Amber Ltd can deduct total CAs from its trading income, of £2,025 (the WDA).

| **Accounting period to 31.12.96** | £ | £ |
|---|---|---|
| Opening balance of pool of machinery brought forward | | 6,076 |
| *Less*: Sale proceeds of 15.9.96 sale | | (3,700) |
| Balance of qualifying expenditure after sale [2] | | 2,376 |
| *Less*: WDA at 25% | | (594) |
| BALANCE OF POOL OF PLANT AND MACHINERY | | |
| FOR CARRYING FORWARD | | 1,782 |

The figure of £1,782 is carried forward as the opening balance of the pool for the accounting period ending on 31 December 1997. For the accounting period ending 31 December 1996, Amber Ltd can deduct total CAs from its trading income, of £594 (the WDA).

| **Accounting period to 31.12.97** | £ | £ |
|---|---|---|
| Opening balance of pool of machinery brought forward | | 1,782 |
| *Less*: WDA at 25% | | (446) |
| BALANCE OF POOL OF PLANT AND MACHINERY | | |
| FOR CARRYING FORWARD | | 1,336 |

The figure of £1,336 is carried forward as the opening balance of the pool for the accounting period ending on 31 December 1998. For the accounting period ending 31 December 1997, Amber Ltd can deduct total CAs from its trading income, of £446 (the WDA).

*Notes:*
1.  This is because, after the 40% FYA has been made, the remaining 60% of the initial expenditure (i.e. £960) is still unrelieved, and WDAs on that £960 still need to be given on it, in the same way as on the rest of the qualifying expenditure in the pool. It is therefore added to the expenditure in the pool, along with the rest of the qualifying expenditure.
2.  There is no balancing charge here, since the disposal proceeds of the plant and machinery in each case are *less* that the qualifying expenditure in the pool. A *balancing charge* is made if the disposal proceeds of the plant and machinery *exceed* the qualifying expenditure in the pool: CAA 1990, s. 24(5). A balancing charge could arise in this way *either* in an accounting period in which the business is continuing, or one in which the business is permanently discontinued. A *balancing allowance* is made only in the accounting period in which the business is permanently discontinued: CAA 1990, s. 24(2)(b).

# CHAPTER THIRTEEN

# REDUCING INCOME TAXATION (5)

## 13.1 Carry-*forward* of Trading Losses

### 13.1.1 INDIVIDUALS AND COMPANIES

#### GORDON & BLAIR LTD v IRC (1962) 40 TC 358 (CS)

A company ceased its brewing trade, before selling beer which was supplied to its specifications by another company.

*Held*: Losses of the brewing trade could not be carried forward and deducted from the selling trade, since the trade of brewing and the trade of selling were different trades.

THE LORD PRESIDENT (CLYDE): — The question in the present case is whether the Appellants were, subsequent to 1 October 1953, carrying on the same trade as before that date so as to entitle them to carry forward to the years subsequent to 1 October 1953, and set off against profits earned in these subsequent years, the losses which they sustained in their trading prior to that date. The question arises out of the provisions of s. 342(1) of the Income Tax Act 1952. The Special Commissioners have held that the Appellants were not entitled to set off these losses against subsequent profits on the ground that their former trading ceased on 1 October 1953, and a new trade then began. If so, it would follow that the Appellants cannot invoke s. 342(1). It is against this determination that the present appeal has been taken.

Prior to 1 October 1953, the Appellants brewed their own beer at their own brewery in Edinburgh. In addition to selling beer in the market, the Appellants supplied their beer to their own managed houses, to tied houses and to certain clubs. As the Appellants were making losses in the period immediately prior to 1953 they decided to cease brewing, and they entered into an arrangement with another company of brewers in Edinburgh, G. Mackay & Co., Ltd, under which, after 1 October 1953, this other company brewed and supplied beer to the Appellants at the specification which the Appellants had used and at prices adjusted between the parties. The beer was delivered in casks provided by the Appellants and marked with the Appellants' name and labels. Where beer was to be bottled for distribution by the Appellants, Mackays were required to deliver the beer in their casks to the Appellants, and they themselves did the bottling. No beer was brewed by the Appellants after 1 October 1953, but the beer brewed under this agreement with this other firm was distributed by the Appellants after that date under the same organisation and to the same type of customers, and in substantially the same way, as the Appellants had been distributing their own beer prior to that date.

It appears to me that in this situation the Special Commissioners were entitled to conclude that the trade carried on by the Appellants before 1 October 1953, was not the same trade as that carried on afterwards. The question is primarily, if not indeed wholly, a question of fact dependent upon the special circumstances of the particular case. It was contended that it was immaterial to the Appellants' trading whether they manufactured their particular brand of beer by the hands of their own workmen or arranged with some other party to manufacture it for them and to their order. In either event, their trade was the distribution and sale for profit of their own particular brand of beer. Upon such an approach to the matter, the trade both before and after 1 October 1953, so it was contended, was the same. But, in my view, this contention involves a misdescription of the real nature of the Appellants' trade. The essence of that trade, as I see it, prior to 1 October 1953, was the manufacture for sale by the Appellants of their own particular brand of beer. Their selling and distribution organisation was merely ancillary to that main trading activity. It is, in my view, quite false to suggest that their trade throughout was essentially the distribution of a special brand of beer, whoever may have been the manufacturer. After 1 October 1953, what had been, in my view, their ancillary activity became the Appellants' sole trading activity, and instead of being brewers of beer, they became distributors of beer which they did not brew but which another firm contracted to brew for them. In these circumstances the Special Commissioners were entitled, in my view, to reach the conclusion to which they came.

A considerable number of previous decisions were quoted to us, but each of these cases largely depends upon its own special facts, and the decisions therefore have no direct bearing upon the problem which we have got to decide in the present case. I do not, therefore, consider it necessary to analyse these decisions in any detail. But there are just two which were mainly canvassed before us and to which I should briefly refer. The first of them is *Fredk. Smith, Ltd* v *Commissioners of Inland Revenue*, 29 TC 419. The appellants' trade in that case was the trade of brewing and selling their own beer. In 1941 they purchased from Millward Brothers Ltd, certain tied houses. Prior thereto, Millward Brothers Ltd, had conducted their trade in regard to these tied houses by buying beer in the market for sale in these tied houses. In substance, the trade or business of Smiths was the same as that of the Appellants prior to 1 October 1953, while the trade or business of Millwards was the same as that of the Appellants subsequent to 1 October 1953. The Special Commissioners, in *Smith's* case, held that the company did not succeed to any part of Millward's trade or business *quoad* these tied houses. Sir Raymond Evershed, MR, in affirming this conclusion said, at page 460:

> . . . I am persuaded by Mr Tucker's argument that there is a real and substantial difference between the two classes of business, that conducted by Millward in regard to these houses and that conducted by Smiths, a difference substantial enough to support the finding of the Special Commissioners.

This appears to me to support the conclusion to which I have come in the present case. It was contended, however, that the distinction between *Smith's* case and the present was that in *Smith's* case Millward bought beer of no particular quality for sale in their tied houses, whereas after 1 October 1953, the Appellants supplied to their tied houses a beer of a specific quality brewed according to their specification. This does not appear to me to be a material consideration. The business of Millward was a non-brewing business, whether they bought their beer from one particular brewer or from several and whether the beer was of one particular quality or of several.

The other case was *Highland Railway Co.* v *Special Commissioners of Income Tax* (1885), 13 R 199; 2 TC 151. In my view that case is really not of assistance in the present instance. It concerned an arrangement between the Highland Railway Co. and Mr David McBrayne in regard to a steamer service previously operated by the Highland Railway Co. The arrangement was treated by the Court as not amounting to the abandonment by the railway company of the steamer branch of their business, which still remained part of their undertaking and which their statutory powers contemplated could be carried on in the way in which they arranged to carry it on with Mr McBrayne. The case, therefore, on its facts, is far removed from the circumstances of the present one.

On the whole matter, in my view, the Commissioners were entitled to arrive at the conclusion to which they came, and the question put to us should be answered in the affirmative.

### *NUCLEAR ELECTRIC PLC* v *BRADLEY* [1996] 1 WLR 529 (HL)

The facts of this case are noted in the *Learning Text* at **13.4.3.2**. His Lordship uses the abbreviation 'NE' for Nuclear Electric plc.

LORD JAUNCEY OF TULLICHETTLE: . . . When does investment income amount to a trading receipt of the taxpayer? The statute provides no guidance on the matter beyond impliedly recognising that it can sometimes do so. Such few authorities as are relevant have refused to lay down any hard and fast rule or draw any distinct line for determining the matter. Thus in *Liverpool and London and Globe Insurance Co.* v *Bennett* [1913] AC 610, Earl Loreburn said, at p. 620: 'I know of no formula which can discriminate in all circumstances what are and what are not profits of a trade.' It must at the end of the day always be a question of fact. In *Bennett* the taxpayer was a United-Kingdom-based insurance company which carried on business both at home and abroad. In certain foreign countries it was required by law to deposit sums of money with the relevant governments and to invest them according to local law. It also invested certain other sums derived from accumulated profits of the business in the country in question and received the interest on all these investments abroad. As this interest was not remitted to the United Kingdom it was only taxable if it was a trading profit for the purposes of Case I of Schedule D. The special commissioners [1911] 2 KB 577 found that the investments in question were made in the carrying on of, and were part of, its business transactions and that the interest therefrom was taxable under Case I. In relation to the compulsory deposits Hamilton J quoted with approval, at p. 593, the following dictum of Wright J in an earlier case (*Norwich Union Fire Insurance Co.* v *Magee* (1896) 73 LT 733):

> If there is a trade which cannot be carried on without making investments abroad, the interest arising on the investments necessarily made for the purposes of the trade is, as it seems to me, part of the gains of that trade.

The judge observed in relation to the voluntary investments, at p. 594:

> And I think it is clear that the investments which this fire insurance company voluntarily makes abroad are made not merely for investment's sake, but for the sake of having a fund readily realisable abroad to meet the liabilities of their business if need should be.

The Court of Appeal [1912] 2 KB 41 affirmed Hamilton J, and Buckley LJ, at p. 60, posed the question as being 'whether the interest and dividends are profits of the business as fruit derived from a fund employed and risked in the business.' This House [1913] AC 610 dismissed the taxpayer's appeal. Earl Loreburn, at p. 619, cited Buckley LJ's above quoted text with approval. Lord Mersey said, at p. 621:

> These temporary investments are also required for the formation of the reserve fund, a fund created to attract customers and to serve as a stand-by in the event of sudden claims being made upon the insurers in respect of losses. It is, according to my view, impossible to say that such investments do not form part of this company's insurance business, or that the returns flowing from them do not form part of its profits.

Lord Parker of Waddington after stating, at p. 622, that the compulsory investments constituted a security to the policyholders should the taxpayer fail to satisfy their claims concluded, at p. 623, that they were made for the purpose of and were 'at risk' in the company's business. He went on to observe that the voluntary investments were easily realisable and 'at any time available for the purposes' of the taxpayer's business. The words 'employed and risked' used by Buckley LJ have been quoted on many occasions but I doubt the utility of the word 'risked' as a word of general application. If it is intended to mean that the investments are at risk because they are available to satisfy the claims of the general creditors that does not advance the matter since all assets of the taxpayer for whatever purposes they may be held are similarly available. If it is intended to mean that the fund is used for the purpose of the taxpayer's business it adds nothing to the word 'employed.' It seems probable that Buckley LJ used the word because the funds of an insurance company are necessarily at risk of claims by policyholders immediately the policies are effected. I do not therefore think it necessary to go further than consider whether funds are employed in the business whereby any income therefrom arises from the trade for the purposes of Case I of Schedule D. What appears clearly from the speeches of Lord Mersey and Lord Parker of Waddington is the importance which they attached to the fact that the investment funds were available at any time during the relevant years of assessment to meet the requirements of the taxpayer's business.

In *Inland Revenue Commissioners* v *Butterley Co. Ltd* [1957] AC 32 Lord Radcliffe, in the context of profits tax, said, at p. 61:

> I do not think it possible to say that a company cannot own beneficially assets which do not belong to any trade or business which it conducts or that it cannot receive income beneficially which nevertheless is not income of such a trade or business.

Finally in *Bank Line Ltd* v *Commissioners of Inland Revenue* (1974) 49 TC 307 the Court of Session held that a fund set aside by a ship-owning company to replace some years hence obsolete ships was not to be treated as trading income for the purposes of the statutory predecessor of section 393 of the Act of 1988: section 58 of the Finance Act 1965. The Lord President, Lord Emslie, after referring at some length to *Liverpool and London and Globe Insurance Co.* v *Bennett* said, at p. 322:

> In my opinion, further, if I am correct in holding that what must be demonstrated by the appellants here is the active current employment and risking of the ship replacement fund in their trade of owning and operating ships in each of the relevant accounting periods, the appellants have failed to do so. This reserve fund was a fund laid aside to be employed and risked in the future, and although the appellants may be right in saying that they had a present and continuing purpose in maintaining this fund, I am quite unable to accept that they accordingly 'employed and risked' it in their business in the relevant periods.

Lord Cameron said, at p. 324:

> The investments of which the interest and dividends are in question were made with a particular purpose in view, replacement of capital assets, and not for the current requirements of the trade carried on by the appellants with the ships owned and operated by them.

He further observed, at p. 325:

> The receipts in question are not the receipts of such trading — on the contrary, they are receipts from the investment of sums which have been withdrawn from trade and dedicated to and drawn upon for the replacement of capital assets. No doubt they are receipts from the investment of sums set aside out of the profits of trading in previous years, and that by providing such a replacement fund the appellants made the continued carrying on of the trade possible, but there is in my opinion a material difference between such investments and the investment of funds which are or can be at call to meet the current demands of the trading activity carried on by the company.

Lord Avonside said, at p. 333:

> Income becomes a trading receipt when it arises from capital activity employed and at risk in the business, capital which is employed in the business because it is required for its support or, perhaps, to attract customers looking to the credit of the business. Trading income is 'the fruit' of the capital employed in the business in a present and active sense.

Like Lord Cameron he also pointed out that the fund, far from being employed in the business, had been created by withdrawing money from it.

All the judges in that case looked at the current use of the capital of the fund during the relevant accounting periods and concluded in the light of the findings of the special commissioners that it was not employed in the business of the shipowners. Mr Aaronson for the taxpayer did not seek to challenge the decision but argued that it was distinguishable because in this case there was in the year of assessment an accrued liability to pay the back-end costs albeit at a future date, whereas in the *Bank Line* case there was no such current obligation on the taxpayer to replace its ships. The answer to this submission may be shortly stated. Although N.E. had incurred a liability to make future payment it was no more obliged to set up a fund to meet this liability than were the shipowners. However, having done so, N.E. during the year of assessment neither used the fund for this purpose nor employed it in any other way in the business of generating electricity. The fact that in future years it might invest the fund in plant producing revenue and hence trading receipts cannot alter the character of its current use. It is the year of assessment that has to be looked at. I can therefore see no grounds for distinguishing the *Bank Line* case which I consider to have been correctly decided.

Whether income from investments held by a business is trading income must ultimately depend upon the nature of the business and the purpose for which the fund is held. At one end of the scale are insurance companies and banks part of whose business is the making and holding of investments to meet current liabilities. It has been suggested that tour operators might fall into this category but without a good deal more information I do not feel able to express an opinion on this matter. At the other end of the scale are businesses of which the making and holding of investments form no part. In between these two ends there will no doubt fall other types of businesses whose position is not so clear. However in this case it is absolutely clear that the business of N.E. was to produce and supply electricity. The making of investments was neither an integral nor any part of its business. Furthermore the investments which it did make were in no sense employed in the business of producing electricity during the year of assessment. It follows that wherever the line may be drawn the income from N.E.'s investment cannot be treated as trading income.

In this case we are dealing with a very large sum of money intended to be invested for a long period. Therefore in reaching the conclusion that this fund was not employed in N.E.'s business I would not wish to be taken as suggesting that sums held by a trader in an interest-bearing account to meet current or short-term trading liabilities should be similarly considered.

For the foregoing reasons I consider that the Court of Appeal arrived at the correct conclusion and that the appeal must be dismissed.

## 13.2   End of Chapter Assessment Question

Refer to the facts concerning Amber Ltd: **2.3**, **5.4**, **6.2**, **11.3** and **12.2**. In the accounting period to 31 December 1998, it has trading income of £250,000. Assume that it has allowable deductions from its trading income of £380,000 (refer to your answer to **11.3**) in the accounting period, plus further allowable deductions of £10,000. In the accounting period ending on 31 December 1998, Amber Ltd makes gross patent royalty payments of £200, in respect of a process used by it in its trade.

Remember that, on 30 November 1998, a gross dividend of £12,000 was declared and paid: see **8.4(a)**.

(a) Calculate the WDA available to Amber Ltd on the qualifying expenditure in its pool of plant and machinery, for the accounting period to 31 December 1998. (You will need to refer to the answer to **12.2** to do this.)

(b) Calculate the mainstream corporation tax liability of Amber Ltd, if any.

(c) Indicate any loss reliefs available to Amber Ltd.

## 13.3   End of Chapter Assessment Outline Answer

| (a)  **Accounting period to 31.12.98** | £ |
|---|---:|
| Opening balance of pool of machinery brought forward | 1,336 |
| *Less:* WDA at 25% | (334) |
| BALANCE OF POOL OF PLANT AND MACHINERY FOR CARRYING FORWARD | 1,002 |

Thus, the WDA available to Amber Ltd on the qualifying expenditure in its pool of plant and machinery, for the accounting period to 31 December 1998 is £334.

**(b)   CORPORATION TAX CALCULATION OF AMBER LTD FOR THE ACCOUNTING PERIOD OF TWELVE MONTHS ENDED 31 DECEMBER 1998**

**(Numbers in square brackets refer to Notes at the end.)**

| | £ |
|---|---:|
| Trading profit (Schedule D, Case I) [1] | NIL |
| *Statutory income* | NIL |
| *Total Profits* | NIL |
| *Less* Charges on income (gross) | (200) |
| *Profits chargeable to corporation tax* | NIL |
| Corporation tax on profits at relevant rate(s) | NIL |
| *Total tax* | NIL |
| *Less* tax deducted at source/credited as paid [2] | (2,400) |
| *Sub-total tax due* | NIL |
| *Plus* tax on charges | 46 |
| *Mainstream corporation tax liability* [3] | NIL |

*Notes*:

[1] There is no trading profit, although there is a trading loss. The trading loss is made up as follows:

|  | £ |
|---|---|
| Trading income | 250,000 |
| *Less*: Allowable deductions | (390,000) |
| *Less*: WDA ((1) above) | (334) |
| *Less*: Charges on income (refer to (3) below) | (200) |

TRADING LOSS IN ACCOUNTING PERIOD ENDED 31 DECEMBER 1998   (140,534)

[2] The gross dividend is £12,000, which means that the ACT credit at Stage Five is £2,400: *Learning Text* at **8.3.1** and above **8.4**. This is available for deduction from mainstream corporation tax in subsequent accounting periods.

[3] Amber Ltd is obliged to deduct and account for the £46 on the royalty payment under ICTA 1988, s. 349 (*Learning Text* at **9.4**), but this is *income tax* of the payee, *not* corporation tax of Amber Ltd.

(c) The trading loss of £140,534 (Note [1] above) includes excess allowable deductions of £(140,000), excess CAs of £(334) and excess charges on income of £(200).

   (1) *Carry-forward (ICTA 1988, s. 393(1))*: The conditions for the company carrying forward its trading loss are:

     (a) the loss has not been fully used up in the accounting period under consideration; *and*

     (b) the trade which the company is carrying on in any subsequent accounting period is the same trade as that carried on by it in the accounting period of the loss: *Gordon & Blair Ltd* v *IRC* (1962) 40 TC 358.

The excess charges on income of £(200) can be included, because they were incurred wholly and exclusively for the purpose of the trade: *Learning Text* at **13.4.2**.

   (ii) *Carry-across (ICTA 1988, s. 393A)*: This relief is applicable because it enables a company to deduct a trading loss incurred by it in the accounting period under consideration from its total profits of the previous accounting period. This deduction is made at Stage Three of Amber Ltd's corporation tax calculation for that previous accounting period. The conditions for the company to be able to carry-across its trading loss in this way are that:

     (a) it must have incurred the loss in carrying on a trade: see ICTA 1988, s. 393A(1); *and*

     (b) it must make the claim in writing, not more than two years after the end of the accounting period in which the loss was incurred by it: ICTA 1988, s. 393A(10); *and*

     (c) it must have carried on the trade in the year of the loss on a commercial basis and with a view to the realisation of profits.

All the indications here are that these conditions are satisfied by Amber Ltd.

# CHAPTER FOURTEEN

# INCOME RECEIPTS (1): OFFICES AND EMPLOYMENTS

## 14.1 Employment Income

### 14.1.1 INTRODUCTION

**CCH Editions Ltd,** *The British Master Tax Guide*, **paras 252 and 253**

**¶253 Employed or self-employed?**

Employees are taxed under entirely different provisions (Schedule E) from those which tax the self-employed (Schedule D). It is therefore necessary to distinguish an employment from a profession, trade or vocation.

In *Davies (HMIT)* v *Braithwaite* [1931] 2 KB 628, Lillian Braithwaite, an actress, claimed that each of her engagements was a separate contract of employment and was not incidental to the carrying out of her profession. The court, however, found that she was merely carrying out her profession and the engagements formed part of it.

On the other hand, in *Fall (HMIT)* v *Hitchen* [1973] 1 WLR 286, a ballet dancer who was engaged by a ballet company to work for a rehearsal period plus 22 weeks and thereafter until the contract was determined by a fortnight's notice by either side, was held to be an employee. The contract provided that Mr Hitchen worked full-time for the ballet company during the 22-week period and thereafter until the contract was determined by notice, but he was allowed to work for others as well with the permission of the ballet company. The ballet company paid Mr Hitchen's National Insurance contributions as though he were an employee. His hours were specified and he worked for a regular salary.

The approach of the court in *Fall* v *Hitchen* (above) is in line with modern labour law cases in deciding whether or not a contract of service exists (see *Warner Holidays* v *Secretary of State for Social Services* [1983] ICR 440). In *Fall* v *Hitchen* the court decided that once a contract of service was found to exist then the taxpayer would be taxed under Schedule E. The Revenue have relied on the case in treating entertainers who made or make their first appearance after 5 April 1987 as employees unless they have a three-year history of Schedule D status (ICAEW Technical Release 796 and ESC A75 . . .). The Revenue have also produced notes listing those grades within the film and television industry which they would regard as indicative of employee status, although a vision mixer succeeded in arguing that he was self-employed (*Hall (HMIT)* v *Lorimer* [1993] BTC 473: see further below).

In deciding whether a contract of service exists, all the relevant facts are looked at and weighed in the balance. Some of the more obvious facts that the court takes into consideration were set out by Cooke J in *Market Investigations Ltd* v *Minister of Social Security* [1969] 2 QB 173; the main considerations are as follows.

| *For employment* | *Against employment* |
|---|---|
| Control by another over the manner in which the work is performed. | No control by another over the manner in which the work is done. |
| The person performing the work is restricted from delegating his work to another. | The person performing the work is free to delegate his duties to another. |
| The person performing the work does not bear the losses nor keep the profits. | The person performing the work bears the losses and keeps the profits. |
| Tax and National Insurance contributions are withheld by the person for whom the work is done. | No tax or National Insurance contributions are withheld from payments. |
| The parties agree employment. | The parties agree self-employment. |
| The person for whom the work is done provides the tools and equipment. | The person performing the work provides his own tools. |
| The person for whom the work is done lays down regular and defined hours of work. | The person performing the work is free to decide when he wishes to work. |
| The person for whom the work is done cannot withhold payment. | The person for whom the work is done is free to withhold payment until the work is performed as agreed. |
| The person for whom the work is done can dismiss. | The person for whom the work is done cannot dismiss the worker or cancel the work once the work is agreed, without compensation. |
| The person for whom the work is done has an obligation to provide work and to pay the 'employee' when no work is available. | There is no obligation to provide the 'employee' with work, or to pay him when no work is available. |

Individually the above points do not prove the existence or otherwise of a contract of employment. Leaflet IR 56 (obtainable free from any Tax Office) gives useful guidance on what the Revenue regard as important criteria. They are, however, points which influence the courts in deciding whether such a contract exists. The list is not exhaustive and any fact which appears relevant in a particular case will be taken into account and considered. The important factor is the actual performance of the contract. In *Ready Mixed Concrete (South East) Ltd* v *Minister of Pensions and National Insurance* [1968] 2 QB 497 it was emphasised that:

> whether the relationship . . . is that of master and servant or otherwise is a conclusion of law dependent on the rights conferred and the duties imposed by the contract (i.e. the real unwritten contract). If these are such that the relation is that of master and servant it is irrelevant that the parties may have declared it to be something else.

In *Hall (HMIT)* v *Lorimer* (above), in the Court of Appeal Nolan J said that to the list of indications set out by Cooke J were to be added other matters, such as whether the person performing the services had set up a business-like organisation of his own; the degree of continuity in the relationship between the person performing the services and the person for whom he performs them; how many engagements he performed and whether they were performed mainly for one person or for a number of different people. He added that the fact that the taxpayer accepted the risk of bad debts was a risk not normally associated with employment, and he incurred expenses in organising his business which were different in nature and scale from the likely expenses of an employee.

Other recent cases related to the following:

- a part-time law lecturer was found to be correctly assessable under Schedule E (*Sidey* v *Phillips (HMIT)* [1987] BTC 121);
- a professional singer who worked four days each week in term time teaching music at a technical college was found to be working under a contract of service and so liable to tax under Schedule E (*Walls* v *Sinnett (HMIT)* [1987] BTC 206); and

■ the leader of a gang of potato pickers who, with others, worked for a potato merchant on an ad hoc basis was not self-employed — *inter alia*, he selected helpers but did not 'hire' them and his position as gangmaster did not yield a profit as the fruits of the work were equally shared among the members of the gang (*Andrews* v *King (HMIT)* [1991] BTC 338).

In the case of workers supplied by agencies who would not otherwise be taxable under Schedule E there are deeming provisions in ICTA 1988, s. 134 which subject them to Schedule E tax. They are generally subject to PAYE procedures even if engaged through a foreign agency which does not have a branch or agent in the UK (via an intermediate employer . . .)

The duties of certain divers performed in the UK or a designated area are statutorily treated as a trade rather than an employment (ICTA 1988, s. 314).

Although Schedule D is more generous to the taxpayer, the loss of job protection legislation, redundancy and unemployment pay may outweigh the tax benefits.

**Typical memorandum from employer to employees, July 1996**
**Travelling and Subsistence Rates (1996/97 tax year)**

### TRAVELLING AND SUBSISTENCE RATES

*Travelling*

The Inland Revenue has determined the 1996/97 tax-free mileage rates and the following revised rates are effective from 1 August 1996:

| Annual Mileage Mileage | Cars up to 1000 cc | Cars 1001 — 1500 cc | Cars 1501 — 2000 cc | Cars over 2000 cc |
|---|---|---|---|---|
| Up to 4000 miles | 27p (27p) | 34p (34p) | 43p (43p) | 61p (60p) |
| Over 4000 miles | 15p (15p) | 19p (19p) | 23p (23p) | 33p (32p) |

Public Transport Equivalent Rates — 23p (23p)

*Subsistence*

The following rates will apply from 1 August 1996:

| | | £ p | £ p |
|---|---|---|---|
| Bed & Breakfast | — Provinces | 61.65 | (60.00) |
| | — London | 75.80 | (73.80) |
| Breakfast | | 3.80 | (3.70) |
| Lunch | | 5.80 | (5.70) |
| Tea | | 2.10 | (2.10) |
| Dinner | — Provinces | 8.40 | (8.20) |
| | — London | 10.00 | (9.80) |

The figures in brackets are the 1995/96 rates.

### 14.1.2  STATUTORILY-DEEMED EMOLUMENTS

Living accommodation: ICTA 1988, ss. 145 to 147.

**Sellwood, A., 'A Job With A Home',** *Taxation,* **30 January 1997, p. 488**

The provision of living accommodation has always been highly valued as a form of remuneration. This may sometimes be because it offers reasonably affluent members of society a higher level of social standing. In other cases, it may afford a basic necessity of life to those who might not otherwise have sufficient means to provide it.

### Two kinds of occupation

One form of occupation by an employee may not be wholly for his own benefit. He may live where he does because his employer needs the employee's presence there for various reasons, such as the security of the premises or their contents or to ensure that someone is continually present to tend livestock when needed or to attend suppliers and to receive customers outside normal working hours. In such a case, the employee's occupation may be representative of his employers rather than to suit his own convenience. It may even be highly inconvenient for him.

When, in earlier days, liability under Schedule E arose only if the remuneration was actually in the form of money or in some way represented money's worth — in the sense that it could be exchanged for cash, the question whether occupation of accommodation was beneficial or representative assumed some importance.

If occupation was beneficial, payments by an employer of such expenses as rent, rates, gas and electricity or garden upkeep were regarded as money's worth in the hands of the director or employee concerned (see *Nicoll* v *Austin* 19 TC 531).

A much earlier case, *Tennant* v *Smith* 3 TC 158, had established that, where the occupation was representative, payment of the expenses of occupation were held not to be money's worth. The occupation in this case was by a bank manager who was required to live in the bank house by the employing bank. In the later case of *Gray* v *Holmes* 30 TC 467, a similar decision was reached with regard to a house occupied rent-free by a colliery manager, who was required to live there by the employing colliery owners.

### Early benefits legislation

Soon after the second world war it was provided by Finance Act 1948 that directors and those who later came to be designated as 'higher paid' employees would be chargeable to tax under Schedule E in respect of benefits-in-kind and allowances for expenses. Benefits-in-kind were not as fully defined as they have since become, but the new rules did mark a departure from the old requirement that, in order to be assessable under Schedule E, an emolument received must constitute money's worth.

The legislation of 1948 contained some references to expenditure connected with living accommodation and produced a further string of cases in the courts, in which it was claimed that expenditure in connection with living accommodation provided for by the employer was not taxable. Most of these claims were unsuccessful. But in *Commissioners of Inland Revenue* v *Luke* 40 TC 630 a managing director had bought a house for his own occupation and for the entertainment of foreign customers. He had later sold it to the company, whilst remaining in occupation and paying the company rent. He was found by the court not to be liable to tax on the sums expended by the company on owners' rates, repairs and other items.

Others fared less well. The managing director in *Doyle* v *Davison* 40 TC 140 who rented a house from his company was held to be liable to tax on the cost of repairs to the house borne by the company. In *Butter* v *Bennett* 40 TC 402 a manager of a paper-mill who was required to live in a house provided by his employers was held to be liable in respect of the payments by the employers for coal, electricity and gardening services for the house. Again, in *McKie* v *Warner* 40 TC 65 a senior employee, who had moved into a London flat and paid a rent of £150 to the company which employed him, was adjudged to be liable to tax on the difference between the rent which he paid and the rent of £500 which the company paid for the flat.

### Representative occupiers

It will be observed that, although the benefits-in-kind legislation disposed, in the case of directors and higher paid employees, of the requirement that an emolument must represent money's worth if it is to be regarded as assessable under Schedule E, it did not alter the position with regard to representative occupation.

It could, of course, still be possible to question whether, in a particular case, occupation is beneficial or representative. The case of *Langley and Others* v *Appleby* [1976] STC 368 reached a final decision in the courts in 1976. It was concerned with the occupation of police houses by members of the police force and gave rise to the Revenue's view that an employee 'must establish affirmatively that for the performance of his duties he must live in that house and no other' if he claims that his occupation is merely representative.

The benefits-in-kind legislation was drastically revised and updated in respect of most forms of benefit in 1976 but, because the *Langley* v *Appleby* case was still before the courts when the new rules were introduced into the legislation of that year, benefits in respect of accommodation were left until the Finance Act of the following year. This legislation established the general principle, discussed in more detail below, that living accommodation provided by reason of a person's employment will, if not otherwise chargeable to tax, give rise to a taxable benefit. But it still contained an exemption (now included in ICTA 1988, s. 145) for employees whose occupation is regarded as truly representative.

### Employees not caught

This exemption from the general charge is given:

(i)     where residence on the premises is necessary for the proper performance of the duties of the employment;

(ii)    where the accommodation is provided for the better performance of the duties of the employment and its provision is customary in that type of employment;

(iii)   where there is a special threat to the employee's security and accommodation is provided as part of special security arrangements.

The exemption also covers any rates paid or reimbused by the employer where the accommodation falls within any of the three categories listed above. The third category covers a very limited field such as Government Ministers. Directors of companies are excluded from claiming under the first two categories unless the company is non-profit making or they are full-time working directors and have no material interest (as defined in ICTA 1988, s. 168) in the company.

The first category listed is fairly straightforward. It covers such employees as care-takers, wardens of sheltered housing, hotel managers and other staff required to reside in the hotel, farm workers living in the farm, resident managers of public houses, etc. The second category is more controversial. It is not always easy to satisfy the test that living in particular premises enables duties to be better performed and it may be even harder to show that to have such accommodation is 'customary'.

In the case of *Vertigan* v *Brady* [1988] STC 91 a nursery foreman, provided by his employers with a rent-free bungalow, was refused exemption. The court indicated that, in deciding whether the provision of accommodation is customary, it should be considered to what extent it is generally accepted by employers in the particular type of business, how long the practice has continued and how common it is statistically. The Revenue has indicated that such persons as camping-site managers or veterinary surgeons assisting in a practice might customarily live at or adjacent to their place of work but it would still have to be shown that the requirement that they do so for the better performance of duties is satisfied.

As will be seen below, the general charge to tax on accommodation as a benefit and the exemption from it relate to all employees and not merely, as in the case of some benefits, to directors and those earning above a certain level of remuneration. But these directors and employees may well be liable to tax on other benefits arising from accommodation, other than the mere occupation of the accommodation itself, by virtue of the special legislation in ICTA 1988, s. 153 *et seq.*

Under ICTA 1988, s. 163, where the employer pays for, or reimburses to, the employee the costs of heating, lighting, cleaning, repairs, maintenance or decoration or the provision of furniture or other effects which are normal for domestic occupation, the amount to be included is not to exceed a specified level. This maximum is 10 per cent of the net emoluments, i.e., the remuneration (excluding the expenditure under consideration) less capital allowances, deductible expenses, superannuation and retirement annuity contributions and, where the expenditure is incurred by someone other than the employee, any sum made good to that person by the employee. The emoluments taken into account in making the calculation are those from the employment in question with the addition of those from any associated company. Where the period under review is less than twelve months, a proportionate reduction is made in the percentage.

### The general charge

Most of the employees who receive the use of accommodation by reason of their employment are not entitled to the exemptions for representative occupation already considered and will, therefore, be subject to a charge to tax under ICTA 1988, s. 145. Where living accommodation is provided to any person by reason of his employment, and, under the original wording, was not otherwise charged to tax, or if it is provided to his family or household by reason of his employment, it will give rise to a taxable emolument equal to the value to him of the accommodation for the relevant period, less any sum paid by him for the use of the accommodation and less any expenses which would have been deductible if they had been paid by the employee out of his taxable emoluments. The charge applies whatever the pay level or position in the company or business of the employee. There are exceptions to this charge:

(i)   where the employer is an individual and it can be demonstrated that the provision of accommodation is made in the normal course of a domestic or family relationship; *or*

(ii)   where the employer is a local authority and the accommodation is not provided on better terms than those available for similar accommodation to persons who are not employees.

The value of the benefit is to be the annual value of the premises as defined in ICTA 1988, s. 837, viz, the gross rateable value which was applicable before the displacement of domestic rates by the community charge. If, however, the person providing the accommodation paid a rent for it in excess of its annual value as defined above, the value of the benefit is equal to the rent. For properties in Scotland there were special provisions in Inland Revenue Extra-statutory Concession A56. As regards the deductions from the value of the accommodation, it is stated in s. 145(*i*) that this value may be reduced by so much as is properly attributable to the provision of any sum made good by the employee to those at whose cost the accommodation is provided. There is some discussion of this point in the case of *Stones* v *Hall* [1989] STC 138 where certain deductions were unsuccessfully claimed.

### Increase in benefit

Property values were increasing very rapidly in the 'seventies' and 'eighties' and this rendered it unlikely that the annual value measure would remain sufficient to cover the benefit actually obtained from the occupation of accommodation. New legislation, now found in ICTA 1988, s. 146, was introduced in 1983. Where living accommodation is provided for a person by reason of his employment and that person is treated — or would be so treated if any contribution made by him were disregarded — as being in receipt of an emolument chargeable to tax under s. 145 and the cost of providing the accommodation exceeds £75,000, he is to be treated as being in receipt of an additional chargeable emolument.

This emolument is calculated by reference to the notional annual rent which would be payable if computed as an 'appropriate percentage' of the amount by which the cost exceeds £75,000. The appropriate percentage is that prescribed by the Treasury, for the purpose of determining the benefit from beneficial loans, under ICTA 1988, s. 160(5), as at the beginning of the relevant year of assessment of the accommodation benefit. If the employee pays a rent for the accommodation in excess of its value as determined by s. 145, that excess may be deducted from the additional emolument as calculated.

The cost of providing the living accommodation is the aggregate of:

(a)   the amount of any expenditure incurred in acquiring the estate or interest in the property held by a relevant person; *and*

(b)   the amount of any expenditure incurred by a relevant person before the relevant year of assessment on improvements to the property.

This aggregate figure is to be reduced by any sum paid by the employee so far as it represents reimbursement of the expenditure or consideration for the grant to the employee of a tenancy of the property. Where the employee's first occupation of the property fell or falls on a date after 30 March 1983 and any estate or interest in the property had been held by a relevant person throughout the six years ended on the date of the employee's first occupation, the open market value (assuming vacant possession and disregarding any options held by the employee) is to be substituted for the cost of acquiring the property.

A relevant person is the employer or other person providing the accommodation or a connected person (as defined in ICTA 1988, s. 839). It was at first assumed by the Revenue that market value could be substituted for cost of acquisition, whether or not the cost exceeded £75,000. But this was later found to be erroneous in law. The practice was changed as from 1987–88 and repayments were made in certain cases.

### Avoidance and counter-avoidance

The charge for the additional benefit under s. 146 could be burdensome, especially when interest rates were high and, not surprisingly, ways of avoiding it were sought. One such way that was discovered was by way of the original wording of s. 145 which imposes the original charge under that section, and consequently also, the additional charge under s. 146. The charge under s. 145(*i*) was imposed where living accommodation is provided for a person in any period by reason of his employment and 'is not otherwise made the subject of any charge to him by way of income tax'. This meant that, if it could be shown that the occupation of the accommodation was already chargeable to tax, it could not be charged under ss. 145 and 146.

A method of having it charged to tax at a much lower figure was found in the decision in *Heaton* v *Bell* 46 TC 211, where an employee sacrificed some salary to have a company car; it was held that the car was a taxable benefit in the amount of salary forgone. This decision has been used to offer accommodation under 'cash alternative' schemes in which the employee could take either the accommodation or a small additional salary. He opted for the accommodation, thus creating a Schedule E liability in respect of the money's worth represented by the extra salary forgone.

Moves to prevent the continuance of such schemes were announced in the Budget of 28 November 1995 and in the press release of that date and found their way into Finance Act 1996 at s. 106. By this section the wording of ICTA 1988, s. 145(*i*) was curtailed by the elimination of the words 'and is not otherwise made the subject of any charge to him by way of income tax' and a new s. 146A was inserted into the Taxes Act 1988 to make a charge on accommodation under ss. 145 and 146 a priority to any other [charge] thereon.

### *Two concessions*

Two new extra-statutory concessions were announced at the same time as the proposed legislation. Under the first it was indicated that, where the same accommodation is provided to more than one director or employee in the same period with the result that each of them may be subject to a charge on it, as from 1995–96 it will be ensured that the total charged will be no more than if a charge were made for the provision of accommodation to a single employee.

The other concession is concerned with the fact that it is possible for a charge based on the open market rental of accommodation to be made with an additional charge also arising under s. 146. This can happen when the accommodation is outside the United Kingdom or where the person providing the accommodation rents it from a connected person who acquired it for more than £75,000. As a result of the concession, no charge will be made under s. 146 where the charge under s. 145 is based on the open market rental.

### Yerbury, P., 'Lump-Sum Payments on the Termination of Employment', *The Tax Journal*, 23 April 1992, p. 10

This extract deals with termination payments (*Learning Text*, Note 4 to Table B). The references to ICTA 1988, s. 188, have been superceded by the amendments made by FA 1998, drawing s. 188 and ICTA 1988, s. 148, together. The points made are equally valid now.

### Payments in lieu of notice

Employers often make payments to employees in lieu of notice. This is a useful tax planning device, especially for senior employees and may in part overcome or avoid the need to negotiate with the Revenue over non-statutory 'redundancy' payments. There are three basic situations to distinguish:

- Where an employee has been given notice and is not given the opportunity by his employer of working out that notice, the payment he receives in lieu of that notice would not in general be taxable, under the principles established in, for example, *Clayton* v *Lavender* 42 TC 607. However, any such payment would be aggregated with any redundancy payments, whether or not statutory, for the purposes of the £30,000 exemption — see s. 188(5).
- Where an employee has been given notice and is given the opportunity by his employer to work out that notice, but chooses not to, and nevertheless receives payment for the notice period, this payment would be subject to income tax in the normal way.
- Where an employee has been given notice and is given the opportunity by his employer to work out that notice, but chooses not to, and the employer nevertheless makes him an *ex gratia* payment, this would not normally be liable to income tax. It would, however, again, be included in the £30,000 computation.

The tax position of the employer is not expressly provided for but the likelihood is that a deduction would be obtained on general principles.

### Ex gratia payments

*Ex gratia* payments are not so frequently made now — presumably because of the clarification of the loss of office termination payments legislation in 1988. However, it is still of importance to consider the principles involved.

The general position is that *ex gratia* payments made by an employer to an employee are not taxable. However, again, any such payments are, subject to exceptions, aggregated with any other payments made for the purpose of determining whether the £30,000 limit is exceeded. To be non-taxable in principle, the payment must be made, for example, as a token of appreciation. If this is not the case and the payment is made, for example, by reference to past services, it may be subject to income tax, because it could be argued that it is derived 'from' the employment and therefore falls directly within the definition of Schedule E in s. 19.

Four principles to be used in determining the nature of such payments were established in *Moorhouse* v *Dooland* 36 TC 1 as follows:

- the test of liability to tax on a voluntary payment made to the holder of an office or employment is whether, from the standpoint of the person who receives it, it accrues to him by virtue of his office or employment or, in other words, by way of remuneration for his services;
- if the recipient's contract of employment entitled him to receive the voluntary payment, that is a strong ground for holding that it accrues by virtue of the office and so, in other words, is remuneration for his services;
- the fact that the voluntary payment is of a periodic or recurrent character affords a further, though less cogent, ground for the same conclusion; and
- on the other hand, a voluntary payment may be made in circumstances which show that it is given by way of a present or testimonial on grounds personal to the recipient, as for example a collection made for the particular individual who is at the time vicar of a given parish because he is in straitened circumstances, or a benefit held for a professional cricketer in recognition of his long and successful career in first class cricket.

In the last case the proper conclusion is likely to be that the voluntary payment is not a profit accruing to the recipient by virtue of his office or employment but a gift to him as an individual, paid and received by reason of his personal needs or by reason of his personal qualities or attainments.

If these principles are followed in determining whether to make *ex gratia* payments or not, together with the intentions of the payer, the tax position of the employee should be relatively clear.

The status of *ex gratia* payments on retirement or death has, however, now been modified by a new Revenue Statement of Practice SP 13/91, which changes the tax treatment of payments made after 31 October 1991. The Revenue now takes the view that such *ex gratia* lump-sum payments are within the separate tax rules for payments under retirement benefits schemes rather than, as before, being taxable under the section 148 rules. In future the Pension Schemes Office will be prepared to approve *ex gratia* schemes and not simply contractual schemes. In the case of an approved scheme, lump-sum payments will now be tax-free instead of being taxable under the section 188 rules. In the case of unapproved schemes lump-sum payments will be taxable in full and not even qualify for the £30,000 exemption.

The Revenue has confirmed that the tax treatment of other *ex gratia* payments is unchanged. It has also stated that employers should always deduct tax under the PAYE system when making taxable lump-sum payments of any kind except, of course, where approved status has been granted.

### Other exemptions

Advantage can sometimes be taken of other exemptions granted by section 188, when payments exceed £30,000. Perhaps the most important of these other exemptions is a payment made in respect of foreign service. Broadly speaking, at least 75 per cent of the period of service must have been foreign service or, in the case of a period of service exceeding 10 years, the whole of the last 10 years, or for periods exceeding 20 years, half of the period including any 10 of the last 20 years. If any of those qualifications is achieved, lump-sum payments received on this basis are exempt from tax.

Other exemptions include payments resulting from death, injury or disability occurring during employment, payments under approved retirement benefits schemes, payments under unapproved retirement benefits schemes where the person has received no tax deduction for his contributions, and payments under certain overseas superannuation schemes — see s. 188(1).

The exemption can also apply to a lump-sum payment made in respect of a foreign pension scheme. In the case of a lump-sum payment made from a United States pension scheme to a United Kingdom resident, for example, such a sum would normally be taxable in the United States unless it is taxable in the United Kingdom, following the provisions of Article 18(1) of the United States/United Kingdom double taxation convention.

It ought to be possible to take advantage of Article 18(1) because such a payment is in principle taxable in the United Kingdom under s. 148, although it is actually exempted by s. 188(1). Doubt had been cast on this argument due to the operation of s. 596A, which provides that no exception is made to a charge under Schedule E for benefits from foreign pension schemes. However, due to a conflict in the legislation, and the opinion that s. 596A might take priority over s. 148, the Revenue decided to issue a Press Release and a revised Extra-Statutory Concession A10 on 8 October 1991, which clarified the position in favour of the priority of s. 148 over s. 596A for these purposes. Thus the rule is as it was prior to the implementation of s. 596A (on 26 July 1989).

### Alternative situations

The one situation to avoid in tax planning for termination is where the contract of employment provides for compensation for loss of office. The analysis generally accepted if that is the case is that the employee has received exactly what he was entitled to under the contract. He has surrendered no rights and so his remuneration is said to have been derived from his contract of employment and thus the payment will be chargeable under Schedule E, not s. 148.

It might be thought that if a new employer offered a payment to an employee of another employer as an inducement to leave that employment and work for the new employer that this would escape a Schedule E liability. However, in *Shilton* v *Wilmshurst* [1991] STC 88 the House of Lords concluded that the emoluments were 'from' an employment, even though they were coming from a third party who had no interest in the contract concerned.

**Timing**

It may well be that in certain situations there will be no choice in determining when a termination payment is to be made. However, if there is a choice — and particularly if the payment can be made in one or other of two tax years — some consideration to timing can produce significant savings. In particular, if there is the possibility of higher tax rates in the next tax year, it may well be advantageous for an employee to receive a termination payment prior to 6 April if his payment is in excess of £30,000.

On the other hand, it may be that the employee is unlikely to be offered new employment quickly and if he obtains a payment in excess of £30,000 but not significantly so, and if no other source of income is likely to spring up in the new tax year, even though higher tax rates may be in prospect it may be better for him to have the payment made after 5 April.

Another possible advantage of receiving a payment in a later rather than an earlier tax year is that the tax return including the payment is then for a later year and the employer's obligation to notify the Revenue, as provided in s. 148(7), is within 30 days of the end of the fiscal year in which the payment was made. Cash flow advantages could arise if there is any dispute.

It is also important that the payment is received after the employee has received his P45. Income tax on any excess over £30,000 will then be deducted at the basic rate, not the higher rate — see Regulation 16 of the Income Tax (Employments) Regulations 1973 (SI 1973/334). If it is paid before the employee has received the P45, a full withholding will have to be made by the employer, unless otherwise authorised by the Revenue.

Normally the payment would be made at the same time as the individual receives his P45 and then he would depart the same day.

The date of termination of the employment is the date when the income is regarded as being received — see s. 148(4) — in the case of a payment for compensation for loss of office. However, in the case where there has been a breach of contract, the date of the breach is, in my view, when the employment is regarded as terminated and not at some later date — see *Micklefield* v *SAC Technologies Ltd* [1991] 1 All ER 275 and pages 13 to 15 of Issue 102 of *The Tax Journal*.

**Conclusion**

The above demonstrates quite clearly that considerable care needs to be exercised in making lump-sum termination payments — both from the employer's and employee's standpoints — but that there are certain areas where tax planning can prove beneficial. Specific advice is, of course, necessary in all situations.

**14.1.3 SPECIAL STATUTORY CODE FOR EMPLOYEES WITH EMOLUMENTS OF £8,500 PER ANNUM OR MORE AND MOST DIRECTORS**

**Masters, C., and Ball, S., 'Driven to Distraction', *The Tax Journal*, 7 July 1997, p. 7**

. . .

Now, what happens when a chap switches cars during the tax year? Does he add up the business miles he does in both cars and then sees whether he clocks up 2,500 or, as the case may be, 18,000 miles; or does he look at the business mileage in each car separately by reference to the thresholds reduced pro rata? This was precisely the point at issue in the recent case of *Henwood* v *Clarke* [1997] STC 789. Mr Clarke was provided with a car by his employer. Part of the way through the year (in August) the employer changed the car for another model. To confuse the picture a bit, in the year in question (1993–94) the cash equivalent was calculated in a different way in that it depended on, among other things, the cylinder capacity of the car and its value. However, it was still relevant to determine whether an employee clocked-up 2,500 (or 18,000) business miles to qualify for a lesser tax charge.

Mr Clarke drove 1,425 miles on business in his first car and 1,452 miles in the second one. His total business miles were therefore 2,877, well over the 2,500 threshold. Mr Clarke therefore thought he was entitled to the lower tax charge. The inspector of taxes disagreed. He said that it was necessary to apportion the 2,500 limit on a time basis between the two cars. If this was done Mr Clarke exceeded the threshold on the first car, but not on the second. In the circumstances of this case, this meant that Mr Clarke's cash equivalent was increased by almost £1,000. The one point for the decision of the court was which of these two bases of calculation was correct. Even though the method of calculating the cash equivalent is now different, this point is still relevant today. The answer given by the judge applies to both the 2,500 and the 18,000 thresholds.

At the date of the case, and under current law, the legislation does not specifically cover the point, so the judge had to make up his mind by reference to the general structure of the company car provisions. He admitted that Mr Clarke's approach had the attractions of common sense and simplicity. However, the judge took the view that the way the legislation was drafted showed that the inspector's approach was the right one. Under the law at the time, a number of variables had to be taken into account in determining the cash equivalent, such as the age of the car, cylinder capacity, and value. It so happened in Mr Clarke's case that the age, cylinder capacity and value were the same, but the judge pointed out that in many cases this would not be the case. In another case the cash equivalent for the two cars might be very different and to lump the two together for the purpose of determining whether the thresholds had been exceeded would give a distorted picture. The judge also referred to the rule explained above which applies where a car is not available for part of the year, where the business mileage threshold is reduced pro rata. In Mr Clarke's case each car had been unavailable for part of the year. It therefore made sense to reduce the thresholds for each pro rata. Accordingly, the judge agreed with the approach of the inspector and rejected Mr Clarke's argument.

### Timing of the switch

This important point is still relevant today. The implications are that, where it is intended that an employee's company car is to be changed during the course of a tax year, care should be taken in calculating whether the proportionately reduced thresholds will be exceeded. The timing of the switch should then be fixed accordingly (if this is practical — it won't be in many cases), because the employee's tax situation could be affected accordingly. Another point to keep in mind is that the employee must be clear, when keeping a record of his business mileage, to show which car he was using at the time, if he changes during the tax year. Given that few changes in company car take place at the end of the tax year, this case is of wide application.

In passing, it should be noted that, in this case which potentially affects many employees, the taxpayer was not professionally represented before the appeal commissioners, and did not even appear before the court (where the Inland Revenue had their arguments presented by a QC). This was unfortunate but perhaps understandable. Mr Clarke may well have taken the view that the amount of tax at stake did not justify the retention of counsel to present his case. It should be noted that, as this case was seen as involving a point of principle on the construction of the legislation, the Inland Revenue did not seek an order for costs against Mr Clarke, so Mr Clarke did not have to pay any of the Revenue's costs before the court. Mr Clarke would still have had to cough up his own lawyer's cost if he had retained legal representation.

### Missed opportunity

At the end of the day, it is not possible to say whether the decision would have been different had Mr Clarke's case been put before the court by counsel, but it is a shame that, in what was essentially a test case affecting many taxpayers, the court did not have the benefit of legal argument on behalf of the taxpayer. In fact, Mr Clarke's employer, which had imposed the change of car on him, was one of the 'high street' banks. Perhaps the employer could have retained counsel on Mr Clarke's behalf (although it should be noted that the report of the court case does not explain the reason why the employer was not involved, and it may well have been for perfectly proper reasons).

## 14.2   End of Chapter Assessment Question

Refer back to **6.2**, and note the following additional facts. The non-pooled car provided for Deborah's general use by the company is retained by her throughout the 1998/99 tax year. It has an 1,800cc petrol-engine, and she is reimbursed by Amber Ltd for the petrol used by her for private purposes. The manufacturer's list price of the car is £28,000, including the CD-player and alloy wheels with which it is fitted. In the 1998/99 tax year, her business mileage for Amber Ltd is 2,000 miles.

Comment on the significance of these facts in terms of Deborah's income tax position in 1998/99.

## 14.3   End of Chapter Assessment Outline Answer

As a director of Amber Ltd, the emoluments of Deborah's office are governed by the special statutory code, irrespective of the fact that she is also an employee. The only directors to whom the special statutory code does *not* apply are ones who do not have a material interest in the company, and *either* (a) are full-time working directors of it; *or* (b) the company is charitable or non-profit making. The fact that Deborah is an employee means that, even if Amber Ltd fell into one or other of these categories, she would still be within the code were her emoluments to be £8,500 per annum or more: ICTA 1988, s. 167(5). For the 1998/99 tax year, therefore, she will have to include in the emoluments of her employment with Amber Ltd the cash equivalent of the car: ICTA 1988, s. 156. The cash equivalent of the car is determined by reference to ss. 157, 159, 159AB and sch. 6, ICTA 1988.

Deborah's car has an 1,800cc petrol-engine. The manufacturer's list price of the car is £28,000, including the CD-player and alloy wheels, and her business mileage for Amber Ltd is 2,000. The cash equivalent of the car is 35% of the manufacturer's list price, reduced by 1/3 if her business mileage is between 2,500 per annum and 17,999 per annum. To claim the reduction, she must be required by the nature of her office to use the car to this extent, however. Deborah's business mileage does not entitle her to this reduction, so the cash equivalent of the car is a straight 35% of the manufacturer's list price, i.e. £9,800.

Deborah is reimbursed by Amber Ltd for all the petrol used by her. The cash equivalent of the private use petrol is determined by reference to a scale charge for the *private use of petrol in* ICTA 1988, s. 158. Under the 1998/99 scales, the 1,800cc engine would produce a cash equivalent of £1,280. Subject to any allowable deductions from her Schedule E income, in relation to which there is no information, her Schedule E income profits for inclusion in Stage One of her income tax calculation for the 1998/99 tax year are therefore £19,080, i.e. £9,800 + £8,000 + £1,280.

# CHAPTER FIFTEEN

# INCOME RECEIPTS (2): TRADES, PROFESSIONS AND VOCATIONS

## 15.1 Income Tax and Corporation Tax: Methods of Calculating Trading Profits

In reading the article below, it is necessary to bear in mind that it was written *before* the amendment introduced by FA 1998, s. 42(1), which applies for accounting periods beginning after 6 April 1999: see *Learning Text* at **15.5.2**.

### 15.1.1 RELATIONSHIP BETWEEN SCHEDULE D, CASE I PROFITS AND GAAP

**Akin, B., 'Accountancy Principles and Case I Profits',** *The Tax Journal*,
**22 September 1997, p. 7**

The Taxes Acts give no clue as to the relevance or otherwise of accountancy principles in arriving at profits for the purposes of Cases I and II of Schedule D. The nearest we get is the statement of the basis of assessment in TA 1988, Section 60 that 'income tax shall be charged under Cases I and II of Schedule D on the full amount of the profits or gains of the year of assessment'. Although the legislation is peppered with provisions treating the results of certain transactions as giving rise to a Case I profit and others as not being deductible in computing it, the legislation simply fails to give a starting point. Although Lord Halsbury was able to say in 1892 in *Gresham Life Assurance Society* v *Styles* (3 TC 185, p. 188), 'The word "profits" I think is to be understood in its natural and proper sense — in a sense which no commercial man would misunderstand', the Courts have been troubled many times with disputes as to how trading profits should be calculated.

The purpose of this Article is to give a brief summary of what appears to be the current status of accounting principles as a determinant of Case I profit and to point out one or two trends which have manifested themselves over recent years.

**The Current Position**
The current position, following *Gallagher* v *Jones* (66 TC 77) and *Johnston* v *Britannia Airways* (67 TC 99) can be summarised as follows:

1.  Where accounting principles point unequivocally to a particular treatment of a transaction or state of affairs, that treatment will usually be followed in ascertaining trading profits.
2.  Where conflicting accountancy principles are potentially applicable or where there is no generally accepted principle the Court will do its best to choose the most appropriate method of arriving at trading profit.
3.  In all cases, the accounting treatment will be subject to statutory or judge made override where appropriate; i.e. where taxation principles dictate a different treatment.

### *Gallagher* v *Jones*

After a century or so of case law, the dominant trend that has emerged in recent years is that the Courts will place considerable emphasis on generally accepted accounting principles when they consider disputes as to the nature of trading profits. Accountancy principles are usually the starting point for arriving at trading profit (see, for example, *Odeon Associated Theatres Ltd* v *Jones* (48 TC 257)).

This approach was illustrated in *Gallagher* v *Jones* where the taxpayer's accounts deducted the full amount of 'front-loaded' rentals payable in the period under finance leases of canal boats, rather than the much smaller amount which would have been deducted in arriving at profits if the accounts had followed Statement of Standard Accounting Practice 21 (SSAP 21). The Special Commissioners accepted the unchallenged expert evidence of the accountancy advisor to the Board of Inland Revenue that the taxpayer's accounts gave a completely misleading picture of the trading results of the business for the period in question. The profits had therefore to be recomputed using SSAP 21, which only permitted a deduction for the amounts (presumably, but not actually stated, the finance charge and notional depreciation) properly attributable to the period, having regard to the useful life of the asset. The taxpayer argued that SSAP 21 was overridden by the principle that actual expenditure properly incurred was deductible in the period in which it falls (see *Vallambrosa Rubber Co. Ltd* v *Farmer* 5 TC 529). In the Court of Appeal, Sir Thomas Bingham MR said: 'I find it hard to understand how any judge-made rule could override the application of a generally accepted rule of commercial accountancy which (a) applied to the situation in question (b) was not one of two or more rules applicable to the situation in question and (c) was not shown to be inconsistent with the true facts or otherwise inapt to determine the true profits or losses of the business.'

This dictum leaves plenty of scope for judges to depart from accountancy principles where appropriate, so the general current of opinion that accountancy principles took on greater importance with the judgment in *Gallagher* v *Jones* may turn out to be an overstatement as accounting principles depart further from legal form.

### *Johnston* v *Britannia Airways*

The question of *conflicting* accountancy principles arose in *Johnston* v *Britannia Airways Limited* where the taxpayer accrued the estimated cost of future engine overhauls. The taxpayer brought expert evidence as to the appropriateness of this accounting treatment when challenged by the Inland Revenue. At the hearing before the commissioners, the Revenue's expert put forward an alternative accounting method based upon the capitalisation of engine overhauls *after* they had been performed and their subsequent amortisation. As a result of this conflict of expert evidence, the Special Commissioners had to choose between accounting methods, and they held that the accruals method used by the taxpayer was the more appropriate.

In the High Court, the Inland Revenue argued that the accruals method was inappropriate to the facts because it dealt with future expenses. By way of example, if the taxpayer had ceased trading before carrying out an overhaul, the accrual would, the Revenue argued, have been unnecessary. That argument would, if successful, have virtually destroyed the accruals concept for taxation purposes. It was not accepted. The Revenue also argued that the accruals method was not, on the facts, sufficiently reliable, as in *Southern Railway of Peru Limited* v *Owen* (36 TC 602).

In the High Court, Knox J treated the Special Commissioners' acceptance of the accruals method as a finding of fact, with which he clearly agreed and which he was not prepared to disturb following the well known principles in *Edwards* v *Bairstow* (36 TC 207).

*Johnston* v *Britannia Airways* is of interest because it shows that in the absence of any overriding legal rule, the potential conflict between possible accounting treatments is likely to be viewed as a question of fact for the Commissioners. To some extent, this is an innovation. In *Duple Motor Bodies Limited* v *Ostime* (39 TC 537) the Commissioners chose one of two conflicting but apparently acceptable accounting treatments but, on appeal to the House of Lords, that treatment was rejected and the competing accounting treatment was adopted. The House substituted its own view as to which accounting principle was correct, treating the matter as one of 'common sense' (per Lord Reid at page 571). The House seems to have considered itself quite free to do this, which makes the issue appear to be one of law, rather than one of fact, which is usually a matter for the Commissioners. This apparent conflict between *Johnston v Britannia* and *Duple* is possibly explained by the rather incomplete findings of fact made by the Commissioners in *Duple*, but *Britannia* certainly suggests a trend away from the judges' substituting their own views on accounting for those of the fact finding body.

This still leaves plenty of scope for disputes in the future. For example, the accruals concept often conflicts with the 'prudence' concept (both are in SSAP 2) and the 'correct' application of these two concepts to any given set of facts is often a matter of fine judgment. The writer is aware of at least one case recently before the Special Commissioners (but not yet decided) where conflicting accountancy principles have played a significant part.

### Legal view or profit

The third situation referred to in *Gallagher v Jones* in which accountancy principles may be overridden is extremely broad. It covers the fairly straightforward situation where the accounting treatment is inappropriate having regard to the actual facts. An illustration of this would be where an equipment lease is accounted for as a finance lease within the meaning of SSAP 21, whereas the facts plainly show it to be an operating lease. However, the override goes much further than this. It permits the court to apply a 'legal' view of what constitutes 'profit' for the generally accepted accounting view. A striking example, given the result in *Gallagher v Jones*, is the taxation of finance lessors. SSAP 21 treats finance lessors as not being the owners of leased assets, but as providers of finance. Each payment of lease rental is treated as including an element of principal and an element of interest.

Accordingly only a portion of each rental is taken to the profit and loss account of the lessor. As is well known, tax law is assumed to take a totally different view, treating the entire rental income as income of the trade and hence forming part of profits. Even though the accounting treatment is generally accepted, it is generally assumed not to be appropriate for tax purposes. It is interesting to ask why this is the case. SSAP 21 takes a view of the distinction between capital and revenue which does considerable violence to the principles developed in case law. It treats most of the lease rental as a capital receipt. This feature (and the fact that SSAP 21 would not prevent a finance lessor from claiming capital allowances on the equipment) is arguably sufficient to bring the override into action. But SSAP 21 *was* regarded as appropriate for establishing the quantum of the deduction for finance lease rentals payable by finance lessees in *Gallagher v Jones* even though the lessee is treated by SSAP 21 as paying a mixture of financing charges and notional loan principal, rather than rent. This difficulty was not explored in the Courts in *Gallagher v Jones*. In practice, of course, lessees will rely on Inland Revenue Statement of Practice 3/91 to secure a deduction for the depreciation charge in respect of the equipment, which generally relieves the capital element of the rentals.

### Trends

It is clear that the law in this area is still developing. This is not surprising, given the enormous developments in accountancy theory over recent years. Lord Halsbury's words quoted at the beginning of this article have become increasingly less true, unless one replaces Lord Halsbury's 'commercial man' with 'chartered accountant'.

There is also a clear trend for the Court to rely more heavily on accountancy evidence. Although this might seem at first to be a reasonable way of preventing the court from having to use its own common sense where the opinion of technical experts is available, there are risks. Accountancy is not a precise science. It involves the exercise of considerable skill and judgment to facts and situations where there is frequently room for conflicting views. Rather than setting up an overriding principle of tax law to defeat the taxpayer's position, the Inland Revenue are now much more likely to dispute the accounting treatment adopted by the use of expert accounting evidence. An illustration of the Revenue's recent thinking can be seen in the Revenue Interpretation issued in February 1997 on Employee Share Ownership Trusts, in which they accept that the timing of a trading deduction for contributions to a non statutory ESOT is governed by UITF 13, which may require the deduction to be taken to the contributor's profit and loss account before the expense is incurred. Specific reference is made to the recent cases as justification for this view.

**Tightly controlled**

A second trend which has emerged is for legislation to prescribe that 'profits' for Case I purposes will follow some form of accounting treatment. The loan relationships legislation in the Finance Act 1996 taxes the profits and gains arising from the loan relationships of a company by reference to the credits and debits to be brought into account in accordance with 'an authorised accounting method'. Section 80 of that Act provides that, to the extent that a company is a party to a loan relationship for the purposes of a trade carried on by it, the profits and gains arising from the relationship are to be brought into account in computing the profits and gains of the trade. Even though, superficially, this legislation appears to adopt accountancy principles in arriving at trading profit, it becomes rapidly clear that the authorised methods are tightly controlled; see s. 85. To the extent that accountancy principles in general give a different result, or evolve over the years, they are always overridden by the precise words of the statutory provisions. This apparent adoption of accounting principles by statute is therefore somewhat misleading.

A third trend which comes out of recent legislation is the adoption of the accountancy based measure of profit where that gives a higher taxable profit than the use of 'conventional' tax rules. This can be seen in the finance leasing legislation in FA 1997, sch. 12. This is not, however evidence of a trend towards the adoption of accounting principles generally when taxing a leasing trade. It is if anything more indicative of the Revenue's increasing interest in curbing what they consider to be a form of tax avoidance — where the trading profit for tax purposes is less than the trading profit disclosed in the taxpayer's financial statements, including group accounts.

A potential danger with this method of legislation, quite apart from its complexity, is its unpredictable effect if accountancy principles change. There are already moves to abolish the distinction between finance and operating leases and for all leases to be capitalised.

**The Future**

Accountancy principles are not static. Nor are they drafted with legal precision. Nevertheless, we are likely to see greater reference to them as the determinant of taxable profit as the British taxation system slowly evolves away from the schedular system. This will not necessarily reduce the incidence of disputes between taxpayers and the Revenue on the correct measure of trading profit. It is, however, likely to shift the emphasis towards disputes between accountancy experts. Given the necessary flexibility of accountancy principles, this is likely to inject a further (and unwelcome) element of uncertainty into our system.

### 15.1.2  BASES FOR CALCULATING TRADING INCOME

**Pye, S., 'Young Bar Exempt From Professional Tax Charge', *The Lawyer*, 24 March 1998, p. 44**

THE INLAND Revenue is to exempt newly-qualified barristers from forthcoming changes to the way lawyers pay tax, after the Bar showered it with objections to the proposals.

In last week's Budget, the Government confirmed it would be pressing ahead with its controversial plan, announced just before Christmas, to tax professionals on their earnings, including work in progress, as opposed to a cash received basis.

However, it deferred the change for a year — to April 1999 — to give barristers and solicitors time to develop adequate accounting systems.

And, in a significant concession to the Bar, it said new barristers would be able to pay tax on the old cash received basis for the first seven years of practice.

In a further concession, the deeply unpopular catch-up charge — tax payable on any bills outstanding in 1999–2000 — can now be paid off over 10, rather than three, years.

Each year, lawyers will pay either a 10th of their catch-up charge, or 10 per cent of normal profits, whichever is smaller.

If, in any year, a sole practitioner makes a loss, they pay nothing towards the catch-up charge.

However, after 10 years the catch-up charge must be paid in full, regardless of profitability.

Both the Bar Council and the Law Society have expressed anger that the plans are still going ahead, but they have welcomed the concessions. The Bar Council is particularly pleased over the extra concession it won.

Of over 600 objections received by the Inland Revenue to the plans, 350 came from barristers.

David Milne QC, a member of the special Bar Council committee looking at the reforms, said there was relief around the Bar. 'It's solved most of the worst problems.'

He added that the Inland Revenue had promised to collaborate with lawyers on the introduction of the reforms, which could lead to further concessions.

Heather Hallett QC, chairman of the Bar Council, was disappointed that the Government had chosen to go ahead, but was 'pleased that they have recognised our concerns, particularly about barristers just starting out'.

Ron Downhill, chair of the Law Society's revenue law committee, said the concessions had saved many high street firms from bankruptcy, although they still faced hardship.

## 15.2 End of Chapter Assessment Question

The three partners of Brown & Co. (see **4.6** and **9.3**) have traditionally calculated their Schedule D, Case II profits on the bills delivered basis.

In their accounting period to 30 November 1998, they are awarded damages for loss of profits of £5,000 against a company of computer consultants. This sum relates to the disruption to their business caused by defective installation of a computer system in January/February 1995.

Advise them:

(a) How FA 1998 will affect them, as to the basis on which their Schedule D, Case II profits are calculated.

(b) Whether the £5,000 damages are a receipt falling under Schedule D, Case II.

## 15.3 End of Chapter Assessment Outline Answer

(a) The bills delivered basis, on which the three partners of Brown & Co. have traditionally calculated their Schedule D, Case II profits, means that their income for any accounting period consists of the bills sent out to their customers in that period. Equally, their expenditure is identified according to the bills received by them in that period. Their trading profit (or loss) for an accounting period is the difference between the two.

FA 1998 requires the profits of a trade, profession or vocation to be computed on an accounting basis which gives a true and fair view, subject to any adjustment required or authorised by law in computing profits for those purposes. With limited exceptions, FA 1998 will therefore apply the earnings basis to all Schedule D, Case I and Case II profits, for accounting periods beginning after 6 April 1999. By contrast with the bills delivered basis, the earnings basis means that the partners will need to take the income earned, rather than the bills sent out, as their income for an accounting period. Their expenditure will be identified according to the expenditure incurred by them, irrespective of whether they have actually paid the bills, and irrespective of whether their clients have paid them. Their income profit (or loss) for an accounting period will again be the difference between the two figures. They will need to ascribe a value to work-in-progress, i.e. unfinished and therefore unbilled work. This means that their income profits will be included in their income tax calculations for an earlier tax year than would have been the case under the bills delivered basis. It also means that bad debts will be deductible from income only in the accounting period when they are actually shown to be bad.

(b) In their accounting period to 30 November 1998, the partners of Brown & Co. are awarded damages of £5,000 for loss of profits. The fact that the damages relate to the disruption to their business is highly significant. Whether the damages are Schedule D, Case II income, so far as the partners are concerned, depends on the relationship between the payment and the business carried on by them. In *London and Thames Haven Oil Wharves Ltd* v *Attwooll* [1967] 1 Ch 772, Diplock LJ said that, if a trader receives compensation for non-receipt of trading income, that compensation is itself to be treated as trading income. These damages represent non-receipt of Schedule D, Case II income, and therefore fall under Schedule D, Case II in the partners' individual income tax calculations.

# CHAPTER SIXTEEN

# INCOME RECEIPTS (3): SAVINGS INCOME

## 16.1   Types of Entitlement to Savings Income

### 16.1.1   BENEFICIARIES OF A TRUST

**McCutcheon, B., 'Interests in Possession Again — s. 31 of the Trustee Act 1925',**
*The Law Society's Gazette*, **1 October 1980, p. 951**

Section 31 of the Trustee Act 1925 has always been important for tax purposes. The introduction of [IHT] with its distinction between settled property in which there is a subsisting interest in possession and settled property in which there is no such interest, coupled with the favoured treatment extended to accumulation and maintenance trusts, had made it even more so. Nevertheless, the full effects of s. 31 often go unappreciated.

The main reason s. 31 is important for tax purposes is that it can dramatically affect in two ways a beneficiary's entitlement to trust income. First, it can remove from a beneficiary, simply because he is a minor, the entitlement to income which he would have under the trust instrument if he were an adult. This is what might be called the 'deferring' effect of s. 31. Second, s. 31 may give to an adult beneficiary an entitlement to income which under the trust instrument he would otherwise lack. This might be called the 'accelerating' effect of s. 31.

The effect of s. 31 on a beneficiary's entitlement to trust income may, in turn, be decisive in determining (*i*) whether or not he has an interest in possession in the trust property for tax purposes, and (*ii*) how income arising to the trustees is to be treated for tax purposes. If the beneficiary is entitled to the income he will have an interest in possession in the trust property, in which case he will be assessable to income tax on income arising to the trust and for [IHT] purposes will fall to be charged under the main [IHT] charging provisions, on the footing that he is beneficially entitled to the property in which his interest subsists. The fact that the beneficiary has an interest in possession may also be relevant for CGT purposes under [TCGA 1992, ss. 72(1) to 76]. If the beneficiary is not entitled to the income he will not have an interest in possession under the trust, with the result that the trustees will be assessable to [the special rate applicable to trusts], on the income arising to them, and the trust will for [IHT] purposes be accorded the rather harsh treatment meted out to discretionary trusts (unless, of course, it is a favoured accumulation and maintenance trust).

. . .

**Kerridge, R., 'The Taxation of Trust Income', (1994) 110 LQR 84, pp. 92–96**

(Note: This article was written when the special rate applicable to trusts was 35%, and the basic rate of income tax was 25%.)

We may start with questions (i) and (ii):

(i)   how should income (generally) be taxed when in the process of being accumulated?

(ii)   should there be any special rule for income accumulated for the settlor?

The two questions are interlinked. There will only be a need for a special rule for income accumulated for the settlor if the standard accumulation rule is relatively generous. If it is possible to devise a standard rule for accumulations which is thought to be reasonably fair, there may be no need for any subsidiary rule to cover what is to happen if income is accumulated for the settlor.

So, what is now the standard rule for accumulations? Is it over-generous? The standard rule at the present time is that income which is being accumulated and to which, during a year of assessment, no individual taxpayer is entitled, shall be taxed at the basic rate of 25 per cent, plus an 'additional rate' of 10 per cent, thus giving a total rate of 35 per cent. Given that there is now only one higher rate of income tax, and that it is 40 per cent, the 35 per cent rate on accumulated income is *not* generous. The accumulation rate is, relatively speaking, much less favourable than it used to be. From the inception of income tax until 1973 accumulated income was taxed at the *standard rate* of income tax, which was the normal rate paid by an individual on his investment income. From 1973 to 1984 it was taxed at the *basic rate* plus the *additional rate* (which was known colloquially as the 'investment income surcharge'); but this combined rate was again the normal rate paid by an individual on his investment income. Since 1984 the normal rate for investment income has been the basic rate by itself, yet income which is being accumulated continues to be subject to taxation at the basic rate *plus* the additional rate. And when the higher rate structure was simplified in 1988, leaving only one higher rate, the effect was that the rate for income which was being accumulated was much closer to the top rate of tax than it was to the basic rate.

Let us compare the figures. In 1920 the standard rate of income tax, which was the normal rate of tax paid by an individual on his investment income, was 30 per cent, the rate for income which was being accumulated was the same, 30 per cent, while the top rate of tax on an individual's investment income was 60 per cent. In 1922 (the year the anti-avoidance provisions were enacted) the rates were, respectively, 25 per cent, 25 per cent and 55 per cent. In 1940 the rates were 42.5 per cent, 42.5 per cent and 90 per cent. In 1941 they were 50 per cent, 50 per cent and 97.5 per cent. So the accumulation rate remained the standard rate and was much lower than the top rate. In 1978 they were 49 per cent, 49 per cent and 98 per cent, in 1983 they were 45 per cent, 45 per cent, and 75 per cent. But in 1984 they were 30 per cent, 45 per cent, and 60 per cent and since 1988 they have been 25 per cent, 35 per cent and 40 per cent. The standard accumulation rate has moved away from being the same as the normal rate paid by an individual on his investment income, and is now nearer to the top rate than to the basic rate, only 5 per cent below the top rate.

So, the current rule is nothing like as generous to income which is being accumulated as the rule used to be 20 years ago. What is wrong with the rule now? Is there any good reason to want to change it? The authors of the Consultative Document set out to consider whether there was 'a satisfactory alternative' to the additional rate system; but the suggestion they put forward was, it is submitted, no improvement on the present system. It seems to have been a question of suggesting change for change's sake. The Consultative Document suggested abolishing the additional rate, the extra 10 per cent, on accumulated income and then taxing accumulation trusts *either* at the basic rate of 25 per cent *or* at the higher rate of 40 per cent. Smaller accumulation trusts would be taxed at the basic rate and bigger ones at the higher rate — this could be achieved by having a threshold of undistributed income, below which income would be taxed at the basic rate and above which it would be taxed at the higher rate.

The proposal can be presented as a simplification. At the present time there are four rates of income tax; the lower rate — 20 per cent; the basic rate — 25 per cent; the basic plus additional rate — 35 per cent; and the higher rate — 40 per cent. The proposal would abolish one rate, which makes for neatness and simplicity; at least, that is the way it is presented by the Consultative Document. The suggestion is not entirely convincing. Of course it is true that the fewer rates there are, the neater the system will be, but neatness is not everything. And if there were particular merit in this sort of neatness, it must have been an error to have introduced the lower rate in 1992, which was not a simplification.

The Consultative Document suggests that abolishing the additional rate and taxing undistributed income at basic and higher rates would also make for administrative simplicity where trustees have a discretion to accumulate or distribute. Under the present system, trustees of accumulation or discretionary trusts pay (25 + 10 =)35 per cent tax on all their income. There is no problem if the income is accumulated, but if it is distributed, it is then distributed with a 35 per cent credit. If the recipient is a higher rate taxpayer, he has to pay another 5 per cent while if he is a basic rate taxpayer he is entitled to a refund of 10 per cent. This is untidy. The Consultative Document implies that changing over to a system where accumulated income is taxed at 25 per cent or 40 per cent somehow avoids a problem which is inherent in the present system. This is not true. The administrative problem arises because trustees of a discretionary or accumulation trust must, as the rules are framed at present, pay the 35 per cent *before* they distribute the income. But there is no reason why the rules could not be modified to provide that they should pay only 25 per cent before distribution and an extra 10 per cent if income is not distributed within a specified period, e.g., before the end of the tax year. That gets rid of the administrative problem. All beneficiaries who receive income would receive it with a tax credit of 25 per cent. Basic rate payers would not have to bother with refunds and would have no more to pay. Higher rate payers would have to pay another 15 per cent.

The problem with the suggestion made in the Consultative Document, that the income from an accumulation trust should pay more tax if it exceeds a particular threshold is that this *must* encourage settlors and their advisers to attempt trust splitting — what the Consultative Document calls 'fragmentation.' If the accumulated income from a trust will be taxed at 25 per cent if it does not exceed £12,000 a year but will be taxed at 40 per cent if it does exceed £12,000 a year then it will obviously be to the beneficiaries' advantage if a trust with an accumulated income of £24,000 p.a. could be split into two trusts, and so on. A number of small accumulation trusts would pay less tax than one large one. The response to this is obvious. There would have to be an *anti-fragmentation* rule. There already exists such a rule for capital gains tax, and what amounts to a completely different anti-fragmentation rule for inheritance tax. If the 35 per cent rate is replaced, there needs to be an anti-fragmentation rule for income tax. So much for simplification. Getting rid of the 35 per cent rate really means replacing one rate with two rates and then having to add an anti-avoidance rule (or rules) to prevent taxpayers from paying at the lower rate when they should be paying at the higher.

If the present structure of income tax rates for individuals is to be retained, with a basic rate of 25 per cent, or even with a basic rate of 20 per cent, and a top rate of 40 per cent, then taxing income which is being accumulated at 35 per cent is probably about right and reasonably fair. Such income will usually end up in the hands of persons who would have paid tax at the higher rate and so there will be a small saving for them. But this is at the expense of having had to wait for the income: in effect it acts as a higher rate taxpayer's tax-effective savings scheme. There is nothing wrong with that, provided the incentive is not excessive. It is submitted that, at 5 per cent, it is not.

If the present structure of income tax rates for individuals (i.e. the rates of 20 per cent, 25 per cent and 40 per cent) is not retained, the suggestion made in the Consultative Document would not work anyway. The issue would have to be reconsidered. If top rates of tax were increased, it would be necessary either to tax accumulated income at a rate somewhere between the basic rate and the top rate, probably closer to the top than to the basic, or to tax the income by reference to the taxpayer to whom it was ultimately distributed, possibly using some form of top-slicing. For example, if income were accumulated for nine years and then paid out to the settlor's adult child, the sum paid out could be divided by the number of years, nine, and the resulting sum added to the beneficiary's income. The extra tax due on it could be calculated and that figure could be multiplied by nine. The final figure would be the tax payable, giving credit for any tax paid during the accumulation period. But none of this need concern us if we stay with the sort of graduation which we have at the present time, and a top rate of tax which is in the 40 per cent range.

What of income which is being accumulated for the settlor? Ever since 1922, the rule has been that income which is being accumulated for the settlor, or which is being accumulated and *may* find its way into the hands of the settlor, will be taxed as the settlor's income. But, to make sure that settlors cannot cheat (and the Revenue appear to take a rather adverse view of settlors) the rule has been expanded to what are now *13 sections* in the 1988 income tax consolidation. There is no doubt that the basic rule could be enacted in a virtually avoidance-proof form without the need for *so many* sections, and the Consultative Document proposes a simplification of the present provisions. Certainly it would be better to simplify the provisions than to leave them as they are; but is it really worth the bother of retaining the basic rule at all? Following on from what has been said above in relation to the standard accumulation rate, could one not simply abolish the rule itself and permit a settlor to accumulate income for himself paying tax of 35 per cent? All he would save would be 5 per cent.

## 16.2   Dividends

**Good, T., and Birkett, S., 'Dividend Income of Trusts and Beneficiaries',**
*The Tax Journal*, **13 January 1994, p. 18**

(Note that, when this article was written, the special rate applicable to trusts was 35%, and the basic rate of income tax was 25%, the 25% rate applying to Schedule D, Case III interest. The personal allowance was £3,445.)

**The Basic Rules**
Trustees are assessed to income tax on trust income in their capacity as trustees and not in a personal capacity. Thus there can be no personal allowances to set against the trust income.

Normally there is no tax deduction for trust expenses unless they comprise fixed remuneration for the trustees, as determined by the trust deed. Fixed remuneration will be treated as a charge on the trust's income, paid net of basic rate tax (see *Baxendale* v *Murphy* 9 TC 76). It will therefore still not be deductible from any source of income. However, any expenses specifically deductible against a source of trust income (for example, letting expenses for a trust property that is let) may be set against that source.

Where the income of the trust is payable to beneficiaries who have an interest in possession, the trustees should provide the beneficiaries with certificates of tax deducted (Form R185E) that show the net payment to the beneficiary, the tax deducted at source by the trustees, and the gross income to be included in the beneficiary's own tax return.

The same basic rules apply to trusts with no interest in possession (that is, discretionary trusts and accumulation and maintenance settlements).

However, in addition to their basic rate liability, trustees of discretionary trusts must pay additional rate tax (10 per cent since 1988/89). Additional rate tax falls due on 1 December following the end of the tax year.

Genuine revenue expenses of the trustees that were disallowed in the calculation of basic rate tax may be deducted (grossed-up for basic rate tax) in calculating the additional rate tax liability. Annuities and charges on trust income will also be allowed at their gross amounts.

**Interest in Possession Trusts**
For 1993/94 and later tax years, trustees of both interest in possession and discretionary trusts will need to deal carefully with dividend income when computing the trust's tax liabilities.

Trusts subject to an interest in possession will enjoy the lower 20 per cent tax rate on dividend income (but obtain a lower tax credit). Because such trusts only pay tax at 20 per cent on dividends, it is only possible to pass to the beneficiary a tax credit at that lower rate. It is therefore essential to analyse the distribution to the beneficiary and distinguish between the amount that can be traced to dividends received by the trust and the amount that arises from other sources. In performing this analysis trustees must set the trust expenses (which, remember, are not tax-deductible) against dividend income rather than other income (see FA 1993, s. 79(3)).

The example which follows illustrates this.

**Example 1**
The Euridice Trust was established by Proserpine, Caronte having a life interest in the whole of the income from the trust assets. The income of the trustees in 1993/94 is as follows:

|  | £ |
|---|---|
| Schedule A rentals, less eligible expenses | 30,000 |
| Building society interest received | 15,000 |
| Dividends received from UK companies | 28,000 |

The trustees incurred eligible expenses amounting to £3,750 during the year. The tax computation of the trust will show:

|  |  | Tax credit |
|---|---|---|
|  | £ | £ |
| Schedule A | 30,000 | Nil |
| Building society interest (£15,000 × $^{100}/_{75}$) | 20,000 | 5,000 |
| Schedule F (£28,000 × $^{100}/_{80}$) | 35,000 | 7,000 |
|  | £85,000 | £12,000 |

The taxable income of the trustees is £85,000, of which £50,000 is taxable at 25 per cent and £35,000 (the Schedule F income) at 20 per cent. Thus total tax borne by the trustees will be £19,500.

The distributable income on which Caronte is to be assessed is calculated as:

|  | Basic rate | Lower rate |
|---|---|---|
|  | £ | £ |
| Income | 50,000 | 35,000 |
| Tax borne | 12,500 | 7,000 |
|  | 37,500 | 28,000 |
| Trustees' expenses |  | 3,750 |
| Distributable | £37,500 | £24,250 |
| Tax credits (at $^{25}/_{75}$ and $^{20}/_{80}$, respectively) | £12,500 | £6,063 |

Caronte (who has no other source of income) is taxed on the gross income of £80,313 (£37,500 + £12,500 + £24,250 + £6,063); after a personal allowance of £3,445 his taxable income is £76,868, of which £2,500 is taxed at 20 per cent, £21,200 is taxed at 25 per cent and £53,168 (including £30,313 of Schedule F income) is taxed at 40 per cent. Total tax borne is £27,067, against which the tax credits totalling £18,563 are set, to leave a net liability of £8,504.

Had the expenses been deducted from the distributable other income rather than the dividends, Caronte would have had a smaller tax credit to recover.

### Discretionary Trusts

Trustees of discretionary trusts within ICTA 1988, s. 686, will, from 1993/94, pay tax at a single rate, the 'rate applicable to trusts', which is equal to the sum of the basic and additional rates (s. 686(1A)). The rate applicable to trusts will also apply to dividend income received in a discretionary trust, so the 20 per cent lower rate of tax is only relevant to such trusts inasmuch as the tax credit on such dividends is at that rate.

The deduction for trustees' expenses 'properly chargeable to income' is extended to deduction for the purposes of the rate applicable to trusts (previously additional rate only). However, the amount of income needed to defray the trustees' expenses will continue to be taxed at basic rate (if such income is not dividend income), or lower rate if the income is dividend income.

Where part of the trustees' income is not chargeable to United Kingdom tax (by reason of the trustees being treated as not resident in the United Kingdom) the expenses must be apportioned over the taxable and non-taxable income and only the amount apportioned to taxable income will be so allowable.

### Example 2

The Orfeo Trust is a discretionary trust established by Plutone. The income and expenses of the trustees for 1993/94 are as for the Euridice Trust above, except that, instead of dividends, the trustees receive debenture interest of £27,000.

The tax computation of the trustees is:

| | £ | Tax credit £ |
|---|---|---|
| Schedule A | 30,000 | Nil |
| Building society interest (£15,000 × $^{100}/_{75}$) | 20,000 | 5,000 |
| Debenture interest (£27,000 × $^{100}/_{75}$) | 36,000 | 9,000 |
| | 86,000 | £14,000 |
| Trustees' expenses (£3,750 × $^{100}/_{75}$) | 5,000 | |
| | £81,000 | |
| Tax at the rate applicable to trusts (35 per cent) | 28,350 | |
| Tax at basic rate on the expenses 25 per cent × £5,000 | 1,250 | |
| | 29,600 | |
| Less: tax credits suffered and imputed | 14,000 | |
| Tax payable by direct assessment | £15,600 | |

The real fun starts where the expenses are paid out of dividend income. If a discretionary trust receives nothing but dividends, the income needed to defray the expenses will be income taxed at the lower rate only and so the expenses should be grossed up for a 20 per cent rather than a 25 per cent rate.

**Example 3**
A discretionary trust receives net dividends of £12,000 (£15,000 gross) and incurs expenses of £1,200. Because *all* of the income is dividend income the expenses are grossed up at 20 per cent and become £1,200 × 100/80 = £1,500. The trust tax is therefore £13,500 × 35 per cent + £1,500 × 20 per cent = £5,025.

If instead the £12,000 (£16,000 gross) had been net building society interest the expenses would be grossed up at 25 per cent to £1,600 and the trust tax would be £14,400 × 35 per cent + £1,600 × 25 per cent = £5,440.

If the income had been £6,000 (£7,500 gross) of dividends and £6,000 (£8,000 gross) of building society interest, section 79(3) ensures that the expenses are deemed to come out of the dividend income first and so would be grossed up to £1,500. The trust tax would be £14,000 × 35 per cent + £1,500 × 20 per cent = £5,200.

We wonder what the tax position would be if the income consisted of £900 net dividends and £11,100 net building society interest.

**Discretionary Trust Beneficiaries**
Since the trustees have paid tax at 35 per cent on the distributable income, the tax credit that can be passed to the beneficiary with any income that is distributed will continue to be at the rate of 35/65 of the net distribution. It does not matter what the source of the income is — it can only be distributed if the rate applicable to trusts has been paid (either under s. 686 or under *ibid*, s. 687) and so the 35 per cent credit applies.

## 16.3   End of Chapter Assessment Question

Refer to the facts involving Amber Ltd and its shareholders: **2.4** and **8.4**. In 1998/99, Deborah receives interest on securities held for her by Georgina and Harry, who are the trustees of Deborah's uncle Frederick's will trust. Deborah has a life interest in possession under the will trust. In the 1998/99 tax year, she receives £800 net in interest from the debentures in Megabucks plc (see **8.4**). Under Charlie's will, cash gifts of £2,000 each are made to Alan, Bertram and Deborah. The will provides for them to receive interest on their cash gifts, from Charlie's death (on 28 September 1998), to the date of the receipt of the separate cheques for the gifts and the interest in March 1999.

(a)   Having calculated the amounts for inclusion in Deborah's 1998/99 income tax calculation (see **8.4**), comment on the total income tax due from the trustees, on the basis that the trust has no other source of income in 1998/99.

(b)   On the assumption that the cheques for £2,000 are paid over to Alan, Bertram and Deborah on 1 March 1999, together with cheques for interest of £150 each, comment on the income tax position of each of the beneficiaries in relation to the interest received.

## 16.4   End of Chapter Assessment Outline Answer

(a)   Uncle Frederick's will trust is not a trust to which ICTA 1988, s. 686 applies, since Deborah has a life interest in possession under it. Georgina and Harry, as trustees, are therefore liable to pay only basic rate income tax on the taxable income of the trust. The only income of the trust is savings income, so their basic rate liability is satisfied by the lower rate income tax deducted at source by Megabucks plc: ICTA 1988, s. 349. Deborah receives a tax credit for the lower rate tax deducted at source: see **8.4**.

(b)   Since the interest will be received gross by them, the whole £150 will be included in Stage One of their income tax calculations for 1998/99. There is no credit to be given at Stage Six, since no income tax will have been deducted at source by Bertram, the executor. The capital amounts of £2,000 each do not, of course, enter their income tax calculations at all.

However, were Deborah not actually to receive the interest from Bertram, she would not include it in Stage One at all. This is shown by *Dewar* v *IRC* [1935] 2 KB 351, where the Court of Appeal held that, since a general legatee had not actually received the interest to which he was entitled, it must not be included in his statutory income for the tax year under consideration.

# CHAPTER SEVENTEEN

# INCOME RECEIPTS (4): INCOME FROM LAND

## 17.1  Rents

### 17.1.1  INDIVIDUALS

**Williams, D., 'Income From Property', *The Tax Journal*, 22 June 1995, p. 12**

(Note: the figures given for rent-a-room relief are now superseded.)

The new régime completely rewrites section 15(1). It starts by saying that Schedule A applies to 'the annual profits or gains arising from any business carried on for the exploitation, as a source of rents or other receipts, of any estate, interest or rights in or over any land in the United Kingdom' (paragraph 1(1) of the new Schedule A in section 15). Paragraph 1(2) goes on to deem any transaction entered into by any person for the exploitation of any such estate, etc, as such a source to be a transaction in the course of such a 'business'. Paragraph 1(3) then says that 'receipts' in that definition includes:

- payments in respect of licences to occupy or otherwise use land;
- payments for the exercise of any other right over land; and
- rentcharges, ground annuals, feu duties and other annual payments reserved in respect of land or charged on it. Interest, profits from woodlands (still tax-free) and the specific land-related matters which fall within Schedule D by statute, such as farming, mineral rents, etc, are then excluded from Schedule A by paragraph 2.

Furnished lettings are also specifically included (see below), as are caravan and houseboat lettings (paragraph 3 of the new Schedule A). Commercial woodland rents are, of course, still exempt from income tax.

By section 145, which was added in Standing Committee, mineral and similar rents (within ICTA 1988, section 119) paid after 1 May 1995 are payable gross, though one half is still regarded as capital under *ibid*, section 122. . . .

**Implications**

The Inland Revenue is thought to take the view that this restructuring does not remove any types of income from Schedule A (it adds several, as noted below). In particular, where income from land is concerned, the old case law distinction between the passive exploitation of property rights to produce income (Schedule A) and the active occupation of land for profit (Schedule D, Case I or II) is apparently intended to be reflected in the new wording (see cases such as *Salisbury House Estate Ltd* v *Fry* 15 TC 266, which will remain relevant).

The use of the phrase 'annual profits or gains' in paragraph 1(1) of the new Schedule A indicates that items of a capital nature are still excluded (compare *McClure* v *Petre* [1988] STC 749, concerning one-off payments for tipping rights). The new reference to 'any licence to occupy or otherwise use any land' in paragraph 1(3)(*a*) is apparently intended as a catch-all for any payments of an income nature involving giving rights over land and seems to be intended to replace the former paragraph 1(c) of section 15(1), which referred to 'other receipts arising to a person from or by virtue of his ownership of an estate', etc.

### A 'business'

There is no definition of a 'business' for this purpose and this could cause some problems. The Inland Revenue is likely to refer to the VAT cases on the meaning of the phrase 'in the course or furtherance of any business' in VATA 1994, section 4(1). These naturally give the word a very wide meaning — for example, 'the deliberate carrying on, continuously, of an activity . . . [it] does not require that what is done must be done commercially, in the popular sense, or with the object of making profits' (see *Commissioners of Customs and Excise* v *Morrison's Academy Boarding Houses Association* [1978] STC 1).

There could be scope for some interesting argument, however, especially bearing in mind the *dictum* of Lord Diplock in *American Leaf Blending Co. Sdn Bhd* v *Director-General of Inland Revenue* [1978] STC 561, at page 565:

> In the case of a private individual it may well be that the mere receipt of rents from property that he owns raises no presumption that he is carrying on a business.

Presumably, the intention of paragraph 1(2), which deems any transaction entered into for the exploitation as a source of rents, etc, of an interest in land, to be in the course of a business, is to defeat any such argument, and in practice it is difficult to see how any income currently within Schedule A is going to escape. It will not help to argue that lettings are casual, or not organised in a 'businesslike' manner.

### Furnished lettings included

As expected, paragraph 4 of the new Schedule A brings furnished lettings into Schedule A in respect of all payments, whether for the use of the premises or the furniture. This does not apply where the activity amounts to a trade (paragraph 4(2)).

None of these changes appears to disturb the position of:

■ furnished holiday lettings within the special rules in ICTA 1988, section 503 — paragraph 21 of Schedule 6 adapts these rules so that they will still operate in the same way as before, in particular ensuring that full 'trader' treatment as regards loss relief, earned income status, rollover relief and retirement relief will remain available; and
■ 'Rent-a-room' relief — paragraph 38 of Schedule 6 adapts this legislation so that rental income not exceeding £3,250 is still exempt. However, if the income from such lettings exceeds £3,250, the first £3,250 is part of the Schedule A 'business' result.

The previous right to elect for the 'furniture' rent to be taxed under Schedule A (section 15(2)) has, of course, been overtaken by these rules (see paragraph 1 of Schedule 6).

. . .


## 17.2   Other Relevant Taxes

### 17.2.1   VALUE ADDED TAX

**Pickering, J.C.G., 'VAT on Property', *Solicitors Journal*, 15 April 1994, p. 370**

The matters concerning value added tax on property are covered by [VATA 1994, sch. 9, Group 1]. This group has caused more disputes and more difficulties between Customs and Excise and the business community than any other. There was a fundamental review of the law by the Finance Act 1989 which has tidied up the legislation and made it more logical.

This article does not seek to be a detailed review of the legislation, but merely to draw one or two points to the notice of the solicitor who is not usually involved in questions of VAT on land.

### Construction

From 1 April 1989 the supply of all goods and services in connection with non-qualifying construction work is standard-rated. All commercial construction, alteration or maintenance of new or existing buildings is standard-rated. The definition of qualifying buildings includes domestic buildings designed as dwellings as well as buildings which are intended for use solely for a relevant residential or charitable purpose.

There are obviously problems with buildings that are built for mixed purposes, as well as with some of the definitions within the section relating to residential or charitable purposes. Care also has to be taken where there is a change in use from a qualifying to a non-qualifying use of a building within 10 years of its construction. A VAT charge will arise, even if the owner is not currently registered for VAT.

Thus where a charity owning a hospice which was built for it sells the building to a private clinic, it will be required to register and pay VAT on the sale price. This is not a problem if the sale agreement included VAT, but could be considerably embarrassing if the charity had to pay VAT out of the proceeds of sale and was unable to recover the tax from the purchaser.

### Letting

So much for the construction of buildings, what about the letting of them? Leases of qualifying buildings are always exempt from VAT, unless it is a lease of at least 21 years by the person who constructed it. In this case, the lease is likely to be zero-rated. Only the premium, or the first payment of rent, is so treated; thereafter, payments of rent revert to being exempt.

The granting of any lease in relation to commercial property is exempt from tax. This is the case whether or not the building is a new or a refurbished building. However, the owner of the building or the landlord can waive this exemption. Such a waiver is known as the option to tax. The election must be made in writing, and normally covers a period commencing not more than 30 days prior to the written notification of the election being received by the Customs and Excise. The Commissioners have power to extend this time, effectively back-dating the election, but such power is entirely discretionary and should not be relied upon.

### Pros and cons of option to tax

Why should such an election be made? Providing the election is made in good time, then the VAT on the costs of purchase, building or refurbishment can be reclaimed. The election, however, is irrevocable, and a number of points flow from the election.

The rule is that the election applies on a plot by plot, or building by building, basis. Thus it is possible to pick and choose which plots or buildings are registered for VAT. Equally, just because a person has one building registered for VAT, it does not mean that any future buildings purchased are automatically registered.

It should be noted, however, where two buildings are linked by a bridge or subway, they are treated as one building. Likewise individual units in a shopping precinct are all treated as one building. In these circumstances care should be taken to ensure that the election is suitable for all the linked buildings or units.

The consequences of an election are that VAT must be added to all rent charges and VAT must be added to the sale price of the building. Obviously if the likely tenant or purchaser is also registered for VAT, then there is no problem. The VAT is simply reclaimed by the tenant or purchaser in the normal way. However, if the likely tenant or purchaser is exempt from VAT (a financial institution for example), they will not appreciate VAT at the standard rate being added to their outgoings.

It is true, of course, that if the building is to be let to an exempt tenant, and therefore an election is not made, a higher premium and rent may be claimed to cover the unrecoverable VAT on building or refurbishment.

### Prophetic skills needed

It would seem that most of those involved in the purchase, sale or letting of property need a crystal ball when deciding how to deal with the VAT question. The solicitor should be especially careful when his client asks for his predictions of the future.

Sinfield, G., and Davis, A., 'VAT and Property Transactions', Part 4, *The Tax Journal*, 10 December 1992, pp. 6, 9

## COMMERCIAL AND NON-COMMERCIAL PROPERTY TRANSACTIONS

| Type of transaction | VAT treatment as at November 1992 |
|---|---|
| **COMMERCIAL PROPERTIES** | |
| Freehold sale of 'new' building (that is, less than three years old) | 17.5% (compulsory) |
| Freehold sale of building not yet completed (whether or not preceded by a letting) | 17.5% (compulsory) |
| Freehold sale of 'new' civil engineering work | 17.5% (compulsory) |
| Freehold sale of civil engineering work not yet completed | 17.5% (compulsory) |
| Separate grant of facilities for parking a vehicle, playing sports or housing aircraft | 17.5% (compulsory) |
| Grants of certain rights in respect of theatre boxes, hotels, holiday accommodation, caravans and camping facilities and rights to take fish, game and timber | 17.5% (compulsory) |
| Any sale of a lease preceded by election to waive exemption | 17.5% (compulsory) |
| Payment of capital sum to prospective tenant to induce him to take up lease | 17.5% (compulsory) |
| Payment for release of restrictive covenant or easements | 17.5% (compulsory) |
| Sale of leasehold of 'new' building or building not yet completed or 'new' civil engineering work or civil engineering work not yet completed | Exempt (election available) |
| Grant of lease for a premium or at a rent (whether of 'new' building, one not yet completed or otherwise) | Exempt (election available) |
| Letting pursuant to a 'developmental lease', licence or tenancy | 17.5% (compulsory) |
| Any sale of a lease where option not exercised | Exempt (election available) |
| Sale of existing (old) building whether freehold or leasehold | Exempt (election available) |
| Exercise of power of sale by mortgagee (whether or not mortgagor has exercised option over mortgaged land) | Supplies by mortgagee deemed to be made by mortgagor |

. . .

| | |
|---|---|
| **NON-COMMERCIAL PROPERTIES** | |
| Grant of a major interest (which is also the first supply) in a new non-commercial property by 'person constructing' | Zero-rated |
| Grant of a major interest in a non-commercial property by someone other than 'person constructing' | Exempt |
| Grant of any other interest in a non-commercial property | Exempt |
| Self-supply on change to *commercial* use (not dwellings) | 17.5% (compulsory) |
| **GENERAL** | |
| Transfer of a going concern | No supply for VAT purposes |

## 17.3   End of Chapter Assessment Questions

(a)  Hugh, the barrister (see **7.4**), is one of three trustees of The Smallpiece (1998) Discretionary Trust. None of the income profits of the trust have been appointed to any of its class of beneficiaries in 1998/99. For 1998/99, the trust accounts show *expenditure* totalling £2,400, made up as follows:

| | |
|---|---|
| Auditors' remuneration | 750 |
| Other administrative expenses | 50 |
| Allowable deductions under Schedule A | 1,600 |

In 1998/99, the trust has Schedule A income of £9,200, and receives *net* dividends from its shareholding in Moneybags Ltd of £3,000.

Calculate the total income tax due from Hugh and his fellow-trustees for 1998/99.

(b)  Refer to **2.4**. Will Deborah be liable to pay income tax on the rental of £150 per month from Edwina?

## 17.4   End of Chapter Assessment Outline Answers

(a)             INCOME TAX CALCULATION OF THE TRUSTEES OF THE
       SMALLPIECE (1998) DISCRETIONARY TRUST FOR THE TAX YEAR 1998/99

(Numbers in square brackets refer to Notes at the end.)

| | £ |
|---|---|
| Profit from let properties (Schedule A) [1] | 7,600 |
| *Plus* Dividends (Schedule F) [2] | 2,750 |
| *Statutory/Total income* | 10,350 |
| | |
| £10,350 at 34% | 3,519 |
| | |
| *Total tax* [3] | 3,519 |
| | |
| *Less* Tax credited as paid [4] | (550) |
| | |
| TOTAL INCOME TAX DUE | 2,969 |

*Notes*:
[1]   i.e. £9,200 − £1,600.
[2]   i.e. £3,000 − £800 = £2,200 × 100/80. [The £800 is £750 + £50.]
[3]   In the absence of income tax reductions, the figure for tax liability is the same as for total tax.
[4]   i.e. £2,750 × 20/100 = £550.

(b)  No. Deborah's rental income from Edwina is only £1,800 per annum. The rent-a-room scheme exempts up to £4,250 per annum.

# CHAPTER EIGHTEEN

# INCOME TAXATION: ANTI-AVOIDANCE ISSUES

## 18.1 Schedule D, Case VI: the Specific Element

### 18.1.1 CERTAIN TRANSACTIONS IN LAND: ICTA 1988, SECTION 776

#### PAGE v LOWTHER [1983] STC 799

The facts of this case closely resembled those of **Activity 37**, *Learning Text*. The judge is discussing ICTA 1970, s. 488, which was the predecessor of ICTA 1988, s. 776. Trafalgar was the name of the development company.

SLADE LJ: . . . I now turn to the second principal submission of counsel for the trustees on the wording of the section. This was, in effect, that no gain of a capital nature has been obtained by the trustees from the relevant disposal of the land within the meaning of s. 488(2). It is common ground that the relevant 'disposals' (if any) were the underleases granted by Trafalgar, which were the disposals of the land when developed. Though I think counsel for the trustees accepted that the ordinary dictionary meaning of the word 'from' is wide enough to include a reference to what he called a secondary source, he submitted that, in its present context, it denoted only the primary source of the relevant gain, and that the primary source of the gain obtained by the trustees in the present case was not the subsequent underleases, but the lease of 1971. He pointed out that, as he put it, the lease of 1971 generated the right of the trustees to the gain which, at the date of the grant of that lease, was as yet unquantified, but nevertheless ascertainable in due course by reference to the formula contained in it. In those circumstances, he contended that a construction which treated the trustees as having obtained any gain 'from' the underleases subsequently granted by Trafalgar would fail to take account of the purpose and scope of the section as indicated by the sidenote and sub-s (1). The gain, he submitted, was a gain obtained solely 'from' the lease of 1971.

In support of this submission relating to the construction of the word 'from', counsel for the trustees referred us to a passage from Vinelott J's judgment in the *Chilcott* case ([1982] STC 1 at 21) but, since that passage was directed to a case where para. (*c*) was not in point, I find it of very limited assistance in the present case. The same comment may be made in relation to a number of hypothetical examples which counsel for the trustees put forward, for the purpose of showing that the Crown's construction of the word 'from' and, indeed, its construction of the word 'arrangement', would lead to hardship and injustice. None of them related to a case where land had been developed for the sole or main object of realising a gain from the disposal of the land when developed, and the first relevant question would accordingly be whether a gain of a capital nature had been obtained from the disposal of the land when developed. It seems to me that questions relating to the meaning of the word 'from', or indeed to the meaning of the word 'arrangement', in that context may well give rise to considerations different from those that apply where sub-s (2)(*a*) and (*b*) are in point.

In considering the second principal submission of counsel for the trustees, I agree with the judge that the simple question one has to ask is: did the trustees obtain any gain of a capital nature from the disposals effected by the underleases? I think that the only possible answer to this question is 'Yes'. The execution of each underlease was not merely the occasion when the trustees received substantial extra payments, according to the formula agreed with Trafalgar and included in the lease of 1971; it was the first occasion on which the trustees' entitlement to such a payment arose as against the person who was actually going to pay them, that is to say the underlessees. In these circumstances, to hold that they had obtained no gain from the disposals effected by the underleases would, in my opinion, be to fly in the face of reality and the ordinary use of language.

To sum up, if one applies the relevant words of s. 488(2) to the facts of the present case, three points, in my opinion, stand out. First, this land was 'developed' — that is to say by Trafalgar — with the 'sole or main object of realising a gain from disposing of the land when developed'. That is not disputed. Secondly, a 'gain of a capital nature' was obtained by the trustees from the disposal of the land when developed, as and when completed houses or flats were sold by Trafalgar to underlessees and the trustees received premiums from such purchasers. Thirdly, the trustees were parties to an 'arrangement effected as respects the land' (that is to say the lease to Trafalgar) which 'enabled a gain to be realised by them' (that is to say the premiums) by an 'indirect method' (that is to say by procuring Trafalgar to impose on the purchasers an obligation to pay such premiums to the trustees) or by a 'series of transactions' (that is to say the various underleases granted by Trafalgar to the purchasers or, in the alternative, the 1971 lease and the underleases together). It seems to me, in these circumstances, that the facts of the present case fall clearly and indisputably within the words of s. 488(2).

With all respect to the very careful argument of counsel for the trustees, I think there is no room for construing the phrases 'arrangement' and 'from the disposal of the land' in the very restricted senses which he suggests. While sub-s (1) may be regarded as being of the nature of a preamble, stating in general terms the nature of the mischief at which the section is aimed, its wording is not, in my opinion, nearly sufficiently clear to enable the court to give a construction to sub-s (2) which would enable the trustees to escape the net of taxation under s. 488 in the present case. If it had expressly limited the operation of the section to transactions specifically designed to avoid tax, the position might have been quite different.

. . .

## 18.1.2 TRANSFERS OF ASSETS ABROAD: ICTA 1988, SECTIONS 739 AND 740

### Dearden, P., 'The Evolution of S. 739—62 Years Old and Still Growing', *Taxation Practitioner Offshore Supplement*, March 1998, p. 14

Section 739 of the Income and Corporation Taxes Act 1988 is one of the Revenue's favourite weapons for countering the avoidance of tax using offshore vehicles. This article reviews some of the changes that have taken place both in statute and in the courts and considers the effect of these changes to this very important piece of legislation.

This article concentrates on changes rather than the main thrust of the legislation and for a reminder of how s. 739 operates the reader should review an earlier article in the May 1997 edition of *Taxation Practitioner*.

*Overview*
The broad effect of s. 739 is to levy a tax charge on UK ordinarily resident individuals in respect of income accruing to offshore entities such as trusts and companies. The charge will only apply where a UK ordinarily resident individual has made a transfer of assets to an offshore entity *and* where he has the 'power to enjoy' funds representing that income.

There is a sister provision, s. 740, which applies where the 'transferor' does not have the 'power to enjoy' funds representing the income. In this case s. 740 may levy a tax charge on the individuals who eventually receive a benefit out of those funds. This will apply for example in the case of an offshore trust set up by an individual in the UK for the benefit of his children or his grandchildren. If the settlor is 'excluded' from benefiting under the terms of the trust then he would not be subject to tax charge under s. 739. However, the actual beneficiaries would be subject to a charge under s. 740 as and when they received the benefit out of the trust.

*Recent events*

Section 739 was originally enacted in 1936 and has long been an effective counter measure to the use of offshore vehicles for the avoidance of income tax. The Revenue are keen to protect the effectiveness of s. 739 and as soon as any weaknesses are identified they are quickly rectified. This has been particularly noticeable in the last year.

*Finance Act 1997*

The Finance Act 1997 introduced two amendments to s. 739. These resulted in the insertion of sub-section 1A which now provides that the 'transferor' need not be ordinarily resident in the United Kingdom at the time he transferred assets to an offshore structure for s. 739 to be in point.

This makes it clear that where an individual has transferred income earning assets to an offshore structure prior to the commencement of residence in the United Kingdom he will, on subsequently becoming UK resident, be within the scope of s. 739.

This amendment arose out of a decision in *IR Commrs* v *Willoughby* [1997] BTC 393. One of the defences put forward by Mr Willoughby's Counsel was that s. 739 could not apply where the transferor had been non-resident at the time he made a transfer of assets to a non-resident entity. The Revenue were obviously very unhappy at the thought of such a defence prevailing and thus an amendment was provided in the 1996 Budget and enacted in the Finance Act 1997. The Revenue were wise to be pessimistic about the chances of their case before the House of Lords as this was one of the points on which they lost when the judgment of the Lords was delivered on 10 July 1997.

It may seem academic to consider an amendment which puts the legal position back to the position which the Revenue had maintained existed prior to the *Willoughby* case. In fact, the *Willoughby* case is important as a number of taxpayers will have been treated in accordance with the Revenue's view of the legislation which has now been held to be in error.

A further amendment was intended to make it clear that avoiding *any* tax is sufficient to bring a transfer within s. 739 and it will not be a defence to assert that, for example, the structure was put in place to avoid inheritance tax or capital gains tax but not income tax so that s. 739 should not be in point. This amendment confirms the decision in *Sassoon* v *IR Commrs* 25 TC 154 in which it was held that 'avoiding taxation' includes the avoidance of death duties.

*The Willoughby case*

The details of the *Willoughby* case have been examined in many earlier articles. Here we will focus upon the lasting effects of the case. Mr Willoughby was a resident of Hong Kong. In order to create himself a pension, he invested a lump sum he received from his employers on retirement into a number of single premium bonds offered by an Isle of Man insurance company.

The Revenue contended that s. 739 applied to income accruing within the bonds so that income earned by the life company, which increased the value of the policies, should be taxable on Mr Willoughby as that income arose.

A number of issues were raised, which were upheld by the special commissioners and the Court of Appeal. However, in the House of Lords, the Lords found in favour of the clients on two principle issues and did not feel it necessary to consider the remaining issues.

As described above it was held that the income from bonds that had been purchased by Mr Willoughby prior to the commencement of UK residence could not fall within s. 739 as he had not been resident in the UK when he purchased the bonds. This ruling has been amended by the Finance Act 1997. Additionally, the Lords found it difficult to come to terms with the Revenue's view that, as Mr Willoughby and other holders of similar bonds had a greater amount of influence over the investment policy adopted by the life company this rendered the bonds vulnerable to s. 739. The Revenue had long contended that the holders of so called 'personalised' bonds should be subject to s. 739. The House of Lords agreed with the taxpayer that as he fell within legislation that Parliament had specifically enacted to levy tax on profits arising from such products (the 'chargeable event' legislation), s. 739 should not be in point. The Lords also agreed that a particular investment strategy did not make a bond-holder more or less a tax avoider. Thus the defence in s. 741(a) which relies on the particular transfer not being effected for the purpose of avoiding taxation was held to apply.

This is very reasonable result as Mr Willoughby does not appear to have been attempting to avoid tax when he bought his policies. However, it will be interesting to see how far this logic can be taken. Individuals who invest via offshore companies will eventually be subject to tax in a manner determined by Parliament (on distribution or liquidation) but I would not be optimistic about a similar defence applying in such a scenario.

### IRC v Botnar

The judgement of the Chancery Division was delivered on 10 November 1997 in the case of *Inland Revenue Commissioners* v *Botnar* [1997] BTC 613. The *Botnar* case is interesting for a number of reasons, not least being the amount of tax at stake. In the *Willoughby* case the numbers were relatively small, although the principles were quite important. The numbers in the *Botnar* case are extremely large. At stake was tax on income arising in the years of assessment from 1974–75 to 1987–88 of £144,417,997 on which tax had been assessed of £50,198,328. The essence of the case was that Mr Octav Botnar had settled shares in Datsun UK Limited upon an offshore structure on terms that he was not directly able to benefit from the trust assets although there was, in certain circumstances, a possibility that he may one day benefit.

This case may serve to destroy a few golf-club myths. It is often said that s. 739 will not apply if the transferor is not a beneficiary of an offshore trust, although he may at some time become a beneficiary. It is also often said that taxation will not apply until or unless the income is paid back into the UK. These myths, which never stood up to much scrutiny, can now be dispelled.

The case revolved around the interaction of cl. 23 and cl. 3(c) of the offshore settlement. Clause 23 provided that, 'excluded persons' which included Mr Botnar and his wife could not benefit under the terms of the settlement. However, cl. 3(c) of the settlement gave the trustees the power to transfer funds to a new settlement which would not be bound by the same restrictions as the original settlement. Thus it may have been possible for the trustees to transfer the trust assets to a new settlement under the terms of which Mr Botnar or his wife might have been able to benefit. Indeed, there was documentary evidence from the time of creation of the settlement that this was indeed the intended strategy. The Revenue contended that Mr Botnar had 'power to enjoy' the income of the offshore trust. The special commissioners allowed Mr Botnar's appeal holding that he didn't have any 'power to enjoy' as he and his wife were excluded from benefiting. Unfortunately for Mr Botnar it was held, in Chancery Division, that as the taxpayer and his wife were potential beneficiaries by virtue of the cl. 3(c) power the Revenue's appeal would be allowed.

The Revenue have always held that 'power to enjoy' had a very wide meaning and this case shows that the courts are also prepared to interpret this phrase in its widest sense.

### McGuckian

The decision in *Inland Revenue Commissioners* v *McGuckian* [[1997] 3 All ER 817] was delivered on 12 June 1997, only four weeks prior to the decision in *Willoughby*. However, in this case the House of Lords was in an altogether more intolerant mood.

The essence of the case is that Mr McGuckian and his wife transferred their shares in a company incorporated in the Republic of Ireland to a Guernsey company as trustee of an offshore settlement. Mr and Mrs McGuckian were both beneficiaries and the income of the settlement was payable to Mrs McGuckian.

Dividends were declared by the Irish company but before they were paid the trustees sold their rights to receive the dividends for a capital sum which turned out to be 99 per cent of the dividend receivable. The issue before the Lords was whether or not the sum received by the trustees as consideration for the right to receive a dividend could be treated as income and thus taxed upon Mr McGuckian under what is now s. 739. On the surface the sum received would appear to be a capital receipt. The Revenue relied upon the Ramsay principle to contend that the artificial step (the sale of the right to receive the dividend) should be ignored.

The courts took a rather liberal interpretation of the legislation and may have been influenced by the attitude of the taxpayer and his advisors. The Crown contended that the assignment of the right to a dividend was an inserted step with no commercial purpose and that following the principle which had first been enunciated of in *Ramsay (WT) Ltd* v *IR Commrs* [1982] AC 300, the inserted step could be ignored so that the dividend could be taxable upon Mr McGuckian. It was in fact held that the sale of the dividend could be ignored on these grounds.

One of the taxpayer's arguments was that he should have been assessed under ICTA 1988, s. 730 and thus could not be assessed under s. 739. It was also noted that it was at this time, too late to raise an assessment under s. 730. The House of Lords does not appear to have been happy to accept this argument. . . .

## 18.2 End of Chapter Assessment Question

Refer to the facts involving Amber Ltd and its shareholders: **2.4** and **8.4**. In Amber Ltd's accounting period ending on 31 December 1998, Bertram, who is short of money, proposes that Amber Ltd makes him an interest-free loan of £10,000, repayable in full on 31 December 2002. Alan and Deborah are amenable to the proposal, provided any company law requirements are complied with, although they are concerned about its tax implications.

Advise them.

## 18.3 End of Chapter Assessment Outline Answer

Amber Ltd is a close company, being a company under the control of five or fewer participators: ICTA 1988, s. 414(1). As at 31 December 1998, each of Alan, Bertram, Deborah, and Charlie's estate are participators in Amber Ltd, since they have a share or interest in the capital of the company: ICTA 1988, s. 417(1). The proposed loan of £10,000 by Amber Ltd to Bertram will be treated, in general terms, as if it were a dividend: ICTA 1988, s. 419. The making of the loan will mean that it is treated as if it had declared and paid a dividend, and it will have to pay an amount representing ACT of 1/4 of the loan, i.e. £2,500.

So far as Bertram is concerned, the £10,000 will not be treated as income of his, and he will be entitled to no credit for the 'ACT' which Amber will have to pay. In addition, he will be treated as receiving Schedule E income in each tax year the loan is outstanding, equal to the cash equivalent of the interest-free loan: ICTA 1988, s. 160. The cash equivalent will be the difference between the official rate of interest on the loan, and the amount actually paid by him. Although the special statutory code treats him in this way for income tax purposes, the value of the waived interest on the loan will *not* count as part of his earnings for the purposes of Class 1 NICs.

# CHAPTER NINETEEN

# INCOME TAXATION: COMPLIANCE AND APPEALS

## 19.1   Income Tax

### 19.1.1   TAX INSPECTORS AND TAX COLLECTORS

**The Adjudicator's Office, 'Using the Adjudicator', *Taxation Practitioner*, April 1998, p. 12**

The Adjudicator acts as an impartial, independent and accessible referee. She looks at complaints from people and businesses about the way the Inland Revenue (including the Valuation Office Agency), Customs and Excise or the Contributions Agency have handled their affairs.

Complaints can be about, for example, mistakes, delays, the behaviour of staff, quality of service and the way in which an organisation has exercised discretion. Her services are free.

The Adjudicator does not look at issues of law or tax liability, because the procedures for resolving these problems are already well established; for example, the General and Special Commissioners (for Inland Revenue disputes) and VAT tribunals (in Customs and Excise cases).

She also will not look at matters relating to a criminal investigation or prosecution brought by the Inland Revenue, Customs and Excise or the Contributions Agency until the completion of the investigation and of any court proceedings.

The Adjudicator does not look at complaints about government policy (which is a matter for ministers and Parliament), or complaints that have already been investigated, or are under scrutiny, by the Parliamentary Ombudsman, or that are, or have been, before the courts.

And in the case of the Contributions Agency, the Adjudicator would not look at an appeal against a decision made by the Secretary of State for Social Security about someone's national insurance liability.

*Practical considerations*
The Adjudicator looks at complaints about the Inland Revenue relating to problems arising after 1 April 1993, and complaints about Customs and Excise and the Contributions Agency relating to problems arising after 1 April 1995.

The Adjudicator will not normally look at a complaint if she receives it more than six months after a senior manager from the Inland Revenue, Customs and Excise or the Contributions Agency has given the complainant a response to their complaint with which he or she is not satisfied.

Before we take on a complaint for investigation, we give the Inland Revenue, Customs and Excise or the Contributions Agency a chance to resolve the problem at a senior level. This level is usually a Director of the Inland Revenue (or the Chief Executive of the Valuation Office Agency), a Collector in Customs and Excise or the Chief Executive of the Contributions Agency.

Some people come to the Adjudicator's Office before the organisation has had a chance to resolve their problem at a senior level, or with a query which is outside the Adjudicator's remit. We try to help these individuals and businesses sort out their problems with the organisation — through their internal complaints systems — or through other bodies which we feel can best help them with their query.

If someone tells us that they remain dissatisfied after a senior manager in the Inland Revenue, Customs and Excise or the Contributions Agency has looked at their complaint, and the complaint is one that we can consider, we take it on for investigation.

### Investigation procedures

To investigate a complaint we begin, if necessary, by asking the person or business having problems with the organisations to set out the details of their complaint. This helps make sure that we look at all the complainant's concerns. After this, we ask the organisation involved for a full report on the complaint and all their files on the complainant's affairs.

We review this material — along with any material the complainant has provided — to see how the complaint should in our view, be settled. Where possible, we will try to mediate a settlement of a complaint by discussing the matter with the organisation and the complainant and encouraging a fair settlement. Otherwise, the Adjudicator will make a formal recommendation in writing to the complainant and the organisation: the Adjudicator has final responsibility for making recommendations.

Sometimes, we need to interview complainants, their agents or officials. And sometimes the Adjudicator holds a hearing so that she can hear the details of a case herself from these parties before making a decision.

Complainants can be represented by a relative, friend or agent, but to protect their confidentiality, we ask complainants for their written permission that we can disclose information about them and their affairs to a third person, before we begin an investigation. And where the Adjudicator believes she needs to interview a complainant at the Adjudicator's Office as part of her investigation, the interview cannot be conducted through another person, although the complainant can be accompanied by a relative, a friend or an agent.

Where the Adjudicator feels that the organisation has provided someone with a poor service, she can recommend that they take a number of actions to put things right. For example, that they apologise, pay compensation (for actual financial loss and for distress), and write off tax and interest. She may also ask the organisation to review their operations or management practices to ensure that similar problems do not recur.

### Are our decisions binding?

On organisations, no. The organisations have undertaken to accept the Adjudicator's recommendations in all but exceptional cases. To date the organisations have accepted all the Adjudicator's recommendations.

The Adjudicator does not make recommendations that complainants take, or desist from taking, any action. And she does not look at agents' work.

If a complainant is unhappy with the factual content of a recommendation the Adjudicator may re-consider her decision if the complainant provides new evidence in support of their view or identifies important factual error(s) in the Adjudicator's recommendation which could lead her to change her view. The Adjudicator will not re-consider a complaint if a complainant is unhappy with the Adjudicator's judgment of a complaint.

Complainants who are dissatisfied with the Adjudicator's decision(s), or with any other aspect of our performance, can ask a Member of Parliament to put their complaint to the Parliamentary Ombudsman.

### How, where, and when to contact us

The Adjudicator's Office is open from 09.00 to 17.00, Monday to Friday except public holidays.

We can be contacted at: The Adjudicator's Office, Haymarket House, 28 Haymarket, London SW1Y 4SP. Tel: (0171) 930 2292; fax: (0171) 930 2298; e-mail: adjudicator@gtnet.gov.uk

### 19.1.2   TAX RETURNS AS A SOURCE OF INFORMATION

**Inland Revenue Corporate Communications Office, 'Guidance for employees about the employment records they may need to keep', February 1996**

The term 'employees' includes directors or other office holders.

From April 1996, all employees must keep records so they can complete a Tax Return fully and accurately if requested to do so. The same records will also be needed where claims are made, for example for business expenses.

Employees should keep any information and documents they have received, or have prepared, from which they have to work out what to put on their Tax Returns or claims.

It helps to organise and retain records in an orderly fashion.

Normally employees will have to retain records for 22 months from the end of the tax year — for example, for the tax year ended 5 April 1997, records will normally have to be retained until 31 January 1999. There are exceptions — in some circumstances records have to be retained for longer.

The Tax Office has the right to enquire into Tax Returns and claims and may want to see the supporting records.

Failure to keep records can result in a penalty (maximum £3,000 in the most serious cases).
. . .

**Records for income, benefits in kind and expenses payments**
Examples of records employees may need relating to income, benefits in kind and expenses payments from an employment are

- form P60, a certificate from the employer after 5 April (the end of the tax year) giving details of pay and tax deducted
- any form P45 (Part 1A), a certificate from a former employer showing details of pay and tax in that employment
- any form P160 (Part 1A) from an employer when an employee retires and goes on to a pension paid by that employer
- payslips or pay statements (plus certificates or other proof of any foreign tax paid on employment income)
- forms P11D or P9D or equivalent information from all employments during the year, showing any benefits in kind and expenses payments received
- certificates for any Taxed Award Schemes in which an employee participated
- information from any other person or company who provided benefits in kind in connection with the employment
- a note of the amount of any tips or gratuities and details of any other taxable receipts or benefits not included in any of the above records. These should be recorded as soon as possible after receipt, and not simply estimated at the end of the year.

It would also be sensible to keep forms P2 (PAYE Coding Notices) — they may help to keep track of any earlier underpayments of tax that are being collected through PAYE.
. . .

**Own car used for business travel**
There are two reasons why employees may need to work out the costs of using their own cars for business travel

- to know if they made a taxable profit on the car allowances and motor mileage allowances paid to them, or
- to support a deduction for business motoring expenses.

One way to work out the costs is for records to be kept of the motoring costs during the year and the business and total mileage. The proportion of the costs that relate to business motoring can then be worked out.

The other way is to use the tax free mileage rates which the Tax Office sets each year for the Fixed Profit Car Scheme (FPCS). Here, employees only need to keep a record of business miles. The tax free rate for the car engine size can simply be multiplied by the number of business miles travelled. That gives employees the business motoring costs for the year without having to keep details of actual motoring costs. . . .

However motoring costs are calculated, tax relief may still be available for interest paid on a hire purchase agreement or a loan to buy a car. Relief is limited to the business proportion of any interest payable within three years of the end of the tax year in which the hire purchase agreement of loan was arranged.

### Claims to other expenses

For other expenses claimed, employees will need to keep the necessary records to support them. For example, if it is established that part of an employee's home has to be used for work, sufficient records will need to be kept to support the proportion of heating and lighting costs that relate to employment and to private use.

### 19.1.3 COLLECTION OF INCOME TAX: EMPLOYEES AND PAYE

### *IN RE SELECTMOVE LTD* [1995] 2 All ER 531 (CA)

PETER GIBSON LJ: This is an appeal by Selectmove Ltd (the company) from the order made on 19 January 1993 by Judge Moseley QC, sitting as a judge of the Companies Court, whereby on the petition of the Commissioners of Inland Revenue (the Crown) as creditors he compulsorily wound up the company. The issue before us, as it was before the judge, is whether the debt of the company to the Crown is disputed in good faith on substantial grounds.

There is no doubt as to the correct approach to that issue. The jurisdiction of the Companies Court to wind up companies is not for the purpose of deciding a factual dispute concerning a debt which is sought to be relied on to found a petition. Until the petitioner can establish that he is a creditor, he is not entitled to present a petition based on a claimed debt. Accordingly, the practice of the Companies Court is to dismiss a creditor's petition based on a debt which is disputed by the company in good faith and on substantial grounds (see e.g. *Stonegate Securities Ltd* v *Gregory* [1980] 1 All ER 241 at 243, [1980] Ch 576 at 580 per Buckley LJ).

In July 1991 the company owed the Crown substantial amounts of tax (PAYE) which it had deducted from the emoluments of its employees under the PAYE system and national insurance contributions (NIC), the arrears going back to the previous fiscal year. On 15 July 1991 Mr ffooks, the managing director of the company, met Mr Polland, a collector of taxes, at the latter's office. Mr ffooks' account of what occurred is contained in a letter dated 11 October 1991 from him to the Crown and is verified by his affidavit of 27 November 1992. In that letter he said that he explained to Mr Polland that the company was having cash flow problems, but that the company's bank was being supportive. He said that he suggested to Mr Polland that it could not be in anyone's interest for the company to be put into compulsory liquidation when the typesetting market in which the company was engaged usually picked up after the summer, and that the company had been trading 'marginally profitably' since the start of the financial year. Mr Polland, he said, asked him if he was in a position to put forward a proposal to pay back the arrears of PAYE and NIC and told him that any proposal should include the prompt payment of any future PAYE and NIC as they fell due. He further said that he told Mr Polland that because of the lengthy credit terms usual in the publishing industry, even if the company continued to trade at a profit, this would not be reflected in cash coming in to the company for four or five months. He continued:

> I therefore proposed that the company would pay any future PAYE and NIC liability as it fell due commencing with the liability for August (due September) and this has been done. I further proposed that the arrears of PAYE and NIC would be paid at a rate of £1,000 per month from the 1st February 1992. Mr Polland said that such a proposal went further than he would have liked and that he would have to seek approval from his superiors to whom he would recommend it considering the support that both I and our bankers were giving the company. He said he would revert to me if it was unacceptable. To date I have not heard from him and as I have made the two

payments which were due under the agreement it is clear that this agreement has come into existence.

The Crown disputes that Mr Polland made any agreement with Mr ffooks. However, it was accepted that for the purpose of the hearing before the judge the company's version of the facts of what occurred should be taken as correct, and the same assumption has been common ground on this appeal.

The company did not hear further from the Crown until 9 October 1991. By then, on 19 August 1991, it had duly paid PAYE and NIC for August 1991 amounting to £2,309, but it had not paid PAYE and NIC for September 1991 although that had become due on 19 September 1991. On 9 October 1991 the Crown wrote to the company, demanding payment of PAYE and NIC arrears totalling £24,650 and threatened a winding-up petition if payment was not made. It was to that letter that Mr ffooks was responding by his letter dated 11 October 1991 in which the agreement between Mr ffooks and Mr Polland was alleged. On 11 October 1991 the company paid the September PAYE and NIC in the sum of £1,821. On 22 November 1991 a further payment of PAYE and NIC for October and November in the sum of £2,699 was made, again late. In 1992 seven cheques of £1,000 each were paid to the Crown, the first two on 3 March 1992. Again there were failures by the company to honour what Mr ffooks said was agreed with Mr Polland, viz the payment of £1,000 per month from 1 February 1992. On 18 October 1991 the employees of the company were given notice of dismissal and on 24 October 1991 the company sold all its work-in-progress to another company, the intention of the sale agreement being, according to the company's solicitor, Mr Stockler, to provide £1,000 per month to settle the Crown's claim. However, the Crown continued to press for payment and served a statutory demand for payment of £19,650.15. On 7 September 1992 the Crown presented its winding-up petition based on a claimed debt of £17,466.60.

On behalf of the company it was contended before the judge that it had an arguable case that the Crown had accepted the proposal put by Mr ffooks to Mr Polland on 15 July 1991. The Crown took two points on this contention, each of which was accepted by the judge. The first was that no agreement was concluded by the silence of the Crown in response to Mr ffooks' proposal. The second was that if there was an agreement there was no consideration therefor. The company also argued in the alternative that by reason of the agreement between Mr ffooks and Mr Polland the Crown is estopped from relying on the debt as due. That argument too was rejected by the judge on the ground that there was no agreement or promise by the Crown to give rise to any estoppel.

Similar contentions were advanced by Mr Nugee for the company before us, and I shall consider in turn the following issues. (1) Was there an acceptance by the Crown of Mr ffooks' proposal? (2) If there was an agreement, was it supported by consideration moving to the Crown? (3) If there was no agreement, is the Crown estopped from asserting that its debt is due?

### (1) *Acceptance*

The judge referred to the affidavit evidence of Mr ffooks in which he had stated what had occurred at the meeting with Mr Polland on 15 July 1991 and the absence of any communication from the Crown at any time before 9 October and had asserted that the offer had been accepted. The judge said: 'It is not asserted . . . that Mr Polland said anything to the effect, "if you do not hear from me, take it that there is an agreement between us".' But that seems to me to be what necessarily is the effect of Mr ffooks' assertion of the acceptance of the offer.

The question is whether an agent who makes clear to an offeror that he lacks the principal's authority to accept the offer can, by indicating that he would refer the offer to his principal and that he would come back to the offeror only if the offer was not acceptable, bind the principal to accept the offer by the agent's subsequent silence. Mr Charles, for the Crown, drew our attention to the general rule that silence will not normally amount to acceptance of an offer since acceptance cannot be inferred from silence alone 'save in the most exceptional circumstances' (see *Allied Marine Transport Ltd v Vale do Rio Doce Navegacao SA, The Leonidas D* [1985] 2 All ER 796 at 805 per Robert Goff LJ). But the authorities that support the general rule are cases where an offeror sought to impose on the offeree a term as to acceptance by silence. For my part, as at present advised, I would accept the observation of Evans J in *Gebr Van Weelde Scheepvaartkantor BV v Cia Naviera Sea Orient SA, The Agrabele* [1985] 2 Lloyd's Rep 496 at 509:

> The significance of silence, as a matter of law, may also be different when there is an express undertaking or an implied obligation to speak, in the special circumstances of the particular case.

Where the offeree himself indicates that an offer is to be taken as accepted if he does not indicate to the contrary by an ascertainable time, he is undertaking to speak if he does not want an agreement to be concluded. I see no reason in principle why that should not be an exceptional circumstance such that the offer can be accepted by silence. But it is unnecessary to express a concluded view on this point.

The more substantial objection taken by Mr Charles is as to the want of authority of Mr Polland. That he had no authority to agree to the proposal Mr Polland had made clear to Mr ffooks. It is not suggested by Mr Nugee that Mr Polland had actual authority to conclude the agreement or otherwise to bind the Crown by his silence. He has to assert that Mr Polland had ostensible authority and he submits that such authority extended to conveying his principal's acceptance by his subsequent silence. The difficulty that I have with this submission stems from the fact that it is trite law that ostensible authority involves a representation by the principal as to the extent of the agent's authority and no representation by the agent as to the extent of his authority can amount to a holding out by his principal (see eg *Bowstead on Agency* (15th edn, 1985) p. 286). In *Armagas Ltd v Mundogas SA, The Ocean Frost* [1986] 2 All ER 385 at 391, the House of Lords expressly approved the following remarks by Robert Goff LJ:

> . . . the effect of the judge's conclusion was that although Magelssen [the defendants' chartering manager and vice-president] did not have ostensible authority to enter into the contract he did have ostensible authority to tell Jensen and Dannesboe [two shipowners who controlled the plaintiffs] that he had obtained actual authority to do so. This is, on its face, a most surprising conclusion. It results in an extraordinary distinction between (1) a case where an agent, having no ostensible authority to enter into the relevant contract, wrongly asserts that he is invested with actual authority to do so, in which event the principal is not bound, and (2) a case where an agent, having no ostensible authority, wrongly asserts after negotiations that he has gone back to his principal and obtained actual authority, in which event the principal is bound. As a matter of common sense, this is most unlikely to be the law.' (See [1985] 3 All ER 795 at 803).

In the present case I am not aware of any fact which would enable Mr ffooks reasonably to believe that the superiors to whom Mr Polland referred were themselves making a representation that Mr Polland had their authority to accept the offer or to convey their acceptance by his silence. Accordingly, I would hold that the judge was right to conclude that there was no acceptance, though my reasons differ from those of the judge.

### (2)   Consideration

There are two elements to the consideration which the company claims was provided by it to the Crown. One is the promise to pay off its existing liability by instalments from 1 February 1992. The other is the promise to pay future PAYE and NIC as they fell due. Mr Nugee suggested that implicit in the latter was the promise to continue trading. But that cannot be spelt out of Mr ffooks' evidence as to what he agreed with Mr Polland. Accordingly, the second element is no more than a promise to pay that which it was bound to pay under the fiscal legislation at the date at which it was bound to make such payment. If the first element is not good consideration, I do not see why the second element should be either.

The judge held that the case fell within the principle of *Foakes v Beer* [1881–5] All ER Rep 106. In that case a judgment debtor and creditor agreed that in consideration of the debtor paying part of the judgment debt and costs immediately and the remainder by instalments the creditor would not take any proceedings on the judgment. The House of

Lords held that the agreement was nudum pactum, being without consideration, and did not prevent the creditor, after payment of the whole debt and costs, from proceeding to enforce payment of the interest on the judgment. Although their Lordships were unanimous in the result, that case is notable for the powerful speech of Lord Blackburn, who made plain his disagreement with the course the law had taken in and since *Pinnel's Case*, [1558–1774] All ER Rep 612 and which the House of Lords in *Foakes* v *Beer* decided should not be reversed. Lord Blackburn expressed his conviction that—

> all men of business, whether merchants or tradesmen, do every day recognise and act on the ground that prompt payment of a part of their demand may be more beneficial to them than it would be to insist on their rights and enforce payment of the whole. (See [1881–5] All ER Rep 106 at 115.)

Yet it is clear that the House of Lords decided that a practical benefit of that nature is not good consideration in law.

*Foakes* v *Beer* has been followed and applied in numerous cases subsequently, of which I shall mention two. In *Vanbergen* v *St Edmunds Properties Ltd* [1933] All ER Rep 488 at 491 Lord Hanworth MR said:

> It is a well established principle that a promise to pay a sum which the debtor is already bound by law to pay to the promisee does not afford any consideration to support the contract.

More recently in *D & C Builders Ltd* v *Rees* [1965] 3 All ER 837 at 841, this court also applied *Foakes* v *Beer*, Danckwerts LJ saying that the case—

> settled definitely the rule of law that payment of a lesser sum than the amount of a debt due cannot be a satisfaction of the debt, unless there is some benefit to the creditor added so that there is an accord and satisfaction.

Mr Nugee, however, submitted that an additional benefit to the Crown was conferred by the agreement in that the Crown stood to derive practical benefits therefrom: it was likely to recover more from not enforcing its debt against the company, which was known to be in financial difficulties, than from putting the company into liquidation. He pointed to the fact that the company did in fact pay its further PAYE and NIC liabilities and £7,000 of its arrears. He relied on the decision of this court in *Williams* v *Roffey Bros & Nicholls (Contractors) Ltd* [1990] 1 All ER 512, for the proposition that a promise to perform an existing obligation can amount to good consideration provided that there are practical benefits to the promisee.

In that case the defendant, which had a building contract, sub-contracted work to the plaintiff at a price which left him in financial difficulty and there was a risk that the work would not be completed by the plaintiff. The defendant agreed to make additional payments to the plaintiff in return for his promise to carry out his existing obligations. The plaintiff sued for payment under the original agreement and the further agreement. The defendant argued that its promise to make additional payments was unenforceable and relied on *Stilk* v *Myrick* (1809) 170 ER 1168, in which Lord Ellenborough CJ held to be unenforceable for want of consideration a promise by a ship's captain to seamen, hired to crew the ship to and from the Baltic, of extra pay for working the ship back from the Baltic after two men had deserted. This court rejected that argument without overruling *Stilk* v *Myrick*. Glidewell LJ, with whom Purchas and Russell LJJ agreed, expressed the law to be this:

> . . . (i) if A has entered into a contract with B to do work for, or to supply goods or services to, B in return for payment by B and (ii) at some stage before A has completely performed his obligations under the contract B has reason to doubt whether A will, or will be able to, complete his side of the bargain and (iii) B thereupon promises A an additional payment in return for A's promise to perform his contractual obligations on time and (iv) as a result of giving his promise B obtains in practice a benefit, or

obviates a disbenefit, and (v) B's promise is not given as a result of economic duress or fraud on the part of A, then (vi) the benefit to B is capable of being consideration for B's promise, so that the promise will be legally binding. (See [1990] 1 All ER 512 at 521–522.)

Mr Nugee submitted that although Glidewell LJ in terms confined his remarks to a case where B is to do the work for or supply goods or services to A, the same principle must apply where B's obligation is to pay A, and he referred to an article by Adams and Brownsword 'Contract, Consideration and the Critical Path' (1990) 53 MLR 536 at 539–540 which suggests that *Foakes* v *Beer* might need reconsideration. I see the force of the argument, but the difficulty that I feel with it is that if the principle of *Williams'* case is to be extended to an obligation to make payment, it would in effect leave the principle in *Foakes* v *Beer* without any application. When a creditor and a debtor who are at arm's length reach agreement on the payment of the debt by instalments to accommodate the debtor, the creditor will no doubt always see a practical benefit to himself in so doing. In the absence of authority there would be much to be said for the enforceability of such a contract. But that was a matter expressly considered in *Foakes* v *Beer* yet held not to constitute good consideration in law. *Foakes* v *Beer* was not even referred to in *Williams'* case, and it is in my judgment impossible, consistently with the doctrine of precedent, for this court to extend the principle of *Williams'* case to any circumstances governed by the principle of *Foakes* v *Beer*. If that extension is to be made, it must be by the House of Lords or, perhaps even more appropriately, by Parliament after consideration by the Law Commission.

In my judgment, the judge was right to hold that if there was an agreement between the company and the Crown it was unenforceable for want of consideration.

### (3) Estoppel

Mr Nugee submitted that if the agreement was unenforceable for want of consideration the Crown is nevertheless estopped by the doctrine of promissory estoppel. As I understood him, he was saying that the Crown could not go back on its implied promise not to enforce the debt, given as it was in return for the company's promise to pay the future PAYE and NIC as they fell due and to pay the arrears by monthly instalments of £1,000 from 1 February 1992. He said that the company had acted on the Crown's promise and it would be inequitable to allow the Crown to renege on its promise.

Mr Charles did not accept that the Crown could be estopped as a matter of private law from performing its statutory duty, but he accepted that as a matter of public law the Crown could be prevented from acting unfairly. He did not suggest that an objection of unfairness could not be taken in the present proceedings.

It is unnecessary to consider the rival arguments in further detail as in my opinion Mr Nugee's submission cannot succeed for at least two reasons. First, as Mr Polland had no actual or ostensible authority to make the agreement claimed by the company, he had no authority to make the promise said to found the estoppel against the Crown. Second, because the company failed to honour its promise to pay the September PAYE and NIC as they fell due, it was not inequitable or unfair for the Crown on 9 October 1991 to demand payment of all the arrears, nor, in the light of the further late payments of the October and November PAYE and NIC and of various of the monthly instalments of £1,000, was it unfair or inequitable to serve a statutory demand and present a winding-up petition to enforce the debt.

For these reasons, despite the able and well-sustained arguments of Mr Nugee, I would dismiss this appeal.

STUART-SMITH LJ: For the reasons given in the judgment of Peter Gibson LJ I agree that this appeal should be dismissed.

BALCOMBE LJ: I agree. For the reasons which are given in the judgment which has been handed down this appeal will be dismissed.

*Appeal dismissed. Leave to appeal to the House of Lords refused.*

**Inland Revenue Leaflet IR 34, *PAYE — Pay As You Earn*, August 1994**

(Note: The figures for personal reliefs given here have now been superseded.)

*What is PAYE?*
It stands for Pay As You Earn. Most of us pay our income tax under this system. PAYE is a way of spreading your income tax over the tax year. The tax year starts on 6 April of one year and ends on 5 April in the next. Under PAYE your employer takes tax from your weekly or monthly earnings and pays it over to the Inland Revenue.

You don't pay tax on all your income. Everybody can earn or receive a certain amount in each tax year free of tax. This amount is called a 'personal allowance'. The Chancellor sets the amounts of the allowances each year in the Budget. . . .

There are other allowances. From 6 April 1994, these reduce your tax bill by a certain amount. . . .

*How does PAYE work?*
Normally under PAYE the total of your allowances is divided by the total number of pay days in the tax year. So if you are paid weekly, your allowances are divided by 52, and if you are paid monthly, by 12. This gives you your 'tax free pay' for each pay day. For example, in the tax year 1994–95, if you get the basic allowance of £3,445, you receive £66.25 a week (£3,445 ÷ 52) tax free if you are paid weekly. You receive £287.08 a month tax free (£3,445 ÷ 12) if you are paid monthly.

If you don't get paid for some time, you will not lose your tax free pay for those weeks or months. Usually it builds up until the next time you get paid. In the same way, if you start work part way through the tax year and have not had any income up to then, you still get all your tax free pay up to that date. . . .

*How does my employer know how much tax to deduct from my pay?*
We produce 'tax tables' for your employer to use every pay day. These show the tax free pay for each week or month and how much tax to deduct.

By the end of the tax year, you will normally have had all your tax free pay and received all your allowances. If your earnings are less than your allowances at any time, you pay no tax and may get back some of the tax you paid earlier in the tax year.

*How does my employer know what my allowances are?*
Your Tax Office gives your employer a PAYE code. This represents the total of your allowances, but not how they are made up, which is confidential between you and your Tax Office (see below).

*What does a PAYE code look like?*
It is normally a number followed by a letter (but can be a letter followed by a number). The number is simply your total allowances, without the last figure. For example, if your total allowance is £3,445, your code will be 344 followed by a letter.

The letters show which allowances are included in the number. These are the most common

L    includes the basic personal allowance for a person under 65
H    includes the basic personal allowance **and** the married couple's allowance for a person under 65, or the additional personal allowance **and** also shows that we estimate you are liable at the basic rate of tax
P    includes the personal allowance for a person aged 65 to 74
V    includes the personal allowance for a person aged 65 to 74 **and** the married couple's allowance for a person aged 65 to 74 **and** also shows that we estimate you are liable at the basic rate of tax
K    (followed by a number) is used where your state pension or benefits from your employment (for example, the value of a company car) are greater than your allowances. The tax on the amount by which your state pension or benefits exceeds your allowances will be collected from your earnings or pension from a previous job.

**With the letters L, H, P and V, your employer can change your tax when allowances are changed by a Budget.**

T   is for all other cases where the number stands for the allowances. You can ask your Tax Office to use this letter if you do not want your employer to know that your code should end in one of the other letters.

There are also three special codes

BR   means your pay will be taxed at the basic rate
D   (followed by a number) means that your pay will be taxed at a higher rate of tax.

These codes are mainly used if you have a second job. The whole of your pay will be taxed at a single rate of tax (either the basic or the higher rate) because all your tax allowances will be used against the income you get from your main job.

NT   means that no tax will be taken from your pay or pension.

*If I am starting work for the first time, how do I get a PAYE code?*
If you go straight to a job when you leave school or college, your new employer will give you a form P46 which you can sign. You can then be given a PAYE code based on the personal allowance for people under 65. Your employer will use this code on your first pay day and send the P46 to the Tax Office to let them know you have started work.

   You should make sure you tell your employer your National Insurance (NI) number as soon as you start work or change jobs. You will also need to quote it whenever you get in touch with the Tax Office because they use it as a tax reference number. If you do not know your NI number, ask at any DSS office.

*What if I want to claim any other allowances?*
You must get in touch with your Tax Office (your employer can give you the name and address). Please quote your National Insurance number. . . .

*If I am already working, how do I find out my PAYE code?*
Before the beginning of the tax year, you may receive a notice of coding from your Tax Office. You will normally only get such a notice if your code changes. This shows the amount of your allowances and your PAYE code. There are some notes with it to help you.
. . .

*What happens if I have other income as well as my earnings?*
The Tax Office sends out forms at the end of each tax year asking for information on income. These are called tax returns. If you are sent one, you must enter details of all the income you receive. If you do not get a tax return and receive other income as well as your earnings, you should contact your Tax Office and ask for one. If the income is not taxed before you get it, or if you are paying tax at a higher rate, your PAYE code may need to be changed. This is so you can pay any tax due on the additional income at the same time as the tax on your earnings.
. . .

### 19.1.4   APPEALS AGAINST INCOME TAX ASSESSMENTS/AMENDMENTS TO SELF-ASSESSMENTS

**Oliver, S., 'Reshaping Tax Appeals', Part 1, *The Tax Journal*, 13 April 1995, pp. 8, 9**

**Ingredients of a Good System**
. . .
I shall conclude this first part of my article by identifying what I see as the essential ingredients of any good tax appeal system.

   First and foremost, it must serve the taxpayer, because it is the taxpayer who institutes every appeal. For this the Tribunal hearing the appeal must stand as a professional, fair and impartial court of law. But the diversity of taxpayers — and here I am referring to subjects affected by every national tax and duty and by European Union impositions, such as agricultural levies and customs duties — makes it imperative that the tax appeal system should be flexible at the first instance level, both in the nature of its judiciary and the places where it sits to hear appeals. It must be in a position to resolve the almost infinite diversity of issues that can now be raised before it. At one end of this spectrum it must have the capacity to deal fairly with the small trader on a 'mark-up' appeal, for whom English is a second language; at the other end it must have the expertise to deal with specialised duties and taxes, such as insurance premium tax and petroleum revenue tax, and it must have the ability to handle appeals from large commercial organisations, lasting for many months, where the tax at stake can — and frequently does — run into hundreds of millions of pounds.

Second, it must serve the taxes. A good tax system, to plagiarise a well-remembered expression of Professor Wheatcroft, breathes through its appeal system. In this respect the Court or Tribunal must not only be a Court for hearing appeals and judging them on the law, it will also have to carry out an administrative and, still further, a social function. A dissatisfied taxpayer must have an absolute right, however hopeless his case may be, to have the opportunity of letting off steam before an impartial forum. That is the social rôle. The administrative function I have already mentioned — it is to review the numerous classes of decisions taken by Customs and Excise and specified in the Value Added Tax Act 1994 and, so far as they relate to excise and custom duties and insurance premium tax matters, in the Finance Act 1994, as well as reviewing all so-called 'prior decisions' (to which VATA 1994, section 84(10) applies). It also extends, in an Inland Revenue tax context, to the advance review of decisions to issue notices under TMA 1970, section 20, and to the review of decisions — for example, to withhold capital gains tax relief on mergers.

Third, the tax appeal system needs to have the wherewithal of a Court with criminal jurisdiction that hears cases without a jury. Both Customs and Excise and the Inland Revenue have increasingly chosen to go for civil penalties in cases of so-called civil fraud, rather than venturing into the criminal Courts. In practice, though not as a matter of strict law, it is the revenue body that brings the appeal, because the burden lies on it. The issues involve fraud and are similar to and often more complex than those found in criminal jury trial cases. The 'Judge' in the VAT and Duties Tribunals has to apply notoriously complicated statutory provisions; he has to decide the legal issues, as well as playing the jury's rôle and deciding the factual questions.

## 19.2 End of Chapter Assessment Question

Refer to the facts relating to Deborah: **2.4**, **4.6(b)**, **5.4**, **9.3**, **14.2**, **15.2**, **16.3** and **18.2**. Advise her:

(a) Whether she is obliged to submit a tax return for 1998/99.

(b) The date by which it must be submitted.

(c) Whether there is any danger that she will have to make payments on account in 1998/99.

(Assume that Deborah has elected to self-assess.)

## 19.3 End of Chapter Assessment Outline Answer

(a) *Whether you are obliged to submit a tax return for 1998–99*: If you are liable to pay income tax for any tax year, you are obliged to notify the Revenue, unless you are within an exceptional category: TMA 1970, s. 7(1). Assuming you are obliged to notify the Revenue, you have a six-month period after the end of the tax year to request a return form: TMA 1970, s. 7(1). Failure to do so attracts a penalty.

You are *not* obliged to notify the Revenue where your total income consists of: (a) income from which tax has been deducted at source by your employer under PAYE; (b) income (e.g. interest) from which tax has been deducted at source by the payer, provided you are not a higher-rate taxpayer; or (c) income (e.g. dividends) on which tax has been credited as paid, subject to the same proviso: TMA 1970, ss. 7(1) to 7(4).

In your situation, you *will* therefore need to submit a tax return for 1998/99.

(b) *The date by which you must submit it*: As you have elected to self-assess, the deadline for submitting your personal return depends on whether or not the Revenue issues you with the return form before 31 October 1999: TMA 1970, s. 8(1). If it does do so, then the deadline is 31 January 2000. If it does not do so, the deadline is the last day of the three-month period beginning with the day on which your return form was sent to you.

(c) *The need to make payments on account*: Section 59A, TMA 1970 may oblige you to make payments on account to the Revenue. This will mean making income tax payments for 1998/99 before 5 April 1999. TMA 1970, s. 59A does *not* apply to 1998/99, however, if in 1997/98:

   (i) Your whole income tax and NIC liability, less tax deducted at source or tax on dividends, was less than £500; *or*

   (ii) Over 80% of the whole of the income tax and NICs paid by you for 1997/98 was deducted at source or credited as paid.

Of these, (a) does not apply, although (b) may apply, depending on your situation in 1997/98. There is not enough information to verify that (b) applied in 1997/98, but it is likely that it did. On this basis, at least two equal payments on account, plus a possible third, will be required from you:

   (i) on 31 January 1999;

   (ii) on 31 July 1999; *and*

   (iii) possibly on 31 January 2000.

The 31 January 2000 payment will be any difference between the total income tax due, according to your self-assessment under TMA 1970, s. 9, for 1998/99; *and* the total of any payments on account made by you in respect of that tax year, and any income tax which, in respect of that year, has been deducted at source: TMA 1970, s. 59B(1). It is due and payable on or before 31 January 2000: TMA 1970, s. 59B(4).

# CHAPTER TWENTY

# INVESTMENT TAXATION: INTRODUCTION AND SCOPE

## 20.1 Investment Taxation

### 20.1.1 THE DISTINCTION BETWEEN CAPITAL AND INCOME

*JOHN SMITH & SON* v *MOORE* [1921] 2 AC 13 (HL)

A son bought a colliery business, including certain forward contracts, from the trustees of his father's will trust. The son already carried on a trade, the income profits from which fell within Schedule D, Case I.

The House of Lords held that the expenditure on the business was capital expenditure, and therefore not an allowable deduction under Schedule D, Case I.

VISCOUNT HALDANE: My Lords, profit may be produced in two ways. It may result from purchases on income account, the cost of which is debited to that account, and the prices realised therefrom are credited, or it may result from realisation at a profit of assets forming part of the concern. In such a case a prudent man of business will no doubt debit to profit and loss the value of capital assets realised, and take credit only for the balance. But what was the nature of what the appellant here had to deal with? He had bought as part of the capital of the business his father's contracts. These enabled him to purchase coal from the colliery owners at what we were told was a very advantageous price, about fourteen shillings per ton. He was able to buy at this price because the right to do so was part of the assets of the business. Was it circulating capital?

My Lords, it is not necessary to draw an exact line of demarcation between fixed and circulating capital. Since Adam Smith drew the distinction in the Second Book of his Wealth of Nations, which appears in the chapter on the Division of Stock, a distinction which has since become classical, economists have never been able to define much more precisely what the line of demarcation is. Adam Smith described fixed capital as what the owner turns to profit by keeping it in his own possession, circulating capital as what he makes profit of by parting with it and letting it change masters. The latter capital circulates in this sense.

My Lords, in the case before us the appellant, of course, made profit with circulating capital by buying coal under the contracts he had acquired from his father's estate at the stipulated price of fourteen shillings and reselling it for more, but he was able to do this simply because he had acquired, among other assets of his business, including the goodwill, the contracts in question. It was not by selling these contracts, of limited duration though they were, it was not by parting with them to other masters, but by retaining them, that he was able to employ his circulating capital in buying under them. I am accordingly of opinion that, although they may have been of short duration, they were none the less part of his fixed capital. That he had paid a price for them makes no difference. Indeed the description of their value by the accountants, in the words I have earlier referred to, as of doubtful validity in the hands of outsiders, emphasises this conclusion. The £30,000 paid for the contracts or its equivalent, therefore, became part of

the appellant's fixed capital and could not properly appear in his revenue account. If that be so, then it was a sum employed as capital in his trade, and has to be excluded as a deduction from the profits on which he is assessed.
. . .

### IRC v CHURCH COMMISSIONERS [1976] 2 All ER 1037 (HL)

A charity owned leasehold properties which were let to a company on long leases. The charity then sold the reversions to the tenant company, in consideration of 10 annual instalments of £96,000, payable under a rentcharge reserved by the charity out of the land.

The £96,000 represented the annual rental, plus an amount which would have produced an equivalent amount to the total annual rental income at the end of the ten-year period, if it had been invested. The question was whether the annual payments were income or capital payments.

LORD WILBERFORCE: I shall not go through the long list of cases in which the courts have considered the problem of 'income' or 'capital' in relation to terminable payments. . . . all rest on the basis that there are two alternatives — instalments of capital, or production of an annual payment and that the task of the court is to find which it is. That this basis is a solid one is borne out by the fact that most of these decisions, as well as that in the *Wesleyan & General Assurance Society* case [1948] 1 All ER 555, bear the authority, or contain the judgment of Lord Greene MR — a hallmark of gold.

I cannot, therefore, for these reasons accept that the Crown's proposition either represents, or ought to represent, the existing law, and I now must consider their alternative particular argument.

This argument involves the proposition that, even though it may be impermissible to predicate, in general, that payments of a purchase price, spread over a number of years, contain a capital element and an interest element, this 'dissection', as it has come to be called, is permissible where the true legal character of the bargain or transaction, calls for it. Dissection is, at least as a plain case, permissible if the parties who are buying and selling a capital asset, having agreed on a price, then make provision for payment of that price by instalments, the amount of which is so calculated and shown to be so calculated as to include an interest element. Whether there are other possible cases of dissection, i.e. apart from the case where a lump purchase price has been agreed on, may be a debatable area.

There is no doubt, in my opinion, that the plain case is recognised by authority: *Scoble v Secretary of State for India* [1903] AC 299. There was an agreed purchase price for the railway but the Secretary of State had an option, instead of paying the lump sum, of making payment by an annuity spread over a long period 'the interest used in calculating the annuity being determined' as prescribed. There was no difficulty whatever in deciding that, under the bargain between the parties, there was a (taxable) interest element and a capital element, and the fact that the word 'annuity' was used, did not prevent the capital element being recognised, and consequently not taxed.

This case has never been doubted or qualified; if it has not been much followed, that is because it is seldom that the case for dissection is so clear as it was there. . . . *Vestey v Inland Revenue Comrs* [1961] 3 All ER 978 is much more directly relevant, and is the decision on which the Crown chiefly relies. The agreement in that case was for a sale of shares for £5,500,000, to be paid without interest by 125 yearly instalments of £44,000. On the face of it — a face with some cosmetic reconstruction — this was a case of a principal sum payable over a period of years, within Lord Greene MR's first category, and not admitting of dissection. However, evidence was given and admitted (i) that the value of the shares at the time of transfer was approximately £2 million and (ii) that on an actuarial basis, the annual sum payable over 125 years, equivalent to a present value of £2 million and taking interest at 2 per cent was £43,670. On this, Cross J felt able to decide that the case was one for dissection of each annual payment between capital and income. This case represents, so far, the high water mark of dissection cases, and the Crown seeks to apply it here. I would, for myself, accept this decision as correct, even though I would be unable to follow those portions of the judgment in which the learned judge appears to favour a general rule of dissection wherever there is a deferred payment of a purchase price. And on that basis I will consider whether on the same principle the Crown can succeed in the present case.

. . .

The essential feature of the negotiations and of the bargain, as shown by the documents, was that Land Securities did not wish, on any account, to pay a lump sum for the properties. This is so found in terms. The Church Commissioners, on their side, wished to maintain their existing income by rentcharges for a longer period. The figure of £720,000 was not an agreed purchase price, or even an agreed valuation. It was, as I understand it, simply a checking figure in the calculations, worked out on the basis of 18 years' purchase (corresponding to 5½ per cent) of the existing rents of £40,000. The bargain was always thought of in income terms, and was concluded on income terms, and there is nothing in the documents which gives to the transaction, or to any element in it, a capital character. The resemblance to the facts of *Vestey* (itself a borderline case), though at first sight striking, is, in the end, more superficial than real, and the essential 'true' character found to exist in *Vestey* is missing here. A fortiori, the present case differs from the clear factual situation in *Scoble's* case. In the end, the decision in the present case rests on a narrow point but I find that it does not come within a dissection principle. I agree with both courts below and I would dismiss the appeal.

## 20.2 Persons and Capacities

### 20.2.1 CAPACITIES

#### 20.2.1.1 Partners

**Good, T., 'Partnerships and Capital Taxes', *The Tax Journal*, 1 February 1990, p. 16**

(Note: References are to the Capital Gains Tax Act 1979.)

**The legislation**
The Taxes Acts are almost silent on the subject of taxing partnership capital gains. The main statutory reference is in section 60, CGTA 1979, which states that 'gains in respect of partnership assets shall be assessed on the partners separately'.

The practical approach to partnership capital gains is contained in the Inland Revenue Statement of Practice SP D12, which was issued on 17 January 1975. The treatment of indexation allowance is further considered in SP 1/89, dated 1 February 1989.

Under SP D12 there are six possible occasions of charge, as follows:
(1)   disposal of a partnership asset to a third party;
(2)   division of a partnership asset amongst the partners;
(3)   changes in the partnership sharing ratios with no adjustment through the accounts;
(4)   revaluations of partnership assets followed by a change in partnership sharing ratios;
(5)   payments between partners outside the accounts; and
(6)   transfers involving partnership assets other than at arms' length.
Each of these will now be considered in turn.

**Disposals to third parties**
The basic premise is that each partner is treated as making a disposal of his fractional share of the partnership asset. The proceeds (or market value) are split according to the partnership asset-sharing ratio. Each partner will set his own allowable expenditure (which may be a fractional share of the original acquisition cost or an amount paid on admission to the partnership) against his share of proceeds. Indexation allowance is calculated as normal on the fractional shares.

**Example**

A, B and D share capital surpluses and losses equally. They dispose of a capital asset for £60,000, which the partnership had acquired for £39,000. D joined the partnership after the asset was acquired and paid C, a retiring partner, £15,000 for his share in the asset.

On disposal the unindexed gains will be calculated as follows:

|                        | A       | B       | C       |
|------------------------|---------|---------|---------|
|                        | £       | £       | £       |
| Proceeds               | 20,000  | 20,000  | 20,000  |
| Allowable expenditure  | 13,000  | 13,000  | 15,000  |
| Unrealised gain        | £7,000  | £7,000  | £5,000  |

## Division of assets

Where a partnership asset is divided in kind amongst the partners (where, for example, one of the partners takes over the asset from the others), gains are calculated in the same way as for disposal to third parties. A partner disposing of the asset will be assessed whilst the partner who receives the asset reduces his deemed cost carried forward by his share of the gain on disposal. This effectively means that the receiving partner carries forward his share of the gain.

## Example

Details are as above except that partner A takes over the asset at its agreed market value of £60,000. Partners B and D realise and will be assessed on unindexed gains of £7,000 and £5,000, respectively. Partner A has an unrealised gain of £7,000, which is deducted from his cost carried forward. A's cost for future disposals will be £60,000 minus £7,000 = £53,000.

If a loss arises when an asset is divided between the partners, those making a disposal may obtain relief for the loss whilst any partner receiving the asset carries forward a base cost increased by his share of the loss.

## Changes in ratio

Where there is a change in the partnership sharing ratio (including occasions on which a partner joins or leaves the partnership), a partner whose share reduces has made a disposal and a partner whose share increases has made an acquisition. However, if no adjustment is made through the partnership accounts, the disposals and acquisitions are at a deemed consideration equal to the capital gains tax base cost, so that there is neither a gain nor a loss.

Prior to 6 April 1988, a partner whose share was reduced could establish an allowable loss equivalent to the indexation allowance on his base cost. SP 1/89, issued on 1 February 1989 removes, *inter alia*, the possibility of establishing such a loss.

Capital contributions on a change of profit-sharing ratio (for example, a payment by an incoming partner) are irrelevant to the treatment described above.

## Example

L and M have traded in partnership for several years sharing profits and losses equally (including those on capital assets). N is admitted to the partnership on 2 January 1990.

He contributes capital of £10,000 and becomes an equal partner. The only capital assets owned by the partnership are a freehold, which cost £60,000 in June 1985 and goodwill, which is not valued in the partnership accounts.

On the admission of N, L and M are treated as disposing of part of their share in the freehold. The computations for each will be:

|                          | £      |
|--------------------------|--------|
| Cost                     | 10,000 |
| Indexation (say 0·250)   | 2,500  |
| Deemed consideration     | 12,500 |
| Gain                     | NIL    |

N acquires a one-third interest in the freehold for a deemed cost of £25,000.

### Revaluations

Where a partnership asset is revalued upwardly in the accounts, this is not of itself an occasion of charge. However, a subsequent change in profit-sharing ratio will result in a disposal by a partner whose share reduces and an acquisition by a partner whose share increases.

The partner whose share reduces is treated as making a fractional disposal of his interest in the asset. The unindexed gain is calculated by taking:

|  | £ |
|---|---|
| F × revalued amount | x |
| Less: F × original cost | x |
| Unindexed gain | x |

where F is the fraction by which the partner's share is reduced.

Similarly, a partner whose share is increased has a corresponding increase in his acquisition cost carried forward.

The increase in cost will be F′ multiplied by the revalued amount, where F′ is the fraction by which his share is increased.

### Example

Assume that in the previous example the goodwill is now valued at £45,000, having cost nothing when L and M formed the partnership in 1983. They decide to value it in the accounts on the admission of N. L and M each have a realised gain of:

|  | £ |
|---|---|
| ⅙ × £45,000 | 7,500 |
| Less: cost | NIL |
| indexation | NIL |
|  | £7,500 |

N has a deemed acquisition cost of ⅓ × £45,000 = £15,000.

### Outside the accounts

If payments between the partners are made outside the accounts on a change in profit-sharing ratio, such payments are treated as consideration for the disposal of a partner's share in partnership assets. This may be in addition to any actual consideration within the partnership.

The partner making the payment may treat it as allowable expenditure in respect of a subsequent disposal of his share of the partnership assets or when he leaves the partnership or subsequently reduces his partnership share.

The partner receiving the payment may set against it his share of the cost of any partnership asset if the payment is clearly made in respect of that asset.

### Non-arms's-length transfers

If a transfer of a share in partnership assets is made between persons not at arm's length, it may be treated as having been made at market value and will then be dealt with in the same way as payments outside the accounts (see above).

This provision might well apply when the offspring of a partner is admitted to the partnership on favourable terms. The Revenue's attempt to assess such gains could, however, be rebuffed if it can be shown that the terms under which the offspring was admitted were not in fact preferential but would equally apply on the admission of a similar but totally unconnected partner.

### 20.2.1.2   Trustees

### TAXATION OF CHARGEABLE GAINS ACT 1992

**60.   Nominees and bare trustees**

(1)   In relation to assets held by a person as nominee for another person, or as trustee for another person absolutely entitled as against the trustee, or for any person who

would be so entitled but for being an infant or other person under disability (or for 2 or more persons who are or would be jointly so entitled), this Act shall apply as if the property were vested in, and the acts of the nominee or trustee in relation to the assets were the acts of, the person or persons for whom he is the nominee or trustee (acquisitions from or disposals to him by that person or persons being disregarded accordingly).

# CHAPTER TWENTY-ONE

# INVESTMENT TAXATION: LIABILITY AND CALCULATION

## 21.1 Liability to Pay CGT and Corporation Tax on Chargeable Gains

### 21.1.1 MAKES A CHARGEABLE DISPOSAL

#### TAXATION OF CHARGEABLE GAINS ACT 1992

**22. Disposals where capital sums derived from assets**

(1) Subject to sections 23 and 26(1), and to any other exceptions in this Act, there is for the purposes of this Act a disposal of assets by their owner where any capital sum is derived from assets notwithstanding that no asset is acquired by the person paying the capital sum, and this subsection applies in particular to—

(a) capital sums received by way of compensation for any kind of damage or injury to assets or for the loss, destruction or dissipation of assets or for any depreciation or risk of depreciation of an asset,

(b) capital sums received under a policy of insurance of the risk of any kind of damage or injury to, or the loss or depreciation of, assets,

(c) capital sums received in return for forfeiture or surrender of rights, or for refraining from exercising rights, and

(d) capital sums received as consideration for use or exploitation of assets.

(2) In the case of a disposal within paragraph (a), (b), (c) or (d) of subsection (1) above, the time of the disposal shall be the time when the capital sum is received as described in that subsection.

(3) In this section 'capital sum' means any money or money's worth which is not excluded from the consideration taken into account in the computation of the gain.

> **de Souza, J. '*Chaloner* v *Pellipar Investments Ltd*: No Transfer of Possession, No Section 22(1)(d) Deemed Disposal', [1996]** *Private Client Business* **156**

Read the summary of the facts and the commentary here, before moving on to the extract from Rattee J's judgment below.

This was a case about the application of 1982 rebasing under the Finance Act 1988.

On August 7, 1987, the taxpayer entered into a Development Agreement under which, in the events which happened, the developer was granted a lease of Blackacre in return for a cash premium and the erection of a building on Whiteacre, which the taxpayer had retained in its own ownership. That building was completed in 1991.

It was common ground between the parties that the contract was not a conditional one and that the cash premium fell to be taxed pursuant to Schedule 8 on August 7, 1987. It was also agreed that, because *money's worth* was not within the definition of premium contained in paragraph 10(2) of it, Schedule 8 could not apply to the consideration which took the form of the erection of the building of Whiteacre.

The taxpayer contended that, in consequence, and by virtue of section 22(2), the disposal date in relation to the consideration in money's worth took place in 1991. In order to establish that there was a different time of disposal under this provision, it was necessary for the taxpayer to show that the transaction fell within section 22(1)(d): *capital sums received as consideration for use or exploitation of assets.*

The Special Commissioner held that it did, applying the speech of Lord Wilberforce in *Marren* v *Ingles*. The Revenue's primary submission throughout the case was that these remarks were *obiter*, and that section 22(1) ought not to apply where an asset was acquired by the payer of the capital sum. Lord Wilberforce had put forward as examples of transactions within section 22(1)(d) sums paid for the grant of a licence or a profit. The Special Commissioner held that the grant of a lease was within the same category.

Rattee J took a different view, holding that, while a grant of a lease of land included the right for the tenant to use or exploit the land in question, a conveyance of the freehold would also and this could not seriously be argued in the context of section 22(1). He saw the words of paragraph (d) as apt to include a licence or a profit, which left the freeholder's rights to the land unaffected in the sense that he remained entitled to full possession of it, but not a lease, which involved the transfer of possession. Accordingly, section 22(1)(d) did not apply and the disposal took place on August 7, 1987.

In the course of his examination of the arguments of the parties, Rattee J came to the conclusion that there was no justification for having a different date of disposal in a case where the premium was payable in cash. It seems unlikely, however, that the point would be material in many cases since, if a landlord had wished to defer the date of disposal, he would have been more likely to resort to some form of cross-option, rather than seek to litigate this point with the Revenue.

It would follow from view expressed by Rattee J, however, that it would be possible to defer the disposal date in the event of a transaction by way of licence, irrespective of whether consideration for the licence was in cash or money's worth. In recent years some landed estates have been seeking to bring arrangements involving the extraction of gravel or the tipping of waste within the licence concept in order to avoid the attribution of a Schedule A element. Pursuant to ICTA 1988, s. 34(1)] Rattee J's judgment appears to confer an additional tax advantage in such cases.

Two notes of caution need to be voiced:

(a)  Although there have been cases where commercial transactions have been held to have taken place by way of licence, one cannot turn what is in reality a lease into a licence by describing it as a licence. Very often the critical issue is whether exclusive possession has been ceded.

(b)  Where tipping is concerned, a waste management licence under section 35 of the Environmental Protection Act 1990 will almost certainly be required. The appropriate licence is likely to be under section 35(2)(a) and the person required to obtain it is the one who is in *occupation* of the land. Because the concept of exclusive possession has a bearing on this, that person is more likely than not to be the owner where a licence, rather than a lease, has been granted.

   The significance of this lies in the new Landfill Tax, which is to be assessed by reference to weight rather than (as originally intended) price. The accountable party is the holder of the waste management licence. If, therefore, the landowner disposed of the tipping rights in return for a capital sum without having reserved the right to collect the Landfill Tax from the tipper independently, he could well find himself in difficulties.

### CHALONER v PELLIPAR INVESTMENTS LTD [1996] STC 234

The discussion of Rattee J set out below involved the predecessor of TCGA 1992, s. 22(1)(d), i.e. s. 20(1)(d) of the Capital Gains Tax Act 1979.

RATTEE J: Mr Bramwell's explanation [i.e. counsel for the taxpayer's explanation] for his submission that a cash premium was not within s. 20(1)(d) was, as I understood it, that the effect of a premium being required for the grant of a lease of land was expressly provided for by para. 2 of sch. 3 to the 1979 Act. That paragraph provided that the effect is a part disposal of the freehold. It only applied, according to Mr Bramwell's argument, where the premium required was in cash. For this last proposition Mr Bramwell relied on the definition of 'premium' in para. 10 of sch. 3. In Mr Bramwell's submission, since the grant of a lease for a cash premium is expressly dealt with by sch. 3, it should not be treated as also within the more general provisions of s. 20(1)(d).

Mr Bramwell accepted that the result of this argument is that the timing of the relevant disposal was different depending on whether the capital consideration for the grant of a lease was in cash or kind. Not surprisingly, as I have already said, Mr Brennan relied on this apparently bizarre consequence of the argument as indicating that it must be wrong.

I agree with Mr Brennan that this consequence of the taxpayer's argument does seem to be irrational. While it does not follow that the argument is wrong, it does, in my judgment, cast some doubt upon it.

However, I do not consider that any great weight should be placed on this point, because I was not persuaded by Mr Bramwell's argument that, because the grant of a lease for a cash premium was within para. 2 of sch. 3 to the 1979 Act, it was not also within s. 20(1)(d). As was recognised by Lord Fraser of Tullybelton in *Marren (Inspector of Taxes) v Ingles* ([1980] STC 500 at 505, [1980] 1 WLR 983 at 989), it is not uncommon in fiscal legislation for there to be some overlapping of the effect of two or more provisions. If the taxpayer's primary argument, namely that a capital sum received as consideration for the grant of a lease was within s. 20(1)(d), is correct, I see no reason why this should not apply to a cash premium as defined in sch. 3, just as much as to any other 'capital sum' within the definition in s. 20(3). Thus I do not think that the apparently irrational distinction drawn by the taxpayer's argument between a case where the capital sum was cash and a case where (as in the present case) it was in kind really helps to answer the question whether any such capital sum received as consideration for the grant of a lease was within s. 20(1)(d).

So, I come back to the words of s. 20(1)(d) themselves — 'capital sums received as consideration for use or exploitation of assets'. In *Marren (Inspector of Taxes) v Ingles* [1980] STC 500 at 503, [1980] 1 WLR 983 at 986, Lord Wilberforce gave two examples of such a capital sum in the case of land — namely, sums received as consideration for the grant of a licence or a profit. He did not suggest a sum received as consideration for the grant of a lease as a further example. This does not, of course, amount to any authority for the Crown's contention that such a sum is not such, but Lord Wilberforce's failure to mention a lease in the same context as a licence or profit is consistent with what seems to me to be an essential distinction between a lease on the one hand and a licence or profit on the other hand. A lease gives the grantee the right to actual possession of the land concerned. A licence and a profit do not. What they do give is a right to use or exploit land the right to possession of which remains vested in the grantor. The right enjoyed under a licence is to use another's land. The right enjoyed under a lease is to full possession of the land itself. The grant by a freeholder in possession of land of a licence or a profit leaves his rights to the land unaffected, in the sense that he remains entitled to full possession of the land. A grant of a lease is very different. It has a fundamental effect on the grantor's rights, which no longer extend to possession of the land.

In my judgment, in the context of s. 20 of the 1979 Act, the words of para. (d) are apt to include the former but not the latter. Those words are apt to include capital sums received as consideration for the use or exploitation of assets title to which remains unaffected in their owner referred to in the opening words of s. 20(1), but are not apt to include capital sums received as consideration for a grant of the owner's title to the assets, whether in perpetuity or for a term of years. Of course, a grant of a lease of land *includes* the right to use or exploit the land concerned, but so does a conveyance of the freehold of the land. Yet I do not think it could be seriously argued (and certainly Mr Bramwell did not argue) that an outright sale of land was within s. 20(1)(d).

For these reasons, in my judgment, the learned Special Commissioner was wrong to allow the taxpayer's appeal before him on the only ground argued in support of that appeal, namely that the benefit to the taxpayer of the development of site A was a capital sum within s. 20(1)(d) of the 1979 Act.

## 21.1.2 OF A CHARGEABLE ASSET

An asset can be a chargeable asset, even though it cannot be bought or sold.

*O'BRIEN* v *BENSON'S HOSIERY (HOLDINGS) LTD* [1979] 3 ALL ER 652 (HL)

A director of the company had a seven-year service contract. In order to be released from his contractual obligations, he paid the company £50,000. The Revenue argued that the receipt of the £50,000 was consideration for the disposal by the company of a chargeable asset.

The House of Lords held that it was irrelevant that the company's rights under the contract could not be assigned by it, thus agreeing with the Revenue's argument.

LORD RUSSELL OF KILLOWEN: My Lords, at first glance I find it difficult to see why the rights of the taxpayer under the contract of service was not an 'asset' of the taxpayer within the unrestricted language of [TCGA 1992, ss. 1(1) and 22]. The Court of Appeal in deciding this case in favour of the taxpayer (and reversing Fox J) relied greatly on the reasons for the decision of this House in *Nokes* v *Doncaster Amalgamated Collieries Ltd* [1940] 1 All ER 549. The question there was whether on the occasion of the approval by the court under the Companies Act 1929 of a scheme for the amalgamation of companies an employee's contract of service was automatically transferred to the new entity, the statutory language stating the relevant effect, on existing contracts and rights, of the order approving the amalgamation being of a width amply sufficient, prima facie, to embrace contracts of employment. This House however declined, despite the width of that language, to include within it contracts of employment; the reason was that to do so would breach a fundamental principle of the law that such contracts were not *assignable*, and that something more particular was needed than mere generality of language (however widely expressed) if such a breach of principle was to be accepted as being intended by Parliament.

My Lords, I do not accept that that decision affords guidance to a decision under the capital gains tax legislation which deals not merely with assignments but with disposals. To treat the events which took place in the instant case as coming within the wide generality of the language of [ss. 1 and 22], and in particular of s. 22(1)(*c*), cannot be regarded as breaching any fundamental principle of the law that a contract of personal service is not assignable. Similarly I derive no guidance from the cases in bankruptcy law of *Bailey* v *Thurston & Co Ltd* [1900–03] All ER Rep 818, which decided that rights under a contract of personal service did not vest in the trustee in bankruptcy, and *Sutton* v *Dorf* [1932] All ER Rep 70, which similarly decided in the case of a statutory tenancy.

It was contended for the taxpayer that the rights of an employer under a contract of service were not 'property' or an 'asset' of the employer, because they cannot be turned to account by transfer or assignment to another. But in my opinion this contention supposes a restricted view of the scheme of the imposition of the capital gains tax which the statutory language does not permit. If, as here, the employer is able to exact from the employee a substantial sum as a term of releasing him from his obligations to serve, the rights of the employer appear to me to bear quite sufficiently the mark of an asset of the employer, something which he can turn to account, notwithstanding that his ability to turn it to account is by a type of disposal limited by the nature of the asset. In this connection I would also refer to the provisions of s. 22(1)(*a*) which appear to me apt to cover a case where damages are recovered by an employer from a third party for wrongful procurement of breach by the employee of his contract of service.

Reliance was placed by the taxpayer and the Court of Appeal on the provisions of [TCGA 1992, ss. 17 and 272] which in certain circumstances introduce the concept of a market value, the contention being that the rights of the employer under the contract of service being non-transferable they could have no market value. In my opinion it is erroneous to deduce from [TCGA 1992, s. 17], the language of which has no direct application to the present case, a principle of general application for the purposes of capital gains tax that an asset must have a market value. This appears to me to be a preferable answer to the alternative contention of the Crown of analogy with the estate duty cases such as *Inland Revenue Comrs* v *Crossman* [1936] 1 All ER 762 in which a market value could be found notwithstanding restrictions on transfer of shares in a private company. It appears to me that there is a distinction to be drawn between a case in which the asset has the essential character of transferability but subject to restrictions imposed by the contract contained in the articles of association and the asset in the instant case which lacks that essential character.

# 21.2   Calculating the *CGT due* from an Individual

## TAXATION OF CHARGEABLE GAINS ACT 1992

### 38.   Acquisition and disposal costs etc.

(1)   Except as otherwise expressly provided, the sums allowable as a deduction from the consideration in the computation of the gain accruing to a person on the disposal of an asset shall be restricted to—

(a)   the amount or value of the consideration, in money or money's worth, given by him or on his behalf wholly and exclusively for the acquisition of the asset, together with the incidental costs to him of the acquisition or, if the asset was not acquired by him, any expenditure wholly and exclusively incurred by him in providing the asset,

(b)   the amount of any expenditure wholly and exclusively incurred on the asset by him or on his behalf for the purpose of enhancing the value of the asset, being expenditure reflected in the state or nature of the asset at the time of the disposal, and any expenditure wholly and exclusively incurred by him in establishing, preserving or defending his title to, or to a right over, the asset,

(c)   the incidental costs to him of making the disposal.

(2)   For the purposes of this section and for the purposes of all other provisions of this Act, the incidental costs to the person making the disposal of the acquisition of the asset or of its disposal shall consist of expenditure wholly and exclusively incurred by him for the purposes of the acquisition or, as the case may be, the disposal, being fees, commission or remuneration paid for the professional services of any surveyor or valuer, or auctioneer, or accountant, or agent or legal adviser and costs of transfer or conveyance (including stamp duty) together—

(a)   in the case of the acquisition of an asset, with costs of advertising to find a seller, and

(b)   in the case of a disposal, with costs of advertising to find a buyer and costs reasonably incurred in making any valuation or apportionment required for the purposes of the computation of the gain, including in particular expenses reasonably incurred in ascertaining market value where required by this Act.

(3)   Except as provided by section 40, no payment of interest shall be allowable under this section.

(4)   Any provision in this Act introducing the assumption that assets are sold and immediately reacquired shall not imply that any expenditure is incurred as incidental to the sale or reacquisition.

## 21.3 End of Chapter Assessment Question

In 1990, Edward bought a derelict cottage in Worcestershire, with a view to rebuilding it and letting it to tenants. The cottage cost him £20,000 and he incurred a solicitors' fee of £400, excluding VAT.

He did part of the work of rebuilding the cottage himself, between 1992/93, estimating the market value of the work at £18,000. However, he also paid contractors to instal a new roof, which cost him £12,000 plus VAT in 1994. Also in 1994, he incurred an architect's fee of £500, including VAT, for the design of an extension, planning permission for which was subsequently refused by the local authority. In addition, he incurred a solicitors' fee of £3,080, including VAT, in 1995 in relation to a boundary dispute, in which he was victorious before the Lands Tribunal. He has never got round to letting the property.

He has now decided that the cottage is more trouble than it is worth, and contracted to sell it for £100,000 on 1 November 1998. His estate agent is proposing to charge a commission of 2% of the selling-price plus advertising fees of £40 (both figures exclusive of VAT). In addition, solicitors' fees on the sale will be £850 plus VAT.

In the 1998/99 tax year, he has gross Schedule E income of £37,000. He makes no other chargeable disposals in the tax year, and he has no carried forward allowable losses.

(a) Explain how the CGT due from him for 1998/99 will be calculated. Do *not* attempt the calculation itself.
(b) Explain whether the conveyance will need to be stamped by the purchaser and, if so, what amount of stamp duty will be chargeable.

## 21.4 End of Chapter Assessment Outline Answer

(a) CGT is charged on the gains chargeable to CGT of a chargeable person in a tax year. Edward is a chargeable person if he is resident or ordinarily resident in the UK in 1998/99: TCGA 1992, s. 2(1). There is nothing here to suggest that Edward is not a chargeable person.

The sale on 1 November 1998 is a chargeable disposal for CGT purposes. TCGA 1992, s. 28(1) provides that the chargeable disposal takes place at the date of the contract. Edward makes no other chargeable disposals in 1998/99. The disposal proceeds of the cottage are £100,000. From these is deducted the base cost of the cottage, determined according to the rules of TCGA 1992, s. 38.

The base cost of the cottage consists of the following:

(i) *Acquisition cost of £20,000*: This is the amount or value of the consideration, in money or money's worth, given by him wholly and exclusively for the acquisition of the asset: TCGA 1992, s. 38(1)(a).

(ii) *Solicitors' fee of £400 (excluding VAT)*: Including VAT, this would have amounted to £470. This·VAT-inclusive amount is an incidental cost of the acquisition, and forms part of the base cost under TCGA 1992, s. 38(1)(a).

(iii) *New roof costing £12,000 plus VAT*: Including VAT, this would have amounted to £14,100. This VAT-inclusive amount is expenditure wholly and exclusively incurred by him for the purpose of enhancing the value of the asset. It will form part of the base cost if it is reflected in the state or nature of the asset at the time of the disposal: TCGA 1992, s. 38(1)(b).

(iv)   *Architect's fee of £500 (including VAT):* This cannot be included in the base cost. Since the expenditure proved abortive, it is not reflected in the state or nature of the asset at the time of the disposal.

(v)    *Solicitors' fee of £3,080 (including VAT):* This is part of the base cost of the asset, under TCGA 1992, s. 38(1)(b). It is expenditure wholly and exclusively incurred by Edward in establishing, preserving or defending his title to the asset.

(vi)   *Estate agent's commission of 2% (excluding VAT):* This forms part of the base cost by virtue of TCGA 1992, s. 38(1)(c) and (2). The base cost can include the incidental costs of making the disposal: TCGA 1992, s. 38(1)(c). The incidental costs of making the disposal is expenditure wholly and exclusively incurred for the purposes of the disposal: TCGA 1992, s. 38(2). It specifically includes the commission of an auctioneer or agent.

(vii)  *Advertising fees of £40 plus VAT:* The position here is as for (f). The costs of advertising to find a buyer are specifically referred to in TCGA 1992, s. 38(2)(b).

(viii) *Solicitors' fees on the sale of £850 plus VAT:* This is remuneration paid for the professional services of a legal adviser. It is specifically included in the base cost of the asset by TCGA 1992, s. 38(2).

The base cost does not, however, include the market value of the work done himself: *Oram v Johnson* [1980] 2 All ER 1.

The total of (a) to (h) is the cottage's base cost and is deductible from the disposal proceeds of £100,000, to find the unindexed chargeable gain. The indexation allowance is then deducted from this gain, to produce the indexed chargeable gain. The indexation allowance is calculated from the month of acquisition to April 1998. For a disposal on 1 November 1998, no taper relief is available, since this is a non-business asset and the necessary qualifying holding period will not have elapsed from 6 April 1998 to the date of the disposal. CGT will be charged on the indexed chargeable gain, less the annual exempt amount (currently £6,800). The CGT due will be calculated by first applying the lower, basic and higher rates of income tax rate to Edward's taxable income of £37,000, and charging the gain chargeable to CGT at the higher rate.

(b)   The conveyance on sale will need to be stamped by the purchaser, as the purchase consideration in the deed is £100,000. Since this exceeds £60,000, but is less than £250,000, duty will be chargeable at 1%, i.e. £1 for every £100 of the consideration. Stamp duty will be £1,000 therefore.

# CHAPTER TWENTY-TWO

# REDUCING INVESTMENT TAXATION (1)

## 22.1 Provisions Making Gains Exempt Gains

### 22.1.1 PRIVATE RESIDENCE RELIEF

If you sell the land *after* the dwelling-house has been sold, you will lose the benefit of the relief.

### *VARTY* v *LYNES* [1976] 3 All ER 447

An individual had sold a house with only part of its garden in June 1971. He sold the remainder of the garden in May 1972, with the benefit of outline planning permission.

Brightman J held that the chargeable gain on the sale of the remainder of the garden in May 1972 was not protected by the relief. The chargeable gain on its disposal was not merely the gain accruing between June 1971 and May 1972, but the gain accruing whilst the remainder of the garden had still been occupied and enjoyed with the residence.

BRIGHTMAN J: This is an appeal by the Crown from a decision of the General Commissioners. The short point at issue is the capital gains tax position where the taxpayer is the owner of a dwelling-house and a garden, the dwelling-house being his only residence; he sells off his dwelling-house and a small piece of the garden; then, at a later date, he disposes of the remainder of the garden. Is the gain resulting from the disposal of the remainder of the garden a taxable gain? The question is a short one . . . and is not in my view susceptible of any very satisfactory answer. [TCGA 1992, s. 1] provided that tax should be charged in respect of chargeable gains accruing to a person on the disposal of assets. All forms of property are assets for this purpose . . . There are a few exceptions from the tax. The exception with which I am concerned is that which applies . . . to certain private residences. Before I go to the section in detail, I will recount the brief facts.

The dwelling-house was known as 'Dalesford', at Hailsham in the county of East Sussex. It was acquired by the taxpayer, who appears before me in person, in 1968. He paid a total of £6,920 for it, including costs. The total area of the house, including the garden, was less than an acre. The property was intended for use as a private residence and was in fact so used by him. In June 1971 he sold the house and a part of the garden at a price of £10,000. Thereupon, of course, it ceased to be his private residence. He retained the remainder of the garden and sold it in May 1972 for a like sum of £10,000. It appears that at the time when he sold off the dwelling-house and the small part of the garden he was informed by the local planning authority that favourable consideration would be given to a planning application for the development of the remainder of the garden. He applied for outline planning approval, which he obtained in January 1972, and sold the remainder of the garden a few months later.

On those facts the inspector of taxes assessed the taxpayer to capital gains tax in respect of a chargeable gain which the inspector maintained the taxpayer had secured

on selling the remainder of the garden. When the matter came before the General
Commissioners, the taxpayer maintained that [TCGA 1992, s. 222], to which I will refer
in detail in a moment, did not expressly deal with the case of the disposal of a property
in two parts, and that the exemption afforded by that section was equally applicable
whether the whole of the property was the subject of a single disposal or of two separate
disposals. . . .

The qualification for the exemption, which applies to the two items within [s. 222], is
defined accordingly by reference to one only of those items; there is no mention in
[TCGA 1992, s. 223(1)] of the garden. The exception of 'all or any part of the last [36]
months of that period' may perhaps have been inserted in order to take into account the
not uncommon case where a person who is changing his residence buys and enters into
occupation of the new residence before he has been able to sell the previous residence.
[TCGA 1992, s. 223(2)] deals with apportionment in a case where the dwelling-house
was the only or main residence for part only of the period of the taxpayer's ownership,
leaving aside the [36] months period covered by [TCGA 1992, s. 223(1)].

. . .

As I have already said, the contention of the taxpayer was that the exemption afforded
by [s. 222] was equally applicable whether the house and garden were sold off in the
course of one or two separate transactions. In particular, he contended that the phrase
in sub-s (1)(b) 'land which he has' did not necessarily imply 'at the date of disposal'. He
submitted that the phrase should be interpreted as meaning land which he had while
owning the residence. In the instant case, the remainder of the garden was quite clearly
land which the taxpayer had for his own occupation and enjoyment with the dwelling-
house as its garden during the whole period of his ownership of the dwelling-house.
Therefore, the taxpayer submits, there is much reason and good sense in saying that it
should fall within the exemption afforded by [s. 222].

The contention of the Crown before the General Commissioners was that the words
'has for his own occupation and enjoyment' refer only to the moment of disposal.
Accordingly, the garden would not be exempt in any case where it was disposed of at a
time when the taxpayer no longer owned the dwelling-house to which the garden had
been attached. It was contended by the Crown that there was no provision in the section
which would allow for an apportionment of the gain on some sort of time basis in
relation to the garden comparable with the apportionment which is appropriate in
certain circumstances in the case of the dwelling-house. The commissioners expressed
themselves very shortly in their decision in favour of the taxpayer. They held—

> that the exemption contained in sub-section (2) of Section 29 of the Finance Act, 1965,
> applied having regard particularly to the words contained in the last part of that
> sub-section. We therefore found in favour of the [taxpayer] and reduced the assess-
> ment to Nil.

The General Commissioners, as they said, placed great emphasis on the concluding
words of [TCGA 1992, s. 223(1)]. It will be recalled that [s. 223(1)] grants exemption
where the dwelling-house was the taxpayer's only residence throughout his period of
ownership but allows one to disregard the last [36] months of that period. To fall within
[s. 223(1)], the house must be the only or main residence throughout the period of
ownership, or throughout the period of ownership except for all or any part of the last
[36] months of that period'. I think that the General Commissioners must have said to
themselves this: 'It was clearly the intention of Parliament that the dwelling-house
should be exempt notwithstanding that a few months before sale the taxpayer went out
of occupation. If, therefore, we, the General Commissioners, do not accede to the
taxpayer's argument, we shall in effect be saying that Parliament intended that a garden
should not qualify for exemption in a case where the taxpayer goes out of residence a
month before he sells; and that,' the commissioners may have said to themselves, 'would
be an absurd construction.'

The point of interpretation is a short one. I think it can be summarised in exactly the
way that the taxpayer put it in his contentions before the General Commissioners,
namely should the court read the words 'land which he has for his own occupation and
enjoyment with that residence as its garden or grounds' as meaning land which he has

at the date of the disposal or land which he has at any time while owning the residence? The contentions advanced by the taxpayer before me are really exactly the same as the contentions advanced before the General Commissioners.

Counsel for the Crown has, I think quite rightly, not regarded it as any part of his duty to seek to justify the anomalies which may be thrown up by the Crown's construction, of [s. 222(1)(b)], nor, indeed, does he seek to deny that anomalies could be said to exist. The anomaly which I find most striking on the Crown's construction is the anomaly which I think impressed itself on the General Commissioners, namely the disregard for the purposes of [TCGA 1992, s. 223(1) of the last 36 months] of the period of ownership in respect of the dwelling-house. Why, I ask myself, should that exemption not equally cover the garden? On the construction advanced by the Crown it must follow, I am disposed to think, that if the taxpayer goes out of occupation of the dwelling-house a month before he sells it, the exemption will be lost in respect of the garden. That, however, is merely my impression, and I do not intend so to decide because it is not a matter for decision before me. . . .

On the other hand, there would also seem to be anomalies thrown up by the construction advanced by the taxpayer. The taxpayer, in his short submission to me, did not shrink from conceding that his construction might produce anomalies. Take the case of a taxpayer who buys his dwelling-house and garden in 1960, sells off his dwelling-house in 1970 and retains the garden for future disposal. That garden is sold off, perhaps, 20 years later as a desirable and extremely valuable building site. In those circumstances, is the garden (or the former garden, as perhaps I should describe it) to fall within the exemption?

I accept counsel for the Crown's submission that in these circumstances all that the court can do is to look at the wording adopted by the legislature and decide whether or not the remainder of the garden in the present case falls or does not fall within the description in sub-s. (1)(b). If it does fall within that description, then it qualifies for exemption under [TCGA 1992, s. 223(1)]; if it falls outside that description, then it does not. It is no good counting up anomalies on one side and the other and twisting the language in order to produce what may seem to be, on balance, the most sensible result, and the one which perhaps Parliament might have preferred if all the various combinations of circumstances had been fully debated. The words [of s. 222(1)] are:

> This section applies to a gain accruing to an individual so far as attributable to the disposal of, or of an interest in . . . land which he has for his own occupation and enjoyment with that residence [i e a dwelling-house or part of a dwelling-house which is, or has at any time in his period of ownership been, his only or main residence] as its garden or grounds . . .

The difficulty of relating the expression 'land which he has for his own occupation and enjoyment with that residence as its garden or grounds' to any moment except the actual time of disposal is that para. (a) is clearly looking both to the present and the past — 'a dwelling-house or part of a dwelling-house which is, or has at any time in his period of ownership been, his only or main residence' — while by contrast para. (b), as a matter of language, is looking only to the present, namely 'land which he has for his own occupation and enjoyment with that residence as its garden'. In the face of that comparative wording, it does not seem to me possible, without doing violence to the language of para. (b), to read it in the manner desired by the taxpayer.

In these circumstances it seems to me that I am bound to accept the argument advanced by the Crown and allow the appeal. I appreciate that this construction can produce anomalies and perhaps injustices. I am slightly comforted by the fact that the alternative construction would have had its own crop of anomalies. Accordingly, I allow the appeal.

The land you dispose of might not be for occupation and enjoyment with the residence.

### *WAKELING* v *PEARCE* [1995] STC (SCD) 1996

T.H.K. EVERETT, Special Commissioner: . . . The taxpayer and her predecessor in title had cultivated a garden in the top left hand corner of field 528 and had maintained a washing line there. A shed which was used as a summer house was also erected in that area of the field. In the top right hand corner of field 528 there was a lean-to shed used by the taxpayer's predecessor for storage of gardening tools.

The taxpayer is now aged 87 years and owing to advancing years and ill health she has been unable to cultivate the garden in field 528 since 1980/81. The clothes line was taken down in 1986 and in the same year the shed/summer house was removed from field 528 and re-erected in the front garden of Cartref.

Field 528 was much used by the taxpayer, her friends and family for relaxation. Her grandchildren played and camped there. Although use by the taxpayer's family gradually declined over the years it continued in reduced form until the taxpayer disposed of the land.

The inspector made two submissions. First, he contended on the authority of *Varty (Inspector of Taxes)* v *Lynes* [1976] STC 508 that it was not possible to look at the history of the land disposed but only at the conditions prevailing at the moment of sale.

Secondly he contended that the language of s. 101 presupposed that the land disposed of should not be separated from but should adjoin the taxpayer's residence.

In my judgment, on balance, I find that the taxpayer's appeals succeed. It is clear that she always regarded field 528 as part of the garden or grounds of Cartref and continued to do so until it was sold. I accept the evidence of the taxpayer and her son, despite the production by the inspector of aerial photographs from which he sought to show that field 528 was not used at various dates in the manner described by the taxpayer and her son. In my judgment the photographic evidence produced by the inspector was not sufficiently clear to disprove the evidence of the taxpayer and her son.

In my judgment the fact that the building plots did not adjoin Cartref is not fatal to the taxpayer's appeals. There is no statutory requirement that the land sold should adjoin or be contiguous with the taxpayer's residence. The distance between Cartref and field 528 was never stated in evidence but having inspected Cartref and viewed the now developed building plots from the road I would estimate the distance at between 25 and 30 feet. I do not believe that that distance is sufficient to disqualify the taxpayer from claiming the relief available pursuant to s. 101.

The words of the statute are 'with that residence'. On the facts of these appeals I find that the taxpayer enjoyed field 528 with Cartref as its garden or grounds until the building plots were sold.

The inspector has submitted, in reliance upon *Varty* v *Lynes*, that the determinative date was the date of the sale of each plot and that by 1987 and 1988 field 528 had ceased to be enjoyed by the taxpayer as the garden or grounds of her residence.

*Varty* v *Lynes* was concerned with a taxpayer who sold his house and part of his garden in June 1971. He obtained outline planning approval for the remainder of the garden in January 1972 and sold it in May 1972. It was therefore quite apparent that the land which he sold in May 1972 was not, at that time, the garden or grounds of his former residence which he had sold in June 1971. Had the taxpayer sold Cartref and at a later date sold all or part of field 528, she would have been in a similar position to Mr Lynes, but she did not do that. She used field 528 as the garden or grounds of Cartref for many years and although that use declined over the years owing to her age and infirmity I have little doubt that the field still formed part of the grounds of Cartref up to the time of sale.

The taxpayer's appeals succeed and I discharge the two estimated assessments.

### Soares, P.C., 'Selling land enjoyed with the principal residence — when the gain is not tax free', 16 *Property Law Bulletin*, p. 30

The relevant exemption is to be found in the Taxation of Chargeable Gains Act (TCGA) 1992, s. 222(1). This exempts from capital gains tax a gain accruing to an individual if he disposes of a dwelling house which has been his main residence or gardens or grounds which he occupied and enjoyed with that residence up to 0.5 of a hectare (inclusive of the site of the dwelling house).

It is not sufficient to show that the land was 0.5 of a hectare or less to get the relief: it is necessary to show that the land was occupied and enjoyed with the residence as its garden or grounds.

If the land is larger than 0.5 of a hectare then it may, nevertheless still benefit from the capital gains tax exemption provided that regard being had to the size and character of the dwelling house, that larger area is required for the reasonable enjoyment of it as a residence.

### Garden or grounds less than 0.5 of a hectare must be occupied and enjoyed with the residence

The situation may arise where the taxpayer has a house with a small garden and other land which is physically separate but is nevertheless occupied and enjoyed with the residence (see Fig 1 below).

The Revenue sought to argue before the Special Commissioners in *Wakeling* v *Pearce* [1995] STC (SCD) 1996 that in such a situation the capital gains tax exemption cannot be available. The Revenue's argument failed. The parcels were separated by 25 to 30 feet. On the separate land the taxpayer had maintained a small garden with a washing line and had erected a shed thereon and it was used by friends and family for relaxation purposes. Due to the advancing age of the taxpayer, the taxpayer's use of the separate parcel had declined in the years leading up to the sale. It was held that the fact that the land may be separate from the house was not fatal to the availability of the capital gains tax relief. Following that case the Revenue issued a Tax Bulletin (Bulletin 18 August 1995) (reproduced in (1995) STI 1313) under which they accepted that decision and stated:

> Disposal of land which is physically separated from the residence may cause problems. The Revenue does not accept that land is garden or grounds merely if it is in the same ownership as the residence and is used as a garden. However, land which can be shown objectively, on the facts, to be naturally and traditionally the garden of the residence, so that it would normally be offered to a prospective purchaser as part of the residence, will be accepted. An example of this is where, as in some villages, it is common for a garden to be across the street from the residence. The separation itself would not be regarded as a reason for denying relief.
>
> It must be stressed that these cases will be rare and if land is separated from the residence by other land which is not in the same ownership as the residence, it will usually not be part of the garden or grounds. For example, land bought some distance from the residence due to an inadequate garden at the residence and which is cultivated and regarded as part of the garden will not qualify for relief.

*Fig 1   Full CGT relief should be available*

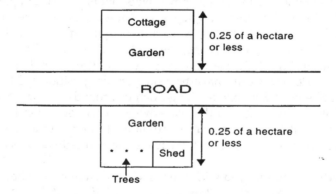

### Garden or grounds exceed 0.5 of a hectare

In order for the area of land exceeding 0.5 of a hectare to qualify for the exemption it is necessary to show that the land has been occupied by the taxpayer and enjoyed by the taxpayer with that residence as its garden or grounds and that the larger area (ie, the area exceeding 0.5 of a hectare) is *required* for the reasonable enjoyment of it as a residence regard being had to the size and character of the dwelling house.

The critical word is 'required': it is necessary to show the larger area is required for the reasonable enjoyment of the particular residence taking into account the house's size and character.

It is generally felt that if the taxpayer, for example, has a largish house with a garden area (surrounded by a fence or hedge) of say 2.5 hectares that there should be no difficulty in satisfying this requirement provided it is clear that the area is enjoyed with the house.

However, in the Inland Revenue Tax Bulletin of February 1992, p. 10, the Revenue indicated that a narrow interpretation is to be given to the word 'required' so that it lies nearer to the word 'indispensable' or 'needed' as opposed to the word 'desirable'.

There is no direct judicial guidance available and the Revenue look to the compulsory purchase case of *Re Newhill Compulsory Purchase Order 1937, Payne's Application* [1938] 2 All ER 163. Du Parcq J said at p. 167C:

> 'Required' I think in this section does not mean merely that the occupiers of the house would like to have it or that they would miss it if they lost it, or that anyone proposing to buy the house would think less of the house without it than he would if it was preserved to it. 'Required' means I suppose that without it there will be such a substantial deprivation of amenities or convenience that a real injury would be done to the property owner.

The Revenue state that the District Valuer's opinion will be based on a comparison of the size of the garden and grounds held with other houses in the locality which are of a comparable size and character to the subject house.

It is clear from the Revenue's view that if one took out part of the garden and this did not result in a substantial deprivation of amenities or convenience resulting in real injury to the property owner then the relief will not be available (see Fig 2 below).

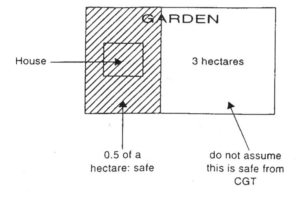

Taxpayers are warned of possible problems in this area.

It is not clear whether the Revenue's strict interpretation will ultimately be found to be the correct one (see, for example, *Re Ripon (Highfield) Housing Order 1938, Applications of White and Collins* [1939] 3 All ER 548).

**Warning**
Solicitors should take special care when advising taxpayers on the application of the capital gains tax exemption available on the sale of the principal residence in cases where grounds or gardens are being sold which are physically separate from the residence in question and in cases were the land exceeds 0.5 of hectare. Do not assume that just because the land is laid out as a garden and has been enjoyed as a garden that the relief will automatically be available.

## 22.2   End of Chapter Self-Assessment Question

Discuss the circumstances in which a gain on the disposal of the garden or grounds of a residence will *not* be an exempt gain.

## 22.3   End of Chapter Assessment Outline Answer

Under TCGA 1992, s. 222, any gain arising on the disposal of a chargeable person's only or main residence is exempt from CGT. This includes a disposal of gardens or grounds of up to half a hectare, or such larger area as is required for the reasonable enjoyment of the dwelling-house as a residence, having regard to the size and character of the house. In the case of the first of these, half a hectare includes the site of the dwelling-house and, in order to obtain the relief, the disponer must show that the land was occupied and enjoyed with the residence as its garden or grounds. The wording of TCGA 1992, s. 222 makes it clear that it is referring to the factual situation at the date of the disposal only. There are a number of situations in which a gain on the disposal of the garden or grounds will not be exempt from CGT.

First, if the disponer disposes of the land after the dwelling-house has been sold, he or she will lose the benefit of the relief. This is clear from *Varty* v *Lynes* [1976] 3 All ER 447. In that case, the disponer sold the house and part of the garden. Afterwards, he sold the remaining part of the garden, with planning permission. Brightman J held that the second disposal was not exempt, the chargeable gain apparently including any gain which had accrued when the garden was occupied with the house. Certain dicta of Brightman J suggest that, even if the disponer were to go out of occupation of the dwelling-house a month before it was sold, the relief would be lost in relation to the garden or grounds. The Revenue has indicated that it does not propose to rely on these dicta.

Secondly, the land you dispose of might not be for occupation and enjoyment with the residence. *Wakeling* v *Pearce* [1995] STC (SCD) 1996 involved a layout of a house and garden of a type commonly encountered in English villages. In that case, an individual had put up a washing line and maintained a garden in a field ('Field 528') which was separated from her residence by another property not in her ownership. The gain on the disposal of Field 528 was held to have the benefit of the relief. The Special Commissioner held that it was not necessary for the land to be contiguous with the residence nor to adjoin it. Following that case, the Revenue has indicated that only land which can be shown objectively, on the facts, to be naturally and traditionally the garden of the residence, so that it would normally be offered to a prospective purchaser as part of the residence, will be accepted as qualifying for the relief.

Finally, it might not be possible to show, where the grounds are more than half a hectare, that the larger area is required for the reasonable enjoyment of the residence, taking into account the size and character of the residence: TCGA 1992, s. 222(3). 'Required' means indispensable. It does not mean desirable. The Revenue uses a dictum of Du Parcq J in *Re Newhill* [1938] 2 All ER 163 as the basis of this argument. It means that the relief is not available unless the disposal results in a substantial deprivation of amenities or convenience resulting in real injury to the owner of the property.

Each of the situations where the gain will not be an exempt gain give rise to difficult factual issues.

# CHAPTER TWENTY-THREE

# REDUCING INVESTMENT TAXATION (2)

## 23.1 Provisions making Gains Exempt Gains

### 23.1.1 RETIREMENT RELIEF

The business might not be the business of the individual making the disposal.

*PLUMBLY v SPENCER* [1997] STC 301

Farming land had been owned by the individual claiming retirement relief. He had let it to the family farming company, of which he was a major shareholder, rent free. The question which arose, on the disposal of the land at a considerable gain, was whether the gain was covered by retirement relief. The problem was that the business in which the land was used was not the individual's business but that of the company in which he was a major shareholder.

Lightman J held that the relief was not therefore available on the disposal of the land. In the following extract, he discusses an earlier version of the retirement relief rules, in ss. 69 and 70, FA 1985, plus sch. 20 thereof.

LIGHTMAN J: . . . Section 69 provides for retirement relief on a disposal of a business or of part of a business or of assets used for the purposes of a business or of shares in certain types of family company by an individual who at the time of the disposal has attained the age of 60 years. Section 70 provides for retirement relief in the case of disposals by employees, trustees, partners and directors of assets which they allowed to be used for the purposes of a business. The two sections are designed to operate independently of each other and the relief available under the two sections may be very different. In this case, as set out in the agreed facts, Mr Harbour granted a lease of land to a company (the company) which at all material times was a trading company and his family company and a company of which he was at all material times a full-time working director; the letting was for use for purposes of its trade and the company paid rent; and within one year of the company ceasing to carry on its trade Mr Harbour disposed of the land. The question to be considered is whether s. 69(2)(b) is applicable in respect of Mr Harbour's disposal of the land. For this disposal to qualify for relief four conditions must be satisfied. (a) First there must be a disposal by an individual who attained the age of 60. This condition is satisfied. (b) Secondly the asset disposed must be a business asset. This is the critical issue. This depends on whether upon the true construction of s. 69(2)(b) use for the purposes of the business carried on by the company was sufficient for this purpose, or whether it was necessary that it was used for the purposes of a business of Mr Harbour himself. (c) Thirdly the disposal must be a 'material disposal' as defined in the section. If the second condition was satisfied and use for the purposes of the business carried on by the company was sufficient, the third condition is also satisfied. (d) Fourthly the land must not have been held as an investment within the meaning of para. 12(2) of sch. 20. The Revenue concede that, if the second condition is satisfied, the fourth condition is also satisfied.

It was common ground before the commissioners and (at least initially) before me, and the decision of the commissioners proceeded on the basis, that the starting point was reading on its own the wording of s. 69(2)(b) and that, when so read, on its face s. 69(2)(b) required only a disposal of an asset used for the purposes of 'a business', and not 'a business of the individual making the disposal'; and that the onus was placed on the Revenue to justify reading into the section the words 'of the individual making the disposal' or some like formula. The argument focused on the rules governing the implication of words into a statute, and most particularly such an implication in a taxing statute in favour of the Revenue. This approach, however, is flawed, for it has the serious shortcoming that it concentrates on looking at s. 69(2)(b) in isolation without due regard to its context and its place in the scheme of the relevant legislation as a whole. The starting and (in this case) the finishing point is reading the section in its context and in its place in such scheme. There is no need or reason to look further afield.

On the true construction of s. 69(2)(b) read in its context and with due regard to its place in the scheme of the Act (and in particularly ss. 69 and 70 and sch. 20) I have without hesitation concluded that the reference is to the business of the individual making the disposal, and accordingly in this case the second condition for qualifying for relief is not satisfied. My reasons are as follows.

(1)   It is clear (and indeed common ground) that the words in s. 69(2)(a) 'a disposal of the whole or part of a business' mean, and can only mean, 'a disposal of the whole or part of a business of the individual claiming the relief'. Section 69(2)(a) is concerned with the situation where the individual on attaining the age of 60 disposes of the whole or part of his business as a going concern. Section 69(2)(b) is concerned with the situation where the individual on attaining the age of 60, instead of disposing of the business as a going concern, ceases to carry on the business and sells one or more assets previously used in the business. In short s. 69 in the two subsections is concerned with two different scenarios, either of which may occur when the businessman decides to retire from his business: he may dispose of his business as a going concern or he may merely dispose of the assets used in such business. The tax relief is rendered available in both cases. In both cases the expression 'a business' is used to denote any business of the individual making the disposal.

(2)   The situation arising where the individual makes a disposal of an asset used by someone else for the purpose of that other person's business is specially catered for in s. 70(6) and (7). Subject to the conditions there laid down, relief may be obtained for 'an associated disposal of assets'. Under these provisions, if Mr Harbour at the same time as he disposed of his land (which the company used for the purposes of its business) had made a material disposal of his shares in the company, Mr Harbour's disposal of the land might have been an 'associated disposal' within the meaning of s. 70(6) and relief might have been available on that basis. It is not to be expected that sale of an asset used in another's business should fall within s. 69(2)(b) when it is the subject of express provision in s. 70(6) and (7).

(3)   Paragraph 6 of sch. 20 provides that gains on disposals of 'chargeable business assets' (and nothing else) shall be entitled to the grant of relief. Paragraph 12(2) excludes from the definition of chargeable business assets 'shares or securities or other assets held as investments'. This paragraph is of general application, extending both to disposals within s. 69 and associated disposals within s. 70. The meaning of the words 'held as investments' would appear to mean 'held for the purpose of obtaining a profitable capital or income return', (see *Cook (Inspector of Taxes)* v *Medway Housing Society Ltd* [1997] STC 90). It is a question of fact for what purpose an asset is held: the return obtained is relevant but not decisive. As I have already stated, the Revenue accept that on the facts of this case Mr Harbour did not hold the land as an investment. What is to be noted is that para. 12(2) makes no specific reference to rent. This is entirely consistent with the view which I have adopted of the true construction of s. 69(2)(b), namely that the person making the disposal of the asset used in the business must be the person carrying on that business. For no question of rent could arise in that situation: there could be no lease or hire of the asset disposed of to the person using the land or asset for the purposes of his business, because there can be no lease or hiring by a man to himself or any liability for rent from a man to himself. By way of contrast para. 10, which applies only in cases of associated transactions and accordingly in situations in which the owner of the asset

used in the business and the person carrying on the business will be different, makes specific provision for cases where rent (as there widely defined) is payable. This, as it seems to me, underlines the fact that the owner and the user in his own business must be the same person in the cases covered by s. 69(2)(b), in contrast to the situations arising in cases of associated transactions where the persons will be different.

I should add that it is clear (and common ground) that the provisions in s. 69(3) and (4), to which some detailed consideration was given in course of the argument, contain nothing which militates against this construction. The provisions allow for the requirements as to ownership during the qualification period to be satisfied by the ownership being vested in certain types of family company instead of the individual making the disposal. I have also been taken through the provisions of s. 69(8) relating to partnerships. I can see nothing in s. 69(8) which affords any contra-indication and indeed none was suggested.

*V. Conclusion*

For the above reasons, I have concluded that Mr Harbour did not qualify for relief under s. 69(2)(b) because the land was not used for the purposes of a business carried on by him. I dismiss the appeal.

## 23.2 Provisions Postponing a CGT Charge on Gains Chargeable to CGT

### 23.2.1 REPLACEMENT OF BUSINESS ASSETS: TCGA 1992, ss. 152–159

#### *WATTON* v *TIPPETT* [1996] STC 101

An individual had acquired freehold land and buildings, the whole of which was known as Unit 1, for an unapportioned consideration. Retaining what he designated Unit 1B, he then sold part of the same freehold land and buildings, designating the part sold Unit 1A. There was a chargeable gain on the disposal of Unit 1A. He claimed roll-over relief under the predecessor provisions to sections 152–159, TCGA 1992 in relation to the disposal of Unit 1A.

Sir John Vinelott held that the relief was not available.

SIR JOHN VINELOTT: . . . As Mr Henderson QC, for the Crown, points out, the difficulty which confronts the taxpayer is that the sale of Unit 1A was strictly a part disposal of Unit 1 and not a disposal of part of Unit 1. The disposal of Unit 1A having been a part disposal of Unit 1, it cannot be said that the consideration arising from the sale of Unit 1A was applied in the acquisition of 'other assets'.

Moreover, it cannot be said that any quantifiable part of the consideration for the disposal of Unit 1A was 'applied' in the acquisition of the retained part of Unit 1, whatever meaning is given to the word 'applied'. Under s. 35(1) and (2) the cost of the acquisition and enhancement of Unit 1 must be apportioned between Unit 1A and the retained part of Unit 1 for the purpose of ascertaining the amount of the gain realised on the part disposal. However, there is nothing in s. 35 which would enable an apportioned part of the consideration for the disposal of Unit 1A to be treated as part of the consideration for the acquisition or enhancement of Unit 1 as a whole.

Mr Bramwell QC, who appeared for the taxpayer, relied on s. 35(5) which provides (so far as material) that s. 35—

> . . . and all other provisions for apportioning on a part disposal expenditure which is deductible in computing a gain, are to be operated before the operation of, and without regard to . . . (b) [section] 115 . . . but without prejudice to the provisions of subsection (8) of the said section 115.

Section 115(8) provides that the provisions of the 1979 Act—

> . . . fixing the amount of the consideration deemed to be given for the acquisition or disposal of assets shall be applied before this section is applied.

These provisions do not, I think, meet the difficulty pointed out by Mr Henderson. The provisions of s. 35 are directed to the ascertainment of the amount of the gain on a part disposal. There is nothing in s. 35(5) or s. 118(1) which justifies the division of a single asset into old and new assets and enables the consideration given for the asset to be apportioned between them.

The Special Commissioner was impressed by what he considered to be the absurd results of the Crown's interpretation of s. 115. He said at para. 9 of his decision (at 20):

Let us suppose that the facts had been slightly different and that the two parts of the premises had at all times constituted two quite separate pieces of property, albeit that these had been purchased by the taxpayer from the same vendor at the same time and for a single unapportioned consideration. Had that been the situation, there would appear to be no grounds for refusing the relief under s. 115. Why, as a matter of common sense, should it make any difference that the premises were not divided into separate pieces of property until one part was disposed of?

The answer to that apparent absurdity is that it is not the fact that Unit 1 was not divided into two separate pieces of property until Unit 1A was disposed of which presents what, in my judgment, is an insuperable objection to the taxpayer's claim. It is that the consideration for Unit 1 cannot be severed and treated as paid in part for Unit 1A and in part for the retained part of Unit 1. So, an example given by Mr Henderson, if a taxpayer were to buy from the same vendor two adjacent properties under two separate but contemporaneous contracts, there would be no reason in principle why the sale of one should not be treated as the sale of old assets and the retained part as new assets for the purposes of s. 115. The description of assets as 'old' and 'new' is functional and not temporal. It may be that the result would be the same if the two properties were acquired under the same contract and at a time when they were not physically separated, provided that they could be treated as separate assets and that the consideration was apportioned between them at the time of sale. That case can be considered when it arises. The insuperable difficulty in the instant case is that Unit 1 was acquired as a single asset and for an unapportioned consideration.

## 23.3  End of Chapter Assessment Question

Refer to the facts concerning Amber Ltd: **2.4**, **6.2** and **8.4**. It is 1 December 1998. The four shareholders in the company have been approached by Megabrackets plc with an offer hard to refuse. Megabrackets plc has offered to buy all of the issued share capital of Amber Ltd from each of the four shareholders. In spite of Amber Ltd's relatively poor trading performance recently, each of the four would make a profit in the region of £500,000. Alan, who will be 62 on 3 March 1999, and Bertram, who is 45 but in poor heath, are keen to accept the offer, since they would both like to retire. Deborah, 35, wishes to devote more time to her work as a partner in Brown & Co., so she is also amenable. Bertram, in his capacity as the executor of Charlie's estate, has no qualms about accepting the offer. All four shareholders acquired their shareholdings on the incorporation of Amber Ltd, on 20 April 1990.

Advise Alan, Bertram and Deborah whether any reliefs from CGT would be available to shelter the gain on the disposal of the shares, and the effect of those reliefs. (Advise Bertram in his personal capacity only.)

## 23.4  End of Chapter Assessment Outline Answer

The CGT relief relevant to Alan and Bertram is retirement relief: TCGA 1992, ss. 163, 164 and sch. 6. Retirement relief is designed to shelter chargeable gains on the disposal of a business or an interest in a business on retirement at 50, or on grounds of ill-health before then. The relief is applicable to a disposal of shares in a personal company. The most important issue here is whether Amber Ltd is such a company, so far as Alan and Bertram are concerned. Deborah will not qualify for retirement relief, but it might be possible for her to shelter the gain by making use of the Enterprise Investment Scheme ('EIS').

Retirement relief turns some or all of what would otherwise have been a chargeable gain into an exempt gain, provided the conditions for the relief are satisfied. TCGA 1992, sch. 6 provides for the way in which the relief takes effect. This varies, depending on the length of time for which a shareholder in a personal company has held the shares disposed of. In the case of an ownership period of ownership of 10 years or more, it makes the whole of a gain up to £250,000 exempt from CGT, and it exempts half of any gain between £250,000 and £1 million. Where the shares have been owned for less than 10 years, the relief is reduced by 10% for each year during which the disponer did not own the interest. Subject to the points discussed below, Alan and Bertram will be disposing of shares in their personal company, so a special formula is used to decide how much of the gain on the disposal of the shares is attributable to chargeable business assets of the company and, therefore, how much of the gain is covered by the relief. Neither Alan nor Bertram will be entitled to the relief in full, since neither of them has owned his shares for the full 10-year period.

Retirement relief applies if four conditions are satisfied. The disponer must have owned the interest in the business for a minimum of one year; be 50 or over or being forced to retire on grounds of ill-health; be making a material disposal; and be disposing of chargeable business assets. Material disposals include a disposal of shares or securities in a personal company: TCGA 1992, s. 163(2)(c), (5)–(7). A personal company is one in which the disponer exercises at least 5% of the voting rights. It must either be a trading company, or a company which is a member of a group of companies, the holding company of which is the disponer's personal company. In addition, the disponer must be a full-time employee or officer of your personal company, required to devote substantially all his time to the service of the company or another company in the group, if relevant. The Revenue seem to regard working 30 hours per week as satisfying this condition. Amber Ltd is both Alan and Bertram's personal company, since they each exercise 25% of the voting rights in it. The only one of these conditions which is problematic, therefore is the ill-heath condition in relation to Bertram. The conditions he will have to satisfy are in TCGA 1992, sch. 6, para. 3. He must satisfy the Revenue that he has retired because of ill-health, and that he is likely to remain incapable of being able to perform work of the kind on which he was engaged previously.

It might be possible for Deborah to shelter her gain through the Enterprise Investment Scheme ('EIS'). This would give her the benefit of an income tax deduction from her total tax, as well as providing a way of sheltering the gain. Briefly, EIS enables an individual who has realised a chargeable gain to postpone liability to pay CGT by re-investing that gain in a qualifying investment (TCGA 1992, sch. 5B, para. 1(1)(c)), i.e. a subscription for eligible shares in an EIS company. The selection of a suitable EIS company will be a matter for her and her advisers, and there will be an element of commercial risk for her in using the relief. Gains on disposals of the EIS shares thus acquired are exempt if they have been held for at least five years: TCGA 1992, ss. 150A(2) and 150B. There may be other possibilities for sheltering the gain open to Deborah, in addition to EIS.

Note: As to all the shareholders, see *Learning Text* at **24.6.2.2** (takeovers), especially Deborah.

# CHAPTER TWENTY-FOUR

# INVESTMENT TAXATION: PARTICULAR TYPES OF CHARGEABLE ASSET

## 24.1 Options

### 24.1.1 SOLUTIONS PROVIDED BY THE CGT RULES

#### *GOLDING v KAUFMAN* [1985] STC 152

VINELOTT J: This is an appeal by way of case stated from a decision of the Special Commissioners. It raises a short question relating to the capital gains tax legislation. Although the amount at stake is small, the question is I understand of general importance. It is whether a sum paid to a person (the option holder) who has the right to call on another to sell property to him (a call option) or to call on another to purchase property from him (a put option) for the release of the option is a capital sum derived from an asset (the option) which falls to be brought into account in computing his chargeable gains.

The question arises in the following circumstances. In July 1965 the respondent, Zacharias Mendel Kaufman (the taxpayer), and one Chaim Saul Kaufman owned the entire issued share capital, comprising 60,000 ordinary shares of £1 each, of a company called Burrell & Maurice Ltd (the company). By an agreement dated 23 July 1965 they agreed to sell 33,000 of the shares to a company called Inter-City Investment & Holding Co Ltd (Inter-City) and 12,000 to a company called Cloverhill Investments Ltd (Cloverhill). It was a term of the agreement that on completion each of the Kaufmans would enter into a service agreement with the company, and that the taxpayer, Inter-City and Cloverhill would enter into an option agreement in the form of a draft agreement set out in the fourth schedule thereto. I pause to observe that under the agreement Mr C S Kaufman sold all his shares in the company. The taxpayer retained 15,000 (that is 25%) of the issued shares. No completed copy of the option agreement was produced to the Special Commissioners, and I understand that none can now be found. However, it is accepted by the Crown that an agreement in the terms of the draft was executed, and, indeed, if it had not been executed the provisions of the draft would none the less have been binding on the parties as a contract.

Under cl. 1(1) of the option agreement, the taxpayer agreed that if within six years from the date of the agreement his employment by the company should cease for any reason, Inter-City or, if his employment ceased for any reason other than his own misconduct or default, the taxpayer would be entitled to give notice in writing, within eight weeks from the date of cesser, requiring that the whole but not part of the taxpayer's shares be transferred to Inter-City at a price to be ascertained by a formula which in effect attributed asset value to the shares but without the inclusion of any figure for goodwill. Thus, if the taxpayer ceased to be employed within the specified period Inter-City had a call option; if he ceased to be employed within that period otherwise than by reason of his misconduct or default he had a put option. It was provided by cl. 1(2) that if the options had not been exercised within six years from the date of the agreement then either the taxpayer or Inter-City should have the right at any time to give notice requiring that Inter-City purchase within eight weeks the whole but not part of the taxpayer's shares at the option price. So, again, the taxpayer had a put option and Inter-City a call option. By cl. 1(3) the taxpayer covenanted that while he or Inter-City or Cloverhill remained shareholders he would not transfer or dispose of his shares or any interest in them to any person other than Inter-City or Cloverhill. Inter-City and Cloverhill similarly covenanted that they would not transfer the shares to which they were respectively entitled save to each other or to the taxpayer. By cl. 3 Inter-City was given the right by notice in effect to substitute Cloverhill for itself for the purposes of the options.

A further agreement was entered into on 27 July 1966. It was recited that the taxpayer had transferred 3,750 of his shares to his wife and 7,500 to the trustees of a settlement, and it was agreed in summary that the provisions of the option agreement should apply to each separate holding of shares held by the taxpayer, his wife and the trustees respectively.

In 1969 the taxpayer's term of office under his service agreement (six years from 1 August 1965) was nearing its end. Cloverhill had agreed to sell its shares to Inter-City. Inter-City had negotiated a sale of its shares to another company, Vantona Ltd. The taxpayer also wished to transfer his shares to a United States company. It was clearly in the interests of Inter-City to negotiate a release of the taxpayer's put option. Otherwise, it might find that having parted with its shares to Vantona it could be compelled to buy a 25% minority holding at asset value.

In these circumstances a further agreement dated 12 March 1969 was entered into between the taxpayer, his wife and the trustees (together described as 'the option holders'), Inter-City and Cloverhill (these two companies being described as 'the Vendors'). By cl. 1 of that agreement each of the parties released the others from the covenants in the earlier agreements not to transfer or dispose of shares held by them. Clause 2 reads as follows:

> In consideration of the sum of £10,000 now paid by Inter-City as to £5,000 to Mr Kaufman and to Mrs Kaufman to be divided between them as they shall decide or in default of agreement in equal shares and as to £5,000 to the trustees (the receipt whereof is hereby acknowledged) and in consideration of the Vendors abandoning their option under the Option Agreement and the Supplemental Agreement to purchase the shares in the Company held by the option holders the option holders and each of them hereby abandon their options to sell to the Vendors on the cessation of Mr Kaufman's employment with the Company their shares in the Company.

As a matter of construction, the extinction of the option holders' put options did not extend to the put options exercisable (under cl. 1(2) of the option agreement) at any time after six years from the execution of the original agreement, which options were not options exercisable only on the cessation of the taxpayer's employment by the company. However, it is clear that that was the intention; Inter-City's call options before and after the six-year period were both extinguished. It is accepted by the Crown that it was the intention of the parties that all the options should be extinguished and that Inter-City could if necessary have the agreement of 12 March 1969 rectified to give effect to this intention.

The assessment against which the taxpayer appealed is an assessment to capital gains tax in respect of the £5,000 paid to him and his wife, no election for a separate assessment having been made.

. . .

[His Lordship then referred to the relevant provisions of FA 1965, the predecessors to the current provisions: see *Learning Text* at **24.3.2**.]

If the words 'abandoned' and 'abandonment' are construed solely in the context of para. 14 it is, I think, difficult to reach any confident conclusion as to the precise meaning to be attributed to those words. The difficulty cannot be resolved by reference to dictionaries or even to other contexts in which these words are used. As with other words in common use, the words 'abandoned' and 'abandonment' are of indefinite scope and may cover a range of related meanings. Their precise scope or connotation can only be ascertained by examination of the particular context in which they are used. Examination of para. 14 by itself to my mind yields no compelling reason to adopt one or the other of the constructions contended for. However, in this court the Crown has advanced an alternative contention. That contention places para. 14(3) in a wider context which in my judgment resolves the difficulty.

The alternative contention, which was not advanced before the commissioners, is shortly as follows. Section 22(3) applies where a capital sum is derived from an asset notwithstanding that no asset is acquired by the person paying the sum and in particular where the asset is lost, destroyed or dissipated or, where the asset is a right, where it is forfeited or surrendered. It fastens on the receipt of a capital sum derived from an asset including one which is then or which has previously been destroyed or which otherwise ceases or has ceased to exist as a distinct asset and which cannot therefore be said to have been disposed of in the ordinary sense of those words. Section 23(3) deals with the loss, destruction, dissipation or extinction of the asset; these events are similarly to be treated as the disposal of the asset for the purposes of giving rise to an allowable loss. So, for example, if a valuable picture comprehensively insured is destroyed by fire the destruction of the picture is treated as the disposal of it and gives rise to an allowable loss. The receipt of the proceeds of the insurance also falls to be treated as a receipt on the disposal of the picture although the picture has then ceased to exist. The two events may be widely separated in time and may not occur in the same fiscal year — for instance if the claim under the policy is disputed.

Looked at in this light para. 14 is naturally read as qualifying s. 23(3) (where it is expressly referred to) and not s. 22(2) (where it is not). Paragraph 14(2) and (3) deal comprehensively with all the circumstances in which an option may cease to exist as a distinct asset. It may be extinguished in one of three ways. It may be exercised, in which event it merges in the contract or transfer and ceases to exist as a distinct asset; it may be released or surrendered or otherwise cease to be exercisable before the expiry of the time limited for its exercise; or it may simply expire. Sub-paragraph (2) and the second limb of sub-para (3) deal with the first of these possibilities; they provide that if the option is exercised the grant and the acquisition of the option, and the transaction entered into by virtue of the exercise of the option between the grantor of the option and the option holder, are to be treated as a single transaction. The first limb of para. 14(3) makes it clear that neither the exercise of the option nor its extinction are to be treated as amounting to its disposal. It is immaterial whether, if the option is simply allowed to expire, it can be said to have been abandoned within the first limb of para. 14(3). As counsel for the taxpayer pointed out, at the time of expiry its written down value will necessarily be nil.

Counsel for the taxpayer submitted that this severance between the receipt of a capital sum derived from an asset which ceases to exist in the circumstances specified in s. 23(3) and the disappearance of the asset — the receipt of the capital sum being treated as a disposal within s. 22(3) and the disappearance of the asset as a disposal within s. 23(3) — is artificial. Although an asset may be said to have been disposed of notwithstanding that no asset is received by the person paying the capital sum there must none the less be a disposal of an asset before a chargeable gain can arise; chargeable gains are gains 'accruing to a person *on* [my emphasis] the disposal of assets' (s. 19(1)). Paragraph 14 is one of the provisions of Part III to which s. 22(3) is expressly made subject and under para. 14(3) the abandonment of an option is *not* to be treated as the disposal of it. Turning to the example given by counsel for the Crown he submitted that the apparent difficulty disappears if s. 22(3) is read together with s. 22(9). The insurance claim which arises at the time of the destruction of the picture represents money or money's worth within s. 22(9); the value of the claim is thus brought in as a capital receipt within s. 22(3); when the claim is settled the payment is a further capital payment derived from the claim within s. 22(3)(*b*). In the particular example given by counsel for the Crown this may be so. The relationship between s. 22(3) (in particular para. (*b*)) and s. 22(9) is not clear and I express no opinion on the point. However, it is not difficult to imagine a case where at the time of the loss of a picture the owner has no claim capable of constituting money or money's worth within s. 22(9) but where he may subsequently receive a capital sum which may be said to have been derived from it — for instance if a picture is stolen and if the owner subsequently recovers damages for conversion from someone who has dealt with it.

The Crown's alternative argument, as I see it, produces a rational and coherent scheme. It explains why s. 23(3) applies whether or not a capital sum is received and why s. 23(3) is and s. 22(3) is not expressly made subject to the provisions of para. 14. Paragraph 14 creates an exception to the general rule that the extinction of an asset is to be treated as a disposal for the purposes of creating an allowable loss. Looked at in that wider context the words 'abandoned' and 'abandonment' in para. 14 are I think clearly used in the wider sense contended for by counsel for the taxpayer.

Counsel for the taxpayer submitted that if this result had been intended para. 14(3), like para. 14(1), would have been expressed to be subject to the provisions of s. 22. The answer to that submission is I think that para. 14(1) is dealing with a different subject matter — the creation of an option. It modifies (though it does not supplant) s. 22(1) (see the decision of Peter Gibson J in *Strange* v *Openshaw (Inspector of Taxes)* [1983] STC 416).

Counsel for the taxpayer submitted that this construction gives rise to other anomalies. If an option is released for value the written down value of the consideration given for it can be deducted in calculating the chargeable gain; if the option has become valueless the release of it does not give rise to an allowable loss. Moreover, an allowable loss clearly arises if instead of being released for value the option is sold to a third party for less than its written down value. It seems to me that these anomalies are the inevitable consequence of denying a claim for a loss where it arises from the extinction of an option. That is the course which the legislature has chosen. The Crown's alternative argument avoids the consequence that a capital sum received on the release of an option escapes capital gains tax and in my judgment gives a rational purpose and meaning to para. 14.

### Soares, P.C., 'Pay Tax at your Option', 16 *Property Law Bulletin*, p. 47

An option is an asset for capital gains tax purposes (Taxation of Chargeable Gains Act (TCGA) 1992, s. 21(1)(a)).

The grant of an option, in particular the grant of an option in which the grantor binds himself to sell, is the disposal of an asset, namely the option, and thus *prima facie* when the monies are received for the option, there is a disposal of a separate asset with virtually no base cost and with a charge to capital gains tax. However, that general rule is subject to provisions in s. 144(2) which treat the grant of an option as part of a larger transaction.

If an option is exercised, the grant of the option and the sale under the option (of the land) shall be treated as a single transaction and the monies paid for the option and the consideration received for the sale of the land comprise the sale consideration.

It is clear the sale takes place, i.e. the disposal takes place, at the time when the option is exercised (see Figure below).

### Note

Even though the vendor has the £10m on day one the CGT disposal is deemed to take place on day 1095 (three years later). The vendor may avoid a tax charge altogether if he is not resident and ordinarily resident in the UK in the year the option is exercised.

That line of analysis fits in with TCGA 1992, s. 28 which states that if a contract is conditional, and in particular if it is conditional on the exercise of an option, the time at which the disposal and acquisition is made is the time when the condition is satisfied.

In *Whiteman on Capital Gains Tax* (4th edn) at 21–02 it is stated that in practice the Revenue does not normally assess taxpayers on the grant of an option if it is of short duration and/or of a relatively small consideration as compared to the eventual sum which would be payable upon the option being exercised. The Revenue is said to be content to await the exercise of the option whereupon the grant and exercise are viewed as a single transaction. Finally the editors state: 'An assessment on granting is the exception not the rule'. That has also been the Tax Editor's experience if the option period is relatively short such as three years.

In *Simon's Direct Tax Service* at C2.1007 an example is given where a prior assessment is made and then discharged when the option is ultimately exercised. It envisages a very short option also and so it may be that some inspectors do not wait. It may be that the taxpayers should appeal any such assessment on the basis that the disposal could become part of a larger transaction and hopefully by the time the matter comes to appeal the option will have been exercised and the assessment would be discharged.

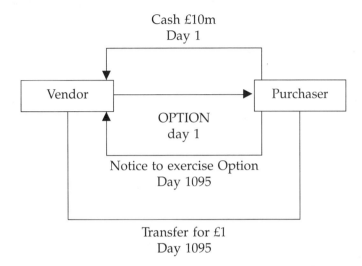

## 24.2 Wasting Assets

### 24.2.1 SOLUTIONS PROVIDED BY THE CGT RULES

A lease is still a wasting asset, even if there is a statutory right of extension beyond 50 years.

#### *LEWIS* v *WALTERS* [1992] STC 97

MUMMERY J: This is a case stated under s. 56 of the Taxes Management Act 1970 by the General Commissioners for the division of Sidmouth. The question raised is whether they were correct in law in holding on 12 December 1989 that the leasehold interest in a house called Red Lodge, 11 Elwyn Road, Exmouth, Devon (the property) was 'a wasting asset' for the purposes of the Capital Gains Tax Act 1979 (the 1979 Act).

The commissioners were required to state a case by Mr Nicholas Lewis (Mr Lewis), who, as one of the executors of the late Mr Frederick Lewis (the deceased), failed in his appeal against an assessment of a capital gain of £50,000 for the year 1987–88. The commissioners decided that the leasehold interest was 'a wasting asset'. They disallowed the appeal, though they reduced the assessment of gain to £40,364 in accordance with the calculations of the inspector of taxes.

Mr Lewis conducted his case in person both before the commissioners and in this court. He said that there was a point of principle involved, namely, the correct construction of the relevant provisions of the 1979 Act. The amount of tax in dispute is small. Mr Lewis has already paid the amount of capital gains tax calculated by the inspector on the revised assessment. If the appeal succeeds, it is agreed that the sum of £929.70, with interest, should be repaid.

The facts were agreed before the commissioners. The property was the house of Mr Lewis's parents, Mr and Mrs Frederick Lewis. The freehold was owned by Mrs Lewis but was subject to a lease in favour of the deceased for a term of 99 years commencing on 29 September 1904 and expiring on 29 September 2003, at an annual rent of £8.

Mrs Lewis died on 22 December 1982. The freehold interest was inherited by and became vested in her two children, Mr Lewis and Mrs Susan Reader.

The deceased died almost three years later, on 21 August 1985. At the date of his death the unexpired term of the lease was 18 years and 2 months. By his will the deceased appointed Mr Lewis and Mrs Reader as his executors and they inherited the leasehold interest.

Neither Mr Lewis nor Mrs Reader were resident in the property at the date of the deceased's death or subsequently. During the tax year ended 5 April 1987 they let the property furnished.

On 5 November 1987 they sold the 16 years left of the leasehold interest and the freehold interest to the same purchaser for £107,500. The leasehold and freehold interests merged.

At the date of the death of the deceased the leasehold interest was valued by the district valuer at £40,000. On the sale of the property the district valuer and the executors agreed that the sale proceeds should be apportioned £82,500 in respect of the leasehold interest and £25,000 in respect of the freehold interest.

The question of law is whether the lease was 'a wasting asset' within the meaning of the 1979 Act and, in particular, for the purposes of the provisions of sch. 3, which, by virtue of s. 106, have effect as respects leases of land.

Section 155 of the 1979 Act is the interpretation section and provides that 'unless the context otherwise requires . . . "wasting asset" has the meaning given by section 37 above and paragraph 1 of Schedule 3 to this Act'.

Section 37(1) defines 'wasting asset' as 'an asset with a predictable life not exceeding fifty years'.

Paragraph 1(1) of sch. 3 provides: 'A lease of land shall not be a wasting asset until the time when its duration does not exceed fifty years.'

Paragraph 8 of sch. 3 contains provisions which have effect 'in ascertaining for the purposes of this Act the duration of a lease of land'.
Sub-paragraph (5) provides:

Where the terms of the lease include provision for the extension of the lease beyond a given date by notice given by the tenant this paragraph shall apply as if the term of the lease extended for as long as it could be extended by the tenant, but subject to any right of the landlord by notice to determine the lease.

Sub-paragraph (6) reads:

It is hereby declared that the question what is the duration of a lease is to be decided, in relation to the grant or any disposal of the lease, by reference to the facts which were known or ascertainable at the time when the lease was acquired or created.

The inspector's calculation of a capital gain of £40,364 was made on the basis that the lease of the property disposed of by the executors on 5 November 1987 was a wasting asset. It was submitted that that was the correct basis because at the date of disposal the lease had an unexpired term of 16 years. It therefore had a predictable life 'not exceeding fifty years' within the meaning of s. 37(1). As its duration did not exceed 50 years at the date of disposal, it was a wasting asset within the meaning of para. 1(1) of sch. 3.

This was, therefore, a case in which the rate at which expenditure was assumed to be written off should, instead of being a uniform rate as provided by s. 38, be a rate fixed in accordance with the table set out in para. 1(3) of sch. 3 and the gain accrued on the disposal of the lease should be computed having regard to the formula in para. 1(4).

The application of the relevant provisions produced an unindexed gain of £43,447, subject to an indexation allowance of £3,083, resulting in an indexed gain of £40,364.

Mr Lewis challenged the correctness of this approach. He submitted that the lease disposed of by him and his sister as executors on 5 November 1987 was *not* a wasting asset and that the inspector had fallen into error because he had disregarded or misconstrued the effect of para. 8(5) and (6) of sch. 3. He argued that the effect of those provisions was that in order to ascertain the duration of the lease, it was necessary to refer to the facts which were known or ascertainable at the time when the lease was acquired by those whose disposal of it gave rise to the charge to capital gains tax.

In this case Mr Lewis and his sister acquired the lease of the property in their capacity as executors on the death of the deceased on 21 August 1985.

In reliance on para. 8(5) of sch. 3 it was then argued that, as at that date, the reality of the situation was that there could be an extension of the lease beyond a given date by notice given by the tenant, because the Leasehold Reform Act 1967 gave to a tenant the right to extend his lease for a further term of 50 years. In those circumstances, it was argued that the effect of para. 8(5) was that the paragraph applied for the ascertainment of the duration of the lease as if the term of the lease extended for as long as it could be extended by the tenant, subject to any right of the landlord to give notice to determine the lease. The overall result was that at the date of disposal the duration of the lease for capital gains tax purposes was not 16 years but 66 years, that is, the unexpired term of 16 years plus the extension of 50 years under the Leasehold Reform Act 1967. A lease of that length had a predictable life exceeding 50 years. It was not, therefore, a wasting asset and the provisions of sch. 3 relating to a wasting asset did not apply.

Mr Lewis developed his arguments clearly and concisely but they do not, in my judgment, accord with the true construction of the statutory provisions. I accept the three arguments relied on by Mr Ter Haar for the Crown to show that para. 8(5) does not apply to the facts of this case and that the lease is not to be treated as extended for a period of 50 years.

First, Mr Lewis agreed that the lease of the property as granted on 30 September 1904 did not contain any express term providing for the extension of the lease beyond a given date by notice given by the tenant. In my judgment, the words in para. 8(5), read in their ordinary and natural way, require that the provision for the extension of the lease should be included among 'the terms of the lease'.

The provision for extension relied on by Mr Lewis is not in 'the terms of the lease'. It is in the Leasehold Reform Act 1967. Omitting immaterial words, s. 1(1) of the 1967 Act provides that the Act 'shall have effect to confer on a tenant of a leasehold house, occupying the house as his residence, a right to acquire on fair terms . . . an extended lease of the house'. It is clear that the right is conferred by statute directly on a tenant who satisfies the prescribed conditions. The right to an extended lease is not conferred either by an express term in the lease as granted in 1904 or by a term to that effect implied into the lease by the Leasehold Reform Act 1967.

Second, even if the statutory right in the Leasehold Reform Act 1967 is to be regarded as a 'term of the lease' for this purpose, it would not constitute a provision 'for the extension of the lease beyond a given date' within the meaning of para. 8(5). Although the statutory right is referred to in s. 1(1) of the 1967 Act as a right to acquire 'an extended lease', it is clear from ss. 14 and 15 of the 1967 Act, which deal with extension, that what is described as 'an extended lease' is a grant which the landlord is bound to make of a 'new tenancy of the house and premises for a term expiring fifty years after the term date of the existing tenancy' and is 'in substitution for the existing tenancy' (see s. 14(1)). The new tenancy is on the same terms as the existing tenancy as those terms apply at the relevant time, but with such modifications as may be required or appropriate to take account of various prescribed matters (see s. 15(1)).

In my judgment, that new tenancy would not be an 'extension of the lease' within the meaning of para. 8(5). It would be a new and separate lease acquired for the first time on the occasion of a grant to the tenant under s. 14 following the giving by the tenant to the landlord of written notice of his desire to have an extended lease.

This approach accords with the decision of Browne-Wilkinson J in *Bayley (Inspector of Taxes) v Rogers* [1980] STC 544, where it was held that a lease granted under the Landlord and Tenant Act 1954 was a new lease and not a part of or a continuation of the original tenancy. When the taxpayer tenant later disposed of the lease he was disposing of the new tenancy and, for the purposes of the capital gains tax provisions of the Finance Act 1965, the new tenancy was a new asset acquired when the lease was granted and the provisions for the gain to be time apportioned did not therefore apply.

Third, the effect of the application of para. 8(5) is a deemed extension of the term of the lease 'for as long as it *could* be extended by the *tenant*' [emphasis added]. On the facts of this case the term of the lease acquired by Mr Lewis and his sister as executors could not be extended by them. The deceased had not during his lifetime given notice to the landlord of his desire to have any extended lease. The executors could not therefore claim that a right of the deceased arising from service of a notice by him as tenant inured for their benefit as executors (see s. 5(1) of the Leasehold Reform Act 1967). The executors, after the death of the deceased, could not claim the right to acquire an extended term as members of his family succeeding to the tenancy on his death. Such a right is only available in cases where, on the death of the tenant while occupying the house as his residence, a member of his family 'resident in the house' becomes tenant of it under the same tenancy (see s. 7(1)). Both executors were members of the family of the deceased but neither of them was resident in the property on his death. The result is that, although Mr Lewis and his sister acquired the lease and became tenants on the death of the deceased, the terms of the lease could not be extended by them either under the terms of the lease or under the provisions of the Leasehold Reform Act 1967, whether they were acting as executors or whether they were claiming as members of his family succeeding to the tenancy on his death.

For all these reasons I dismiss the appeal. Mr Lewis contended that as the appeal was on a point of principle I should not make any order for costs against him. The Crown asked for the normal order that the appeal be dismissed with costs. There is no special factor in this case which would justify me in departing, in the exercise of my discretion, from the general rule that costs should follow the event.

*Appeal dismissed with costs.*

## 24.3   Shares

### 24.3.1   SOLUTIONS PROVIDED BY THE CGT RULES

#### 24.3.1.1   Takeovers

### TAXATION OF CHARGEABLE GAINS ACT 1992

**135.   Exchange of securities for those in another company**
   (1)   Subsection (3) below has effect where a company ('company A') issues shares or debentures to a person in exchange for shares in or debentures of another company ('company B') and—
   (a)   company A holds, or in consequence of the exchange will hold, more than one-quarter of the ordinary share capital (as defined in section 832(1) of the Taxes Act) of company B, or
   (b)   company A issues the shares or debentures in exchange for shares as the result of a general offer—
      (i)   which is made to members of company B or any class of them (with or without exceptions for persons connected with company A), and
      (ii)   which is made in the first instance on a condition such that if it were satisfied company A would have control of company B, or
   (c)   company A holds, or in consequence of the exchange will hold, the greater part of the voting power in company B.
   (2)   Subsection (3) below also has effect where under section 136 persons are to be treated as exchanging shares or debentures held by them in consequence of the arrangement there mentioned.
   (3)   Subject to sections 137 and 138, sections 127 to 131 shall apply with any necessary adaptations as if the 2 companies mentioned in subsection (1) above or, as the case may be, in section 136 were the same company and the exchange were a reorganisation of its share capital.

### Offering Circular for the Recommended Cash Offer for East Midlands Electricity on Behalf of DR Investments

. . .

**8.   United Kingdom taxation**
The following paragraphs, which are intended as a general guide only, are based on current legislation and Inland Revenue practice. They summarise certain limited aspects of the UK taxation treatment of accepting the Offer and the Loan Note Alternative. The information relates only to the position of East Midlands Electricity Shareholders who

hold their East Midlands Electricity Shares as investments and (except to the extent that express reference to the position of non UK residents is made) who are resident in the United Kingdom for taxation purposes.

**If you are in any doubt as to your taxation position or if you are subject to taxation in any jurisdiction other than the United Kingdom, you should consult an appropriate independent adviser without delay.**

**(a)  Taxation of chargeable gains**

Liability to United Kingdom taxation of chargeable gains will depend on the individual circumstances of each East Midlands Electricity Shareholder and on the form of consideration received.

*Cash*

To the extent that an East Midlands Electricity Shareholder receives cash under the Offer, this will constitute a disposal, or part disposal, of his East Midlands Electricity Shares which may, depending on the shareholder's individual circumstances, give rise to a liability to United Kingdom taxation of chargeable gains.

*Loan Notes*

(i)   Holdover

Any East Midlands Electricity Shareholder who, together with persons connected with such shareholder, does not hold more than 5% of any class of shares in or debentures of East Midlands Electricity will not be treated as having made a disposal of East Midlands Electricity Shares for the purposes of United Kingdom taxation of chargeable gains to the extent that such shareholder receives Loan Notes in exchange for East Midlands Electricity Shares. Any gain or loss which would otherwise have arisen on a disposal of East Midlands Electricity Shares at market value at the time of that exchange will be 'held over' and deemed to accrue on a subsequent disposal (including a redemption) of the Loan Notes. No 'indexation allowance' will be available for the period during which any gain is 'held over' in this way.

Any East Midlands Electricity Shareholder who, either alone or together with persons connected with such shareholder, holds more than 5% of any class of shares in or debentures of East Midlands Electricity is advised that an application for clearance has been made to the Inland Revenue under Section 138 of the Taxation of Chargeable Gains Act 1992 in respect of the Offer. If such clearance is given, any such East Midlands Electricity Shareholder will be treated in the manner described in the preceding paragraph. Neither the Offer nor the Loan Note Alternative is conditional on such clearance being obtained.

(ii)   Disposal of Loan Notes

The Loan Notes will be 'qualifying corporate bonds' for the purposes of United Kingdom taxation of chargeable gains. Accordingly, except to the extent that a chargeable gain or allowable loss previously 'held over' in respect of East Midlands Electricity Shares is deemed to accrue as described in (i) above, any gains and losses arising on a disposal (including a redemption) of the Loan Notes will not give rise to chargeable gains or allowable losses for the purposes of United Kingdom taxation of chargeable gains.

Holders of Loan Notes within the charge to corporation tax are also referred to paragraph 8(b)(iii) below.

**(b)  Taxation of income**

*Loan Notes*

(i)   Withholding tax

Interest on the Loan Notes will be paid subject to deduction of United Kingdom income tax (currently at the rate of 20%) by the Offeror unless the

Offeror has previously been directed by the Inland Revenue in relation to a particular holding of Loan Notes to make a payment free of deduction or subject to a reduced rate of deduction by virtue of relief available to the holder of those Loan Notes under an applicable double taxation treaty. Such a direction will only be issued following a prior application to the Inland Revenue in the appropriate manner by the holder of those Loan Notes. The Offeror will not gross up payments of interest on the Loan Notes to compensate for any tax which it is required to deduct at source.

(ii)    Individual holders of Loan Notes
Subject to the above, the gross amount of interest on the Loan Notes will form part of the recipient's income for the purposes of United Kingdom income tax, credit being allowed for the tax withheld. Individuals who are taxable only at the lower or basic rate will have no further tax to pay in respect of the interest. In certain cases, holders of Loan Notes may be able to recover from the Inland Revenue an amount in respect of the tax withheld at source.
   Under the 'accrued income scheme', a charge to tax on income may arise on a transfer of Loan Notes in respect of interest on the Loan Notes which has accrued since the preceding interest payment date.

(iii)   Corporate holders of Loan Notes
For a Loan Note holder within the charge to corporation tax, all profits, gains and losses measured and recognised in accordance with an appropriate accounting method in respect of the Loan Notes will be taxed or relieved as income.

(c)   **Stamp duty and stamp duty reserve tax ('SDRT')**
(i)    *Acceptance of the Offer*
No stamp duty or SDRT will be payable by East Midlands Electricity Shareholders as a result of accepting the Offer (including the Loan Note Alternative).

(ii)    *Loan Notes*
No stamp duty or SDRT will be payable on a transfer or sale of, or an agreement to transfer or sell, Loan Notes.

(d)   **Other taxation matters**
Special taxation provisions may apply to East Midlands Electricity Shareholders who have acquired or acquire their East Midlands Electricity Shares by exercising options under the East Midlands Electricity Share Option Schemes, including provisions imposing a charge to income tax.

### 24.3.1.2   Reorganisations of share capital

**Demerger Document on the Rights Issue by Zeneca Group plc on 12 May 1993**

**6   Taxation in relation to the Zeneca Demerger Shares**
**The following summaries are based upon the current law and local taxation authority practice in the particular jurisdictions to which each relates. Each is only a general guide and applies only to ICI Shareholders resident in those jurisdictions for tax purposes. ICI Shareholders who are in any doubt as to their tax position should consult their own independent professional tax adviser immediately.**

*(a)   UK*
No UK taxation liability will arise for ICI Shareholders solely by reason of the Demerger.
   The receipt of Zeneca Demerger shares will not be regarded as a distribution taxable as income in the hands of ICI Shareholders. The Inland Revenue has granted a clearance confirming that, under Section 215(1) of the Income and Corporation Taxes Act 1988, the

distribution of Zeneca Demerger shares pursuant to the Demerger will be treated as an exempt distribution within the meaning of Section 213 of that Act.

Clearance has been obtained under Section 138 of the Taxation of Chargeable Gains Act 1992 in consequence of which the Board has been advised that ICI Shareholders should be treated for UK tax purposes as having exchanged their holdings in ICI for those held in each of ICI and Zeneca as a result of the Demerger and will not be treated as disposing of their ICI Ordinary shares. The base cost of an ICI Shareholder's existing holding in ICI will become the base cost of that shareholder's holdings in both ICI and Zeneca and will be apportioned between the ICI Ordinary shares and the Zeneca Demerger shares by reference to the market quotations of an ICI Ordinary share and a Zeneca Demerger share on the first day of dealings in the Zeneca Demerger shares, as derived from the London Stock Exchange daily official list.

A liability to taxation may arise on a subsequent disposal of ICI Ordinary shares or Zeneca Demerger shares.

In relation to ICI Shareholders who are trustees, although regard must be had to the terms of each particular trust, the decision in *Sinclair* v *Lee* . . . indicates that, for trustees of trusts governed by English law, the Zeneca Demerger shares will generally be regarded as a capital receipt. Provided this is the case, the tax position of trustees will be the same as that of individual shareholders.

If for any reason, however, the Zeneca Demerger shares are regarded in relation to any particular trustees as an income receipt, the tax implications may be significantly different.

## 24.4 Debts on a Security

### 24.4.1 SOLUTIONS PROVIDED BY THE CGT RULES

#### *TAYLOR CLARKE INTERNATIONAL* v *LEWIS* [1997] STC 499

Robert Walker J considered the characteristics of a debt on a security.

ROBERT WALKER J: . . . The principal characteristics or features which the courts have so far had to consider in this context can be identified as follows.

(1)  First there are the indicia of loan stock issued by an institution (in the Lord President (Emslie)'s phrase) with a view to it being dealt in on a stock exchange or some other established market. These indicia were noted by Templeman LJ in *Ramsay* ([1979] STC 582 at 588) as stock which (i) as the result of a subscription (ii) is issued, the stock being transferable (iii) on a register and (iv) in small, convenient units. In *Ramsay* Templeman LJ was able to find that each of those four tests was satisfied, although in a much less formal way than they would have been in relation to loan stock intended to be dealt with on a stock exchange. It is quite clear that stock exchange requirements are irrelevant here. But one irreducible minimum requirement is that the debt should be capable of being assigned, and assigned so as to realise a gain for the original creditor.

(2)  In order to be capable of realising a gain for the original creditor the loan must carry interest (or provide for a premium on repayment which is broadly equivalent to interest). A loan for a fixed term at a fixed rate of interest provides the possibility of a gain for the original creditor, if interest rates fall or the borrower's credit rating improves (or both). I accept Mr Aaronson's submission that a fixed rate of interest, although exemplified in Templeman LJ's illustration in *Ramsay* ([1979] STC 582 at 587), is not absolutely essential: even if the rate of interest is linked to some known variable (here, 1% over LIBOR) changes in the borrower's credit rating (or in the market's willingness to acquire securities of a particular term until maturity) still import the possibility of gain or loss for the original creditor.

(3)  The third characteristic to which attention has been drawn, especially in *Ramsay*, is what Lord Wilberforce (in a passage which I have already set out) called a structure of permanence. Similarly Lord Fraser (in a passage which I have already summarised) emphasised the long-term nature of the interest-bearing debt (L2) which gave it

marketability. That loan could be paid off before its 31-year term (and had to be paid off if the debtor company went into liquidation) but it could not then be paid off at par if its market value (as a long-term interest-bearing loan) was greater. That point was very important to the decision in *Ramsay*.

Those three characteristics have been considered in the authorities. There is a fourth which was not considered, the provision of some proprietary security. It is common ground that its provision is not necessary, and I have on the first issue held that its provision is not sufficient, to give a debt the quality of being a debt on a security. Nevertheless the presence of proprietary security in the form of a fixed or floating charge (sometimes in favour of trustees for debenture-holders) may make marketable securities more readily acceptable to the market, and any perceptible changes in the adequacy of the proprietary security may affect their market value.

## 24.5   End of Chapter Assessment Question

The source of the dividend income possessed by Hugh the barrister in 1998/99 (see **7.4**) is his shareholding in Superlucre plc. He originally bought 5,000 ordinary shares in Improvements Ltd on 31 March 1986, for £5,000. In 1986, Improvements Ltd was becoming increasingly successful, and it was taken over by Superlucre plc on 1 September 1992, on the basis of a one-for-one share exchange. On 1 April 1994, there was a one-for-one rights issue by Superlucre plc at £2 per share, which was taken up by Hugh. Finally, on 6 June 1997, Superlucre plc made a one-for-one bonus issue to all its shareholders.

Explain the CGT implications of each of these events so far as Hugh is concerned.

## 24.6   End of Chapter Assessment Outline Answer

All of Hugh's shareholding in Superlucre is regarded as forming one pool of expenditure called a Section 104 Holding. This Section 104 Holding of shares in Superlucre plc is effectively frozen at 5 April 1998. Were he today to dispose of any of them, the shares disposed of would be matched in accordance with the rules in TCGA 1992, s. 106A.

The basic acquisition cost of Hugh's shares in Superlucre plc is the £5,000 spent on 5,000 ordinary shares in Improvements Ltd on 31 March 1986. The one-for-one share exchange on 1 September 1992 would have made no difference to this cost, TCGA 1992, ss. 135–137 having provided roll-over relief on the takeover. Sections 135–137 deem there to have been no disposal on the takeover, and assume that the replacement shares are one and the same asset as Hugh's original shareholding in Improvements Ltd. There is no indication here that the conditions for ss. 135–137 applying, relating to the degree of control Superlucre plc consequently exercises over Improvements Ltd have not been satisfied, nor is there any indication that the takeover was effected for tax-avoidance motives or as part of a tax-avoidance scheme. Accordingly, it is assumed that ss. 137–139 apply.

The one-for-one rights issue, on 1 April 1994, which was taken up by Hugh at £2 per share, will have produced the following result. There will have been no disposal of the shares, but the 5,000 new shares, acquired at £2 per share, will have affected the base cost of Hugh's other shares in Superlucre plc. Obviously, their cost will have increased the base cost of the other shares in the Superlucre Section 104 Holding by £10,000. As to the bonus issue, on 6 June 1997, this was a reorganisation within TCGA 1992, s. 127, and thus will have involved no acquisition or disposal by Hugh. Instead, the previous £10,000 shares owned by Hugh, taken as a single asset and the new shares, taken as a single asset are treated as the same asset acquired as the original shares were acquired. This means that his shareholding has increased, as a result of the bonus issue, by 10,000 shares, without any corresponding increase in the base cost of the shares as a whole.

# CHAPTER TWENTY-FIVE

# INVESTMENT TAXATION: ANTI-AVOIDANCE ISSUES AND COMPLIANCE

## 25.1 Removing One of the Four Elements Needed for a CGT Charge

### 25.1.1 NO CHARGEABLE PERSON

#### *R v IRC, EX PARTE FULFORD-DOBSON* [1987] STC 344

MACNEILL J: . . . Concession D2, as I have said, is to be found in the booklet 'Extra-Statutory Concessions in Operation at 8 August 1980'. Inside the front cover of the booklet the following appears:

> The concessions described within are of general application, but it must be borne in mind that in a particular case there may be special circumstances which will require to be taken into account in considering the application of the concession. A concession will not be given in any case where an attempt is made to use it for tax avoidance.

It is the latter sentence which is central to the argument. The passage itself has for convenience during the hearing been called the 'rubric' and I adopt that word.
. . .

The facts are short and simple. Mr Fulford-Dobson was married. He had been in the Merchant Navy, but early in 1980 he was without employment. In 1977 his wife had inherited a property called 'Hardings Farm'. During 1980 she was considering the sale of the property. A letter from accountants acting, it appears, for both Mr and Mrs Fulford-Dobson, dated 7 December 1983 to HM Inspector of Taxes makes it clear that the proposed sale had generated 'a vast amount of correspondence', and involved considerable organisation, in relation, for example, to contracts of employment of farm workers, obtaining vacant possession of farm cottages, termination of grazing rights, investigation of rights of way and the like.

During the same period in 1980, Mr Fulford-Dobson was negotiating employment with a German firm of publishers at Herrsching. His contract of employment was concluded and signed on 18 August 1980. He was thereby required to work and reside in Herrsching and to commence work on Monday, 15 September 1980. On 29 August 1980, that is, eleven days after the contract of employment, Mrs Fulford-Dobson transferred Hardings Farm to her husband by deed of gift. On 13 September he left for Germany. On 17 September Hardings Farm was sold by auction.

In his affidavit of 21 May 1985, Mr Fulford-Dobson was wholly frank. He said at para. 9:

> The purpose of the gift by my wife to me was to avail ourselves of Concession D2 and to provide me with funds which I could invest outside the United Kingdom during my employment abroad without liability to United Kingdom Tax.

. . .

Counsel for the Revenue submitted that the rubric was to be construed as part of the concession, and I have already indicated that I so regard it. As I have said before, the rubric is part of each concession and is so to be read. I am reinforced in that view by his submission that if they give a concession the commissioners are entitled to take reasonable steps to prevent the abuse of the concession. They must act fairly and evenhandedly in the administration of the scheme, but there is no abuse or excess of power if they do what they have done here. It is not without significance that neither Mr Fulford-Dobson in his affidavit, nor the accountants in the correspondence ever suggest unfair treatment or discrimination.

As to tax avoidance, counsel for the Revenue submitted, Mr Fulford-Dobson and the accountants in the passages I have already read from the affidavit and the correspondence make it abundantly clear that the purpose and intent of what was done was to avoid tax. What the Duke of Westminster did was, according to Lord Templeman, tax avoidance. Questions have been raised as to whether that case would now be decided in the same way. Whatever the answer to those questions may be, Mrs Fulford-Dobson is very much, said counsel for the Revenue, in the position of the Duke. If she had not given Hardings Farm to her husband and the auction had continued while it was still in her name, she would undoubtedly have been chargeable to tax on her gain. The clear inference from the papers was that that was in contemplation until her husband was offered the job in Germany. Then, on advice, things moved quickly. Although Lord Templeman uses the word 'arrangement' repeatedly in the course of his speech, the word 'arrangement' clearly encompasses both the complicated arrangements described, for example, in the *Ramsay* and *Burmah* cases, but also the very simple arrangement here, that is to say, the gift to the husband, the departure of the husband to Germany, and the sale four days afterwards.

The question, I am bound to say, remains in my mind: did the advisers recognise the significance of the rubric? The trigger to the whole arrangement or operation, misconceived as I am now satisfied it was, was the prospect of saving the capital gains tax on the sale of the farm once the husband was to become non-resident before the date of the auction. That was the tax advantage which could not otherwise be secured. The gift, as counsel for the Revenue put it, lacked all elements of bounty. It was part of a scheme devised by the accountants and the bankers to avoid tax.

It seems to be plain as a pikestaff upon the facts that this was tax avoidance as that term is used in the rubric. The taxpayer here, Mr Fulford-Dobson, suffered no reduction in income, suffered no loss, incurred no expenditure (save his professional advisers' fees and expenses), nothing which, in Lord Templeman's words on the legislation there in point, Parliament intended to be suffered by any taxpayer qualifying for a reduction in his liability for tax. I repeat that from the passage I have already read.

I return to Lord Tomlin's much quoted sentence:

Every man is entitled if he can [and again I stress those three words 'if he can'] to order his affairs so that the tax attaching is less than it otherwise would be.

It is plain to me, using the same words, that on the facts here it cannot be done, or, more accurately, that the taxpayer, Mr Fulford-Dobson, could not so order his affairs as to attempt to use concession D2 to avoid tax. What was done was done deliberately for the admitted purpose of tax avoidance, but in total disregard of the clear words limiting the availability of the concession.

*Note:* ESC D2 has been modified, to take account of changes made by FA 1998, for departures from the UK on or after 17 March 1998: *Learning Text* at **25.3.1.1**.

## 25.2  Manipulating Allowable Losses, Reliefs and Exemptions

*WT RAMSAY LTD v IRC* **[1981] 1 All ER 865 (HL)**

The facts of this case are discussed in the *Learning Text* at **25.4.1**.

LORD WILBERFORCE: . . . Your Lordships are invited to take, with regard to schemes of the character I have described, what may appear to be a new approach. We are asked, in fact, to treat them as fiscally a nullity, not producing either a gain or a loss. Counsel for Ramsay described this as revolutionary, so I think it opportune to restate some familiar principles and some of the leading decisions so as to show the position we are now in.

1.    A subject is only to be taxed on clear words, not on 'intendment' or on the 'equity' of an Act. Any taxing Act of Parliament is to be construed in accordance with this principle. What are 'clear words' is to be ascertained on normal principles; these do not confine the courts to literal interpretation. There may, indeed should, be considered the context and scheme of the relevant Act as a whole, and its purpose may, indeed should, be regarded . . .

2.    A subject is entitled to arrange his affairs so as to reduce his liability to tax. The fact that the motive for a transaction may be to avoid tax does not invalidate it unless a particular enactment so provides. It must be considered according to its legal effect.

3.    It is for the fact-finding commissioners to find whether a document, or a transaction, is genuine or a sham. In this context, to say that a document or transaction is a 'sham' means that, while professing to be one thing, it is in fact something different. To say that a document or transaction is genuine, means that, in law, it is what it professes to be, and it does not mean anything more than that. I shall return to this point.

Each of these three principles would be fully respected by the decision we are invited to make. Something more must be said as to the next principle.

4.    Given that a document or transaction is genuine, the court cannot go behind it to some supposed underlying substance. This is the well-known principle of *Inland Revenue Comrs* v *Duke of Westminster* [1935] All ER Rep 259. This is a cardinal principle but it must not be overstated or over-extended. While obliging the court to accept documents or transactions, found to be genuine, as such, it does not compel the court to look at a document or a transaction in blinkers, isolated from any context to which it properly belongs. If it can be seen that a document or transaction was intended to have effect as part of a nexus or series of transactions, or as an ingredient of a wider transaction intended as a whole, there is nothing in the doctrine to prevent it being so regarded; to do so is not to prefer form to substance, or substance to form. It is the task of the court to ascertain the legal nature of any transactions to which it is sought to attach a tax or a tax consequence and if that emerges from a series or combination of transactions, intended to operate as such, it is that series or combination which may be regarded. . . .

For the commissioners considering a particular case it is wrong, and an unnecessary self-limitation, to regard themselves as precluded by their own finding that documents or transactions are not 'shams' from considering what, as evidenced by the documents themselves or by the manifested intentions of the parties, the relevant transaction is. They are not, under the *Duke of Westminster* doctrine or any other authority, bound to consider individually each separate step in a composite transaction intended to be carried through as a whole. This is particularly the case where (as in *Rawling*) it is proved that there was an accepted obligation, once a scheme is set in motion, to carry it through its successive steps. It may be so where . . . there is an expectation that it will be so carried through, and no likelihood in practice that it will not. In such cases (which may vary in emphasis) the commissioners should find the facts and then decide as a matter (reviewable) of law whether what is in issue is a composite transaction or a number of independent transactions.

The capital gains tax was created to operate in the real world, not that of make-believe. As I said in *Aberdeen Construction Group Ltd* v *Inland Revenue Comrs* [1978] 1 All ER 962 at 996 . . ., it is a tax on gains (or, I might have added, gains less losses), it is not a tax on arithmetical differences. To say that a loss (or gain) which appears to arise at one stage in an indivisible process, and which is intended to be and is cancelled out by a later stage, so that at the end of what was bought as, and planned as, a single continuous operation, is not such a loss (or gain) as the legislation is dealing with is in my opinion well, and indeed essentially, within the judicial function.

# CHAPTER TWENTY-SIX

# TAXATION OF GRATUITOUS TRANSFERS: INTRODUCTION

## 26.1 Categories of Nominal Transfers

### 26.1.1 TRANSFERS BETWEEN TRUSTEES

#### *ROOME* v *EDWARDS* [1981] 1 All ER 736

LORD WILBERFORCE: The Finance Act 1965 contains no definition of 'settlement.' As to 'settled property' section 45 merely states that the words mean, subject to subsection (8) (concerned with unit trusts), any property held in trust other than property to which section 22 (5) applies (property held by a nominee). So a 'settlement' must be a situation in which property is held in trust. But when is a settlement a separate settlement?

There are a number of obvious indicia which may help to show whether a settlement, or a settlement separate from another settlement, exists. One might expect to find separate and defined property; separate trusts; and separate trustees. One might also expect to find a separate disposition bringing the separate settlement into existence. These indicia may be helpful, but they are not decisive. For example, a single disposition, e.g., a will with a single set of trustees, may create what are clearly separate settlements, relating to different properties, in favour of different beneficiaries, and conversely separate trusts may arise in what is clearly a single settlement, e.g. when the settled property is divided into shares. There are so many possible combinations of fact that even where these indicia or some of them are present, the answer may be doubtful, and may depend upon an appreciation of them as a whole.

Since 'settlement' and 'trusts' are legal terms, which are also used by business men or laymen in a business or practical sense, I think that the question whether a particular set of facts amounts to a settlement should be approached by asking what a person, with knowledge of the legal context of the word under established doctrine and applying this knowledge in a practical and common-sense manner to the facts under examination, would conclude. To take two fairly typical cases. Many settlements contain powers to appoint a part or a proportion of the trust property to beneficiaries: some may also confer power to appoint separate trustees of the property so appointed, or such power may be conferred by law: see Trustee Act 1925, section 37. It is established doctrine that the trusts declared by a document exercising a special power of appointment are to be read into the original settlement: see *Muir (or Williams) v Muir* [1943] AC 468. If such a power is exercised, whether or not separate trustees are appointed, I do not think that it would be natural for such a person as I have presupposed to say that a separate settlement had been created: still less so if it were found that provisions of the original settlement continued to apply to the appointed fund, or that the appointed fund were liable, in certain events, to fall back into the rest of the settled property. On the other hand, there may be a power to appoint and appropriate a part or portion of the trust property to beneficiaries and to settle it for their benefit. If such a power is exercised, the natural conclusion might be that a separate settlement was created, all the more so if a complete new set of trusts were declared as to the appropriated property, and if it could be said

that the trusts of the original settlement ceased to apply to it. There can be many variations on these cases each of which will have to be judged on its facts.
. . .

### *BOND* v *PICKFORD* [1983] STC 517 (CA)

SLADE LJ: . . . The concept of persons becoming absolutely entitled as against themselves, on a first introduction, is not an easy one. Nevertheless two points have been common ground on this appeal. (1) It is in principle quite possible for an occasion to arise when the trustees of one settlement become 'absolutely entitled' (in the relevant sense) to settled property as against the trustees of another settlement, even though the trustees of the first-mentioned settlement have no beneficial interest in the property and are acting in a solely fiduciary capacity. Though the phrase 'absolutely entitled to any settled property as against the trustee' of course includes absolute beneficial entitlement, it is not restricted to it; the ability to give a good discharge for the property renders a person absolutely entitled in the relevant sense. This point was decided by Brightman J in *Hoare Trustees* v *Gardner (Inspector of Taxes)* [1978] STC 89 at 107–108, [1979] Ch 10 at 13–14). He also decided that para. 9 of sch. 19 to the Finance Act 1969, though refining the meaning of absolute entitlement as against the trustee, did not introduce a requirement that the person so entitled should have an absolute beneficial entitlement. The correctness of this decision has not been questioned on this appeal. (2) Furthermore, if an occasion arises on which trust assets wholly cease to be subject to the trusts, powers and provisions of one settlement and become subject to the trusts, powers and provisions of another settlement, a deemed 'disposal' of such assets, within s. 25(3) of the 1965 Act, will not be prevented from occurring merely because the trustees of the two settlements happen to be the same persons. This is because s. 25(1) of that Act provides that, in relation to settled property, the trustees of the settlement are to be treated as being a single and continuing body of persons distinct from the actual persons who may from time to time be the trustees: *Hart (Inspector of Taxes)* v *Briscoe* [1978] STC 89 at 102, [1979] Ch 1 at 5 per Brightman J.

Very frequently, as in the present case, settlements confer on the trustees, or other persons, specific powers to alter, in one way or another, the currently operative trusts of the settlement. Two obvious examples of such powers are what are commonly known as powers of appointment and powers of advancement. But the forms which such powers may take are many and various and, as in the present case, they may be difficult to categorise under some well-recognised label. Where the effect of the exercise of such power is to render a person or persons absolutely entitled beneficially to the relevant assets, the applicability of s. 25(3) of the 1965 Act will not be in doubt. Where, however, the effect of the exercise (whatever the label attached to the power itself) is merely to subject the assets to new trusts of a continuing nature difficult questions may arise as to whether this has involved taking them out of the original settlement and putting them into a new one, so as to give rise to a deemed disposal, or whether they continue to be held on the trusts of the original settlement.

Before turning to the recent decisions which give guidance on this point, I would mention what I conceive to be two basic principles of English trust law. First, the office of a trustee being one of personal confidence, it is well settled that a trustee may not delegate the exercise of his trusts, powers and discretions to other persons, save to the extent that he is expressly authorised to do so either by the trust instrument which clothes him with his office or by statute.

Secondly, the ordinary rule is that, when a special power of appointment is exercised, the limitations created under it are treated as written into the original instrument which created the power and *not* as creating a new settlement for trust purposes. Lord Romer in *Muir or Williams* v *Muir* [1943] AC 468 at 483 had this to say in relation to the ordinary special power of appointment, as contrasted with a general power:

> If, for example, property be settled on trust for A for life and after his death on trust for such of A's children or remoter issue and in such proportions as B shall by deed appoint, B has no interest in the property whatsoever. He has merely been given the power of saying on behalf of the settlor which of the issue of A shall take the property

under the settlement and in what proportions. It is as though the settlor had left a blank in the settlement which B fills up for him if and when the power of appointment is exercised. The appointees' interests come to them under the settlement alone and by virtue of that document. These remarks apply equally well to the case where the donee of the power of appointment has not only the power of saying which of the class shall take under the trust, but also the power of saying what interests they shall take.

Of course, it is possible for a person creating a new settlement expressly to confer on the trustees wide powers, which specifically entitle them to execute an instrument, or do some other act, which has the effect not merely of altering the presently subsisting trusts of the settlement in relation to specified assets, but of subjecting those assets to the trusts of an entirely different settlement, in such manner that the trustees exercising the power are to be discharged from any further responsibilities in relation to those assets in their capacity as trustees of the original settlement. Nevertheless in the light of the two principles of trust law already mentioned, I feel no doubt that as a matter of trust law trustees, who are given a discretionary power to direct which of the beneficiaries shall take the trust property and for what interests, do *not* have the power thereby to remove assets from the original settlement, by subjecting them to the trusts of a separate settlement, unless the instrument which gave them the power expressly or by necessary implication authorises them so to do. In the absence of such authority, any exercise of the power, other than one which renders persons beneficially absolutely entitled to the relevant assets, will leave those assets subject to the trusts of the original settlement, in accordance with the principles explained by Lord Romer in *Muir or Williams v Muir*; and the trustees of the original settlement will remain responsible for them accordingly, in that capacity.

Thus, there is in my opinion a crucial distinction to be drawn between (a) powers to alter the presently operative trusts of a settlement which expressly or by necessary implication authorise the trustees to remove assets altogether from the original settlement (without rendering any person absolutely beneficially entitled to them); and (b) powers of this nature which do not confer on the trustees such authority.

I will refer to these two different types of powers as 'powers in the wider form' and 'powers in the narrower form'. The distinction between them is in my opinion of great importance and is reflected in the relevant decisions.

. . .

OLIVER LJ: . . . In my judgment, Nourse J was right to attach importance to the nature of the power. Again, this may not always be conclusive, but there is, in my judgment, a world of difference between an appointment under a special power to appoint to beneficiaries in the classical form (which is frequently found as the primary trust of a discretionary settlement — the discretionary trusts being expressed to apply only until and in default of appointment) and a disposition of the fund under a power which enables or directs the appointors to remove the fund entirely from the trusts and powers of the settlement.

. . .

### SWIRES v RENTON [1991] STC 490

HOFFMANN J: The issue in this appeal from the Special Commissioner is whether the exercise of a power of appointment under a settlement has resulted in a deemed disposal under s. 54(1) of the Capital Gains Tax Act 1979 (the 1979 Act). The settlement was made on 21 January 1954 by Mr Jack Meek (the settlor) and its relevant provisions may be summarised as follows. First, for a period defined by a royal lives clause there was a discretionary trust of income in favour of a class consisting of the settlor's wife, his daughter Isabelle, her husband and her two sons Mark and Anthony. Second, during the period of the income trust the trustees had power under clause 3 to pay or apply capital to or for the benefit of any member of the class 'freed and released from the trusts concerning the same'. Third, there was an ultimate trust of capital for members of the class living at the expiry of the income trust. Fourth, the settlement contained various administrative powers.

The power to apply capital was exercised by a deed of appointment dated 16 June 1981 which was expressed to be supplemental to the settlement. It divided the trust fund into two parts by reference to a schedule of assets. One part was declared to be held on trust for Isabelle absolutely. The other part (called the appointed fund) was to be held to pay the income to Isabelle during her life or for the remainder of the income trust period, whichever was the shorter, with power to pay or apply capital to or for her benefit 'freed and discharged from the trusts affecting the same under the Settlement and this deed'. Subject to the income trust, the capital was to be held for Mark and Anthony in equal shares absolutely. The remaining clauses of the appointment gave the trustees power to disregard the Apportionment Act and declared that the administrative provisions of the settlement were to continue to apply to the appointed fund as far as they were consistent with the other provisions of the deed.

Section 54(1) of the 1979 Act provides that a disposal of assets comprised in a settlement shall be deemed to have taken place when any person has become absolutely entitled to those assets against the trustees. There is no dispute that by virtue of the appointment there was such a deemed disposal of the assets to which Isabelle became absolutely entitled. The issue in this appeal is whether there was also a deemed disposal of the appointed fund. This remained vested in the trustees. But the 1979 Act treats the trustees of settled property as a single continuing body of persons distinct from the actual persons who may from time to time be the trustees. It is conceptually possible for persons acting in their capacity as trustees of a new settlement to become absolutely entitled to assets against themselves as trustees of the old settlement. Therefore, the appeal turns on the question whether the assets remain subject to the trusts of the settlement as varied by the appointment or whether the effect of the appointment was to subject them to the trusts of a new settlement.

The decision of the House of Lords in *Roome v Edwards (Inspector of Taxes)* [1981] STC 96 at 100, [1982] AC 279 at 293, as expressed in the speech of Lord Wilberforce, shows that the question must be answered according to the view which would be taken of the transaction by a person with knowledge of trusts who uses language in a practical and commonsense way. Which description would be considered more appropriate: that new trusts had been grafted onto the old settlement or that a new settlement had been created?

The more recent decision of the Court of Appeal in 1983 in *Bond (Inspector of Taxes) v Pickford* [1983] STC 517 shows that a critical element in deciding how to describe the transaction may be the scope of the power which has been exercised. If that power allows the trustees to define or vary the beneficial interest but not remove the assets from the settlement or delegate their powers and discretions it is difficult to imagine any appointment within the scope of the power which could be construed as the creation of a new settlement. On the other hand, the power may be expressed in terms wide enough to permit the creation of a new settlement, and the question will then be whether this is what the trustees have chosen to do.

The cases show there is no single litmus test for deciding that question. The paradigm case of the creation of a new settlement would involve the segregation of particular assets, the appointment of a new trustees, the creation of fresh trusts which exhaust the beneficial interest in the assets and administrative powers which make further reference to the original settlement redundant (see *Hart (Inspector of Taxes) v Briscoe* [1978] STC 89 at 105, [1979] Ch 1 at 8 per Brightman J). The absence of one or more of those features is not necessarily inconsistent with a resettlement. It seems to me that the question is one of construction of the settlement using the approach recommended by Lord Wilberforce and looking at the documents in the light of the surrounding circumstances. Putting the same thing another way, it is a matter of endeavouring to ascertain the intention of the parties. The Special Commissioner decided that various indications in the deed of appointment led to the conclusion that it declared new beneficial trusts without creating a new settlement in respect of the appointed fund.

Before me counsel for the Crown took what might be called a preliminary point. He said that whatever might be the indications in the deed of appointment as to the intentions of the trustees, the power which they purported to exercise did not permit them to make an appointment otherwise than by way of outright payment or the creation of a new settlement. Just as in *Bond v Pickford* the power in question did not allow the trustees to remove assets from the settlement, so this power did not allow them to do anything else. For that submission counsel relied on the words 'freed and released from the trusts concerning the same' in clause 3 of the settlement. There can be no doubt that that clause empowered the trustees to make an appointment which would remove assets from the settlement altogether. An outright appointment of capital to a beneficiary would obviously have that effect. A further indication is to be found in the proviso that the power should not be exercised during the life of the settlor so as to reduce the capital of the trust fund 'remaining subject to the trusts of the settlement' below £50.

But was that the only way in which the power could be exercised? Such a construction would mean that an appointment which expressly purported only to vary the beneficial capital trust in some relatively minor respect would have to be held ultra vires or else somewhat artificially construed as the creation of a new settlement with all the provisions of the old one together with the variation.

In the absence of clearer language I am reluctant to construe the clause in this all-or-nothing way. It seems to me that 'freed and released from the trusts concerning the same' can easily mean that the assets are to be released from any trust inconsistent with the appointment. There is no reason why such an appointment should necessarily involve the discharge of the assets from all the trust powers and provisions of the settlement.

Counsel for the Crown drew attention to the fact that clause 3 was expressed in language very similar to that of the statutory power of advancement in s. 32 of the Trustee Act 1925. That was the provision which the House of Lords in *Pilkington* v *IRC* [1964] AC 612, 40 TC 416 held could be used to create a fresh settlement for the benefit of an object of the power. But counsel said that one could also infer from the speech of Viscount Radcliffe (see [1964] AC 612 at 630, 40 TC 416 at 434) that he thought any use of the statutory power otherwise than by way of absolute payment would inevitably involve the creation of a new settlement.

However, in my judgment Viscount Radcliffe was dealing with an express proposal to create a fresh settlement and did not address the question whether this was the only way in which the power could be used to achieve the same result. In my view, clause 3 gave the trustees a choice. They could have disposed of the appointed funds to themselves as trustees of the new settlement or declared that it was to be subject to new trusts within the existing settlement. The difference goes entirely to the method adopted and not to the substantial result achieved, which in either case was precisely the same.

In *Bond* v *Pickford* [1983] STC 517 at 525 Slade LJ said that where trustees had what he called a power in the wider form, that is, a power which enabled the trustees to take assets out of the settlement altogether, and they exercised it—

> . . . in such manner as to cause the trusts which currently affect the relevant assets to be wholly replaced by a new set of trusts, the conclusion will probably be irresistible that both the purpose and the effect of the transaction is to create an entirely new settlement.

Counsel for the Crown said that such a conclusion could be drawn in this case because the appointed fund had been made subject to a wholly new set of trusts which exhausted the beneficial interest. However, I rather think that in referring to a new set of trusts Slade LJ had in mind the whole of the trust powers and provisions of the settlement including the administrative powers, much the same as Brightman J said in the passage in *Hart* v *Briscoe* [1978] STC 89 at 105, [1979] Ch 1 at 9 to which I have already referred.

In this case the question whether the administrative powers were intended to survive is part of the question of construction which has to be decided. Furthermore, although Slade LJ said that such a conclusion would probably be irresistible he emphasised elsewhere in his judgment that the purpose and effect of the transaction must be gathered from the whole of the documents and the surrounding circumstances. Nevertheless, I accept, as Nourse J did in *Bond* v *Pickford* [1982] STC 403, that the creation of trusts under a power in the wider form which exhaust the beneficial interest is a powerful indication of an intention to create a new settlement.

It seems to me the question here is whether that inference is rebutted by the language of the deed of appointment. Both sides have drawn attention to various features of the deed which they say favour their construction. For example, the deed is expressed to the supplemental to the settlement. That is said to be an indication that the settlement is intended to survive. In my view, that phraseology carries little, if any, weight because on any view resort to the settlement would have been necessary partly in order to ascertain that the trustees had power to make the appointment and partly because the appointment uses by way of shorthand various definitions contained in the settlement. On the other side, it is said that the creation of a power to disregard the Apportionment Act indicates an intention to make a new settlement. Again, that seems to me to be entirely neutral. There is no reason why an additional power should not be conferred by the exercise of the power under clause 3 without having to recast the entire settlement.

In my judgment, there are only two provisions in the deed of appointment which really matter. First, clause 7 provides that:

> During the subsistence of the foregoing trusts or any of them the administrative and other powers and provisions declared and contained in clauses 7–10 inclusive in the Settlement shall continue to apply to the Appointed Fund so far (but so far only) as the same are consistent with the beneficial provisions hereinbefore appointed.

The more natural effect of the words 'shall continue to apply' is to connote the continuation of the settlement, but standing by itself that clause would not necessarily have been sufficient. The words are also capable of meaning that the administrative clauses in question are to be incorporated by reference in the new settlement. In *Bond* v *Pickford* [1982] STC 403 at 414, Nourse J would have been willing to construe similar words as words of incorporation by reference if the power in question had been in the wider form.

But clause 7 does not stand by itself. The other counter-indication is clause 4(b) which gives the trustees power to appoint capital from the appointed fund to Isabelle during her lifetime 'freed and discharged from the trusts affecting the same under the Settlement and this deed'. The words 'under the Settlement' clearly indicate that the trustees contemplated that there would be provisions of the settlement continuing to be applicable to the appointed fund. That language can be given meaning and effect if clause 7 is construed as words which continue the application of the administrative powers and with them the old settlement.

Counsel for the Crown, while accepting that in a well-drawn settlement these words would carry the implication which I have given them, submitted that the deed of appointment was in a number of respects clearly an inartistically drafted document and that the reference to the trusts of the settlement in clause 4(b) could be treated as surplus words which had merely been put in for greater caution in case, contrary to the actual intentions of the trustees, some part of the settlement could be held to survive. He pointed to various other provisions in the deed which clearly are redundant, for example, clause 4(b) also says that the appointment of capital shall be 'subject as aforesaid and to every exercise of the foregoing power', words which are plainly unnecessary. In addition, the appointment goes on in clause 5 to create an ultimate trust for Mark and Anthony of the capital on the termination of the former income trust when on any view an exactly similar trust would have taken effect under the previous clauses.

However, it does not seem to me to be a permissible method of construction to say that words which are capable of being given an intelligible effect should be rejected as surplusage because the draughtsman has shown a penchant for surplusage in other parts of his document. In my judgment, the reference to the trusts of the settlement in clause 4(b) should be taken at face value and, if so taken, it shows a sufficient intention on the part of the trustees to create new trusts under the old settlement rather than to set up a new one.

The Special Commissioner gave a number of other reasons for coming to his conclusion with which I must not necessarily be taken as agreeing, but I share his view that in the end the question is not an easy one. Like many questions of construction, it is somewhat finely balanced but in the end my conclusion is the same as his and the appeal must be dismissed.

*Appeal dismissed with costs.*

# 26.2   Historical and Political Contexts

**Beard, M.,** *English Landed Society in the Twentieth Century*, **Routledge,
1989, pp. 92 and 133**

Land disposed of for death duties was sold with great reluctance as owners saw the vast sums which it yielded immediately handed over to the Exchequer. Yet in 1950, when the total revenue from all taxation was £2,436 million, death duties on agricultural estates contributed £3.3 million, a tiny fraction of the total. In the countryside, these obligatory land sales could cut an estate in half, bringing about far-reaching changes in the pattern of landownership and the demise of numerous landed families. Yet death duties on agricultural land, through pressure from the Central Landowners' Association, had been given a 45 per cent abatement in 1949. Attracting half the normal liability at death, agricultural land slowly came to be viewed as a shrewd investment, and so arrived the new breed of 'death bed purchasers'. Landowners whose capital had long been tied up in land saw the value of farmland increase from an average of £27 an acre in 1938 to £80 an acre in 1950. But this meant that, despite the 45 per cent abatement, the higher rates of estate duty on increasingly valuable land demanded more revenue at death than ever before.

For those landowners who did not have to pay death duties, taxation itself had an equally devastating impact after the war. The Gowers report of 1950, a Treasury report on houses of outstanding historic and architectural interest, stated that because of high taxation no individual, however much his gross income or whatever its source, would have more than £5,000 a year to spend. Many of the large country houses needed very much more than £5,000 a year just to preserve them and their contents from deterioration. But a rent roll of £140,000 a year was reduced to £3,500 a year by income tax, tithe, surtax, and the expense of maintaining the agricultural estate from which it came. Out of this £3,500 the owner might have to maintain two historic houses as well as himself and his family. Moreover, despite the increased value of agricultural land, rents remained stagnant. This had been reinforced by another piece of legislation which affected landowners everywhere, the 1947 Agriculture Act. Rents were usually revised when farms were relet. With security of tenure, tenants could now negotiate rent increases secure against any threats of dislodgement.

. . .

In the autumn of 1973, following the Yom Kippur war between Israel and the Arab states, higher oil prices were introduced by the Arabs, aimed specifically at crippling the western economy. New militant nationalist regimes had gained power in Algeria, Libya and Iraq, and they soon changed their relations with the multi-national oil companies. The price of oil was now used as a political weapon. As two-thirds of Britain's oil came from the Middle East this had a disastrous effect on the economy. Yet worse was to come. When in February 1974 the Labour Party was narrowly returned to power, the Chancellor of the Exchequer cleverly diverted the nation's attention from the economic crisis by producing a budget which aimed to 'soak the rich'.

It was the first time in the twentieth century that landed society in England was faced with policies aimed specifically at the redistribution of wealth. As far as the Labour government was concerned, their tax proposals were not primarily a means of gaining revenue. In 1974 they were part of a bitter political crusade. The only country which reshapes its tax laws every year, Britain in 1974 had no less than three budgets, in March, July, and November. The first two were specifically aimed at bringing the rich to their knees.

Since the introduction of death duties in 1894 taxation at death had over the years come to be known as 'the voluntary tax'. Despite the occasional glaring examples, when owners had not outlived the five- and the seven-year-rules, death duties could largely be avoided by setting up trusts and through gifts. Realising the disconcerting success with which the rich had managed to sidestep the taxes, the Chancellor of the Exchequer, Denis Healey, tried to reverse this trend. He stated quite clearly that he wanted to reverse 'the unfair advantages enjoyed by generation after generation of the heirs and relatives of wealthy men'. He rallied his parliamentary colleagues by saying that he could not believe that they could reasonably complain if he now took steps to see that 'a tax that has been on the statute book for nearly 80 years is at last made effective'.

Estate duty payable at death was abolished and in its place was created capital transfer tax. This meant that any transfer of wealth, except between a husband and wife, was subject to tax. It was no longer possible to set up trust funds to avoid paying tax. Yet all was not gloom. For farmers, gradually and grudgingly, there were tax reliefs. Similarly, tax relief was given to the owners of historic houses and their surrounding parkland and contents if they were opened to the public for at least thirty days a year. Once again, by careful management and reorganisation, it was possible for landowners to avoid the worst of the new tax.

# CHAPTER TWENTY-SEVEN

# TAXATION OF GRATUITOUS TRANSFERS: GIFTS

## 27.1 Taxation of Absolute Gifts

### TURNER v FOLLETT [1973] STC 148 (CA)

. . .

4.   Evidence was given before the commissioners by the taxpayer who produced and submitted to them the following statement:

When is a capital gain not a capital gain? When it is a gift is the straightforward the obvious answer. I would mention that I am not objecting to the capital gains tax in general but in particular to a gift tax masquerading as a capital gains tax. Having given 100 shares in Hudson Bay Company to each of my three children and notified HM Inspector of Taxes accordingly I am informed that I, the donor, am liable for capital gains tax under the Finance Act 1965. Upon referring to booklet 560 on Capital Gains which he kindly sent to me I read in Paragraph I 'The Finance Act, 1965 provides for Taxation of Capital Gains accruing on the disposal of assets after 6th April 1965'. No gain of capital accrued to me, therefore I should not be liable for tax. Under paragraph 75 of the same booklet I read: — 'The concept of disposal is nowhere defined in detail in the Act; to begin with, therefore it has to be given its natural meaning.' Quite so. Therefore capital gains tax should also be given its natural meaning. Which is simply a tax on a gain of capital. Not at all difficult to define. In giving shares to my children I have in fact made a capital loss to the extent of the full value of the shares and any attempt by the Finance Act [1965] to describe that as a capital gain is gross misrepresentation which I view with the utmost contempt, creating as it does a contradiction in the true meaning of the English Language and consequently an incomprehensible law. In fact it has been clearly stated in the House of Commons by a Government spokesman on more than one occasion that whilst the possibility of a gift tax had been envisaged such a tax statute does not at present exist. I wish to place on record the courteous and helpful manner in which my protest against payment has been treated by the Inspector of Taxes and I much regret that he finds himself in the unenviable position of having to interpret legislation which in a flagrant distortion of words, calls a gift a capital gain, thus antagonising a Tax payer who for 38 years has paid his income tax, surtax and capital gains tax with fortitude and with reasonable promptness. If the Government wants a gift tax it should be properly named as such so that its meaning can be understood and thrifty people thereby warned. Quite deliberately I have not referred to any calculations which under the circumstances are irrelevant, as on the grounds of equity and the rules of natural justice no gain of capital accrued to me and therefore the question of capital gains tax does not arise.

. . .

RUSSELL LJ: . . . The taxpayer has really argued his case on broader lines than I have so far indicated and has used language, although moderate and reasonably temperate, as to the ways of Parliament in misusing language and in effect 'deeming' him into a position which on any ordinary use of the words 'capital gains' was impossible to assert. He in effect says: 'Here is a discreditable manipulation of words. The Act is not truthful. Words ought to mean what they say. If they' [meaning thereby any Government from time to time] 'want to introduce a gift tax, they should not do it by way of stating something to be a tax on capital gains, and then in a subordinate clause, by references in remoter parts of schedules, saying that "in fact, of course, we we do not confine ourselves to capital gains tax; we are going to bring in under this also an element of a gift tax"'. It is not, of course, fully a gift tax, because a gift tax would ordinarily be a percentage of the value of the asset given at the time it was given; and this tax, on any footing, is not that.

We have listened to the taxpayer's criticisms of this method of legislation, particularly this method of fiscal legislation. To say that his criticisms fall on deaf ears would be impolite; but, speaking judicially, our ears cannot but be deaf to such an approach. We can do nothing but construe the Act to the best of our ability, stifling any distaste which out of court we might find ourselves sharing with the taxpayer.

Accordingly, in my judgment, we have no alternative but to dismiss this appeal.

BUCKLEY LJ: I agree. . . . When one reads the Act as a whole, and particularly the provisions to which Russell LJ has referred, it seems to me that the context is so clear in its indication that the intention of Parliament was to treat the gift as a notional sale at the market value of the subject-matter, both from the point of view of the donor and of the donee, that one cannot escape the conclusion that that was Parliament's true intention. . . .

For these reasons, and for those that Russell LJ has elaborated in the judgment which he has delivered, I agree that this appeal cannot succeed and must be dismissed.

ORR LJ: I also agree.

## 27.2   Taxation of Gifts on Trust

### 27.2.1   INHERITANCE TAX AND GIFTS INTO SETTLEMENTS

#### *PEARSON* v *IRC* [1980] 2 All ER 479 (HL)

The facts of this case are discussed at *Learning Text* at **27.4.2.1**.

VISCOUNT DILHORNE . . . We were referred to a considerable number of statutes in which the expression 'interest in possession' is to be found. . . . I saw nothing in them to indicate or suggest, and I see nothing in the Act itself, to suggest, that the phrase should be given any other meaning than that of a present right of present enjoyment. . . .

Here the three sisters' entitlement to income was subject to the trustees' power to accumulate. On reaching 21 they had no valid claim to anything. If there was any income from the settled property, they were not entitled to it. Their right to anything depended on what the trustees did or did not do and the receipt of income by them appears to me to have been . . . at the discretion of the trustees . . .

LORD RUSSELL OF KILLOWEN: My Lords, the settlor Sir Richard Pilkington executed on 30 November 1964 a settlement of 13,333 ordinary £10 shares in Pilkington Brothers Ltd. The settlor had three children only, his daughters Fiona, Serena and Julia, all of whom had attained the age of 21 before the end of February 1974. These three at all times fulfilled the settlement definition of 'the principal beneficiaries'. The settlement also defined 'the discretionary objects' as meaning the principal beneficiaries, their issue whenever born, and the spouses and relicts of the principal beneficiaries and of their said issue. A 'trust period' was defined as the shortest of three periods: (i) the expiration of 20 years from the death of the survivor of the then (30 November 1964) living issue of

King George V, (ii) until the time when there should be no discretionary object in existence, (iii) until the time when the trustees might by deed in their discretion declare the trust period to expire.

Clause 2 conferred on the trustees an overriding power over capital and income of the trust fund by deed or deeds revocable or irrevocable to appoint in favour of any one or more of the discretionary objects in the widest possible terms, restricted only by the need not to infringe the rules against perpetuities and excessive accumulation.

Clause 3 was in the following terms:

In default of and until and subject to any appointment made under the last foregoing clause the Trustees shall hold the capital and income of the Trust Fund upon the Following trusts that is to say: (a) During the Trust Period or the period of Twenty one years from the execution hereof (whichever shall be the shorter period) the Trustees shall accumulate so much (if any) of the income of the Trust Fund as they shall think fit by investing the same and the resulting income thereof in any manner hereinafter authorised as an accretion to the capital of the Trust Fund and as one fund with such capital for all purposes. (b) Subject thereto the Trustees shall hold the capital and income of the Trust Fund UPON TRUST for such of the Principal Beneficiaries as shall attain the age of Twenty one years or marry under that age and if more than one in equal shares absolutely.

In my opinion the provisions of cl. 3 clearly constitute (i) a mere *power* in the trustees to accumulate, and (ii) subject to (a) that power, (b) the cl. 3 power of appointment and (c) (until the death of the settlor which occurred in December 1976) the possibility of partial defeasance by further children being born to him, an absolute trust as to capital and income and any accumulations for the three daughters in equal shares on attaining the age of 21 years which as stated all three had attained by the end of February 1974. It will be observed that this is not a case of a gift of income for the benefit of a discretionary class, as was the case in *Gartside* v *Inland Revenue Comrs* [1968] 1 All ER 121, [1968] AC 553. Ignoring, as for present purposes may admittedly be done, factors (b) and (c), the three daughters were absolutely entitled each to one-third of the income of the trust subject only to a power in the trustees to divert all or part by deciding to accumulate (during a period permitted by law) some or all of the income as it accrued. In fact the trustees accumulated all income accruing. On the one hand the Crown's claim would have been exactly the same if none had been accumulated; on the other hand the trustees' case equally is that it makes no difference that all had been accumulated. It was therefore common ground that the answer to the question posed in this appeal in no way depended on what the trustees did or did not do by way of exercise of their power of accumulation.

The only other clause in the settlement requiring notice was cl. 21, in the following terms:

The Trustees may at any time or times apply any income of the Trust Fund in or towards the payment or discharge of any duties taxes costs charges fees or other outgoings which but for the provisions of this clause would be payable out of or charged upon the capital of the Trust Fund or any part thereof.

The Crown contended that, even without the cl. 3 power of accumulation, this clause contained a power in effect to accumulate which, though not in fact operated, had the same result in terms of the liability for capital transfer tax asserted.

On 8 August 1974 the trustees exercised their cl. 2 power of appointment over a freehold house in London (part of the trust capital) by revocably appointing the income therefrom to Serena for life, she to be entitled to occupy it rent free but paying rates and other outgoings and keeping it in repair and insured.

On 16 September 1974 the trustees exercised their cl. 2 power of appointment over another London house in favour of Fiona.

On 20 March 1976 the trustees again exercised their cl. 2 power of appointment in favour of Fiona, this time over the sum of £16,000 (part of the trust capital); they irrevocably appointed the income thereof to Fiona during her life or during the trust period whichever should be the shorter period. The appointment reserved a power in the trustees to raise and expend capital of the £16,000 fund on repairs etc to the house previously appointed to Fiona. It also provided that if any capital transfer tax should be payable as a result of that appointment it should be raised and paid out of the balance of the trust fund in exoneration of the appointed fund.

It is in connection with this last appointment that the Crown claims that capital transfer tax is payable as its result. Both Fox J and the Court of Appeal decided to the contrary. (There was later in fact a cl. 2 appointment of a freehold house and £16,000 in favour of Julia on similar lines, but revocable as to both.)

The notice of determination under the Finance Act 1975, sch. 4, para. 6 against which the trustees appealed asserted that under the 1976 appointment Fiona became entitled to an 'interest in possession' in the £16,000 part of the settled property 'at a time when no such interest subsisted in that part of the property within the terms of paragraph 6(2) Schedule 5 Finance Act 1975', that a capital distribution was accordingly to be treated as having been made out of that part of the settled property, and that the tax chargeable on that distribution was £444 odd.

I do not propose to rehearse passages from the 1975 Act. They are fully set out and discussed in the judgments at first instance and in the Court of Appeal. The short question is whether the Crown is right when it contends that for the purposes of para. 6(2) of sch. 5 to the Act at the time of the 1976 appointment of £16,000 *no interest in possession subsisted in the £16,000.* As already indicated the Crown contends that the mere existence of the power to accumulate (cl 3) and equally of the power to apply income for 'capital' purposes (cl 21) necessarily involved a situation in which the daughters had no interest in possession subsisting in the trust fund including the £16,000, though it was not contended that the existence of the cl. 2 power of appointment had that effect.

In common with my noble and learned friend Lord Keith I do not find any reliable guidance in this matter from the provisions of the Settled Land Acts, nor from consideration of the estate duty legislation which was superseded by the 1975 Act. Neither do I find it a useful exercise to compare anomalies and 'hard cases' asserted to arise on either solution: such are, I fear, only to be expected in the introduction of such a radical and complicated experiment in fiscal novelty. The crucial question, in my opinion, lies in the well-known distinction between a trust and a power, a distinction recognised by this House in *McPhail* v *Doulton* [1970] 2 All ER 228, [1971] AC 424, and there only regretted as a distinction which might lead in a given case to invalidity of the disposition. As I have already indicated this is clearly a case of a mere power to accumulate, as distinct from a trust to accumulate unless and to the extent to which the trustees exercised a power to pay allowances to the sisters or any of them. The sisters were able to say that as income accrued on the £16,000 they were then entitled to that income, subject to the possibility that the trustees might *subsequently divert* it from them by a decision to accumulate it. (Indeed but for the cl. 2 power of appointment, and the possibility until the death of the settlor in December 1976 of the birth of further children, they were, notwithstanding the power of accumulation, entitled to claim transfer of the £16,000.) Similar considerations apply to the possibility of the exercise of the cl. 21 application of the income for a capital purpose. The case is also distinguishable from the case of a discretionary trust of income among a class, as in *Gartside* v *Inland Revenue Comrs* [1968] 1 All ER 121, [1968] AC 553.

These considerations persuade me that at the time of the 1976 appointment it is not correct to say that no interest in possession subsisted in the three sisters in the £16,000.

My noble and learned friend Lord Keith, in forming the opposite opinion, suggests that otherwise a conclusion follows that the interest goes in and out of possession according as the trustees refrain from accumulating or decide to do so, and to the further conclusion that as the trustees did actually accumulate all the income up to the date of the 1976 appointment, the interest was never in possession. I do not recall that this proposition was advanced for the Crown, which as already indicated agreed (as did the trustees) that the exercise or non-exercise of the powers under cl. 3 or cl. 21 could make no difference to the outcome. I consider, with respect, that the conclusions stated above do not follow from the view which I have, supporting the courts below, formed. The fact that an interest in possession is liable to defeasance by *subsequent* exercise of the power does not deny it that description when the benefit of it is thus subsequently taken away.

The statute contains a 'non-definition' of an interest in possession which does not assist in answering this problem. If the view which I have formed were the correct one on the statute as drafted, and if it runs counter (as I assume from the fact of this appeal it does) to the intentions of those responsible for the legislation, it should be fairly simple to provide expressly that the existence of a mere power of accumulation, or of a power such as is contained in cl. 21, operates to prevent the simultaneous existence of an interest in possession in any property of which the income is subject to such a power. . . .

. . .

## INHERITANCE TAX ACT 1984

**71. Accumulation and maintenance trusts**

(1)   Subject to subsection (2) below, this section applies to settled property if—

(a)   one or more persons (in this section referred to as beneficiaries) will, on or before attaining a specified age not exceeding twenty-five, become beneficially entitled to it or to an interest in possession in it, and

(b)   no interest in possession subsists in it and the income from it is to be accumulated so far as not applied for the maintenance, education or benefit of a beneficiary.

(2)   This section does not apply to settled property unless either—

(a)   not more than twenty-five years have elapsed since the commencement of the settlement or, if it was later, since the time (or latest time) when the conditions stated in paragraphs (a) and (b) of subsection (1) above became satisfied with respect to the property, or

(b)   all the persons who are or have been beneficiaries are or were either—

(i)   grandchildren of a common grandparent, or

(ii)   children, widows or widowers of such grandchildren who were themselves beneficiaries but died before the time when, had they survived, they would have become entitled as mentioned in subsection (1)(a) above.

(3)   Subject to subsections (4) and (5) below, there shall be a charge to tax under this section—

(a)   where settled property ceases to be property to which this section applies, and

(b)   in a case in which paragraph (a) above does not apply, where the trustees make a disposition as a result of which the value of settled property to which this section applies is less than it would be but for the disposition.

(4)   Tax shall not be charged under this section—

(a)   on a beneficiary's becoming beneficially entitled to, or to an interest in possession in, settled property on or before attaining the specified age, or

(b)   on the death of a beneficiary before attaining the specified age.

. . .

(6)   Where the conditions stated in paragraphs (a) and (b) of subsection (1) above were satisfied on 15th April 1976 with respect to property comprised in a settlement which commenced before that day, subsection (2)(a) above shall have effect with the substitution of a reference to that day for the reference to the commencement of the settlement, and the condition stated in subsection (2)(b) above shall be treated as satisfied if—

(a)   it is satisfied in respect of the period beginning with 15th April 1976, or

(b)   it is satisfied in respect of the period beginning with 1st April 1977 and either there was no beneficiary living on 15th April 1976 or the beneficiaries on 1st April 1977 included a living beneficiary, or

(c)   there is no power under the terms of the settlement whereby it could have become satisfied in respect of the period beginning with 1st April 1977, and the trusts of the settlement have not been varied at any time after 15th April 1976.

(7)   In subsection (1) above 'persons' includes unborn persons; but the conditions stated in that subsection shall be treated as not satisfied unless there is or has been a living beneficiary.

(8)   For the purposes of this section a person's children shall be taken to include his illegitimate children, his adopted children and his stepchildren.

**Precedent Accumulation and Maintenance Settlement,** *The Encyclopaedia of Forms and Precedents,* **5th ed, London: Butterworths, 1993, prepared by John Child, BA, LLB, Barrister**

'THIS SETTLEMENT is made the ................... day of ................... BETWEEN (1) (*settlor*) of (*address*) ('the Settlor') and (2) (*original trustees*) of (*addresses*) ('the Original Trustees')

WHEREAS

The Settlor wishes to make the settlement set out below and has paid or transferred into the joint names of or placed under the joint control of the Original Trustees the assets described in the first schedule to be held on and with and subject to the following trusts powers and provisions

NOW THIS DEED WITNESSES as follows:

**1   Definitions and interpretation**

1.1   In this settlement the following expressions have where the context permits the following meanings:
    1.1.1   'The Trustees' means the Original Trustees or other the trustees or trustee for the time being of this settlement and 'Trustee' means each and any of the Trustees
    1.1.2   'the Trust Fund' means the assets described in the first schedule [not reproduced] all assets at any time added to the same by way of further settlement accumulation of income capital accretion or otherwise and all property from time to time representing the same
    1.1.3   'the Principal Beneficiaries' means:
    1.1.3.1   the two present grandchildren of the Settlor namely (*name*) (who was born on (*date*)) and (*name*) (who was born on (*date*)) and
    1.1.3.2   all future grandchildren of the Settlor born in the future other than any born after the first to occur of the following dates namely:
    1.1.3.2.1   the date on which the first grandchild (whether now living or born in the future) of the Settlor to attain the age of 18 years attains that age and
    1.1.3.2.2   the date of expiry of the Accumulation Period (as such expression is defined below)
    and 'Principal Beneficiary' has a corresponding meaning
    1.1.4   'the Accumulation Period' means the period of 21 years commencing with the date of this deed
    1.1.5   'the Ultimate Date' means the date on which shall expire the period of 80 years commencing with the date of this deed (which date shall be the perpetuity period applicable to this settlement and to the dispositions made by it)
    1.1.6   the expression 'interest in possession' has the same meaning as is now given to such expression for the purposes of inheritance tax

1.2   References in this settlement to the income of the Trust Fund shall (without any allocation or apportionment in favour of the Settlor) extend to any income now accrued or accruing but not yet actually payable in respect of the assets specified in the first schedule [not reproduced]

**2   Principal trusts**

2.1   The Trustees shall stand possessed of the Trust Fund and the income from it upon trust for such of the Principal Beneficiaries as shall either attain the age of 35 years before or upon the Ultimate Date or shall be living under that age upon the Ultimate Date and if more than one in equal shares
2.2   PROVIDED always that if any Principal Beneficiary shall die under the age of 35 years before the Ultimate Date leaving a child or children who shall either attain the age of 25 years before or upon the Ultimate Date or shall be living and under

that age upon the Ultimate Date then such child or children of that deceased Principal Beneficiary shall take (and if more than one in equal shares between them) the share of the Trust Fund and the income from it to which such deceased Principal Beneficiary would have been entitled if he or she had attained a vested interest

## 3 Powers of maintenance and advancement

The trusts contained in clause 2 above shall carry the intermediate income and the statutory powers of maintenance accumulation and advancement contained in the Trustee Act 1925 sections 31 and 32 (as amended by the Family Law Reform Act 1969) shall apply to this settlement but with the following modifications:

3.1 in the case of the said section 31 the substitution in subsection (1)(i) of the words 'the trustees in their absolute discretion think fit' for the words 'may in all the circumstances be reasonable' and the omission of the proviso to subsection (1) and

3.2 in the case of the said section 32 the omission of the words 'one-half of' from proviso (a) to subsection (1) and the insertion of a further proviso to the effect that in any case where the said statutory power of advancement contained in the said section is exercised so as to apply capital money for the advancement or benefit of a person who immediately prior to such exercise does not have an interest in possession in the capital money in question then such capital money must be vested either absolutely or for an interest in possession in the person in question immediately upon such application being made or (if such person is then under the age of 25 years) before he or she shall have attained the age of 25 years and in such manner that conditions (a) and (b) of the Inheritance Tax Act 1984 section 71(1) shall be satisfied

## 4 Failure of living beneficiaries before class closes

PROVIDED that if and so often as during the Accumulation Period and before the closure of the class of the Principal Benficiaries and before any Principal Beneficiary or child of a deceased Principal Beneficiary has attained a vested interest under the above trusts there shall be any period or periods during which no Principal Beneficiary or child of a deceased Principal Beneficiary is for the time being living then during such period or periods the income of the Trust Fund shall not for the time being be subject to the above trusts but rather shall be held upon trust to accumulate the same at compound interest by investing it and the resulting income of the same in any of the investments authorised by this settlement (other than the purchase of land only) and to add such accumulations as an accretion to the capital of the Trust Fund and as one fund with it for all purposes

## 5 Ultimate trust

Subject to all the trusts powers and provisions of this settlement (and each and every exercise of such powers) the Trust Fund and the income from it shall be held upon trust for the two existing grandchildren of the Settlor namely (*name*) and (*name*) in equal shares absolutely

## 6 Administrative powers

6.1 Subject to the provisos contained in clauses 6.2 and 6.3 below the Trustees shall until the Ultimate Date and during such further period (if any) as the law may allow have the additional powers set out in the second schedule [not reproduced]

6.2 PROVIDED always that none of the additional powers contained in the second schedule shall be capable of being exercised in such a way as:

    6.2.1 would or might prevent an interest in possession of any beneficiary from subsisting or continuing to subsist in the whole or any part of the Trust Fund in any case where such an interest otherwise would subsist or continue to subsist or

    6.2.2 would prevent the Inheritance Tax Act 1984 section 71 (or any statutory modification or re-enactment of it) from applying in respect of the whole or any part of the Trust Fund in any case where that section (or modification or re-enactment of it) otherwise would so apply

6.3 And PROVIDED further that the Trustees (being not less than two in number or a trust corporation) may at any time or times before the Ultimate Date by deed extinguish (or restrict the future use of) all or any of the additional powers (but not any of the restrictions applicable to them) conferred by clause 6.1 above

. . .

**11 Exclusion of the Settlor and spouse from benefit**
Notwithstanding anything in this settlement expressed or implied no money or other assets subject to the trusts of this settlement shall in any circumstances whatever be paid or transferred beneficially (except for full consideration) to or lent to or applied (whether directly or indirectly) for the benefit of the Settlor or any spouse of the Settlor'

(There would then follow in the 'real thing' provisions relating to excluding apportionment, trustees' charges and remuneration, corporate trustees, trustees' protection, appointment of trustees and administrative provisions relating to various other matters.)

# 27.3  Taxation of Undervalue Sales

### 27.3.1  INHERITANCE TAX AND UNDERVALUE SALES

#### *IRC* v *SPENCER-NAIRN* **[1991] STC 60 (CS)**

The facts of this case are summarised in the *Learning Text* at **27.5.2.1**.

THE LORD PRESIDENT (HOPE): . . . The fact that the transaction was for less than the open market value cannot be conclusive of the issue at this stage, otherwise the subsection would be deprived of its content. The gratuitous element in the transaction becomes therefore no more than a factor, which must be weighed in the balance with all the other facts and circumstances to see whether the onus which is on the transferor has been discharged. I mention this point at the outset because much emphasis was laid in the argument for the Crown on the fact that the diminution in value which had occurred in this case was very great. It was said that the fact that there was a sale at less than open market value was clear in this case, and that a very careful approach to the facts was required.
. . .

In my opinion the facts which are of particular significance . . . are that at the time of the sale both the transferor and Mr Burgess were unaware that they were dealing with a connected person in selling the farm to Domaine and that, judged against the yardstick of the advice which Mr Strang-Steele would have given in an arm's length transaction, Mr Burgess's advice was sound and that the actions of the transferor were reasonable in all the circumstances. The first point is important because, in my view, a good way of testing the question whether the sale was such as might be expected to be made in a transaction between persons not connected with each other is to see what persons who were unaware that they were connected with each other actually did. That there was, in fact, a connection was of no significance in this case as to the way in which the sale was effected or the price which was achieved. The second point is important because, in my opinion, it goes a long way towards answering the Crown's argument that the commissioner did not apply an objective test to the facts. His decision is, I agree, open to the criticism that he did not in terms make the comparison which, at the outset of this part of his decision, he described. But I think that the conclusion to be drawn from the evidence which he accepted from Mr Strang-Steele is that the comparison with what might be expected to have taken place objectively is to be found in that evidence. If the yardstick of Mr Strang-Steele's advice in an arm's length transaction is applied, Mr Burgess's advice was not only sound and reasonable but it was advice which might be expected to be given in the circumstances in which the transferor was placed at the time.

The two propositions seem to me to go hand in hand, if I may use that metaphor, since Mr Strang-Steele's test of what was sound and reasonable was what he would have done in a transaction at arm's length.

Various other detailed points were made in support of the argument that the commissioner erred in law in holding that the sale of Domaine was not such as might be expected to be made in a transaction at arm's length. I agree with what your Lordships say about them and I need add only a few words of my own. The fact that no advertising took place and that no professional advice was taken other than that which was given by Mr Burgess was said to be inconsistent with a transaction of that kind. It was pointed out that no legal advice was sought about the landlord's obligation for renewal of the piggery, although this was obviously a matter of importance to the decision whether to sell and if so at what price. But I agree with counsel for the transferor that the facts found by the commissioner were sufficient to entitle him to decide the case as he did. The question which he had to resolve . . . was whether the sale to Domaine was such as might be expected to be made on the hypothesis which that paragraph describes. The only assumption which had to be made to compare what actually happened here with what might be expected to happen on the statutory hypothesis was that the seller and the purchaser were not connected with each other and that they were dealing at arm's length. The words 'might be expected' suggest that there may be no single answer to this question, and that in the end the question is one of fact for the commissioner assuming that he was properly instructed as to the relevant law. I think that he was entitled to conclude that the sale to Domaine at the price in question was one which might be expected to be entered into on the statutory hypothesis, given the circumstances in which the transferor found himself at the time and that he acted on what has been judged to be sound advice.

## 27.4   End of Chapter Assessment Questions

(a)  In a single sentence for each point, comment on the IHT and CGT implications of each of the following events:

| | |
|---|---|
| 1 April 1993 | Alexandra gave £2,999 to Belinda in cash. |
| 28 February 1994 | Alexandra transferred her shareholding of 10,000 £1 ordinary shares in Megabucks plc, then worth £250,000, to the trustees of a discretionary trust. The shares were all acquired by her on 30 November 1985. |
| 23 June 1995 | Alexandra gave £56,000 of loan stock to her son Charles. The loan stock was a QCB for CGT purposes. |
| 1 April 1999 | Alexandra died. |

Ignore any exemptions and reliefs, and assume that Alexandra is a chargeable person for CGT purposes. In relation to the CGT aspects of this question, you will need to refer to material from earlier in the book.

(b)  Turn to **27.2.1**, and read IHTA 1984, s. 71. Also read **7.6.1** and **18.4.3** of the *Learning Text*. Comment briefly on the income tax, CGT and IHT implications of the following clauses in an accumulation and maintenance settlement:

> The Trustees shall stand possessed of the Trust Fund and the income from it upon trust for such of the Principal Beneficiaries as shall either attain the age of 35 years before or upon the Ultimate Date or shall be living under that age upon the Ultimate Date and if more than one in equal shares.
> . . .
>
> 'the Principal Beneficiaries' means:
>
> (a)   the two present grandchildren of the Settlor [the deed gives their names]
> . . .

'The Ultimate Date' means the date on which shall expire the period of 80 years commencing with the date of this deed (which date shall be the perpetuity period applicable to this settlement and to the dispositions made by it).

## 27.5   End of Chapter Assessment Outline Answers

(a)  For IHT, the gift of £2,999 to Belinda in cash, on 1 April 1993, is a PET by Alexandra: IHTA 1984, s. 3A(1). She is not liable to pay CGT on the gift since, even though she is a chargeable person, sterling is not a chargeable asset.

The gift on trust to the trustees of the discretionary trust, on 28 February 1994, is not a PET, but a transfer immediately chargeable to IHT. For CGT purposes, Alexandra has made a chargeable disposal of a chargeable asset, and is deemed to have received the market value in return: TCGA 1992, s. 17.

The gift of the loan stock is a PET for IHT purposes: above. In addition, Alexandra is not liable to pay CGT on the disposal of the loan stock, since it counts as a QCB, gains on the disposal of which are exempt from CGT: TCGA 1992, s. 115.

There is a chargeable transfer of the whole of Alexandra's estate immediately before her death on 1 April 1999, for IHT purposes. In addition, the PETs and the transfers chargeable immediately to IHT all become subject to IHT at the death rate. Alexandra's death is not a disposal for CGT purposes. Instead, her estate is acquired by her PRs at its market value at the date of death: TCGA 1992, s. 62(1)(a).

(b) An accumulation and maintenance settlement offers a favourable IHT treatment, designed to equate the IHT treatment of a gift into trust for the maintenance, education or benefit of an infant beneficiary with an absolute gift to an adult. The three conditions which an accumulation and maintenance settlement must satisfy are set out in IHTA 1984, s. 71. The first condition is that one or more beneficiaries must become beneficially entitled to an interest in possession in the settlement before attaining an age not over 25. Although the stipulated age here is 35, the beneficiaries would obtain interests in possession in the trust income at 18, by virtue of TA 1925, s. 31. There must be no interest in possession in the settled property, the income of the fund must be accumulated, to the extent that it is not applied for the maintenance, education or benefit of a beneficiary. The final condition, that all the beneficiaries must have a common grandparent is met here. The settled fund is settled property for CGT purposes (TCGA 1992, s. 60(1)), and the trustees will be liable to CGT at 34% on chargeable gains. The trustees will be liable to pay income tax at 34%, and any income paid out to unmarried minor children, or for their benefit, is deemed to be the settlor's income under ICTA 1988, s. 660B.

Note: As required by the question, discussion of possible exemptions and reliefs is omitted from (a) and (b) above.

# CHAPTER TWENTY-EIGHT

# TAXATION OF GRATUITOUS TRANSFERS: NOMINAL TRANSFERS

## 28.1 Transfers between Trustees

### 28.1.1 CAPITAL GAINS TAX IMPLICATIONS

#### Inland Revenue Statement of Practice 7/84 IR131 (1996)

The Board's Statement of Practice SP 9/81, which was issued on 23 September 1981 following discussions with the Law Society, set out the Revenue's views on the capital gains tax implications of the exercise of a Power of Appointment or Advancement when continuing trusts are declared, in the light of the decision of the House of Lords in *Roome & Denne* v *Edwards*. Those views have been modified to some extent by the decision of the Court of Appeal in *Bond* v *Pickford*.

In *Roome & Denne* v *Edwards* the House of Lords held that where a separate settlement is created there is a deemed disposal of the relevant assets by the old trustees for the purposes of TCGA 1992, s. 71(1) (CGTA 1979, s. 54(1)). But the judgments emphasised that, in deciding whether or not a new settlement has been created by the exercise of a Power of Appointment or Advancement, each case must be considered on its own facts, and by applying established legal doctrine to the facts in a practical and commonsense manner. In *Bond* v *Pickford* the judgments in the Court of Appeal explained that the consideration of the facts must include examination of the powers which the trustees purported to exercise, and determination of the intention of the parties, viewed objectively.

It is now clear that a deemed disposal under s. 71(1) cannot arise unless the power exercised by the trustees, or the instrument conferring the power, expressly or by necessary implication, confers on the trustees authority to remove assets from the original settlement by subjecting them to the trusts of a different settlement. Such powers (which may be powers of advancement or appointment) are referred to by the Court of Appeal as 'powers in the wider form'. However, the Board considers that a deemed disposal will not arise when such a power is exercised and trusts are declared in circumstances such that—

(a) the appointment is revocable, or
(b) the trusts declared of the advanced or appointed funds are not exhaustive so that there exists a possibility at the time when the advancement or appointment is made that the funds covered by it will on the occasion of some event cease to be held upon such trusts and once again come to be held upon the original trusts of the settlement.

Further, when such a power is exercised the Board considers it unlikely that a deemed disposal will arise when trusts are declared if duties in regard to the appointed assets still fall to the trustees of the original settlement in their capacity as trustees of that settlement, bearing in mind the provision in TCGA 1992, s. 69(1) (CGTA 1979, s. 52(1)) that the trustees of a settlement form a single and continuing body (distinct from the persons who may from time to time be the trustees).

Finally, the Board accept that a Power of Appointment or Advancement can be exercised over only part of the settled property and that the above consequences would apply to that part.

## 28.2 Transfers from Personal Representatives to Legatees

### 28.2.1 CAPITAL GAINS TAX IMPLICATIONS

#### *IRC* v *MATTHEWS* [1984] STC 386

. . .

LORD CAMERON: . . . I turn first to the provisions of that settlement. The taxpayers are appointed both as executors and trustees, with a descriptive narrative of the powers to be available to them in their capacity as trustees. In the next place the testator's disposal of his estate was 'in trust only for the ends and uses and purposes aftermentioned'. These are: (1) payment of the debts, funeral expenses, all government duties payable on death and expenses of administration and winding up his estate, (2) a pecuniary legacy to his brother 'to be paid as soon as possible after my death' and (3) for division and payment of the residue equally among 12 charitable bodies. There were no trust purposes which required the retention of the whole or any part of the estate for any other purpose. Therefore the sole function and duty of the taxpayers was to ingather the testator's estate, discharge his liabilities and thereafter distribute the estate in accordance with the provisions of his will.

. . .

## 28.3   End of Chapter Assessment Questions

Re-read **21.8** and **24.9** in the *Learning Text*. Then analyse *both* the CGT and IHT implications of each of the following:

(a)   Terry dies on 1 November 1998, aged 102. On 20 May 1998, he sold 2,000 ordinary shares in Umberto Ltd, at a loss of £10,000. He has no chargeable gains in the tax year of his death, but his chargeable gains for 1997/98 were £15,000.

(b)   It is 1 December 1998. Tom and Theo are the trustees of a settlement constituted by Damon's will, under which his two grandchildren, Beatrix and Ben, are to receive the settled fund in equal shares absolutely, on attaining the age of 18. Ben is 16 and Beatrix is 17. Both beneficiaries are rather immature for their ages. The settled fund consists of 100,000 ordinary shares in Utopia plc, worth £500,000 in total, as at 1 December 1998. The will trust contains a power for the trustees, in their discretion, to remove the whole or part of the settled fund from the will trust, and to transfer it to the trustees of another settlement. They are contemplating whether to transfer 90% of the settled fund to an identical settlement, with an age contingency of 25.

(c)   Alison is the remainderman under a life interest trust set up by her uncle Jake in 1980. The life tenant is 21 and in excellent health. Either:

   (i)   Alison sells her interest to her schoolfriend, Brenda, for £10,000; or

   (ii)   the life tenant is killed in a mountaineering accident.

## 28.4   End of Chapter Assessment Outline Answers

(a)   Terry's death on 1 November 1998 is a chargeable transfer for IHT purposes. The value transferred by this chargeable transfer will obviously not include the 2,000 ordinary shares in Umberto Ltd sold by Terry on 20 May 1998. For CGT, death is not a disposal. Terry's PRs acquire his estate at its market value at the date of his death, however: TCGA 1992, s. 62(1)(a). A loss on the disposal of shares is an allowable loss. Under TCGA 1992, s. 62(2), Terry's PRs can carry back the allowable loss and deduct it from his 1997/98 chargeable gains of £15,000.

(b)   The settled fund is settled property for CGT purposes. Neither Ben nor Beatrix would be absolutely entitled to the settled fund but for their infancy, they would be contingently entitled only: TCGA 1992, s. 60(1). The crucial question for CGT purposes is whether the removing of the 90,000 ordinary shares from the original settlement is a re-settlement for CGT purposes. If it is, the trustees of the new settlement will become absolutely entitled to the settled fund as against the original trustees: *Hoare Trustees* v *Gardner* [1978] 1 All ER 791. This means there will be a deemed disposal, and a possible CGT charge under TCGA 1992, s. 71(1). This is undesirable, so Tom and Theo will need to be sure that what they propose to do is *not* a re-settlement. The guidance on this issue is to be found in *Roome* v *Edwards* [1981] 1 All ER 736, *Bond* v *Pickford* [1983] STC 517 and *Swires* v *Renton* [1991] STC 490. SP 7/84 also provides guidance. According to *Bond* v *Pickford*, the power possessed by Tom and Theo here is a power in the wider form. According to SP 7/84, there is unlikely to be a resettlement where such a power is exercised and duties in regard to the appointed assets still fall to the trustees of the original settlement in their capacity as trustees of that settlement. This is not exactly the case here, and there must be a risk of a re-settlement being held to have taken place here, especially in the light of Hoffman J's comments in *Swires* v *Renton*.

As to IHT, both the existing and the proposed settlements are accumulation and maintenance settlements. The proposals do not involve either beneficiary in attaining an interest in possession in a settlement other than an accumulation and maintenance settlement, and should therefore have no disadvantageous IHT consequences for Beatrix and Ben.

(c)    If Alison sells her interest in remainder to Brenda for £10,000, she will not be liable to pay CGT. Although she is a chargeable person, and there is a gain, the gain is exempt from CGT because Alison's interest has never been acquired for money or money's worth: TCGA 1992, s. 76. Alternatively, if the life tenant is killed in a mountaineering accident, Alison not having sold her interest, TCGA 1992, s. 71(1) will apply, and whether there is a CGT liability will depend on whether uncle Jake claimed hold over relief on setting-up the settlement. There is no question of an IHT liability in (i), since there is no transfer of value: IHTA 1984, s. 10. In (ii), the life interest will form part of the value transferred by the chargeable transfer on the death of the life tenant.

# CHAPTER TWENTY-NINE

# TAXATION OF GRATUITOUS TRANSFERS: AUTOMATIC TRANSFERS

## 29.1  The Survivorship Principle

### 29.1.1  INHERITANCE TAX IMPLICATIONS

#### INHERITANCE TAX ACT 1984

**4.  Transfers on death**

(1)  On the death of any person tax shall be charged as if, immediately before his death, he had made a transfer of value and the value transferred by it had been equal to the value of his estate immediately before his death.

(2)  For the purposes of this section, where it cannot be known which of two or more persons who have died survived the other or others they shall be assumed to have died at the same instant.

## 29.2    End of Chapter Assessment Question

Comment on the IHT and CGT implications of the following, ignoring the availability of hold-over relief. It is 1 September 1998. Sugden transfers 100,000 ordinary shares in Olympic plc to Terence and Tara, who are the trustees of the Sugden 1998 Interest in Possession Settlement. Under the terms of the settlement, the shares are to be held for Bella for life, remainder to Charlotte, remainder to Douglas absolutely. Bella is 28, Charlotte is 30, and Douglas is 27. Charlotte sells her interest to her cousin Frank for £60,000, its open-market value, on 20 November 1998. On 1 December 1998, Bella is drowned in a fishing accident, dying intestate. Besides being the life tenant of the Sugden 1998 Interest in Possession Settlement, Bella was the co-owner of Makepiece Hall, under a joint tenancy, with Bill, her husband. At her death, Makepiece Hall was worth £550,000, and the shares in Olympic plc, £100,000.

## 29.3    End of Chapter Assessment Outline Answer

Sugden's gift on trust of the 100,000 ordinary shares in Olympic plc to Terence and Tara is a chargeable disposal for CGT purposes. Sugden is deemed to have received the market value of the shares in return, and will be liable to pay CGT on this deemed gain, unless holdover relief is available, which is unlikely on these facts: TCGA 1992, s. 17. Since the settlement has an interest in possession, the gift counts as a PET for IHT purposes, which means that IHT would only be charged were Sugden to die within the period of seven years, beginning with 1 September 1998.

As life tenant of the settled property Bella, who is now deceased, is treated as having owned the whole capital of the settled property. On the death of Bella, on 1 December, this amount therefore forms part of the value transferred by the chargeable transfer on her death. On the assumption that Bill is domiciled in the UK, however, the chargeable transfer on her death is entirely exempt from IHT by IHTA 1984, s. 18. Under the intestacy rules, her estate other than Makepiece Hall, is automatically transferred to her PRs. Her interest in Makepiece Hall is automatically transferred by survivorship to Bill. Bella's life interest in the settled fund is worth £100,000, and it passes automatically to Frank, as the purchaser of Charlotte's reversionary interest. There is no indication of what amount Bella's PRs will be holding as a statutory legacy for Bill.

The gain realised by Charlotte on the sale of her reversionary interest to Frank is exempt from CGT: TCGA 1992, s. 76, it never having been acquired for money or money's worth. There is no question of an IHT liability on this sale since her transaction with Frank was obviously a commercial one, the sale having been made for the reversionary interest's market value. It is therefore unnecessary to consider the question of the reversionary interest being excluded property for IHT purposes.

# CHAPTER THIRTY

# TAXATION OF GRATUITOUS TRANSFERS: CALCULATIONS (1)

## 30.1 Calculating the IHT Liability on Lifetime Transfers

### 30.1.1 TRANSFERS WHERE THE GIVER ASSUMES THE IHT BURDEN

#### INHERITANCE TAX ACT 1984

**7. Rates**

(1)  . . . the tax charged on the value transferred by a chargeable transfer made by any transferor shall be charged at the following rate or rates, that is to say—

(a)  if the transfer is the first chargeable transfer made by that transferor in the period of seven years ending with the date of the transfer, at the rate or rates applicable to that value under the Table in Schedule 1 to this Act;

(b)  in any other case, at the rate or rates applicable under that Table to such part of the aggregate of—

(i)  that value, and

(ii)  the values transferred by previous chargeable transfers made by him in that period,

as is the highest part of that aggregate and is equal to that value.

TABLE [SCHEDULE 1]

| Portion of value | | Rate of Tax |
|---|---|---|
| Lower Limit £ | Upper Limit £ | Per cent |
| 0 | 223,000 | NIL |
| 223,000 | — | 40 |

## 30.2 Calculating the IHT Liability on Transfers on Death

### 30.2.1 PROBLEMS OVER WHO IS TO BEAR THE BURDEN OF THE IHT

#### *RE BENHAM* [1995] STC 210

The facts of this case are discussed in the *Learning Text* at **30.4.3.2**.

R.M.K. GRAY, QC: The second question in the originating summons raises the problem to which s. 41 of the Inheritance Tax Act 1984 (the 1984 Act) gives rise, given that one of the beneficiaries in list A is a charity and exempt, the other beneficiaries being close friends and relatives of the testatrix, and of the list B beneficiaries several are charities (the others being acquaintances), and those charities in list B are also exempt.

Section 41 of the 1984 Act reads as follows:

Notwithstanding the terms of any disposition—
    (a)   none of the tax on the value transferred shall fall on any specific gift if or to the extent that the transfer is exempt with respect to the gift, and
    (b)   none of the tax attributable to the value of the property comprised in residue shall fall on any gift of a share of residue if or to the extent that the transfer is exempt with respect to the gift.

There seem to me to be three possibilities: (1) that the non-charitable beneficiaries receive their respective share, subject to inheritance tax, which would mean they would receive less than the charitable beneficiaries; (2) that the non-charitable beneficiaries are entitled to have their respective shares 'grossed up' so the net result is that equality is achieved between charitable and non-charitable beneficiaries; (3) that the executors should pay the inheritance tax as part of the testamentary expenses under cl. 3(A) of the will and distribute the balance equally between the exempt and non-exempt beneficiaries.

This type of problem is the subject of observations in McCutcheon *Inheritance Tax* (3rd edn, 1988) para. 7–84, p. 263–264 which summarises the difficulty with admirable succinctness in these terms:

When drafting wills, it is important to make sure that the burden of tax falls in the intended way. Section 41 precludes the burden of tax falling on exempt specific gifts at all, and also precludes tax attributable to a chargeable share of residue falling on any exempt share of residue. It does not preclude tax attributable to chargeable specific gifts falling on exempt shares of residue. A will should therefore be drafted in such a way as (a) makes clear exactly how tax is to be borne, and (b) is not rendered ineffective for that purpose by section 41.

Then the learned editors give an example of an approach which they commend and then they go on at the second break to say:

It is important to note that the common form of residuary gift directing the usual trusts for conversion, payment of debts, etc., and tax, and then directing a division of what remains can give rise to difficulties of construction. The point can best be illustrated by an example. Suppose a will provides as follows: 'I give all my property both moveable and immoveable of whatever nature and wherever situated subject to and after payment of my funeral and testamentary expenses and debts and all inheritance tax payable in respect thereof on my death to my wife and my son in equal shares absolutely.' The testator, it might be thought, intends an equal division between his wife and his son of what is left after payment of all expenses, etc. and [inheritance tax]. How is this to be achieved? Clearly it is inadmissible for the executors to ascertain the value of the estate, pay [inheritance tax] on half that value, and split the balance between the widow and the son. Such a course is precluded by section 41, because it would involve the widow's exempt share bearing some of the tax attributable to the son's chargeable share. Is the proper approach therefore to divide the residue before [inheritance tax] in half, with the son bearing all the tax on his half, so the widow receives more than the son? This is a possible construction, but not, in the authors' view, a correct one. Instead, a gift in the above terms should, it is thought, be construed as a gift in unequal shares of the residue before [inheritance tax], the son's share being of an amount such that, after payment of [inheritance tax] out of that share, his share and the widow's share are equal. This yields a result consistent with: 1. the testator's probable intention, 2. the express terms of the will . . ., and 3. the provisions of section 41 itself . . .

Miss Baker, who appears for a charity in list B, submitted that the possibility at (3) above is precluded by s. 41 of the 1984 Act. I agree. Miss Baker further submits that on a proper construction of the will, the testatrix can be seen as intending the charitable beneficiaries to have the benefit of their exempt status with the result that there is at the end of the day inequality in the amount the non-charitable beneficiaries and the charitable beneficiaries receive. That would accord, says Miss Baker, with a presumed intention by the testatrix that her estate should pay as little inheritance tax as possible. Miss Baker further submits that such a construction would accord with the anticipation of the 'ordinary person' that the extent to which each beneficiary receives an equal share will depend on that beneficiary's status as exempt or non-exempt.

I am afraid I cannot agree with Miss Baker's submissions on those points. I agree with Sir Patrick Sinclair and Mr Caddick that the plain intention of the testatrix is that at the end of the day each beneficiary, whether charitable or non-charitable, should receive the same as the other beneficiaries in the relevant list. That result is consistent with the express terms of the will and the statutory provisions that apply. I therefore answer the second question in the originating summons in the sense that the non-charitable beneficiaries receive grossed-up shares so that the sum each of the beneficiaries receives as between themselves in the relevant list is the same.

. . .

### Caddick, N., 'Drafting Charitable Bequests after *Benham*' [1995] *Private Client Business* 381

The tax aspects of the recent decision of the High Court in *Re Benham* have given rise to much comment — most of it adverse. The three main questions which have been asked are:

(a)   Was the decision correct?
(b)   How does one carry out the necessary calculations?
(c)   How should one draft wills as a consequence?

### The decision in *Benham*

In *Benham* the testatrix by clause 3 of her will provided that the executors should hold her residuary estate upon trust:

(A)   to pay thereout all my just debts funeral and testamentary expenses
(B)   as to the residue after such payment aforesaid to pay the same to those beneficiaries as are living at my death and who are listed in List A and List B hereunder written in such proportions as will bring about the result that the aforesaid beneficiaries named in List A shall receive 3.2 times as much as the aforesaid beneficiaries named in List B and in each case for their own absolute and beneficial use and disposal.

Both List A and List B contained exempt beneficiaries (charities) and non-exempt beneficiaries (relations and friends).

The Court considered there to be three possible constructions, namely:

(1)   That the non-charitable beneficiaries receive their respective share, subject to inheritance tax, which would mean that they would receive less than the charitable beneficiaries;
(2)   That the non-charitable beneficiaries are entitled to have their respective shares 'grossed up' so that the net result is that equality is achieved between charitable and non-charitable beneficiaries; and
(3)   That the executors should pay the inheritance tax as part of the testamentary expenses under clause 3(A) of the will and distribute the balance equally between the exempt and non exempt beneficiaries.

In this article, references to a numbered construction are references to the relevant one of these constructions.

The Court found that construction (3) was precluded by IHTA 1984 s. 41(b) and that construction (2) was the correct construction on the basis that the 'plain intention of the testatrix is that at the end of the day each beneficiary, whether charitable or non-charitable, should receive the same as the other beneficiaries in the relevant list. That result is consistent with the express terms of the will and the statutory provisions that apply.'

### Was the decision correct?
The correctness of the decision in *Benham* has been questioned in an article by Robert Grierson in *Taxation* on 20 April 1995.

In his article (at p. 54 and 55) Mr Grierson argues that, on the true construction of the will, the testatrix thought that her estate should be dealt with in the way set out in construction (3). However, as that construction is precluded by section 41(b), he argues that the Court should have adopted construction (1) rather than construction (2).

A similar conclusion is implicitly reached in another article, by Margaret Stirling in the last issue of *Private Client Business*.

On the facts of *Benham*, I am not at all sure that their arguments are correct.

First, it is true that the fact that the main residuary gift (clause 3(B)) comes after the provision for the payment of testamentary expenses (clause 3(A)) initially points to construction (3). However, the terms of the will are nevertheless consistent with either construction (2) or construction (3). Under both constructions, the end result is that the exempt beneficiaries in each list 'shall receive' the same amount as the non-exempt beneficiaries in their list.

Secondly, given that the will is consistent with either construction, why should the court assume that the testatrix intended construction (3), which was precluded by section 41(b), rather than construction (2), which was not? Particularly where the will was evidently professionally drafted.

Thirdly, even if the precluded construction (construction (3)) was what the testatrix intended, it may be argued that, when that construction was found to be precluded by section 41(b), the Court should adopt instead construction (2) rather than construction (1). Construction (2) at least gives effect to what the Court has found to be the testatrix's intention — namely that the exempt and non-exempt beneficiaries 'receive' the same amounts. It could be argued against this (and against what I say in the second point above) that construction (2) looks dangerously like an attempt to construe one's way around section 41(b) and that for the Court to accept a construction which requires the grossing up of non-exempt gifts would require much clearer wording than that in *Benham*. However, the judge in *Benham* was satisfied that, on those facts, construction (2) was not precluded by section 41(b).

### The calculations
The next question which has arisen from *Benham* has been how to calculate the grossed-up sums to be paid to the non-exempt beneficiaries. This is dealt with in Margaret Stirling's article and on the facts of *Benham* at least presents few difficulties.

Taking a simple example where, after payment of all debts, funeral and testamentary expenses, the residue of the estate (which amounts to £600,000) is to be divided such that the testator's widow and daughter receive equal shares.

The calculation is as follows:

Assumed that £'X' is the grossed-up amount which the daughter is to receive:
Then, £(0.6)'X' is the amount which the widow is to receive
And, £(0.4)'X' is the amount of tax payable.

$$'X' + (0.6)'X' = 600,000$$
$$(1.6)'X' = 600,000$$
$$'X' = \frac{600,000}{1.6}$$
$$'X' = 375,000$$

So, the daughter's share is £375,000;
The widow's share is £(0.6)(375,000) = £225,000
And the tax on the daughter's share is £(0.4)(375,000) = £150,000
So, the widow and the daughter each receive £225,000

As commented above, the facts of my example (and of *Benham* itself) are simple and I have heard tales of mathematical horror involving pages of calculations in trying to give effect to the decision in *Benham* where the facts are more complicated (for example where there is double grossing up as required by section 38). It may be that difficulties of calculation would affect the view which a Court would take of the construction of the particular will in question. In any event, I am sure that this publication would welcome feed back on difficulties encountered.

### Drafting

The decision in *Benham* followed from the Court's finding that it was the testatrix's 'plain' intention that the exempt and non-exempt beneficiaries should receive the same amounts. On the facts of *Benham*, this finding followed from the testatrix's use of phrases such as 'to pay' and 'shall receive'.

A further question which arises is whether less specific (but commonly used) wording — such as a gift of 'the residue after payment of debts, funeral and testamentary expenses to my wife and daughter in equal shares absolutely' — would lead to the same result.

On such wording, it is plainly questionable whether the initial assumption underlying *Benham* (namely that the exempt and non-exempt beneficiaries should receive the same sums) would be justified. Certainly *McCutcheon on Inheritance Tax* (3rd ed.) has argued that it would be justified and the relevant passage from that book (para. 7–84) was quoted by the judge in *Benham* without adverse comment. However, it is clearly the case that many wills have been drafted on the assumption that such a clause would allow the widow to have the benefit of her exempt status and it may be that *Benham* can be distinguished on the basis that it involved gifts to more distant relatives, friends and charities rather than to close family.

*Benham* has not, therefore, finally resolved how such clauses should be construed and the only safe course would be to ensure that, in drafting, the will makes clear whether or not the exempt beneficiaries are intended to have the benefit of their exempt status.

If a *Benham* result is intended, the will may provide:

> that after payment of all debts, funeral and testamentary expenses, the residue of the estate be divided between [the relevant beneficiaries] in such shares that after deduction of inheritance tax all beneficiaries receive the same sum

If, however, the exempt beneficiaries are intended to have the benefit of their exempt status, the will may provide (for example):

> that after payment of all debts, funeral and testamentary expenses, the residue of the estate be divided equally (subject to that the incidence of inheritance tax) between [the relevant beneficiaries] and, for the avoidance of doubt, it is not intended that, after the incidence of inheritance tax, the sums received by those beneficiaries to whom gifts are exempt from inheritance tax be the same as those gifts received by those beneficiaries to whom gifts are not so exempt

or

> that after payment of all debts, funeral and testamentary expenses, the residue of the estate be divided equally between [the relevant beneficiaries] but so that any inheritance tax in respect of non-exempt shares of residue is borne by those shares only

or

> that after payment of all debts, funeral and testamentary expenses the residue of the estate be divided equally between [the relevant beneficiaries] and, for the avoidance of doubt, it is not intended that the construction applied in *Re Benham* [1995] STC 210 shall apply

Finally, I should say that in any case, no one should act or refrain from acting on the basis of the views and suggestions set out in this article as each case must turn on its own facts.

### 30.2.2   CALCULATING THE IHT LIABILITY ON THE TRANSFER ON DEATH

Cattell, J., 'Precedent for a Modern Will', *Solicitors' Journal*, 28 November 1997, p. 1132

#### Sample Will

I, [*Testator's name*] of [*Testator's address*], revoke all my former wills and codicils and declare this to be my last will ('my Will').

#### Part 1 — Operative Provisions

#### 1. Appointment of executors
I appoint [*names and addresses of executors*] to be the executors of my Will.

#### 2. Interpretation
I declare that in my will, where the context admits, the definitions and rules of construction contained in Part 3 shall apply.

#### 3. Personal chattels legacy
I give all my personal chattels not otherwise specifically gifted by my Will or any codicil, [free of] [subject to] [*delete as appropriate*] inheritance tax, to [*details of beneficiary*].

#### 4.   Nil Rate Band Legacy
4.1   I give the Nil Rate Band Legacy to the Trustees to hold upon the following trusts.

4.2   The Trustees shall have power to appoint the whole or any part of the capital and/or income of the Nil Rate Band Legacy Fund upon trust for or for the benefit of such of the Discretionary Beneficiaries, at such ages or times, in such shares, upon such trusts (which may include discretionary or protective powers or trusts) and in such manner generally as the Trustees shall in their discretion appoint. Any such appointment may include such powers and provisions for the maintenance, education or other benefit of the Discretionary Beneficiaries or for the accumulation of income, and such administrative powers and provisions as the Trustees think fit.

4.3   No exercise of the power conferred by sub-clause 4.2 shall invalidate any prior payment or application of all or any part of the capital or income of the Nil Rate Band Legacy made under any other power conferred by my Will or by law.

4.4   Any trusts and powers created by an appointment under clause 4.2 may be delegated to any extent to any person whether or not including the Trustees or any of them.

4.5   Any appointment under sub-clause 4.2 shall:
    (a)   be subject to the application, if any, of the rule against perpetuities; and
    (b)   be by deed, revocable during the Trust Period or irrevocable, and executed during the Trust Period.

4.6   The provisions of this sub-clause shall apply until, subject and in default of any appointment under sub-clause 4.2.
    (a)   The Trustees shall pay or apply the income of the Nil Rate Band Legacy Fund to or for the benefit of such of the Discretionary Beneficiaries as shall for the time being be in existence, in such shares and in such manner generally as the Trustees shall in their discretion from time to time think fit.
    (b)   Notwithstanding the provisions of sub-clause 4.6(a) Trustees may at any time during the Accumulation Period in their discretion accumulate the income by investing any investments authorised by my Will or by law and, subject to sub-clause 4.6(c), shall hold such accumulation an accretion to capital.
    (c)   The Trustees may apply the whole or any part of the income accumulated under sub-clause 4.6(b) as if it were income arising in the then current year.

4.7   Subject as above, the Trustees shall hold the capital and income of the Nil Rate Band Legacy Fund [upon the like trusts as are contained in clause 7 in relation to the Trust Fund, as if references to the '**Trust Fund**' were references to the Nil Rate Band Legacy Fund] [*Insert details of default trusts. These may be in favour of a named individual or, as here, provide for the legacy to be held on similar trusts to residue.*].

4.8   I declare that:
   [(a)]   [*Consider including if agricultural property is included in the gift. Where liabilities have been incurred for the purpose of the agricultural enterprise, unlike the position in relation to business property, relief can be given on the whole value of the agricultural property with the deduction for the liability being allowed against other property which is charged to support it. Sub-clause 4.8(b) ensures this will occur.*] this gift shall only take effect if the gift to my [Husband/Wife] [*delete as appropriate*] in sub-clause 7.1 shall take effect and qualify, or would apart from this sub-clause have taken effect and qualified, in its entirety for exemption under s. 18 of the Inheritance Tax Act 1984 [; and
   (b)   for the avoidance of doubt, where any liability of mine is secured on property which is not Agricultural Property, such liability shall not be discharged out of Agricultural Property]. [*Consider including if agricultural property is included in the gift. Where liabilities have been incurred for the purpose of the agricultural enterprise, unlike the position in relation to business property, relief can be given on the whole value of the agricultural property with the deduction for the liability being allowed against other property which is charged to support it. Sub-clause 4.8(b) ensures this will occur.*]

## 5.   Administration of my Estate

My Executors shall hold my Estate upon trust to pay, discharge or provide for my debts, funeral, testamentary and administration expenses and to give effect to legacies.

## 6.   Transfer to trustees

Subject to the trusts declared above, my Executors shall transfer to the Trustees, or otherwise place under their control, the Trust Fund to be held upon, with and subject to the following trusts, powers and provisions of my Will.

## 7.   Residuary gift — substantive trusts

7.1   Subject as above, the Trustees shall hold the Trust Fund upon trust for my [Husband/Wife] [*delete as appropriate*] absolutely.

7.2   Subject to the provisions of sub-clause 7.1, the Trustees shall hold the Trust Fund for such of my children as shall survive me and attain the age of 25 years before the end of the Trust Period, or shall be living and under that age at the end of the Trust Period, and, if more than one, in equal shares absolutely.

7.3   If any child of mine shall die in my lifetime or before attaining a vested interest leaving issue who shall attain the age of 25 years before the end of the Trust Period or be under that age and living at the end of the Trust Period, then such issue shall take the share of the Trust Fund which such child would otherwise have taken. If there shall be more than one of such issue they shall take in equal shares per stirpes, but so that no one shall take a share if his or her parent is alive and takes a share.

7.4   Subject as above, the Trustees shall hold the capital and income of the Trust Fund upon trust for [*insert name of long-stop beneficiary*] absolutely.

## 8. Survivorship provision

Every person who would otherwise benefit under my Will but who fails to survive me by [*insert length of period which should not exceed six months*] calendar months shall be treated for the purposes of my Will (but not for the purposes of clauses 1 and [*insert reference to Trustee charging clause in administrative provisions*]) as having died in my lifetime.

**9. Extended power of maintenance**

The statutory provisions for maintenance and education shall apply but so that the power of maintenance shall be exercisable at the absolute discretion of the Trustees and free from the obligation to apply part only of the income for maintenance where other income is available.

**10. Extended power of advancement**

The statutory provisions for advancement shall apply but so that the power of advancement shall extend to the whole rather than one half of the share or interest of the person for whose benefit the advancement is made.

**11.   Trustees' and Executors' powers**

11.1   Without prejudice to all statutory powers and immunities, the provisions set out in clauses 9 and 10 and in Part 2 shall apply:

(a)   to the Trustees in relation to the Trust Fund; and

(b)   to my Executors in relation to my Estate, as if all references to the **'Trustees'** and the **'Trust Fund'** were references to my Executors and my Estate.

11.2   All the provisions of clauses 9 and 10 and Part 2 shall apply to the Nil Rate Band Legacy Fund as if (in the case of Part 2) the expression the **'Nil Rate Band Legacy Fund'** was substituted for the Trust Fund where the latter expression occurs.

11.3   No power conferred on the Trustees or my Executors shall be exercised so as to conflict with the beneficial provisions of my Will or with any prior exercise of a power, whether by the Trustees or my Executors.

**Part 2 — Administrative Provisions**

[*Insert administrative powers* — . . . — *running on numbering so that the first power appears as clause 12.*]

**Part 3 — Interpretation**

**[28.]** [*Run on numbering*] **Definitions and construction**

[28.1]   **'my Executors'** shall mean the persons appointed by clause 1 or any other persons who act as my personal representatives.

[28.2]   **'my Estate'** shall mean:

(a)   all my property of every kind, wherever situate;

(b)   all property of every kind, wherever situate, over which I have a general power of appointment; and

(c)   the money, investments and property from time to time representing the above.

[28.3]   The **'Trustees'** shall mean my Executors or the trustees for the time being of the Trust Fund.

[28.4]   The **'Trust Fund'** shall mean:

(a)   my Estate, after the payment of my debts, funeral, testamentary and administration expenses and legacies;

(b)   all money, investments or other property paid or transferred by any person to, or so as to be under the control of, and, in either case, accepted by the Trustees as additions;

(c)   all accumulations (if any) of income added to the Trust Fund; and

(d)   the money, investments and property from time to time representing the above.

[28.5] The **'Trust Period'** shall mean the period ending on the earlier of:

(a) the last day of the period of 80 years from the date of my death, which period, and no other, shall be the applicable perpetuity period; and

(b) such date as the Trustees shall at any time specify by deed, not being a date earlier than the date of execution of such deed or later than a date previously specified.

[28.6] The **'Accumulation Period'** shall mean the period of 21 years from the date of my death, or the Trust Period if shorter.

[28.7] **'personal chattels'** shall have the meaning given by s. 55 (1)(x) of the Administration of Estates Act 1925[, except that it shall include personal chattels used partly, but not exclusively, for business purposes.] [*Delete words in square brackets if personal chattels used partly for business purposes are not to be included.*]

[[28.8] **'business property'** shall mean relevant business property for the purposes of s. 105 of the Inheritance Tax Act 1984, and **'business property relief'** shall mean the relief given by that section.] [*Include if business property is to be included.*]

[[28.9] **'agricultural property'** shall mean agricultural property which attracts relief under Part V Chapter II of the Inheritance Tax Act 1984, and **'agricultural property relief'** shall mean the relief given by that chapter.] [*Include if agricultural property is to be included.*]

[28.10] The **'specified sum'** shall mean such sum as is equal to the upper limit of the nil per cent rate band in the table of rates of tax (applicable on my death) in Schedule 1 to the Inheritance Tax Act 1984, less an amount equal to the aggregate of the amount chargeable to inheritance tax of:

(a) all or any chargeable transfers, including potentially exempt transfers which have become chargeable as a result of my death, made by me during my lifetime in the cumulation period specified by s. 7(1)(a) of the Inheritance Tax Act 1984;

(b) all other gifts, if any, taking effect under my Will or any codicil to the extent that they are not exempt transfers for the purposes of the charge to inheritance tax on my death;

(c) all or any settled property in which, on my death, I have an interest in possession and which is chargeable to inheritance tax by reason of my death; and

(d) all other property, if any, which is treated as property to which I am beneficially entitled immediately before my death (including property subject to a reservation as defined by s. 102 of the Finance Act 1986) and which is chargeable to inheritance tax by reason of my death.

[28.11] The **'Nil Rate Band Legacy'** shall mean:

(a) all of [my business property which qualifies for business property relief at the rate of 100%] [*Include if business property is to be included*] [and] [all of my agricultural property which qualifies for agricultural property relief at the rate of 100%] [*Include if agricultural property is to be included*];

(b) the whole, or such part of, [my business property] [*Include if business property is to be included*] [and] [my agricultural property] [*Include if agricultural property is to be included*] which qualifies for [business property relief] [*Include if business property is to be included*] [or] [agricultural property relief] [*Include if agricultural property relief is to be included*] at a rate of less than 100% as my Executors shall in their discretion decide to allocate to the Nil Rate Band Legacy, provided that the value of such property, after deduction of all or any available reliefs discounts and exemptions, shall not exceed the specified sum; and

(c) the sum which, when added to the value, after deduction of all or any available reliefs, discounts and exemptions, of the property allocated to the

Nil Rate Band Legacy pursuant to sub-clause [28.11(b)], is equal to the specified sum.

[28.12]    The **'Nil Rate Band Legacy Fund'** shall mean:
    (a)    the Nil Rate Band Legacy;
    (b)    all accumulations (if any) of income added to the Nil Rate Band Legacy Fund; and
    (c)    the money, investments and property from time to time representing the above.

[28.13]    The **'Discretionary Beneficiaries'** shall mean:
    (a)    [   ] [('**my Husband'**)/('**my Wife'**)]; [*delete as appropriate*];
    (b)    my children and remoter issue, whether living at my death or born thereafter;
    (c)    the spouses, widows and widowers (whether or not such widows and widowers have remarried) of my children and remoter issue; and
    (d)    Charities. [*The nil rate band legacy is drafted to include all business of agricultural property which qualifies for BPR or APR at a rate of 100%. Care should therefore be taken to ensure that the discretionary class of beneficiaries is as wide as possible to provide sufficient flexibility in relation to the distribution of the property. If charities are not included in the class, delete sub-clause [28.15].*]

[28.14]    **'Beneficiary'** shall mean any person beneficially interested in my Estate.

[[28.15]    **'Charity'** shall mean any trust, foundation, company or other organisation whatever established only for purposes regarded as charitable under the law of England and Wales.]

[28.16]    **'person'** shall include a body of persons, corporate or unincorporate.

[28.17]    References to any statutory provision shall include any statutory modification or re-enactment of such provision.

[28.18]    References to the children, grandchildren and issue of any person shall include his children, grandchildren and remoter issue, whether living at my death or born after it, and whether legitimate, legitimated[, illegitimate] or adopted[, but shall exclude any illegitimate person and his descendants]. [*If 'illegitimate' is included and the final wording in square brackets is deleted, this sub-clause confirms expressly the inclusion (by virtue of the Family Law Reform Act 1987, the Adoption Act 1976 and the Legitimacy Act 1976) of illegitimate, adopted and legitimated children and issue and their descendants. If the testator wishes to exclude illegitimate children and issue, and their descendants, 'illegitimate' should be deleted and the final wording in square brackets should be retained. The wording may be adapted to exclude legitimated or adopted persons.*]

[28.19]    My Will shall be construed as if s. 33 of the Wills Act 1837 had not been enacted.

[28.20]    Words denoting the singular shall include the plural and vice versa.

[28.21]    Words denoting any gender shall include both the other genders.

[28.22]    The clause headings are included for reference only and shall not affect the interpretation of my Will.

**Testimonium and attestation**

Signed by me on

.....................................
Signature of [testator] [testatrix]

Signed by the [testator] [testatrix] in our presence and then by us in [his] [hers]

|  | Witness 1 | Witness 2 |
|---|---|---|
| Signature: | ................................................. | ................................................. |
| Full Name: | ................................................. | ................................................. |
| Address: | ................................................. | ................................................. |
|  | ................................................. | ................................................. |
| Occupation: | ................................................. | ................................................. |

## 30.3 End of Chapter Assessment Question

On 1 September 1988, Angus transferred a cash fund of £258,000 to the trustees of the 1993 Angus Discretionary Trust. On 1 October 1994, he made an absolute gift of his holiday home, worth £150,000, to his daughter Beth. On 1 February 1997, he gave an old master oil painting to his son Chris, at that time worth £264,000. On 31 March 1998, Angus dies, leaving an estate on his death worth £900,000. At his death, he has made no other gifts.

Describe how the IHT liability on his death will be calculated (assuming the spouse exemption does not apply). Ignore the calculation of the estate rate, as well as Angus's annual exemptions. Assume the nil rate band has been £223,000 throughout.

## 30.4 End of Chapter Assessment Outline Answer

It is first necessary to ascertain which PETs were made by Angus in the seven-year period prior to his death. These are the PETs of £150,000 to his daughter Beth, on 1 October 1994, and of £264,000 on 1 February 1997, to his son Chris.

The next stage is to work out Angus's gross cumulative total prior to the earlier of these two PETs. The transfer on 1 September 1988 was a transfer immediately chargeable to IHT. It is not stated whether the IHT on that transfer was borne by Angus or the trustees. IHT is charged on the reduction in value of the giver's estate caused by a transfer of value: IHTA 1984, s. 3(1). If Angus had borne the IHT, the net gift of £258,000 would have had to be grossed-up, in order to give the true fall in value of Angus's estate. If the trustees had borne the IHT, there would have been no need to gross-up the £258,000. Angus's gross cumulative total prior to the 1994 PET would have been the grossed-up equivalent of £258,000, in the former case. In the latter case, it would simply have been £258,000. In the rest of this answer, we shall assume it was £258,000. IHT would have been charged at $20/100 \times £258,000$, insofar as it exceeded the nil rate band.

Both PETs have turned into chargeable transfers, because of Angus's death. It is therefore necessary for Angus's PRs to calculate the IHT on the PET, at the death rate of 40%. The valuation of the holiday home, the property transferred, will be as at the date of the PET, unless it has declined in value by the time of Angus's death: IHTA 1984, s. 131. There is nothing to suggest this is the case, so the value at the time of the PET will be taken. Prior to the PET of 1 October 1994, none of Angus's nil rate band is left, which means that IHT will be charged at 40% on the whole of the value transferred on 1 October 1994. The same comment applies to the PET of 1 February 1997.

On the death, IHT is charged on the gross cumulative total of lifetime chargeable transfers, plus the total value transferred on Angus's death. Angus's gross cumulative lifetime total is £672,000, i.e. £258,000 × £150,000 × £264,000. The value of his estate on death is £900,000. The total amount on which IHT will be calculated is therefore £1,572,000. IHT is calculated at 40%, on the amount by which this exceeds the nil rate band, i.e. £1,349,000, with credit being given for the IHT already paid on the 1 September 1988 transfer.

Taper relief will be available to mitigate the impact of the recalculation.

# CHAPTER THIRTY-ONE

# TAXATION OF GRATUITOUS TRANSFERS: CALCULATIONS (2)

## 31.1  The Valuation Rules

### 31.1.1  LIFETIME TRANSFERS

*BAIRD'S EXECUTORS* v *IRC* **[1991] 1 EGLR 201 (Lands Tribunal for Scotland)**

The tribunal are not persuaded that the present transfer of the lease . . . involved was of no value whatsoever; or that it was an interest so difficult to assess that a nil value should be returned. The appellants' submissions to this effect are really based upon the presence, rather than the disregard, of the landlord's right of veto. What the case of *Crossman* . . . decided was that any such restriction which prevents the application of the open market criterion must be disregarded for the purposes of the *hypothetical* open market sale; although, on such a sale, the property had thereafter to be valued in the hands of the hypothetical purchaser as subject to the same restriction. This is hardly an unfair test to apply, for, as already remarked, such a restriction could be deliberately inserted into articles of association or, as here, into a lease extinguishing its value for tax purposes, whereas in many cases it may in reality be readily transferable with the landlord's consent. . . .

**Barlow, J.S., King, L.C., and King, A.G., 'Wills, Administration and Taxation: A Practical Guide', 7th edn, London: Sweet & Maxwell, 1997, p. 50**

*Unquoted shares*

In the case of shares not listed on the Stock Exchange, although recent bargains will be taken as a starting point, other factors may lead to a different value being adopted (SP 18/80).

The valuation of unquoted shares is factually very difficult but will take into account: the dividend record of the company, the retained earnings (especially where earnings have been retained with a view to increasing the share value), the profitability of the company even if profits have not been used to pay dividends (this is especially relevant where profits have been used to pay high director's fees to a controlling shareholder) and the value of the assets owned by the company (this is especially relevant where the company is likely to be wound up or taken over).

Three special rules apply to the valuation of unquoted shares:

(a) A reduction in value resulting from the death cannot be taken into account if it arises from the fact that the rights attached to the shares are varied as a result of the death (for example, because the articles of the company provide that the shares are then to lose their right to dividend or to vote). (Inheritance Tax Act 1984, section 171(2).)

(b) If the shares are subject to pre-emption rights the market value is to be assessed on the basis that the pre-emption rights do not apply to the hypothetical sale on the open market at the time of death but that they will apply to the hypothetical purchaser (in other words the value is the price which a purchaser would pay knowing that he would be subject to the pre-emption rights in the future). This was established in *IRC v Crossman* (1937) an estate duty case decided on legislation which was in this respect similar to the inheritance tax legislation.

(c)  The value on death is calculated on the assumption that a prospective purchaser would have all the information which a prudent prospective purchaser might reasonably require if he were purchasing from a willing vendor by private treaty and at arm's length (Inheritance Tax Act 1984, section 168(1)).

## 31.1.2  TRANSFERS ON DEATH

### *IRC v GRAY* [1994] STC 360 (CA)

The facts of this case are summarised in the *Learning Text* at **31.3.2.2**. (Mr Clegg, referred to in the extract below, was the District Valuer; Mr Reeves was the taxpayer's valuer.)

HOFFMAN LJ: . . .
*6. First issue: can the two interests be aggregated for the purposes of valuation . . .*

In my judgment the tribunal here misdirected itself as to the true principle which it had to apply. The share in the farming partnership, with or without other property, was plainly not a 'natural' item of commerce. Few people would want to buy the right to farm in partnership with strangers. Nevertheless, s. 38 requires one to suppose that it was sold. The question for the tribunal was whether, on this assumption, it would have been more advantageous to sell it with the land.

The answer which the tribunal would have given to this question appears clearly enough from the answer which it gave to the second issue, namely whether, assuming that aggregation was permissible, the method of valuation adopted by Mr Clegg (which I have described above) was correct. Mr Reeves had said that purchasers would not give any more for the land because of also being able to 'step into the shoes of Lady Fox' and exercise her rights as a partner. 'In reality' he said, 'this reversion was no different from that of any other let farm and purchasers in the market would bid accordingly.'

On this point, however, the tribunal preferred the approach of Mr Clegg. It said:

> On the assumption that in law the Respondent may lot or sell together the freehold reversion and the 92.5% share in the farming partnership as a single unit of property, we are persuaded that the approach to valuation adopted by Mr Clegg pays a realistic regard to the circumstances actually prevailing and likely to have been within the knowledge of the hypothetical purchaser at the relevant date. Whilst the general basis of value to be adopted is prescribed by statute as open market value there is no prescription of the method of valuation to be applied. If adjustment of the agreed value with vacant possession by deductions and/or apportionment is adopted, it falls to be considered on the criterion of whether it produces a realistic answer when judged against the prevailing factual circumstances. On the evidence before us the most likely prospect in March 1981 was that the minority shareholders would negotiate a surrender of the tenancies: as indeed they in fact did during the years 1982–1984.

This passage in my judgment shows that the tribunal was persuaded that in real life, selling the freehold and the partnership share would have produced a greater combined price than selling them separately. There was no evidence that this would have required undue effort or expense. Accordingly I think that if the tribunal had not considered it necessary to find that the aggregate was a 'natural unit', it would have decided this point in favour of the Crown. As the tribunal was also in my view wrong in rejecting aggregation on the basis of the attribution and jurisdiction points, I think that the Crown should have succeeded on the first issue as a whole. . . .

### de Souza, J., [1994] *Private Client Business* 210

. . .

The question which therefore falls to be considered is whether lotting invariably follows in any case in which the deceased has an interest in both the freehold reversion and the tenancy. It is considered that the answer is 'no', for two reasons:

(A)   In Lady Fox's case her partners' livelihoods were not bound up with the continuation of the partnership. In most cases this will be so since the partners will usually be the other members of the family. The findings of fact by the Lands Tribunal in *Walton* suggest that, in such cases, no higher value would actually be realised by lotting, with the result that it ought not to be resorted to. This ought to rule out lotting in cases in which members of the same family hold interests in the family farm, and the tenancy was granted primarily in order to differentiate between those members who were working farmers and those who were passive (and possibly not too willing) investors. It may take further litigation, however, before such a situation is accepted by the Revenue.

(B)   The proprietors of the other interests in the property are actual (whereas the statutory sale and parties to it are notional). The realities have therefore to be taken into account by an operation described by the Court of Appeal as:

> The valuation is thus a retrospective exercise in probabilities, wholly derived from the real world but rarely committed to the proposition that a sale to a particular purchaser would definitely have happened.

It ought to follow from this that where the owners of Blackacre and Whiteacre are in partnership and, to enable the partnership to continue after the death of one of the owners, tenancies of both properties have been granted, the death of the freeholder of Blackacre should not be the subject of a lotting unless the owner of Whiteacre is actually unwilling to continue the farming partnership with the heirs of the owner of Blackacre. The Revenue's attitude to such a situation is, however, unknown at present.

### In the pipeline

The Revenue told the Court of Appeal that 100 other cases awaited the outcome of its decision. It is extremely difficult to believe that there are many, if indeed any, other cases in which a valuation formula could be based on such unusual rights given to the deceased under the partnership agreement.

The question therefore arises as to what types of case were considered to be similar. It is unlikely that those in relation to category (A) above were included. Although there is some confusion about this, a number of corporate tenancies are thought to have been involved. Most of the cases will probably have been of sole freeholders who were farming in partnership. The important point to remember in relation to these is, however, that the valuation formula in Lady Fox's case will not be of general application and that the reservations made by the Lands Tribunal to its application, even in those circumstances, ought to result in District Valuers putting forward very much more conservative computations.

It is almost certain to be claimed that the lotting process itself justifies a *Baird* rather than *Walton* approach to the valuation of the partnership's tenancy. But is this correct? Under *Gray*, it is only permissible to lot if a higher price is likely to result from lotting the two separate items together. If the reality is that the other co-owners are unwilling to co-operate, how can it be said that a higher price would be realised by offering the two assets for sale in a lotted condition? In such a situation, why does one not have to have regard to the evidence of Mr Reeves that a lower price might be received by reason of the unnatural lotting? This is a difficult question to answer because it is of the essence to unnatural lotting that the end-product cannot be checked against actual transactions in the real market. But if the reality is that vacant possession is unlikely to be available, why should 'an anonymous but reasonable vendor, who goes about the sale as a prudent man of business' take such a step into the unknown?

Are there really 100 cases where *all* the other people involved are likely to be willing to be bought out?

## 31.2   End of Chapter Assessment Question

Alice, who died aged 75 on 20 June 1998, had been a successful novelist. At her death, she had a bank account containing royalties of £78,000, for the period from 6 April 1997 to 20 June 1998. She co-owned her freehold house and grounds in Warwickshire, with her husband Arthur, under a joint tenancy. Her executors have valued the house and grounds together at £700,000.

Alice owned a portfolio of shares in quoted companies, i.e. 1,000 ordinary £1 shares in Megabrackets plc, and 2,500 ordinary £1 shares in Utopia plc. On 20 June 1998, the London Stock Exchange quotation for the Megabrackets shares was 220–280p per share, and the Utopia shares 650–680p per share. Alice's personal effects were worth £15,000. Alice was the life tenant under a settlement set up by her uncle George in 1950. The value of the whole capital of the settled fund, consisting of debentures, was £10,000 at Alice's death. Net interest was due to her from the trustees of the settlement, as at 20 June 1998, of £800. Funeral expenses, including a tombstone costing £1,500, were £5,000. Other liabilities were:

(a)   *General household bills*: outstanding water rates, an electricity bill, outstanding council tax and a gas bill totalling £1,000.

(b)   *Outstanding tax*: income tax due from her for 1997/98, and from 5 April 1998 to 20 June 1998, is estimated by her PRs at £16,000.

Under her will, Alice bequeathed legacies of £5,000 to each of three nephews, her personal effects and shares in Utopia plc to her husband, Arthur, and the residue to her son Alan, 40, absolutely.

Calculate the IHT liability, if any, on Alice's death, on the assumption that she made no lifetime transfers. Do not calculate the estate rate. (You may need to refer to the *Learning Text* at **30.5.5** to get started.)

## 31.3   End of Chapter Assessment Outline Answer

The numbers in square brackets refer to the Notes at the end.

IHT LIABILITY ON ALICE'S ESTATE (DIED 20 JUNE 1998) [1]

|  | £ | £ |
|---|---|---|
| *Property owned jointly with husband* | | |
| Interest in house passing to husband under survivorship principle [2] | 350,000 | — |
| | | |
| *Free estate* | | |
| 1,000 shares in Megabrackets plc [3] | 2,350 | |
| 2,500 shares in Utopia plc [3] | 16,450 | |
| Personal effects | 15,000 | |
| Accrued royalties | 78,000 | |
| Accrued interest from settled fund [4] | 800 | |
| | 112,600 | |
| *Less:* Bills, funeral expenses and outstanding tax [5] | (22,000) | 90,600 |
| | | |
| *Less:* Property left to spouse [6]: | | |
| Personal effects £15,000 | | |
| Utopia Shares   £16,450 | | (31,450) |
| | | 59,150 |

*Settled property*
Settled fund                                                                          10,000

*Total value of transfer on death*                                                   69,150

*IHT liability on death [7]*                                                            NIL

**Notes:**

[1]   No layout for this calculation is specified in the *Learning Text*. Provided you follow the rules in *Learning Text* at **30.5.5** and **31.3**, however, feel free to set it out as you wish.

[2]   The automatic transfer under which Alice's interest under the joint tenancy passes by survivorship (*Learning Text* at **29.3**) is covered by the spouse exemption, provided Arthur is UK-domiciled: **27.7**.

[3]   The Megabrackets and Utopia shares are valued at the lower of their mid-price valuation and quarter-up valuation on 20 June 1998.

*Megabrackets plc* (per share)      *Utopia plc* (per share)
Mid-price = 250p                    Mid-price = 665p
Quarter-up = 235p                   Quarter-up = 658p

The Megabrackets holding is therefore valued at £2,350 (i.e. 235p × 1,000), and the Utopia holding is valued at £16,450 (i.e. 658p × 2,500).

[4]   It has been assumed that the £10,000 value of the settled fund does not include any accrued income, the net interest figure of £800 being shown separately.

[5]   The cost of the tombstone is included in the funeral expenses. Total debts are £22,000, i.e. sum of £5,000 + £1,000 + £16,000.

[6]   By her will, she leaves to Arthur her personal effects (i.e. £15,000) and her Utopia shares (i.e. £16,450).

[7]   There is no liability to IHT on Alice, since her gross lifetime cumulative total is NIL, and the value transferred on her death not covered by the spouse exemption is less than £223,000.

# CHAPTER THIRTY-TWO

# REDUCING THE TAXATION OF GRATUITOUS TRANSFERS

## 32.1 Lifetime Transfers

### 32.1.1 CAPITAL GAINS TAX HOLD-OVER RELIEF

**Elwes, S., 'Holdover Relief and Settlements',** *The Tax Journal,* **6 February 1997, p. 17**

There is a deemed disposal of assets forming part of settled property for capital gains tax purposes, when a beneficiary becomes absolutely entitled to those assets (TCGA 1992, s. 71(1)).

The trustees are deemed to have disposed of those of the trust assets to which the beneficiary has become absolutely entitled at market value and immediately reacquired them at the same value.

The deemed reacquisition is deemed to be the act of the person who is absolutely entitled to the fund. Thus, if the beneficiary sells the assets in the future, any gain is calculated by reference to that market value.

There is no deemed disposal where a beneficiary merely acquires the right to the income of a trust. It is only a right to capital that triggers the charge to capital gains tax.

General holdover relief is no longer available. But in this situation the parties may hold over the gain, provided that the transfer by the trustees to the beneficiary would attract an immediate inheritance tax charge (TCGA 1992, s. 260).

This is only the case where the trust which is terminating is a no interest in possession trust, typically a discretionary trust.

(Here, inheritance tax would, of course, be payable on the beneficiary becoming absolutely entitled to the trust fund.)

If, on the other hand, the beneficiary has already become entitled to the income of the fund as a result of Trustee Act 1925, s. 31, then for inheritance tax purposes he is treated as owning that portion of the capital fund (IHTA 1984, s. 49(1)).

He has an interest in possession and, therefore, when he becomes entitled to the capital at a later date, this is not an occasion on which inheritance tax becomes immediately payable. It is rather a potentially exempt transfer. Thus, TCGA 1992, s. 260, is not satisfied and no hold-over relief is available for capital gains tax.

Trustee Act 1925, s. 31 gives the trustees of a settlement power to make payments to the parent or guardian of an infant beneficiary towards that infant's maintenance, education or benefit. Moreover, if the beneficiary, on attaining the age of 21, has not a vested interest in such income, the trustee shall pay the income of the property to him until he obtains a vested interest in the property, or dies.

The Family Law Reform Act 1969 specifically applied to Trustee Act 1925, s. 31 and lowered the age of majority to the age of 18.

Thus, once a beneficiary has attained the age of 18, he will have an interest in possession in the trust income. This will not attract a charge to capital gains tax until he becomes absolutely entitled to the capital, but it means that no holdover relief is available to him under TCGA 1992, s. 260.

Recently, in *Begg-MacBrearty (Inspector of Taxes)* v *Stilwell* [1996] 4 All ER 205 the High Court had to interpret the Family Law Reform Act 1969 to see whether a beneficiary was entitled to an interest in possession of the income of a trust at the age of 18, before his interest in the capital vested at the age of 21.

In this case, a settlor made a discretionary trust in 1959 in favour of his children and grandchildren. A special power of appointment was given to the trustees under the settlement. This the trustees exercised in 1975 by holding the capital thereafter for the three grandchildren of the settlor in equal shares, contingently on their reaching the age of 21.

The appointment incorporated Trustee Act 1925, s. 31, whereby the beneficiaries were to become absolutely entitled at the age of 18 (this age was substituted by Schedule 1 of the Family Law Reform Act 1969 instead of the earlier age of 21).

However, Family Law Reform Act 1969, sch. 3 provides:

(1)   The principal section shall not affect Trustee Act 1925, s. 31:

(a)   In its application to any interest under an instrument made before the commencement date.

The commencement date was 1 January 1970.

The issue in the case was whether the interest of the beneficiary was under an instrument made before this date. Did it arise under the 1959 original settlement, or the 1975 exercise of the power of appointment?

The court found that the appointment and not the original settlement was the relevant instrument under which the beneficiary's interest existed, and the beneficiary became absolutely entitled to the income at the age of 18.

In interpreting sch. 3, the judge made six observations.

Firstly, any interest that is under an instrument made after 1 January 1970 is affected by the changes made to Trustee Act 1925, s. 31 made by the Family Law Reform Act 1969.

Secondly, the wording in sch. 3 is obscure. Does it mean any interest arising under an instrument? This was the meaning given to it by Slade J in *Re Delamere's Settlement Trusts, Kenny* v *Cunningham-Reid* [1984] 1 All ER 584 and is the most obvious meaning.

Thirdly, the scheme of the 1969 Act in relation to non-statutory documents is that those written after 1 January 1970 are subject to majority at the age of 18, but those written before have their words respected in the pre-1970 form.

Fourthly, the common sense approach is that where there are two instruments, the settlement and the appointment, the appointment is the relevant document.

Before the appointment, the beneficiary did not have a relevant interest to which Trustee Act 1925, s. 31 could attach; she was a mere object of a power of appointment.

Fifthly, as the appointment itself must be construed under the 1969 Act, so the trust incorporated by reference to Trustee Act 1925, s. 31 must be similarly construed.

Finally, the fact that the appointment was not actually affected by the 1969 Act, as the words 'full age' and 'infancy' were not used is immaterial. The time the appointment was made determined whether or not the 1969 Act applied to Trustee Act 1925, s. 31.

The judge here found that two cases were particularly relevant to the facts before him.

In *Re Dickinson's Settlements, Bickersteth* v *Dickinson* [1939] Ch 27 the court was concerned with Trustee Act 1925, s. 31(5) which provides, 'This section does not apply where the instrument, if any, under which the interest arises, came into operation before the commencement of this Act'.

A power had been created before the Act came into force, but was executed afterwards. The court found that s. 31 applied, as the appointed interests arose as a result of the appointment.

Also, in *Re de La Bere's Marriage Settlement Trusts, de La Bere* v *Public Trustee* [1941] 2 All ER 533, there was a marriage settlement made in 1919 and the wife covenanted to settle any after-acquired property, except any property regarding which an intention was expressed in the instrument under which the property was acquired that it should be exempt from the covenant.

In 1938, a settlement was made whereby power was given to the trustees to appoint the funds to the wife and her issue and other beneficiaries.

In 1941, the trustees appointed that on the expiry of the trusts declared by the 1938 settlement, the funds should go to the wife and her sisters in equal shares. Here, it was expressly stated that each share should be exempt from the covenant to settle after-acquired property.

The question was whether the property thus appointed was property expressed in 'the instrument under which the property was acquired' to be exempt from the covenant. The instrument creating the power did not express any such intention.

The court found that it was exempt from the covenant.

Simonds J said that, 'Where one has an instrument creating a power and an instrument exercising that power, the interest, created by the exercise of the power, arises under the later instrument, for in fact there never was such an interest until the power was exercised to create it.'

The significance of the *Begg-MacBrearty* case is that whenever a power of appointment is created, if it is exercised after 1 January 1970, the Family Law Reform Act 1969 applies to Trustee Act 1925, s. 31 incorporated in the exercise of that power. This will adversely affect hold-over relief on any capital gains tax liability when the beneficiary is eventually paid his share of the capital fund.

There are two possible ways to avoid this.

Firstly, the settlement should be drafted so that the contingent interest of the beneficiary in the capital vests at the same time as his interest in the income. Thus, if X is given a right to the trust fund contingently on obtaining the age of 18, hold-over relief should still be available to him.

What is to be avoided is a right to income in possession vesting at the age of 18 before a similar right to the capital. For example, a trust to which s. 31 applies, and therefore gives X the right to income at the age of 18, but where X takes absolutely at the age of 25.

Here there is no holdover relief, as there would be no immediate charge to inheritance tax on the twenty-fifth birthday of X, as he has an interest in possession of the income. Thus, TCGA 1992, s. 260 would not apply.

Secondly, it might be possible to vary or exclude Trustee Act 1925, s. 31 in the trust deed. Thus, the deed might typically provide that s. 31 should only apply with the variation that the beneficiary would only be entitled to the income of the trust at the age of 25, or until he became absolutely entitled to the capital, if earlier.

While these courses of action ensure the preservation of holdover relief for capital gains tax, the benefit of that relief must be weighed against the immediate charge to inheritance tax, when the trustees distribute part of the capital of the discretionary trust.

Whether it is worthwhile to take action, depends on the facts of each case and, in particular, the size of the settlement and the inheritance tax reliefs and exemptions available.

## *BEGG-MACBREARTY* v *STILWELL* [1996] 4 All ER 205

KNOX J: . . . I can dispose of the suggestion that para. 5(1)(a) of sch. 3 applies to interests under instruments made both before and after the commencement date and therefore operates to preserve the pre-1970 version of the Trustee Act 1925. That was an argument advanced on behalf of the taxpayer before the Special Commissioner. In my view, para. 5(1) was clearly intended to provide a dividing line between those interests in respect of which s. 31 of the Trustee Act 1925 applied still unaltered and those in respect of which it applied in its post-1969 altered form.

The following points can be made on para. 5(1)(a) of sch. 3. First, the paragraph clearly connotes that the principal section shall affect s. 31 of the 1925 Act in its application to any interest under an instrument made after the commencement date. One has to choose as regards any particular interest whether it is one under an instrument made before the commencement date or not.

Secondly, the paragraph is elliptical in that there is no verb connecting 'interest' and 'under an instrument', although one has to be supplied to obtain the full sense of the provision. The most likely verb that can grammatically be supplied is 'arising' or possibly 'existing'. 'Created' or 'constituted' does not fit very happily.

Thirdly, the scheme of this part of the Family Law Reform Act 1969, in particular s. 1(2), seems to me to be consistent with an approach to resolving questions of construction by treating documents which are not statutory, and which are effectively written after 1969, in the new climate of majority supervening at 18 or as including that concept. A dictionary is provided in which those who speak post-1969 are presumed to use Family Law Reform Act language, but those who spoke before that time have their words respected in their necessarily pre-1970 form. Section 1(7) in its treatment of wills seems to me to emphasise that approach in requiring the rather technical doctrine of republication of wills by confirmation to be ignored in deciding whether or not a will is to be treated as written before or after the commencement date of the 1969 Act.

Fourthly, if for the reasons given above one has to decide, as I believe one does, under which of the two instruments — the settlement and appointment — the beneficiary's interest exists, and one is not allowed to say that it exists under both, the commonsense approach points to the appointment as the relevant instrument. Before the appointment the beneficiary had no relevant interest to which s. 31 of the 1925 Act could attach. It is true that immediately before the appointment she was entitled to a revocable interest, but it was revoked. She was an object of the power of appointment, but s. 31 could never attach to that, even if it is properly describable as an interest. The immediate cause of the existence of a relevant interest is the appointment. Under the settlement alone she had no relevant interest. She was not incidentally entitled in default of appointment. Under the appointment she had the relevant interest. True it is that without the settlement the appointment would not have been made, and to that extent her interest is one under the settlement. But of the two instruments it seems clear to me that the appointment is the one under which the beneficiary's interest arises and to which it directly owes its existence.

Fifthly, since the appointment itself undoubtedly falls to be construed under s. 1(2) in the post-1969 sense that majority is attained at 18, it seems a priori more probable that the trust incorporated by reference to s. 31 of the 1925 Act should be similarly construed.

Sixth and last, para. 9 of sch. 3 of the 1969 Act reads as follows:

The principal section shall not affect the construction of any statutory provision where it is incorporated in and has effect as part of any deed, will or other instrument the construction of which is not affected by that section.

In my view, that paragraph lends support to the view that s. 31 of the 1925 Act as incorporated in the appointment, is affected by the change in the age of majority. The construction of the appointment is affected by the principal section, in the sense that it is clearly within the ambit of s. 1(2). If it had used the words 'full age' or 'infancy' they would have been used as referring to the attainment of the age of 18 as the age of majority. The appointment does not use any of those words, but that does not detract from the fact that the provision for preserving unaltered statutory provisions which are incorporated by reference is limited to those which are incorporated by documents unaffected by the principal section. In my view, this must be a reference to documents falling within the ambit of s. 1(2), that is to say 'any deed, will or other instrument of whatever nature made on or after 1 January 1970', rather than whether or not by accident the words 'full age', 'minority', etc figure in the document in question. Those are my views on the Act unaided by any authority.

### 32.1.2  INHERITANCE TAX EXEMPTIONS AND RELIEFS

#### 32.1.2.1  Small gifts made to any one person

**Feldman, D., 'Capital transfer tax — A note on exemptions' [1977] BTR 164, pp. 171–72**

(Note: The author is discussing the exemptions and reliefs from IHT, originally contained in FA 1975, sch. 6 (hence the reference to capital transfer tax in the article's title). At the relevant time, the annual exemption was £2,000, not £3,000 as now.)

. . .

Enough has been said to show that the relationship between the various exemptions in Schedule 6 is not as simple and straightforward as may be thought at first sight. In particular,

(1)  It is misleading to say that:

The exemptions appear to be cumulative, so that where one transfer falls within two or more exemptions a person can, in effect, elect which exemption applies to that transfer . . .

They will often be cumulative, but it will depend in many cases on the order in which the transfers of value are made;

(2) it is misleading to say that:

Nothing appears to turn on the fact that an exempt transfer is one of value but not chargeable.

On the approach adopted here, a great deal may hinge on that distinction; a transfer of value exempt under paragraph 4 may, because it is a transfer of value still, go to reduce the amount of any subsequent transfer of value in the same year which is eligible for exemption under paragraph 2;

(3) the same applies, it is submitted, to transfers in consideration of a marriage (paragraph 6) and to gifts for political parties, national purposes and the public benefit;

(4) these strange results arise from a misunderstanding of the effects of the term 'transfers of value,' standing unqualified in Schedule 6;

(5) if indeed it was the intention of the government that the exemptions should be cumulative, it should be made clear by amendment of the Finance Act 1975 that this is what was intended. The amendment would be a simple enough matter; the insertion of a few words and a couple of commas would do it. If for example it was desired to make all the exemptions applicable cumulatively, the words 'not being exempt transfers by reason of the operation of any other provision of this Schedule' added to paragraphs 2, 4, 6 and 11 would do the job admirably. (It is only necessary to spell it out in provisions which apply a fixed financial limit to the exemptions which they confer.) If this were done, paragraph 2 (1) for example as amended would read as follows:

Transfers of value made by a transferor in any one year, *not being exempt transfers by reason of the operation of any other provision of this Schedule*, are exempt to the extent that the values transferred by them (calculated as values on which no tax is payable) do not exceed £2,000.

The accomplishment of the purpose of Parliament in relation to a taxing statute ought not to be dependent on the Revenue misinterpreting the statute or on the expectation that the courts would take the same attitude as the Revenue should the matter come before them.

### 32.1.2.2 Payments which are normal expenditure out of income

#### *BENNETT v IRC* [1995] STC 54

The facts of this case are discussed in *Learning Text* at **32.3.2.3**.

LIGHTMAN J: . . . In my view, in the context of s. 21 of the 1984 Act, the term 'normal expenditure' connotes expenditure which at the time it took place accorded with the settled pattern of expenditure adopted by the transferor.

The existence of the settled pattern may be established in two ways. First, an examination of the expenditure by the transferor over a period of time may throw into relief a pattern, e. g. a payment each year of 10% of all income to charity or members of the individual's family or a payment of a fixed sum or a sum rising with inflation as a pension to a former employee. Second, the individual may be shown to have assumed a commitment, or adopted a firm resolution, regarding his future expenditure and thereafter complied with it. The commitment may be legal (e.g. a deed of covenant), religious (e.g. a vow to give all earnings beyond the sum needed for subsistence to those in need) or moral (e.g. to support aged parents or invalid relatives). The commitment or resolution need have none of these characteristics, but none the less be likewise effective as establishing a pattern, e.g. to pay the annual premiums on a life assurance qualifying policy gifted to a third party or to give a predetermined part of his income to his children.

For an expenditure to be 'normal' there is no fixed minimum period during which the expenditure shall have occurred. All that is necessary is that on the totality of evidence the pattern of actual or intended regular payments shall have been established and that the item in question conforms with that pattern. If the prior commitment or resolution can be shown, a single payment implementing the commitment or resolution may be sufficient. On the other hand, if no such commitment or resolution can be shown, a series of payments may be required before the existence of the necessary pattern will emerge. The pattern need not be immutable; it must, however, be established that the pattern was intended to remain in place for more than a nominal period and indeed for a sufficient period (barring unforeseen circumstances) in order for any payment fairly to be regarded as a regular feature of the transferor's annual expenditure. Thus a 'death bed' resolution to make periodic payments 'for life' and a payment made in accordance with such a determination will not suffice.

The amount of the expenditure need not be fixed in amount nor need the individual recipient be the same. As regards quantum, it is sufficient that a formula or standard has been adopted by application of which the payment (which may be of a fluctuating amount) can be quantified e.g. 10% of any earnings whatever they may be or the costs of a sick or elderly dependant's residence at a nursing home. As regards the payees, it is sufficient that their general character or the qualification for benefit is established, e.g. members of the family or needy friends.

There is no need (unlike under the 1910 Act) for the expenditure to be reasonable or that the expenditure is such that an ordinary person might have incurred in similar circumstances, though the existence or otherwise of this characteristic may be relevant in deciding whether the evidence establishes the necessary pattern. The fact that the objective behind the expenditure is tax planning, e.g. to prevent an accumulation of income in the hands of the transferor liable to inheritance tax on his death, is no impediment.

What is necessary and sufficient is that the evidence should manifest the substantial conformity of each payment with an established pattern of expenditure by the individual concerned — a pattern established by proof of the existence of a prior commitment or resolution or by reference only to a sequence of payments.

Turning to the facts of the present case, the evidence now before the court (though not the evidence before the court at the original hearing) does establish that Mrs Bennett when active and healthy, albeit of considerable age, and when death was not seen as imminent, made a considered determination for the residue of her life to give all her surplus income from the trust beyond what she reasonably required for maintenance to her sons, and this determination was implemented by executing the authority, requesting the trustees (who in regard to the income available for distribution to her were bare trustees for her) to act accordingly and their so acting. The trustees did so act, and none the less so because they felt the need to act conservatively in assessing distributable income and accordingly the surplus available to the sons. It seems to me that Mrs Bennett in the circumstances did adopt a pattern of expenditure in respect of the surplus, and the payments to the sons were made in accordance with this pattern and were accordingly part of her normal expenditure within the meaning of s. 21.

If the evidence before the court had remained that which was adduced at the original hearing and the court had been faced merely with the authority and the two payments, that would have been insufficient. The unexplained divergences between the trust income for the years in question and the two payments and between the two payments themselves afforded no sufficient pattern. But the fresh evidence proves the existence on the part of Mrs Bennett of the determination to establish a pattern in relation to the surplus income and explains that there is in fact no inconsistency (let alone incompatibility) between the pattern resolved on and the payments made: Mrs Bennett had a single and continuing intention regarding the surplus and in respect of the assessed surplus this intention was given effect.

In the circumstances, I see no obstacle in what but for the evidence of Miss Buckle might appear to be the disparate (and one-off) character of the payments to the sons. Nor do I find any difficulty posed by the language of the authority or the interposition of the trustees between Mrs Bennett and the sons. The trustees, (as I have already said), held the income received as bare trustees for Mrs Bennett; the authority requested them to pay the surplus to the sons in language adequate (as was plainly understood and intended) to constitute a (polite) direction to them to act in this way; and the reference to 'all or any of the income' contemplates only the possibility that there may or may not be an available surplus in any one year. No discretion was conferred on or exercisable by the trustees regarding the payment to the sons, beyond that of quantifying the surplus available for payment to the sons, and no other discretion was either intended or exercised.

CONCLUSION

For the above reasons, I quash the determinations of the Revenue and declare that each of the payments constituted part of the normal expenditure of Mrs Bennett within the meaning of s. 21 of the 1984 Act.

## 32.2  Transfers on Death

### 32.2.1  VARIATIONS AND DISCLAIMERS

**McCutcheon, B., 'Five Non-Requirements for Deeds of Variation' [1998]**
*Private Client Business* **45**

It may be helpful to remind readers of the following requirements which a deed of variation does not have to satisfy to qualify for favourable inheritance tax or capital gains tax treatment.

1. There is no requirement that the person entering into the deed can only do what the deceased himself could have done. For example the persons effecting the deed can settle the property on trustees of a trust which was not in existence when the deceased died, e.g. which is set up by, or contemporaneously with, the deed of variation. In the same way, the fact that the deceased had a joint interest in property does not preclude a deed of variation being entered into in respect of that property.
2. There is no requirement that the property must go to someone else who benefited under the deceased's Will or intestacy. It can go to someone, for example the person entering into the deed of variation wishes it to go to. It could go to someone, for example who the deceased expressly excluded from benefiting under his will.
3. There is no requirement that the deceased's personal representatives must be parties to the deed. Therefore the deed can be effected before probate is obtained.
4. There is no requirement that the estate must still be in the course of administration. On the contrary, section 142(6) of the Inheritance Tax Act 1984 expressly provides that a deed can be entered into, 'whether or not the administration of the estate is complete or the property concerned has been distributed in accordance with the original dispositions'. Thus, there is no requirement that the property must still be in the hands of the personal representatives, still less that it somehow must pass through their hands on its way from the person entering into the deed to the person intended to benefit under the deed.
5. There is no requirement that the person redirecting the property did not benefit from it. e.g. by receiving dividends.

### *RUSSELL v IRC* **[1988] 2 All ER 405**

KNOX J: . . . It was submitted by Mr McCall [counsel for the taxpayer] that the distinction between variations of the original dispositions taking effect on death, on the one hand, and variations of such variations, on the other, lead to difficulties in distinguishing between the two and that these difficulties were an indication that such a distinction was conceptually uncertain and therefore not to be attributed to Parliament. I accept that there may well often be, and indeed are in the present case, difficulties in drawing the line between the two, but I do not find the distinction in the least unclear in principle. Nor do the difficulties, such as they are, point to any conclusion in favour of the plaintiffs stronger than that Parliament may perhaps not have foreseen this precise point. Equally I do not find the insertion of subsection (1A) into section 47 of the Finance Act 1975 a very general provision whereby events within two years of a testator's death otherwise giving rise to charge to tax under the regime dealing with settlements without interest in possession are effectively regarded as occurring just before the testator died, a reliable guide to solving the present problem. Although the provision is very wide it could only operate once and in any event the problem dealt with is different. . . .

## 32.3   Lifetime Transfers and Transfers on Death

### 32.3.1   BUSINESS PROPERTY RELIEF

*BROWN'S EXECUTORS* v *IRC* **[1996] STC (SCD) 277 (***Current Law Cases* **summary)**

B held nearly all the shares in G Ltd, which carried on business as nightclub operators. The nightclub was sold in January 1985 and the proceeds placed in a deposit account. B investigated various projects for reinvesting these funds in another nightclub, but they all proved abortive. He suffered a heart attack in the autumn of 1986 and died in November. Another project was under active consideration prior to his death. The Revenue contended that business property relief was not available on the shares in G Ltd by virtue of Inheritance Tax Act 1984, s. 105(3). The executors appealed.

Held, allowing the appeal, that there was no change in the nature of the business in view of B's intention to purchase another nightclub, *Gladstone Development Co. Ltd* v *Strick* (1948) 30 TC 131, [1947–1976] 1 CLC 4755 considered. Whether the business had changed on the sale of the nightclub required a consideration of the company's activities, allied with the director's intentions. The facts showed that, although the sale proceeds were held in an income producing account, they were available at short notice to be applied as and when a suitable alternative was found. Therefore no change occurred in the nature of the business between the club's sale and B's death.

MR T.H.K. EVERETT (Special Commissioner): . . . Ms Lawunmi, for the commissioners, directed my attention to the fact that from the date of the sale of the night-club Gaslight [i.e. G Ltd] held most of the proceeds of sale as an investment in a deposit account. She suggested that such action amounted to the holding of an investment. She also pointed to the statement by the directors in the accounts for 1985 to the effect that the principal activity of Gaslight was as a night-club operator until the sale of the night-club. She also drew my attention to a statement in the accounts of Gaslight for 1988, but in my judgment statements made in accounts covering a period later than Mr Brown's death cannot be relevant in this appeal.

Looking at the evidence as a whole, I am unable to accept that the business of Gaslight from the date of the sale of the night-club to the date of Mr Brown's death consisted wholly or mainly of making or holding investments. Although the bulk of the proceeds of sale were held in an income-producing account, they were available at short notice to be applied by Mr Brown when he found suitable alternative premises. He intended to replace the night-club which had been sold with alternative premises and on the evidence of his brother and the evidence of Mr Ufland, he made efforts to find suitable alternative premises for Gaslight and it would appear that those efforts would have come to a successful conclusion but for Mr Brown's untimely illness and death in the later part of 1986.

The office of the company at which Mr Brown's brother dealt with administration and marketing continued to operate throughout 1985 and 1986 and, so far as it is relevant, for some time after Mr Brown's death. . . .

*POWELL AND ANOTHER v IRC* [1997] Simon's Weekly Tax Intelligence 657

T.H.K. EVERETT (Special Commissioner): For many years until her death in 1992 the deceased carried on a business at a caravan park (the park) hiring out caravan pitches on long and short-term lettings and providing ancillary services. The deceased and the personal representatives and other members of her family performed the daily tasks of site maintenance and security and lived at the park. It was essential for the smooth running and security of the park that a representative of the owner should always be in attendance, inter alia, to ensure the delivery of gas bottles for the mobile homes, since all the residents of the park relied on the family for service when electricity or gas supply broke down. The majority of the residents were long-term and many were retired, for whom the family organised social and medical visits. Maintenance included reading meters, cutting grass, ditching, hedging, security, and painting, cleaning and otherwise maintaining site caravans. At the deceased's death 23 of the 33 units were privately owned and the owners paid a pitch fee. Three of the remaining units were occupied on short-term letting. The park was a development of below-average quality and the quality of the letting units was poor. The income of the business was assessed to income tax under Schedule D. The personal representatives appealed against determinations by the Revenue that the business in which the deceased used the park consisted mainly of holding investments within IHTA 1984 s. 105(3) and was not therefore entitled to business property relief, contending, inter alia, that the deceased and her family actively managed the business. The Special Commissioner considered that the tax status of the income of the business was irrelevant in the context of IHT. The availability of business property relief depended entirely on the provisions of IHTA 1984. The personal representatives contended that the holding of investments was a passive activity. The Special Commissioner observed, however, that the question was whether the deceased's business consisted wholly or mainly of holding investments. The whole of the deceased's income was derived from pitch fees paid by long-term residents and rents for hired caravans paid by short-term residents. The whole of the deceased's income fell on the 'holding investments' side of the line. Most of the activities which she carried out were either required under the terms of the lettings or the terms of the caravan licence which governed the lettings. The social visits and organised medical visits were not charged for. Such activities enhanced the goodwill of the business, but also fell on the 'holding investments' side of the line. The position of hoteliers was distinguishable because they offered a high standard of service to their clients and did not merely rent rooms. The hoteliers' services were business activities, not on the 'holding investments' side of the line. The Special Commissioner also considered that it was irrelevant that the business was carried on by the deceased and her family who were in occupation. That made little difference to the end result and it was not relevant that the deceased collected the rents individually from her tenants or licencees rather than the rents being remitted direct to her bank account. The facts of the instant case were broadly the same as in *Hall and another (executors of Hall, decd)* v IRC [1997] STC (SCD) 126 where the Special Commissioner had rejected the executors' claim to business property relief. The Special Commissioner considered that the facts were even less favourable to the personal representatives than in the *Hall* case where there was some evidence of business activity in addition to the receipt of income from caravan rents, since there was no such evidence in the instant case. There was no evidence to support the assertion that the deceased's business 'also involved acting as dealing agent for commission in the assignment of continuing pitch lettings and the connected or unconnected sale of caravans and other mobile residential units'. On the facts of the instant case the Special Commissioner considered that there was little difference in principle between the position of the owner of a portfolio of long leases receiving ground rents, who would be the holder of investments, and the position of the deceased whose main source of income was derived from pitch fees from long-term residents who owned their own caravans. The Special Commissioner did not, however, attach weight to the fact that the park was in a run-down condition, which tended to show that the deceased's activities in managing the business were of low intensity. The Special Commissioner concluded that the deceased was carrying on a business consisting wholly or mainly of the holding of investments.

Accordingly, the appeals would be dismissed and the notices of determination would be upheld.

## 32.4   End of Chapter Assessment Question

Sidney owns 40,000 of the 50,000 ordinary £2 shares in Sidney's Greens Ltd, the company which carries on his family's greengrocers' trade. Sidney has owned his shares since the company was incorporated in 1960. Each share is worth £25. On 1 June 1998, he transfers 60,000 of the shares to Terence and Tom, the trustees of the Sidney 1998 Discretionary Settlement. The settlement deed provides that any IHT is to be borne by the settled property. The gift results in the value of Sidney's retained shares falling to £12 each. On 1 October 1998, Sidney transfers the freehold greengrocer's shop, which is owned by him personally, although used in the business, to his son Sam. The shop is valued at £150,000. Immediately prior to the transfer into the settlement, Sidney had a gross cumulative lifetime total, for IHT purposes, of £300,000. He has made no other transfers, apart from these.

(a)   Comment on the IHT and CGT implications of the transfers on 1 June 1998, and 1 October 1998.

(b)   Calculate the IHT liability, if any, on each transfer on the alternative bases that (i) the IHT is paid by Sidney, and (ii) the IHT is borne by the settled property.

(c)   Comment on how any additional IHT would be calculated if Sidney died on 1 September 2002, assuming that the shop was transferred on 1 October 1998. Mention any relevant relief.

## 32.5   End of Chapter Assessment Outline Answer

(a)   For IHT purposes, the transfer on 1 June 1998 is a transfer chargeable immediately to IHT, since a discretionary settlement is one without an interest in possession. However, BPR is available at 100%, since the shares are unquoted, and they give Sidney control of the company: IHTA 1984, s. 105(1)(b). For CGT purposes, the transfer, a disposal at deemed market value, qualifies for hold-over relief, under either of TCGA 1992, s. 260 or TCGA 1992, s. 165. In the latter case, business assets include shareholdings in personal companies such as Sidney's Greens Ltd. The postponement of the CGT charge means there is no double charge to IHT and CGT.

The gift of the shop, on 1 October 1998, is a PET for IHT purposes: IHTA 1984, s. 3A(1). For CGT purposes, it is a disposal at deemed market value (TCGA 1992, s. 17) and, even though no IHT is immediately chargeable, hold-over relief is available to postpone the gain: TCGA 1992, s. 165.

(b)   No IHT is chargeable in respect of the transfer on 1 June 1998, as 100% BPR is available: (a) above. No IHT is chargeable in respect of the transfer on 1 October 1998 either, since this is a PET.

(c)   If Sidney died on 1 September 2002, the value of the chargeable transfer of his estate immediately before his death, as to which no details are given, would be cumulated with the gross cumulative total of his lifetime transfers. This process would make both PETs and transfers chargeable immediately to IHT, liable to IHT at 40% if made in the seven-year period prior to his death. Thus the gift of the shop, a PET when it was made, becomes chargeable at 40%, unless BPR applies. A question arises from the fact that, at the time the PET was made, Sidney no longer had control of the company: IHTA 1984, s. 105(1)(d). It seems possible that this means that the now-chargeable PET does not have the benefit of BPR, although no concluded view is expressed here. If it does not have the benefit of BPR, taper relief may none the less be available to reduce the IHT chargeable. Where a PET is made three but not more than four years before the death, taper relief is available at 80%. As to the retained shares, if these are still in Sidney's estate at his death, they should qualify for BPR on the transfer on death, by virtue of IHTA 1984, s. 105(1)(bb).

Although there is no disposal of Sidney's estate on his death, it is acquired by his PRs at its market value at his death: TCGA 1992, s. 62(1)(a).

# CHAPTER THIRTY-THREE

# TAXATION OF GRATUITOUS TRANSFERS: ANTI-AVOIDANCE ISSUES AND COMPLIANCE

## 33.1   Anti-avoidance Issues

### 33.1.1   TRYING TO HAVE YOUR CAKE AND EAT IT TOO: GIFTS WITH A RESERVATION

#### *INGRAM* v *IRC* **[1997] STC 1234 (CA)**

MILLETT LJ (dissenting): . . . In my judgment a nominee may grant an effective lease to his principal, and accordingly the lease which Mr Macfadyen granted to Lady Ingram was effective to vest a legal term of years in her. The transaction did not contravene the two-party rule, for there were two parties to the contract. It is true that they were not independent parties dealing with each other at arm's length, and had Lady Ingram been a trustee the lease would not have bound the interests of her beneficiaries; but this does not render the lease a nullity whether as property or contract. In my judgment, once the lease was granted, Lady Ingram was in the same situation as the testator in *Belaney* v *Belaney* (1867) 2 Ch App 138. Pending the execution of the declaration of trust, and while Lady Ingram remained solely and beneficially entitled to the freehold and leasehold interests, the covenants in the lease were in abeyance because of the circuity of action which would be involved in any attempt by either party to enforce them. But she had succeeded in separating the two legal estates, which were in different ownership, and was in a position to deal separately with her beneficial interest in the freehold reversion and her legal estate in the term of years.

I reach this conclusion with satisfaction for two reasons. In the first place, a lease by a nominee to his principal is unobjectionable on any but the most technical grounds and should be upheld if not conceptually impossible. In the second place, a decision to the contrary effect would create new opportunities for fraud. Such a lease would normally contain nothing on its face to indicate any defect — the lease which Mr Macfadyen granted to Lady Ingram did not — and could be used as security to raise money or to enable the lessee to grant an underlease. This was not fully explored in argument, no doubt because the lease to Lady Ingram contained an absolute prohibition against assignment or subletting. But the Revenue's argument must be tested generally; the validity of a lease by a nominee to his principal cannot be made to depend on the presence or absence of such a covenant. If the Revenue are right and the lease is a nullity then the position of a mortgagee or underlessee must be considered. It seems that he can obtain no title; but there is no very obvious reason of legal policy why he should lose the estate. Moreover, it is contrary to principle that a purchaser should have to investigate the beneficial interests in order to satisfy himself as to the legal title.

. . .

I can summarise my reasons for upholding the transaction as follows. (1) A man can convey one of the two legal estates in land, i.e. the fee simple absolute in possession, to a nominee for himself. There is no rational basis for denying him the ability to vest the other, i.e. a term of years absolute, in a nominee for himself. (2) The right to exclusive possession is what distinguishes a lease from a contractual right of occupation. The right is a proprietary right, not a contractual right. (3) A trustee does not contract as agent for his beneficiary but as principal. A contract by a trustee with his beneficiary does not contravene the two-party rule, and is good at law. (4) Before 1873 such a contract would have been enforced by the common law courts, though the action might have been restrained by the Court of Chancery. Today proceedings to enforce such a contract would be stayed for circuity of action. But the contract would not be a nullity, and enforcement would be permitted once the circuity was eliminated by, for example, an assignment. (5) A lease can be validly created even though it achieves nothing beyond the vesting of the legal estate. It is difficult to see why it should be possible to grant a lease which contains no covenants at all but not a lease containing covenants which are temporarily unenforceable on procedural grounds. (6) The law permits a man who acquires the freehold and leasehold interests by different transactions to keep the interests separate by vesting one in himself and the other in a nominee for himself. Such a transaction is very common. Yet it produces the very result which Lady Ingram set out to achieve, and which is stigmatised as nonsensical or whimsical. (7) The lease in question is good on its face. If void, it is a potent instrument of fraud. It should not be necessary for a purchaser to investigate the equitable interests in order to satisfy himself as to the legal title. (8) The principle for which the Revenue contend rests on bare assertion. Neither principle nor authority compels its acceptance. The English authorities relied on in *Kildrummy* [*Kildrummy* v *IRC* [1990] STC 657] when properly analysed, provide no support. . . .

## 33.1.2 ASSOCIATED OPERATIONS: ATTEMPTING TO REDUCE THE VALUE TRANSFERRED

### *IRC* v *MACPHERSON* [1988] 2 All ER 753 (HL)

The facts of this case are summarised in the *Learning Text* at **33.3.2**. (Note: References are to the Finance Act 1975.)

LORD JAUNCEY OF TULLICHETTLE: . . . In determining whether the 1977 agreement was made in a transaction, within the extended meaning, intended to confer gratuitous benefit it is necessary to consider what are 'associated operations' for the purposes of the subsection. The definition in section 44 is extremely wide and is capable of covering a multitude of events affecting the same property which might have little or no apparent connection between them. It might be tempting to assume that any event which fell within this wide definition should be taken into account in determining what constituted a transaction for the purposes of section 20(4). However, counsel for the Crown accepted, rightly in my view, that some limitation must be imposed. Counsel for the trustees informed your Lordships that there was no authority on the meaning of the words 'associated operations' in the context of capital transfer tax legislation but he referred to a decision of the Court of Appeal in Northern Ireland, *Inland Revenue Commissioners* v *Herdman* (1967) 45 TC 394, in which the tax avoidance provisions of sections 412 and 413 of the Income Tax Act 1952 had been considered. Read short, section 412(1) provided that a charge to income tax arose where the individual had by means of a transfer of assets either alone or in conjunction with associated operations acquired rights whereby he could enjoy a particular description of income. Lord MacDermott CJ, at p. 406F-I, upheld a submission by the taxpayer that the only associated operations which were relevant to the subsection were those by means of which, in conjunction with the transfer, a taxpayer could enjoy the income and did not include associated operations taking place after the transfer had conferred upon the taxpayer the power to enjoy income. If the extended meaning of 'transaction' is read into the opening words of section 20(4) the wording becomes:

A disposition is not a transfer of value if it is shown that it was not intended, and was not made in a transaction including a series of transactions and any associated operations intended, to confer any gratuitous benefit. . .

So read it is clear that the intention to confer gratuitous benefit qualifies both transactions and associated operations. If an associated operation is not intended to confer such a benefit it is not relevant for the purpose of the subsection. That is not to say that it must necessarily per se confer a benefit but it must form a part of and contribute to a scheme which does confer such a benefit.

In this case it is common ground that the appointment conferred a gratuitous benefit on Timothy. It is clear from paragraph 17 of the trust solicitor's affidavit that the appointment would not have been made if the 1970 agreement had not been varied by that of 1977. It follows that the 1977 agreement was not only effected with reference to the appointment but was a contributory part of the scheme to confer a benefit on Timothy. So viewed there can be no doubt that the 1977 agreement, being the disposition for the purposes of section 20(4), was made in a transaction, consisting of the agreement and the appointment, intended to confer a gratuitous benefit on Timothy.

Counsel for the trustees argued that if the agreement was a relevant associated operation for the purposes of section 20(4) an anomalous result would follow in as much as double taxation would occur if the order of events which actually took place had been reversed. Thus if the appointment had been made first a charge on the whole value of the sum appointed would have arisen under paragraph 6(2) and when the agreement was subsequently entered into a further charge on the amount of the devaluation would arise under paragraph 6(3). I do not consider that such a result would have ensued. The agreement would undoubtedly have been associated with the appointment within the definition of section 44 but it would not have been a relevant associated operation since it would have contributed nothing to the conferment of the gratuitous benefit which had already been effected by the appointment. It could alternatively be said that the transaction intended to confer gratuitous benefit had already been completed before the agreement had been entered into, therefore although it was an associated operation it could not be said to have been made in that transaction.

It only remains to consider the trustees' argument that the statutory hypothesis in paragraph 6(3) was intended solely to test the transaction referred to in the sub-paragraph and such consequences as might inevitably flow therefrom. Reference was made to the following observations of Lord Asquith of Bishopstone in *East End Dwellings Co. Ltd* v *Finsbury Borough Council* [1952] AC 109, 132:

> If you are bidden to treat an imaginary state of affairs as real, you must surely unless prohibited from doing so, also imagine as real the consequences and incidents which, if the putative state of affairs had in fact existed, must inevitably have flowed from or accompanied it.

The appointment did not flow inevitably from the agreement and therefore fell to be disregarded. I do not read the foregoing observations as limiting the scope of the hypothesis to those events which must follow from the imaginary state of affairs. I agree with Slade LJ that it would be consistent with these observations in testing the 1977 agreement not wholly to exclude consideration of the appointment to which the agreement was intended as a prelude.

My Lords, I do not think that it matters whether, as counsel for the Crown primarily submitted, the statutory hypothesis extends both to the agreement and to the appointment or whether it is restricted to the agreement alone. Having regard to the provisions of section 44 that operations are associated whether they are effected with the same person or with different persons, the agreement and the appointment would be associated by whomsoever they were deemed to have been made. Once it is accepted that the statutory hypothesis does not exclude consideration of the appointment it follows inevitably that the trustees have failed to satisfy the test in section 20(4).

. . .

# 33.2   Compliance

### 33.2.1   INHERITANCE TAX

#### *RE CLORE (NO. 3)* [1985] 2 All ER 819

WALTON J: . . . Knowledge is of many sorts, and a very frequent meaning of the scope of knowledge is something which, although one does not at the moment recollect it, is within a document which one has readily to hand. Indeed, many barristers, even many specialist barristers, may have knowledge of their special law, but on the fifth proviso to sub-s (5) of s. 49 of the relevant Act they would not presume to say that they could, unaided, trill it off in their bath. If they wanted to find it, they would obviously pull down the requisite volume of the statutes to have a look at it; but in that sense they would know it. It seems to me that here there must be a similar extension, because, quite clearly, if a trustee (indeed, even a trustee of a very modest trust fund) is asked, 'Do you know what your trust fund consists of?', his answer would be, 'If you mean can I remember what it consists of, I can make a shot at it, but if you really want an accurate statement then of course I know, it is all here in this list of the trust investments.' So it seems to me that quite clearly here knowledge must extend to the contents of documents.

One then comes on to the question: what documents? Here, I took the liberty of arguing the point to some extent with counsel for Mr Karlweis and I think she was not disposed to resist what seems to me to be inevitable: first of all, documents in the possession of the person concerned; second, documents in his custody; and, third, documents in his power, that is to say documents which are held in general by other people to his order, and that will include in a good many cases solicitors. . . .

I therefore come back to the present case, where the question is: what is the true construction of the words 'to the best of his knowledge and belief'? I have already indicated that it extends to what is contained in any document of the classes that I have indicated. But beyond that, it seems to me that there is nothing whatsoever . . . which requires the person who must deliver the accounts to act as an information gatherer. If it is in his knowledge within the extended definition I have indicated, he must give it. Beyond that, he is entitled to say, 'I am not required by statute to go into the highways and byways and compel anybody, even if that person may be a willing giver of information, to give me the information; because that information is not within my knowledge: it is within the knowledge of somebody else.'